Planning Retirement

 THE OPEN UNIVERSITY

The Open University in association with the Pre-Retirement Association, the Health Education Council and the Scottish Health Education Group

Copyright © 1982 The Open University

Produced and edited in collaboration with
Choice Publications Limited
Bedford Chambers
Covent Garden
London WC2E 8HA

Design/Art Direction: Colin Banks
Layout: Marlon John
Artwork: Tom Greene

Open University Course Team: Allin Coleman, Roger Harrison, Mick Jones, Sheila
Lewis, Pamela Shakespeare

Academic Co-ordinator for Community Education: Nick Farnes

Consultants: D V Bansal, Joanna Bornat, Taylor Brown, William Bytheway,
Monica Darlington, Vincent Duggleby, Edward Eves, Peter Fentem, Maurice
Geller, Irene Gore, J A Muir Gray, Alistair Heron, Lorna Hubbard, Angela Hector,
William Hutchinson, Peter Jarvis, Dorothy Jerrome, Malcolm Johnson, Sidney
Jones, Jane Madders, Tom Moore, Armando Mascarenhas, Heather McKenzie,
Mervyn Morgan, Elizabeth Morse, Steve Murgatroyd, Norman Page, Chris
Phillipson, Rosemary Randall, Jill Sheilds, Victor Sawle, Valerie Talbot, B A Timbs,
Dorothy Walster, Barbara Webb, Alistair Weir, Audrey Wisbey, H Beric Wright

External Assessor: Professor H A Jones

Secretarial support: Lin Dell, Coreen McCarry, Sybil Meacham

Illustrations: Young Artists
Phillip Hood: 7, 67, 135, 185, 198, 191, 195
David Eaton: Pages 8, 11, 18, 19, 22, 28, 32, 34, 37, 40, 82, 92, 100, 102, 147,
154, 155, 169, 207, 223
Susan Hunter: Pages 13, 23, 24, 25, 46, 53, 73, 81, 104, 130, 172, 173, 174, 175,
176, 177, 180, 181, 182, 183, 201, 208, 221, 229, 230, 241
Michael Ogden: Pages 48, 49, 50, 108, 109, 113, 119, 120, 127, 141, 218

Photographs:
All photographs by Mike Levers, except the following; Tony Stone Associates:
Pages 12, 57, 61, 75, 111, 122, 145, 178, 202, 210, 217, 234; Art Directors: Page
12, 128, 132, 213, 224; Picture Post: Page 17; Marathon Pictures: Page 17; John
Watney: Pages 21, 144, 145; Camera Press: Pages 65, 162, 194, 206, 222, 245; E.
A. Doddington: 78, 79, 110; Syndication International: Pages 145, 224; Hilary
Jones: Pages 200, 233; David Lynch: Page 232; Brent Studios: Page 237; Betty
Arlow supplied photograph on page 148

Front Cover by Jonathon De Jongh

British Library Cataloguing in Publications Data

Open University
    Planning retirement.
    1. Retirement — Great Britain
    646.7'9   HQ1064.G7

ISBN 0 906139 09 0

Phototypeset and printed by The Nuffield Press, Cowley, Oxford

Acknowledgements:
The course team would like to thank members of the Bedford Retirement
Centre for their assistance in generating material for this course, and in particular
Angela Hector for her co-operation and advice throughout.

Introduction

This book can be taken up and read at any stage of life. In fact when we were writing it, someone (aged 23) reading through the draft, remarked "This is not just about Planning Retirement, it's all about life!" Perhaps you have given little thought to your retirement. If you are in mid-career, you may think that retirement has nothing to do with you but the very fact that your thoughts are so job-centred may mean that retirement whenever it occurs would take you unawares. You may be approaching retirement soon and tend to push the idea to the back of your mind. Ignoring the fact, will not make it go away.

Five to ten years before the event is not too soon to begin to make plans although most people begin to think more seriously about the matter about eighteen months or so before they leave work. If you are already retired and not too happy about the way things are going, perhaps you should start reading now . . . ?

'Planning Retirement' is about making plans for the rest of your life. Time is a major theme running through the course; people another; you are at the centre.

A well-planned retirement will take into account not only the early years but all those that follow. After all, you are unlikely to feel the same about retirement after say six months as you are ten years later — or when you are eighty! This suggests a considerable time span, inevitable change and the need to adapt to it. For this reason, most of the topics suggest planning for the shorter, medium and longer terms and encourage you to think flexibly about the future.

No one retires in isolation. This implies many changes in relationships with others — associates and colleagues at work, family and friends. Old contacts may be lost, new ones replace them. A number of topics invite you to explore the problems and pleasures that arise out of this, both soon after retirement and much later on.

Before retirement, a work-dominated life may have dictated your range of activities and interests. Whatever your job might have been, many of the skills and much of the expertise developed during those years can be used productively in retirement. In addition, old skills or even new ones can be developed in a new leisure-centred life that allows you more freedom as an active member of the community.

We feel that decisions about retirement must always be personal. So we do not offer a package of information but indicate the kind of questions you need to ask, both about purely practical and more personal matters and the sources from which you can get the facts that are of particular concern to you.

The activities — quizzes, personal profiles, budget assessments etc — will involve you in an active way and help to broaden and deepen your thoughts about your current attitudes and future choices.

The course does not offer a blueprint for the perfect retirement. Everyone who works through the course will come up with a different plan. You are encouraged to draw on your own life experiences, your knowledge of yourself, your preferences, your capacities and your potential in making decisions about what you want to do or who you want to be in retirement.

We feel that retirement opens up a new, rewarding phase of life that needs at least as much preparation as those that went before. We invite you to look at the story of your life so far and actively engage in planning the next stage.

Contents

Taking stock

Some people may start to think about retirement some years before the event, others only months. But wherever you start from, a plan can help and that's what this book is about. It helps you review your current situation; it asks you to think about the changes that will happen when you retire, what changes you want to make, and to work out how to tackle them. It helps you to put your plan into action, think about possible snags and to revise your plan where you need to. Taking stock is something we do from time to time and is a first step to making changes. The topics in this chapter are designed to help you take stock. You are asked to consider how realistic your current ideas about retirement are. Some topics help you to review your health. Some topics help you to work out how to handle your money and what you need to find out about your finances when you retire. Some topics help you explore the area of relationships, to review your life to date, and to consider the importance to you of work and leisure. And finally the chapter looks at retirement day itself.

Do you have a plan?

The success of your retirement will depend, as no period of life before, upon your own personal behaviour. You can treat it as a reward which allows you to move on in freedom to new experiences and opportunities.

This is a time to rediscover the 'real you' that might have become submerged in the business of earning a living.

Another way is to see retirement as a change in life style. It is one of those major changes, like starting school, getting your first job, being called up during the war, getting married, becoming a parent. Expectations are high but there are some doubts and worries. The future beckons and threatens.

Certainly it would be a pity to think of retirement simply as an end of working life and merely a gradual movement into old age.

What do others think

It depends on their age and distance from retirement. Most people wish the retired well. They hope you will be happy, healthy and busy in the ways you want to be but more often than not they give little thought to *how* this can be made to happen.

What do you think

It is tempting to push the thought of retiring out of your mind altogether.
"It will take care of itself when the time comes."
"How can you possibly plan for retirement anyway?"

It may seem foolish to plan if you feel that retirement can only bring tough times.

"What's the use of planning to do this and that when I'll have less money than I've ever had?"

It might seem unnecessary anyway *"Believe me, I can't wait — there isn't going to be enough time in the day to do all I want to."*

It is possible that what you imagine are plans turn out simply to be day-dreams — some possible, some wildly unpractical.

How long is retirement for

The rest of your life. Obviously no one knows how long this will be but given good health everyone has a greater life expectancy than ever before. If you live to a ripe old age, your retirement could last as long as your working life did. This needs thinking about.

Changes

Look back over your working life. You have obviously changed since you started work. Have you ever stopped to think how?

You would probably agree that there have been many changes. They may have been influenced by some or all of the following:
o The places you lived and worked in.
o How much money you earned.
o The way you spent your leisure and working time.
o The people you knew.
o Family changes.

They will have added to your total experience. Think about this as you look forward to retirement.

Some questions to ask

Will your present attitudes towards keeping healthy and occupied change at all as retirement goes on?

Will you always know the same people, live in the same place?

Will you feel the same about retirement after say six months as you are likely to feel:.
o In ten years time?
o When you are 80?

Will you want to go on making changes and responding to them during retirement just as you did before?

'Planning Retirement' does not offer you the perfect plan — it even accepts the fact that some people will never get around to making plans at all! It does offer the means for you, whatever your walk of life, to assess your own attitudes to retirement and to make decisions which will be flexible enough to adapt to changing circumstances and changing personal needs.

Thinking about retirement can make you veer uncomfortably from high spirits to deep depression. There may be a vague feeling of having been let down. *"No one said it would be like this."*

Planning gives you the opportunity to prepare yourself against the occasional emotional unease of the pre-retirement period. It can replace vague dreams with realism.

Time and retirement

You may firmly believe that retirement will take care of itself or that once you've sorted out the finances, everything else will fall into place. There is no doubt, however, that the major change retirement brings is the huge increase in the amount of time at your disposal. You probably have your own ideal pictures of how this will be spent. Often these are just vague, generalised thoughts. You may find that you fret over them or use them to reassure yourself. You could use them to help you plan.

Tick any of the following that you have thought or said:

It's going to be a long holiday.	☐
There won't be enough hours in the day.	☐
I'll spend all my time in the garden.	☐
I'm worried how I'll fill all that time.	☐
The best way to pass time is to keep busy.	☐
I'll wonder how I found time for my job.	☐
It's the hours I used to be at work that worry me.	☐
I'm going to spend all my time decorating the house.	☐
I'm a fishing/bowling (insert your own major interest) person so there's no problem about filling time for me.	☐

All these statements are vague and generalised. The best holidays, long or short, even the ones you spend doing nothing, get their savour from having a time limit. You know the house isn't so huge its maintenance will keep you permanently occupied. You know that the garden lies dormant in the winter. You know that life dominated by one major interest, sport or hobby would be lop-sided.

Planning and day dreaming
Day dreaming doesn't have to be vague and fruitless. Combined with other processes it can be an important part of planning. Once you have taken stock of your situation, set yourself some goals and think about who else is involved, creative day dreaming comes in. It is the time when, in your imagination, you try out different options, run through the possibilities, test what they feel like.

How much time?
Let's look again at the question of time. You need to consider:
O How much time is there?
O Who else is involved?
O What could I do with the time?
O What is realistic?

Before retirement

Hours spent per week:	You	Partner/ Relative Friend	Tom	Alice
At work (including travelling time).			60	—
On domestic chores.			—	50
Asleep.			60	60
On leisure pursuits.			48	58

How do you spend your time now?
There are 168 hours in a week. Most people will spend about 50–60 of these asleep. People in full time jobs will dispose of another 45–60 hours at work, including the travelling time. That leaves about another 50 hours for domestic chores — cooking, cleaning, shopping, washing — and leisure.

On the chart below, fill in how you, if you live alone, or you and your partner relative or friend currently divide your time. As an example we have filled it in for Tom and Alice, a couple approaching retirement.

For most people the increase in leisure time that retirement brings is dramatic. Tom and Alice plan to share the domestic chores when Tom retires. Even so, Tom will have an extra 35 hours at his disposal and Alice an extra 25.

After retirement

Hours spent per week:	You	Partner/ Relative Friend	Tom	Alice
At work (including travelling time).			25	25
On domestic chores.			—	—
Asleep.			60	60
On leisure pursuits.			83	83

Could you fill your extra hours by expanding your current leisure activities? Take paper and pencil and list all the things you currently do in your leisure time. List occasional things such as days out as well as regular pursuits like watching TV. Here are Tom's and Alice's lists. Remember that most people underestimate the time spent watching television.

Tom
Watching TV
Reading science fiction
Visits to the pub
Evening class
Gardening
Seeing relatives
Playing bowls
Caravanning trips
Occasional days out
Decorating the house
Football matches

Alice
Watching TV
Knitting
Visiting friends
Looking after neighbours' children
Writing letters
Seeing relatives
Occasional days out
Red Cross
Caravanning trips

It is unlikely that either of them will be able to fill their extra hours simply by doing more of the same. Tom's leisure activities have been to some extent shaped by his job. Working in a busy, noisy office all day he likes to spend his evenings reading, watching TV or having a quiet pint. After retirement he may need to look for interests that are more active and which would replace the friendship and stimulation found at work. Alice may need to find interests outside the home that will make sure she really does hand over half the domestic chores to Tom.

Does the picture look similar for you? It may be that at the moment you have little idea of how to fill those extra hours beyond a vague notion of 'taking something up'. It would be worth looking at the pros and cons of part-time work, voluntary work, educational opportunities, and joining clubs and organisations so that you will be able to transform dreams into practical ideas about what could and will happen.

How realistic are your ideas

As a first step, take a look at some of your vaguer expectations about filling the extra time of retirement. No one retires in isolation. Almost every decision you make about how to spend your time, even a decision to do nothing, may affect someone else. The closer the relationship, the keener the effect. In making some of your ideas more concrete, see how they match the ideas of those around you.

On the right are some statements that people commonly make about retirement.

o Go quickly through them and circle any of these that might apply to you.
o Then go back and choose one of the statements to work on. Below each statement is a list of questions to answer. The aim of these questions is to make you think in a practical way about what the statement means.
o Think about what the statement implies for people you know. You may find you have to go and talk to other people in order to complete the exercise. This activity should help you to begin to put some detail into your picture of the ideal retirement for you.

If none of the statements applies to you, try to think of one of your own and ask yourself the same kind of questions.

You live with others

It'll be good when I'm home all day.
o What exactly will you do?
o Is your partner going to be pleased?
o Will his/her routine be upset?
o Imagine the events of a typical day's retirement together. What pleasures can you imagine? What problems do you foresee?
o Are there other members of the household at home? How will your retirement affect them and vice versa?

I'll go out most days and avoid getting under his/her feet.
o Where will you go?
o What will you do?
o Is this what your partner/friend wants?
o What will he/she be doing while you're out?
o Imagine the events of typical week in retirement. What occupations can you imagine? What problems do you foresee?

I'll be just as busy in retirement as I was before.
o What exactly will you be busy with?
o How will your partner and friends feel about your 'busy-ness'? Pleased? Fed up you've not much time for them?
o Imagine a typical 'busy' day in retirement. What occupation can you imagine? What problems do you foresee?

We'll do everything together now.
o List the things you might do together.
o List any things you wouldn't enjoy doing together.
o Does your partner want to do everything together?
o Imagine a typical day spent entirely in each other's company. What pleasures can you imagine? What problems do you foresee?
o Do you share all the same friends, some or none?

You live alone

It'll be good when I'm at home all day.

o What steps will you take to make sure you do not become isolated?

o Can you become even more self-sufficient by learning more e.g. cooking, DIY, gardening?

o Imagine a typical month of being at home all day. Will this work for a year or for five years or more? Or do you need to think again?

I'll be able to socialise more once I'm retired.

o Who with?

o Where will you go?

o What can you afford?

o Imagine a typical week's social activities in retirement.

I'll be just as busy in retirement as I was before.

o What exactly will you be busy with?

o How will your friends feel about your 'busy-ness'? Pleased? Fed up you've not much time for them?

o Imagine a typical 'busy' day in retirement. What occupation can you imagine? What problems do you foresee?

Tom's daydream

Here is part of Tom's daydream about the statement 'I'll go out most days and avoid getting under her feet.'

"I'll go out first thing and buy the paper . . . read it over breakfast . . . take Alice tea.

"Monday morning I'll walk into town to the library . . . mm . . . not sure that'll take all morning. Maybe I could look around the shops.

"Or do the shopping for Alice. She'd have lunch ready when I get back. Not sure what else she'd be doing – housework I suppose, or drinking tea with the neighbours.

"Monday afternoon . . . I suppose I could go for a game of bowls, but that would mean trekking back into town . . . I might feel like reading my library books, but then I'd be in Alice's way.

"Well never mind Monday, try Tuesday.

"I could spend Tuesday gardening . . . but what if it rains . . . and anyway Saturday's my usual day in the garden . . . perhaps Tuesday could be my day for taking up something new . . . exactly what, though . . ."

As Tom goes on with his daydream it becomes clear to him that he's not really sure how he'll manage to go out each day. He's not quite sure what Alice wants either. He starts to change his mind about going out so much. He realises that he needs to talk more to Alice about what she wants and to be more precise about how he might spend his time.

You may well find that trying to turn a vague daydream into a more practical statement means that you change your mind. You may have discovered that you need a lot more information. Even the best laid plans can go astray if your partner, family and close friends:

o Are unaware of their existence.

o Have made other apparently good plans of their own.

o Are totally out of sympathy with your decisions.

o Are annoyed about assumptions you have made about what *they* want.

As you develop your plan it is likely that you will change your mind several times. You may change your mind when:

o You look at your assumptions about different aspects of retirement.

o You set yourself goals.

o You think about other people involved.

o You map out a plan.

o You turn a plan or decision into action.

Decisions are never final. Turning a daydream into a plan will mean making some adjustments.

How healthy are you?

Health is important at any time of life. Many people would say health is just the absence of illness, or that it's being fit. Some would say it's surviving a long time; some that it's being able to adapt so that you are on top of things.

Of course health is a mixture of all of these things. It's also something you *can* do something about because it's connected with your life-style.

This topic asks you to think about your health now and in the past. It also asks you to think about what, if anything, you want to do about your health.

What do you think health is?

Try asking your family and friends what they think health is. The chances are that you'll get more than one opinion. The people you talk to might mention

physical health, they might mention mental health, emotional health, or all three. They might have talked about habits and routines, looks and attitudes.

A healthy person is . . . ?

Tick which of the following you think would describe a healthy person. Then ask a couple of other people to do the same.

A person who is healthy:	You	2 Others	
Never goes to the doctor.	☐	☐	☐
Doesn't smoke.	☐	☐	☐
Doesn't drink much.	☐	☐	☐
Takes plenty of exercise.	☐	☐	☐
Has shiny eyes and hair.	☐	☐	☐
Doesn't take any pills or medicines.	☐	☐	☐
Lives to be very old.	☐	☐	☐
Is the right weight for his or her height.	☐	☐	☐
Only gets the odd cold or stomach upset.	☐	☐	☐
Enjoys life.	☐	☐	☐
Is fairly relaxed.	☐	☐	☐
Eats the correct diet.	☐	☐	☐
Doesn't over-indulge.	☐	☐	☐
Takes an interest in everything.	☐	☐	☐
Sleeps well.	☐	☐	☐

Did you all tick the same answers? Do you think that to be a healthy person would involve *all* these things?

Think of someone you know who you think is healthy. What is it that makes you think they are healthy — the way they look, the way they behave, the things they do? Do you think this person works at being healthy, or thinks about it? Do you think he cares for himself, worries about his health? Now think of someone else healthy. Are the features of his health the same as the first person?

Good health for you is the best health *you* can achieve given your own circumstances.

It means:

○ Being aware of the condition of your body, mind, emotions, without being over anxious.

○ Taking some responsibility for your own health care.

○ Paying attention to early warning signals that might mean something is wrong, or that you are pushing yourself too hard.

○ Adapting to any health problems you have and making the best of the situation.

Three health stories

Before you think about your own standard look at these three health stories. Ivan, Cora and Norman are very different individuals. They were all born in the same year and are now 65.

In the chart they have provided details of what they see as the main medical events in their lives.

The social events in their lives provide a further picture of the health of these individuals.

Ivan		Cora		Norman	
Age	Event	Age	Event	Age	Event
3	Whooping Cough	12	Periods started	19	Hernia operation
7	Diphtheria	24	Pregnancy and Childbirth	45	Shingles
10	Pneumonia	27	Pregnancy and Childbirth	45	High blood pressure
17	TB	29	Pregnancy and Childbirth	53	Minor heart attack
28	Bronchitis	51	Menopause	56	Heart attack
37	Pleurisy	63	Touch of arthritis in hands	60	Heart surgery
56	Varicose veins			63	Further heart surgery
63	Bronchitis				

Ivan was a sickly child, one of nine. Two of his brothers died in childhood and several times he wasn't expected to survive. He lived in an overcrowded damp house and his father was frequently out of work. He spent several years in a sanitorium in his late teens where he met and married his wife Edna. Once over TB, and told by his doctor never to smoke, he resumed his former hobbies, cycling and fishing. He and Edna didn't have very much money, they lived in rented accommodation and Ivan cycled to work not being able to afford a car. He lost his job and during the two years he spent unemployed his wife left him and took with her their only child. Ivan became depressed and started to drink during this period. He then had a bad attack of pleurisy at 37 and was forced to take stock of himself. He threw himself into all sorts of activities to take his mind off things.

When his divorce came through he moved to live with his sister who ran a post office and village shop. This arrangement worked quite well. He did the accounts for the shop and took care of the house.

Cora was an only child. She was brought up on a farm. She wasn't sporty but helped on the farm during childhood and adolescence. She married a local farmer and continued to do farm work. Her village shopping and visiting was always done by bicycle or on foot. She always had much to occupy her: three children, a vegetable garden and hens, a little business selling produce at the local market. All that ever made her pause for thought as far as her health was concerned was when she read about the possible dangers of dairy produce five years ago. She decided to cut down on it and has stuck to her decision. In the last couple of years she's had what she calls "twinges of arthritis" in her hands. She hasn't been to the doctor but now makes a deliberate effort to look after her hands.

Norman was the eldest of three children. He was mad about sport as a teenager and won seventeen athletics trophies in six years. He was on active service during the war and when he was demobbed he was slightly underweight but otherwise fit. He got a job in the Civil Service. He got married at 25 to Faye. They had three children in eight years and he was totally absorbed in his family and career. As his prosperity increased he bought a car, started to smoke, drank more alcohol. He was promoted and found himself under some strain at work. It certainly didn't help him smoke less and because he always felt tired after work he tended just to relax and not to think about doing anything active. He was promoted again and felt increased stresses. Norman expected his body to look after itself, partly because he'd always enjoyed good health. He couldn't see any point in giving up smoking, and being overweight at the age of 50 didn't worry him. He put it down to middle age spread. He was shocked when he suffered his first heart attack.

Look back at the stories about Ivan, Cora and Norman and think whether each of them was throughout life:
o Aware of the condition of body, mind and emotions.
o Taking reponsibility for some of their own health care.
o Paying attention to early warning signals of something being wrong.
o Adapting to health problems and making the best of the situation.

Cora's life story shows her to have been fit and healthy throughout. Her style of life contributed a great deal, of course. But what about Ivan and Norman? Ivan's poor health made him more aware of the need to look after himself. A higher standard of living in Norman's case contributed to his decline in physical fitness. After the age of 50 Ivan is in every way fitter than Norman. Yet at every age from the time of his decline Norman could have been fitter if he had wanted to do something about it.

Your health story

Now write down your own health story. Firstly list all the medical events in your life that you think have been significant. Then write a brief sketch of the main social events of your life.

Finally, try and go through things that don't immediately seem to be con-

nected with the list of medical events you've made, but which are nevertherless connected with your health .
o Things that have happened leading you to take more or less exercise.
o Promotion at work.
o Changes in smoking and drinking habits.
o Events which led to alterations in

your diet.
o Alterations in your weight.
o Different kinds of jobs.
o Getting married.
o Things that made you feel depressed or anxious.
o Having a family.
o Moving house.
o Alterations in your income.

Medical events: You

Age	Event

Social events: You

Age	Event	Age	Event

Are there key points in your life when you can remember your level of fitness increasing or declining?

How do you feel about your health now it's down on paper? Do you feel your present health is good? Or do you think you could be healthier?

However your health story reads here are some facts to think about:

o There is evidence that it is more common for health to improve in the year after retirement than for deterioration to occur.

o You do get benefits if you become fitter. And as you get older, the greater these benefits are.

o If fitness has begun to decline, that decline can be slowed down.

o The onset of disease can affect fitness. Nevertheless fitness training when you have a disease can be valuable and may actually slow down the disease process.

o Few parts of the body or mind wear out because they are over-used, and they tend to lose their efficiency if they're *not* used.

o The ageing process is not necessarily accompanied by disease and disability, after all you've been ageing all your life!

o Only a few people ever suffer from the problems which are usually associated with old age.

Your health from now on

It there an elixir of life? The simple answer is no. Ageing is a normal biological process and no substance can slow down the rate of ageing.

However, it is possible to prevent many of the health problems associated with being older because they are not due to ageing itself. They are caused by three other things *disease, unfitness* and *the social problems of growing older.*

These can frequently be prevented or treated.

Look at the chart below. You can't do anything about ageing. But you can make some inroads into any of the other three circles. Body and mind will be more efficient if they're used well. Being fit you'll feel good and be able to do more. Getting the right company will help you with advice and friendship.

Ageing: health and disease

Many unpleasant problems associated with getting older are due to disease.

Dai Evans entered his club in South Wales and walked slowly to the bar taking three or four minutes for the 15 yard journey, because he had to stop for breath. His breathlessness was not due to ageing of the lung tissue but to having smoked 40 cigarettes a day for 30 years. One of the effects was chronic bronchitis.

Dai had had this condition for a long time, and matters had been getting steadily worse in later years. It's easy to confuse disease with the ageing process.

Everyone is aware that the body's vital organs will suffer wear and tear over the years. The difficulty is knowing what is normal and what may be a sign of some disease that requires treatment. If you notice some change in yourself — breathlessness, dizziness, deafness don't assume it's due to your age; seek medical advice. And remember the story of the man who thought the stiffness he got in one leg was due to his age — his other leg was just as old!

Natural biological processes. Cells become abnormal or die completely (e.g. cells in hair roots). Tissues of body become less elastic.

Statistically certain diseases are likely to show themselves in later life e.g. heart disease, arthritis. But this does not mean that you as an individual will suffer any of these once past middle age.

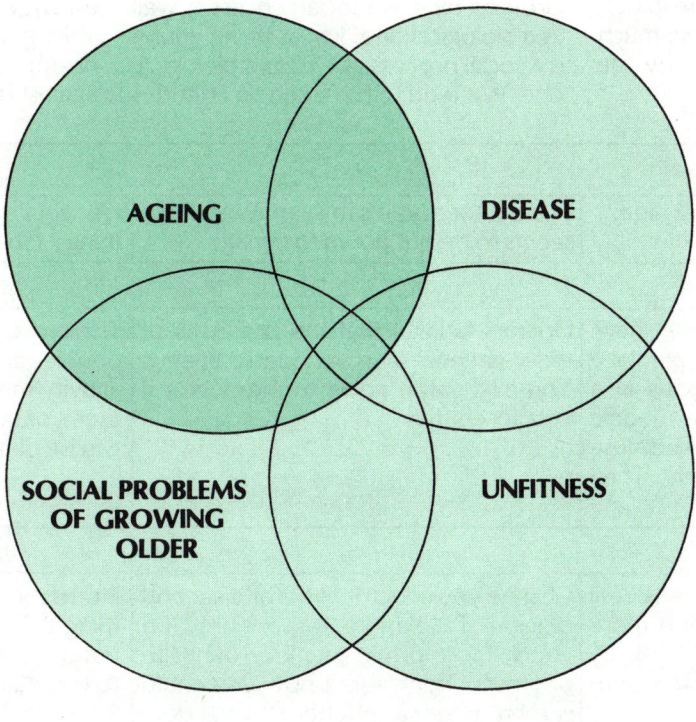

Worried about money or living conditions. Isolated from contact with outside world. Bored with own company. All these are social problems which can affect your state of health both physically and mentally.

If you are unfit you won't be able to walk very far, lift and carry very much. You'll feel tired and lacking in energy. Mentally you will feel less alert. You'll become more inactive and as a result feel old.

Ageing: fitness and unfitness

Fitness is an idea appropriate for any age. It's particularly important to think about fitness at the time of retirement for three reasons:

o Retirement gives you the opportunity to become fitter easily and enjoyably.

o Many of the problems associated with being older are due to unfitness not to disease, not to age. Such problems are therefore preventable.

o As you become older it's easier to become unfit, and more difficult to regain fitness once you've lost it.

There are four aspects of fitness:

Strength
Stamina
Skill
Flexibility

They can all be improved at any age.

Almost everyone who takes exercise regularly reports one other major benefit — they feel better, more confident, less anxious, and less depressed.

But what about fitness and disease?

Many diseases reduce the sufferer's mobility. Immobility then leads to a greater loss of fitness. Someone who stops being as active as he was through illness finds his joints stiffen, his muscles weaken and he becomes breathless more easily. These changes come on more quickly when people are older. Many people are disabled not so much by the disease itself but more by the unfitness which results.

Ageing: its social aspects and problems

Growing older is a social process as well as a biological one. Just as being young is a social process as well as a biological one. We tend to have certain attitudes about how people of different ages should behave.

These are quite extreme examples. Really they are not in the first place to do with the individual who is affected at all. They are about other people's ideas. Taking more responsibility for your health might mean that you do come up against such attitudes.

Attitude		
Swimming or cycling at your age.	The doctor says it's my age. Everything seems to be put down to my age.	He gets so confused and says silly things. (So do we all at times!)
Effect		
Until recently many people have thought it odd if older people take exercise or expose their bodies in a swimming pool. So many people stopped taking exercise simply because they thought it wasn't seemly. Then they became unfit.	Doctors believe that the problems of older patients were all due to ageing. You might stop going to the doctor if you accept this.	The fact that some people think older people are incapable of intellectual activity means they don't really talk to them, or question their statements. This can be damaging to a healthy mind.
Action		
Exercise at home or with friends. Tell yourself that your health matters more to you than what other people think . . . use the swimming pool when few people are there.	Change your doctor. Ask for a second opinion. Take more responsibility on yourself to improve your level of health or fitness. Think about how you could present your case better to your doctor. Get a check up if you are unhappy.	Stretch your mind by tackling something that requires effort and concentration. Show anyone who talks down to you that you don't like it. Stimulation is essential for a healthy mind.

An investment in health

People who retire can expect to live for quite a long time.

If you're . . .	You can expect to live until . . .	
	M	F
50–55	76	80
56–60	76–78	81
61–65	79	82
66–70	79–81	84

How *well* you live is a slightly different matter. When you're 80:

You might be doing this

You probably won't be doing this

You need not be like this

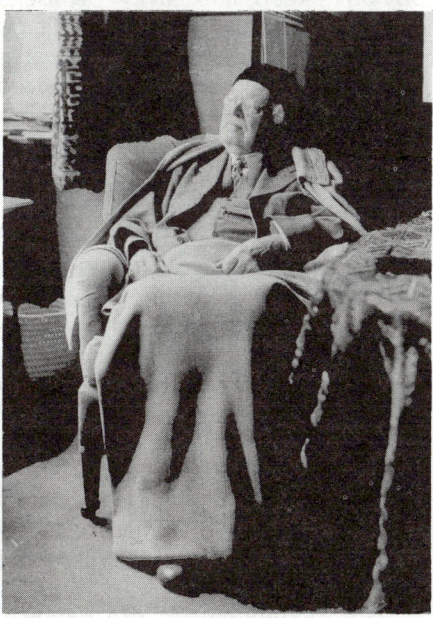

Of course 80 seems a long way off. But how you handle your own health care *now* and from day to day is important for the future.

Think about Norman's health story again. In his mid-thirties and middle age his attitude to health care did have a bearing on what happened to him not so long after.

Good health now is an investment for the future. That's true of all the earlier stages in your life too.

But now you really do have time to take stock, pause and decide how to maintain good health or better still, improve it.

So think about it . . .

How active are you?

When did you last think about keeping active and taking exercise? What do you think being fit means? Can you be sure you're as fit as you think you are? Do you ever get worried about not being fit? What should you be able to do at your age?

Being active, feeling good

Think about the last time when doing something active made you feel really good. Was it during:

o The past week?
o The past month?
o The past year?
o More than a year ago?

What was it that you did that made you feel good? Perhaps it was not an obvious keep-fit activity — although deliberate attempts at keeping fit do pay off surprisingly well. Often it is simply a generally active and balanced life style that aids a feeling of well being.

On the go

Molly Briers, 59, coming up to retirement, would label herself as fairly inactive but fit. She does her housework daily before going to work as a hospital ward auxiliary; keeps her garden tidy when the nights are light and at weekends; walks to the shops and carries a fair weight of groceries home. Her busy life gives ample opportunity for exercise.

Now think of someone you know whom you think is active and healthy for their age and write what you know of their patterns of activity and exercise.

Think of movements like bending, stretching, lifting, carrying, climbing. Is their job physically demanding, or does it offer opportunities for mobility? Are they active at home? Do they seek exercise in the fresh air, say, digging the garden or, in a more organised way, by being an active member of a sporting club?

David, 64, an electrician, works a five day week. His friend Peter wrote down what he knew of David's patterns of activity and exercise:

o David's job does not take much out of him physically but he does do a lot of bending, stretching and climbing.
o Last month David and I and our wives took our grandchildren on holiday.

He played cricket on the beach with the children. Nothing very energetic but he kept at it for a good hour and a half. He also went swimming with them twice.

o He does a lot of gardening. He probably spends an hour a night on the garden when it's fine. He's got a hand lawn-mower and always uses that, and he's got hand shears for the hedge at the front.
o David and his wife Elsie always take the dog out on fine nights, even in the winter. They're away about an hour and a half.
o More occasional events: he always does his own decorating, window cleaning and car maintenance and cleans the car once a week.

Now you've thought about someone else's activity patterns, what about yours?

Do you think that someone else would see you as being active and healthy and do you see yourself in that way?

Sometimes your picture of yourself does not match the picture others have of you.

John Elliott considers himself at 65 healthy and reasonably fit. He is retired and helps his wife who is asthmatic, with jobs that exert her too much — brushing down the stairs, cleaning windows. He walks the dog down to the local most evenings. He plays bowls in the season and, on winter evenings, after his early evening pint or two, he likes his supper in his armchair where he sits watching TV for the rest of the night. He watches more TV than usual at weekends because he likes sport.

Would you see John as being active and healthy?

Mary Morgan does not see herself as unusual though her colleagues would describe her as an athletic 58 year old. She is an active member of a cycling club and cycles most weekends. She likes to keep fit, swims at least once a week and helps at a 'never too late to learn' swimming club for the over 60's. In the large city store where she works as a counter assistant, she usually chooses to use the stairs rather than the lift.

What about Mary, do you see her as being active and healthy?

Putting it to the test

Here are some activities. Tick the ones you think indicate fitness in people of your own age and which ones you think you could do *now* if you were asked.

	Fit for your age	You
Push the car 100 yards on the flat when the battery is flat.	☐	☐
Walk for an hour on the flat on a calm day at three miles an hour.	☐	☐
Walk for an hour on a windy day against the wind at three miles an hour.	☐	☐
Paint the living room ceiling.	☐	☐
Run for the bus (for a minute or so as fast as you can).	☐	☐
Carry a 40 lb suitcase for half a mile.	☐	☐

Think about what you would feel in your present state of fitness if you did any of these things . . .
Would any of the following results occur?

Straight afterwards	**The next day**
Out of breath	Aching muscles
Dizzy	Tired out
Muscle pains	
Tired	

One of the reasons many people think that they are fitter than they are is because they know that they *can* run for a bus or push a car if they are asked to do so, without too many ill effects.

And so they think that they could do a lot more as well if they wanted to.

But short bursts of activity are very different from longer sessions. If you push a car for two minutes, your muscles will work quite well. They don't need your blood to pump extra oxygen to them for activity of this length of time. If you take exercise for a longer period of time your muscles need more oxygen and your heart has to supply the blood for it. If you are unfit your muscles only extract a small proportion of the oxygen from each blood cell.

So if you ticked only the short sharp bursts of activity in the above list, and thought that you might feel distressed if you did any of the others, you could probably be a lot fitter!

Keeping active

Consider the list of activities below. Many people over the age of 60 enjoy them regularly. Perhaps you are among them. If not perhaps you could consider trying one or two.

Activity/Exercise	Tick for yes Cross for no	Others might at 60–65	Myself	Others might at 66–70	Myself
Walk up to a mile a day.					
Garden for an hour a day.					
Cycle to work.					
Cycle to the shops.					
Swim several lengths of the baths once a week.					
Join a veteran's football/rugby club.					
Play: Badminton Tennis Squash } with a partner of own age group and fitness level.					
Choose an activity based holiday, e.g. outward bound for the 60+ Group which offers a choice of learning how to: Ride a horse. Sail a dinghy. Climb rocks.					
Hill walking.					
Go to keep fit classes for own age group.					
Play golf.					
Play bowls.					

Where you have ticked for others and not for yourself, is there a good reason for the difference? Are there real medical indications for your not doing exercise or are you simply opting out? Are you jumping to the conclusion that getting older automatically means decreased activity rather than a matter of selecting activities that best suit your own circumstances?

Improvements

But what would improve if you decided to take more exercise? What would be the benefits?

There are three things that affect your physical condition:

Your age.
Chronic disabilities.
Activity or inactivity.

Your age: as most of us know, there are no elixirs for life. You cannot do anything about your age.

Chronic disabilities: by the age of 65 one in four people have some kind of chronic disability (such as recurrent joint problems, chronic chest or heart diseases). The extent to which the capacity for exercise would be impaired varies considerably from individual to individual. For example, swimming in the local baths, which are usually heated, would ease rheumatic and arthritic joints.
Many forms of chronic disability can be improved or made less painful with medical attention. It is well worth visiting the doctor if you feel you do have a chronic disability about which nothing has yet been done.

Activity or inactivity: this is what you can probably do most about. Physical activity leads to an improvement in your body's performance. and it allows you to do *more* physical activity. If you're out of condition you'll notice improvements very quickly!

What improvements can you bring about

Your lungs
Lungs are subject to age-related changes — they do deteriorate over the years. But generally not so that you would notice. *Except if you smoke.* Age related changes to the lungs are practically nothing compared with the effects of cigarette smoking.

Giving up smoking can slow down the deterioration of your lungs, and reduce the likelihood of recurring bronchitis attacks. Improvements have been noted in people who give up late in life.

Your muscles and your heart
The more active you are, the more useful your muscles become. Although you can't actually improve the condition of your heart you can make its job an easier one and help it to perform better.

Through increased activity your muscles become stronger and able to work harder; they become far more efficient at extracting the oxygen from your blood cells. This takes a load off your heart which doesn't then have to build up so much pressure to pump blood around your system.

But there are plenty of other benefits to be gained from building up your muscles and increasing their usefulness. You want to make sure that they remain strong enough to perform the sorts of movements which are vital to your independence. If you've ever been laid up for a long time you'll know what it's like to find your muscles have become too weak for you to get around the house, even. When that happens your horizons become pretty narrow.

The need to be fit
Your physical condition is something over which you have a lot more control than you might think. It's well within most peoples' capacity to get themselves into good shape — and it's something they must face responsibility for. Being in good shape increases your appetite and your enthusiasm for all good things that life has to offer. Being inactive only leads to still further inactivity. As you start to get out of condition it becomes harder and harder to work up the enthusiasm for doing anything.

And what makes matters worse is the reaction of other people when you get into the state. They may be only too happy to indulge you if you let them. 'Now you mustn't exert yourself' they might say. '*You're not as young as you used to be.*' Their intentions are kindly, of course, but if you allow yourself to be treated like an invalid pretty soon you'll start to feel like one.

So, take steps now. You've seen the list of activities. Have a look now at how much you actually do. If it doesn't seem like very much, see what you can do to increase your level of activity and improve your overall fitness. Get fitter and you'll feel better.

Fit for your age

Nobody works to full capacity all the time. If you start to feel distressed and breathless over a period of time when you're exercising you're working at about 50–70% of *your* capacity. At 30% of your active capacity you'll feel comfortable.

If you watch road labourers leaning on their spades you'll be watching men who are balancing out their work capacity. They do short sharp bursts when they're working at 70%, then they'll take a rest and on the whole they'll end up by working at 30% of their active capacity.

What about You?
Do you think that at your age you can't do as much as you used to be able to do? Well you're right!
A man of 70 has about 50% of the capacity for physical activity that a man of 20 has. So if you're getting older, on the whole you'll be nearer your maximum capacity when a younger person is coping comfortably.
But what does that actually mean for you and your life? It means, forget about the man of 20 and try and make sure you work to the best of *your* abilities.

What could this mean from day to day?
Remember that walking for an hour at three miles an hour is nearer your maximum capacity than it is your daughter's or your grand-daughter's. But if you are fit it won't be as near to your maximum capacity as if you were unfit.

How much do you do

Do a check on the level of your activity.

Think about the past week and write down on the chart what you feel to have been noticeable activity or exercise on your part. Put down any short bursts of activity like running for the bus; noticeable bending and stretching; carrying heavy things.

Try and remember how long each activity took you, how you felt afterwards both on the same day and if you felt any after effects the next day. Here is Eleanor Brent's chart to help you.

Do you find like Eleanor that you did something that perhaps made you feel stretched, tired, breathless?

If so, then in the past week you've probably done something which brought you to 70% of your maximum capacity.

If you're not stretched at all it might be a good idea to see if you can introduce more activity into your daily routine. Once you've done that you'll be able to do more still.

Part of being healthy is being fit. Peoples' health tends to improve anyway in retirement so why not resolve to improve your health by being as fit as *you* can be.

Eleanor Brent's week

	What I did	How I felt
1	Walked to work (25 mins).	Same as usual.
2	Walked to work (25 mins). Went shopping—had to carry shopping to car (½ mile: 15 mins).	Same as usual. Felt as though arms were going to drop off.
3	Walked to work (25 mins). Made love (couldn't see watch!)	Arms ached a bit from yesterday. Same as usual. Pretty good.
4	Walked to work. (just under 20 mins). Walked to the club and back : (½ mile: 15 mins).	Was late on the way so I really pushed myself and felt breathless when I got there. Same as usual.

Your week

Day	What I did	How I felt
1		
2		
3		
4		
5		
6		
7		

What do you eat?

Nutrition, diet and health

Nutrition, more than most other matters connected with health, has been subject to many changes of opinion over the years. Anyone who has been at all interested in the topic could be forgiven for thinking that the 'experts' cannot make up their minds. Most people will agree, however, that diet has a direct effect upon health.

You are what you eat
Eating habits and their effects on your body are an individual matter. The average person swallows about half a ton of food a year and the body is remarkably good at extracting what it needs from this. If you go on eating too much of some things and not enough of others you will eventually get out of condition. If you are eating a varied diet it is almost impossible to go short of proteins, vitamins or minerals.

Find the balance
You can make it easy to stay healthy if you find the right balance for yourself of:
○ Nutrients (proteins, fats, carbohydrates, vitamins, minerals and water) the raw materials for building and repairing the body.
○ Energy (calories) to keep you lively and active.
○ Dietary fibre (a mixture of plant substances) to provide roughage.
Many people nowadays eat much more than they need to. Part of the job of finding the right balance is to also examine the amount of food you are consuming.

Everyone is different
"Mary eats like a horse and never puts on weight. Jim has only a moderate appetite and is always having to watch his weight." How can this be? The tendency to put on weight often runs in families. It may be that the genes Mary inherited determined that this was how her body would react to what she ate. Perhaps, unlike Jim, she had never picked up the habit of eating between meals or a preference for sweet things.

She may, as a busy housewife, be getting the balance right between the food she eats and the amount of exercise she gets. Jim may be travelling from home to office by car, and supplementing his moderate diet with alchohol. Both are likely to put on weight as they get older, however, and Mary will put on proportionally more because of her sex.

Everyone is different. Eating habits, your lifestyle and their effects on your body are an individual matter. How long is it since you thought about the way your diet is affecting your health? If you are having a varied diet, you are certainly getting enough nutrients but, perhaps too many carbohydrates and fats. In most cases only minor adjustments are needed to achieve a healthier diet.

Changing habits

During World War II, despite rationing, the health of the nation improved. There were plenty of vegetables. Bread was coarser and contained more fibre (roughage) than the present white loaf. Meat, eggs, bacon, sugar and fats were strictly rationed as were sweets. Cakes and biscuits were often unobtainable. Only special cases like babies, pregnant women and the sick needed added minerals and vitamins (like iron, cod liver oil or orange juice supplements).

Two war-time menus:

Vegetable Soup
Savoury Omelette
Baked Apples

Tomato Soup
Vegetable Hot-Pot
Sponge (fatless)
and Custard
(made with
dried eggs)

On the whole people are unconcerned about diet and nutrition until some particular event brings them into focus. For example, convalescence might be accompanied by a poor appetite. You might decide you need to slim or you may get short of cash and find you can't afford your usual choice of foods. In each of these cases change may bring concern about diet and health.

Retirement and eating patterns

Retirement will bring changes and these may include altered eating habits. It could be an opportunity for a healthier diet. There isn't one 'right' pattern of eating. You certainly don't have to have three meals a day for instance.

Here's how Mary and Jim, Sylvia and Bert thought about the changes in their eating patterns around retirement.

Before retirement

I'm putting weight on. Have to watch it.

Mary's a great cook. I'm looking forward to a hot midday meal, as well as later in the day!

Wouldn't mind trying my hand at a spot of cooking — I suppose Mary wouldn't want me under her feet in the kitchen.

Hope that Ruth woman doesn't keep coming in and out for cups of tea when I'm at home all day.

Jim

Jim and Mary are married.
Mary decided to bring up the subject of the dreaded cooked lunch as diplomatically as she could one Saturday lunch-time when they were

I like entertaining at home (even if it costs a lot).

I love cooking but once I've cleared breakfast I like to concentrate just on our main major meal in the evening.

I love being free from preparing meals in the day now the children have left.

Dread Jim at home all day — he'll want a cooked lunch and snacks every half hour.

I'd like to try a few vegetarian dishes but Jim likes the old meat and two veg.

Mary

having a pie and a pint at the local pub! It lead to a long talk about their expectations for retirement. They didn't agree on all matters but were able to find some compromises.

After retirement

Although most people would agree in principle that a good diet is important for health, the nutritional side does not always have the biggest effect on what we eat. Work routines, family and social commitments, the cost of food,

I'll have to stop eating out so much.

Not much fun eating on your own though – wonder if I'll get so bored with it that I'll stop bothering with cooking?

Food costs so much – I'll have to cut down if I'm going to be able to afford to go out and about a bit.

I do miss Beryl a lot.

Well, I can boil an egg and make a decent sandwich. I'm going to miss the canteen though.

Glad now I used to do the shopping at weekends with 'B'. At least I know a bit about cost – and quality. I could do with a bit more variety though. I'd love a Sunday roast.

I'm going to go on entertaining but choose less expensive food – think of what is good for us as well as what looks good.

Glad Jim sees the point about me being retired as well. He's made several really nice cold snack lunches this week.

If he gets any better in the kitchen I'll have to look to my laurels.

If I slip in a vegetarian dish once a week Jim'll gradually adjust to the change.

Sylvia

Sylvia lives alone. She decided she needed to think more about her pattern of spending on food and made a note of everything she spent on eating out over a month and found she had to make some minor adjustments.

Bert

Bert recently lost his wife, Beryl, who had always taken care of the cooking. He knew that he would have to fend for himself and that without the works canteen to fall back on he would have problems once he retired.

Mary

the ability to cook will often be of more practical importance.

For each of these four people retirement was an event which triggered off some changes in their eating patterns. All of them found that these patterns continued to change as time went on.

Certain eating patterns drew to a natural conclusion at the onset of retirement and as a result of this the four were presented with opportunities for planning changes. The changes included not only what was eaten and when but also led on to learning new skills, adopting new social routines of eating out, sharing meals with friends and budgeting for new eating habits. All four recognised the fact that there isn't one 'right' pattern so that when they came to organising their new routines, as well as nutritional factors they took into account these other important social considerations.

Mary's right — I enjoy my food much more when I don't eat between meals.

Now that I've lost a bit of weight — I feel much fitter.

Ruth actually stopped talking for five minutes when she saw me getting a fruit salad together this morning. If she keeps coming she might learn something!

I should be able to take up 'holiday Italian' and keep up membership of the drama group.

I'm going to eat at home — it's cheaper and I can have more choice.

Miriam and I can work out some menus together and take it in turns to do the cooking and eat together once or twice a week. We both want to cut down on cost so it should work out quite well.

Glad I joined that class at the adult centre. Fancy them having a 'cookery for men'.

Joe and me are really into this cooking lark now.

I've always liked food — didn't know there was so much to find out about it. I'm getting out of the rut a bit and trying food I've never had before. I'm feeling better lately too.

Jim

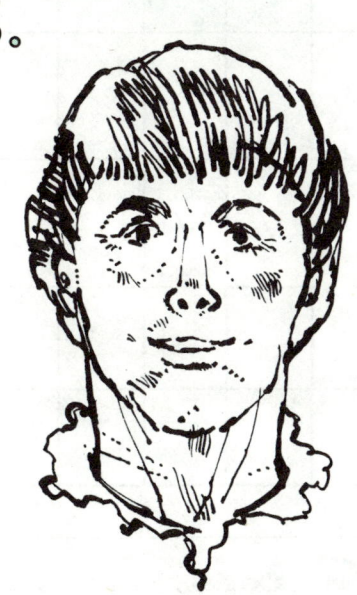

Sylvia

Bert

A chance for healthier eating?

Look at the chart below. Each tick in the 'change' column *could* be an opportunity for a change in a healthier direction. Eating more meals at home and fewer in the works canteen will give you more control and choice. Spending less on food need not mean that you skimp on essential items. If you buy with the nutritional content of the food in mind, you could end up with a better diet. What do your ticks in the 'change' column imply? Can you turn them into opportunities for a healthier diet?

What changes do *you* expect?

Go through the list and tick

	I expect this to stay the same						I expect this to change					
	You	Partner	Mary	Jim	Sylvia	Bert	You	Partner	Mary	Jim	Sylvia	Bert
The meals I eat each day.			✓							✓	✓	✓
The snacks I eat each day.			✓							✓	✓	✓
The times of day I eat.			✓	✓							✓	✓
The meals I eat in a pub, restaurant or canteen.			✓	✓							✓	✓
The meals I eat with friends or relatives.			✓	✓							✓	✓
The meals I cook for guests.			✓							✓	✓	✓
The amount of money I spend on food.				✓	✓				✓			✓
The meals I cook.									✓	✓	✓	✓
The kind of food I eat.									✓	✓	✓	✓

Certain conditions, for example ulcers, diabetes, allergies, blood pressure, digestive disorders, call for special diets. Your doctor will advise you on these.

Handling money

This topic asks you to think about the part money has played in your life — the way you have used it and felt about it. It doesn't try to tell you what is right or wrong. It just tries to remind you of your attitudes so that you will have them in mind when making plans for retirement.

Budgets and plans —handling money

How do you actually deal with your money? Do you live from day to day, or do you budget and plan your expenditure?

On the right are questions about handling money. Think about them in regard to how you have handled your money in the past year.

For each question, tick 'Yes', 'No' or 'Can't Remember'.

You probably won't have had much difficulty in thinking about how you handled money in the past year. Look at the questions and answers again. Do you think that if you had answered these questions 10, 20 or even 40 years ago, your answers would have been the same?

Now think about a year, or more

	Yes	No	Can't Remember
Did you find out what your total net income was for the year?			
Did you keep a full record of your spending?			
Did you deliberately plan your spending?			
Were you saving money in any way?			
Were you saving for a particular purpose?			
Were you able to cope with unexpected bills or emergencies?			

than one year, when something happened that made you think about money more than usual. What did you do? How did you handle your money? Did you use any of the ways mentioned in the questions above?

If you have a partner particularly if he or she has always dealt with the financial affairs in your household discuss the ways that money was handled in the year you are thinking about. See if you can make a list of methods you used.

Past and Future

The year you retire may well be when your finances are in the forefront of your mind. Your financial arrangements will probably change. Think how measures taken in the past when your finances altered could provide pointers to plan this coming year.

Write them down to remind yourself.

Useful points

Here are some of the things to ensure a smooth financial change-over from work to retirement. Consider which ones would be particularly useful to you. Then add to your own list of useful points.

○ For many people being absolutely clear about their new financial situation is a great help. This might be a matter of asking questions of your employer, tax office, insurance companies, social services.

○ Noting spending patterns, listing a budget both for before retirement and after can be a useful exercise in helping to clear up areas of uncertainty.

○ Thinking about savings and investments and what you are worth can be reassuring and help you to plan for the future. Making a will and setting your affairs in order can also be reassuring for all concerned.

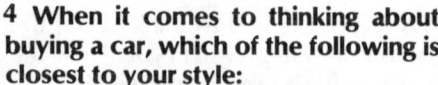

Attitudes to money —personal styles

Your handling of money is a practical thing—but underlying the practical everyday side, you might have certain attitudes towards money which may not be so obvious to you. How do your attitudes to money actually show in day to day life? What effect might they have on how you plan for your retirement?

What I would do if . . .

Here is a quiz about situations where money is involved. Look at each of the questions and circle the letter which marks the answer closest to your own way of going about things. Then ask your partner to look at the questions too and check how close your answers are to each others.

1 You suddenly have a windfall of £250. Would you:
(a) save it for a rainy day;
(b) blow it all on a spree;
(c) put it towards a luxury item;
(d) absorb it in day-to-day living expenses?

2 When it's sales time at the shop, do you:
(a) feel pleased that you've made some really good buys;
(b) feel you inevitably come away with rubbish;
(c) feel satisfied that you've saved money;
(d) feel that you've spent a lot more than you intended to spend?

3 You arrive at the railway station at 11.00 pm on a wet Saturday night after your holidays, your home is two miles away. Would you:
(a) wait for the last bus which doesn't come until midnight;
(b) take a taxi even if it's more expensive after 11.00 pm;
(c) walk home in the pouring rain?

4 When it comes to thinking about buying a car, which of the following is closest to your style:
(a) you look forward to it with pleasurable anticipation and decide to choose a car you'll really love whether you can afford it or not;
(b) you feel you're bound to be swindled whatever you decide;
(c) you examine all the motoring magazines and, after weighing up all the factors, choose your best buy;
(d) you go around all the local dealers and find the cheapest buy available?

5 It's your four-year-old grand-daughter's birthday. Would you decide to give:
(a) a sensible present like a savings certificate;
(b) an outrageous toy like a four-foot high furry panda;
(c) a soap and talcum powder set you received last year which you haven't used;
(d) a silver bracelet you've always loved and which has been in the family for many years?

The quiz, which was mostly about spending money, picked out a number of attitudes.

o Practical approaches to money:
   Organised.
   Disorganised.
   Generous.
   Careful.
o How people feel about money:
   It's enjoyable.
   It's worrying.
o How people see themselves in relation to money:
   Fortunate.
   Unfortunate.

Look back at the answers again. Which answers do you think expressed which attitudes? And which answers did you tick?

Perhaps you found that none of the answers were anywhere near the sort of thing you would have done. So think about what you would have done and see if you can work out what sort of attitudes lie behind your answers.

You may also have found that you had different attitudes to different questions, that in some situations you would be generous, and in others careful. Personal style with money is often a combination of approaches. Few of us are totally consistent.

Money, attitudes and approaches
The attitudes examined in the quiz are written down as a series of statements below.

Next to the statements is a scale with 5 points on it. The scale ranges from *agree strongly* to *disagree strongly*.

Look at each statement and put a tick on the scale to mark down how much you disagree or agree with the statement.

Now look at how you've filled in the scale.

The statements themselves express some quite definite attitudes to money.

Agreeing *or* disagreeing strongly expresses quite definite views of your own too. You have a clear well defined picture of yourself in relation to these attitudes to money. (It might be pessimistic but it is definite!)

If you filled in the scale down the middle then these attitudes obviously don't have much to do with your own attitudes. If that's the case think about what your attitudes are.

See if you can build up a list of your attitudes to money.

Your financial style
Write down the words that you think describe your attitudes to money. Use the ones that have already been suggested if you think they apply, or choose your own.

Now choose one adjective which you think describes one of your attitudes well. You might want to work this out with your partner.

Try and jot down a series of things that you think demonstrate why this word applies to you. Write down an incident that illustrates how the word applies to you, if you think it will help.

Audrey and Frank Jones decided the word 'generous' described their attitude to money well. Their list of activities which made them feel they were generous is as follows:

o Have drinks in our drinks cabinet.
o Feed people who drop in.
o Pay for rounds when out.
o Pay for grandchildren when on outings.
o Take grandchildren on holiday with us.

o Give grandaughter and grandson £10 when they come to visit.
o Give Christmas boxes to the tradesmen.
o Give to any charities at the door.
o Buy a treat for Great Auntie Rene each week.
o Run neighbours, who don't have a car, to the shops for free.

Audrey's and Frank's attitudes have been built up over a lifetime, and have probably developed partly as a result of being fairly well off.

Compare the Jones's ideas about themselves as 'generous' with Joe Leadbetter's description of an incident in which he saw himself as 'careful'.

The last time we went on holiday was to Llandudno a couple of years ago, with Elsie and Dave, our next door neighbours. I thought it would be sensible to keep a note of expenses so we could all square up at the end of the holiday. The scheme fell apart because Elsie and Dave couldn't remember how much they'd paid and they didn't seem very bothered either. My wife Jeanette said not to worry because it was only two weeks and, after all, we have saved for it but, nevertheless, I did feel unhappy about the whole episode, because I don't think you can actually afford to let go for a moment. We don't have very much money, we work hard for it and I don't like to think of it being wasted.

Audrey and Frank viewed their impending retirement very differently from Joe.

Having decided that they wanted to continue to be generous, they came to the conclusion that some of their budgeting and planning had to take account of giving themselves enough leeway to continue to be generous on a day to day level. But they decided to reconsider their larger scale generosity.

Joe decided that he would need to be careful in retirement as he had been throughout his life. He thought that being retired would mean being even more careful.

What about you? How will your attitudes to money have a bearing on your retirement?

Think about each of the words you have written down on your list.

How will these characteristics be carried on into retirement?

	Agree strongly	Agree	No strong opinion	Dis-agree	Dis-agree strongly
I feel I'm quite well organised about money.					
As far as money goes, I see myself as being a generous person.					
Using money is something really enjoyable.					
I feel I have always been fortunate over money.					

Your budget now

Budgeting is especially important when you are planning retirement. Your gross income is almost certainly going to be less than while you are working. To find out if it is going to be sufficient, it is a good idea to make a careful record of what you earn and spend now, to find out how much you might need and what changes are likely when you have retired. Doing this in good time will give you plenty of opportunities to make any changes.

Recording your spending

Start by listing all the things you buy under three main headings.

Regular lump sums—the bills which turn up regularly and which you know you must pay. Your mortgage or rent, rates, fuel bills and car tax.

Day-to-day spending—food, drink, petrol, household supplies and newspapers, for example.

Occasional lump sums—washing machine, refrigerator, carpet, paying for holidays and car repairs.

The checklist will help to ensure you haven't forgotten anything. You may find that you are spending more on some things than you thought. Remember that drawing up this budget should be a joint exercise if there is more than one in your household — it's important that everyone knows the incomings and outgoings in case someone different has to take over the budgeting.

Checklist

Regular lump-sum spending
AA/RAC and other subscriptions
Bank charges (avoidable if required balance is left in account)
Car servicing
Car tax and insurance
Christmas
Christmas clubs, holiday clubs and saving clubs
Fuel (coal, electricity, gas)
College fees
Covenant payments
Ground rent and service charges
HP and other credit payments
House buildings, contents, all-risks insurance
Life insurance
Medical bills insurance

Maintenance and alimony
Mortgage
Oil for central heating
Overdraft interest
Payments to dependants
Personal pension scheme
Private lessons (e.g. music, driving)
Rates (include water rates)
Regular savings
Regular servicing of household equipment
Rent
Season tickets
Telephone
Television licence
Television rental

Day-to-day spending
Books
Cleaning materials
Cosmetics
Cigarettes, matches, lighter fuel
Drink
Drinks and meals out
Dry cleaning, laundry, launderette
Entertainments (e.g. cinema, football)
Fares
Food
Gas and electricity slot meters
General household things (e.g. lavatory paper, cooking foil, light bulbs, batteries)
Hairdresser
Hobbies
Help in the home
Medicines, sticking plaster, etc
Newspapers, magazines
Paraffin, candles, calor gas
Pet food
Petrol and oil for car
Presents
Films for camera, and developing charges
Soap, shampoo and chemists' goods
Stamps, telegrams
Stationery
Sweets, chocolate, ice cream, crisps, peanuts
Shoe repairs
Window cleaning

Occasional lump-sum spending
Car purchase and repairs
Clothes, shoes
Dentist, doctor and other medical
Expenses (including vets)
Garden and allotment (e.g. seeds, plants, fertilisers, tools)
Hobbies and leisure pursuit equipment
Holidays

Home decoration, repairs, alterations
Jewellery
Luggage and leather goods
Major household replacements
Motorcycle, moped, bicycle purchase
Television, radio and stereo equipment

Drawing up your budget

Draw up a budget sheet. Fill in the items on your list that you are able to straight away. You may find that you need to do some 'homework' to complete all the items.

For regular lump sums you will be able to work out most of the items from previous bills and old cheque books.

For day-to-day spending try to keep a spending record for a few weeks. You may find it tedious but it will show up your spending habits very clearly and it will help you to decide where economies can be made.

Occasional lump sums are more tricky precisely because they are occasional and because this year's pattern may not be the same as last year's. It's worth looking back at bills for the past two or three years to give you some ideas of this.

To draw up a budget you will need in addition: The records of your spending covering all the items in your list and an estimate of your total income for the year.

Chief sources of income

Before retirement

Income is the *net* amount you have left over after deducting tax, national insurance contributions and contributions to pension schemes from your gross before deductions pay.

You should also include any other income, for example, child benefit, pensions, interest on investments (after tax), and any other money that will be added to your spendable income. If you know that you will be getting a pay increase during the year then include this — but be realistic about the amount and remember to take into account the usual deductions for tax, national insurance and pensions.

After retirement

Your income is likely to be made up from:
o Your State Retirement Pension.
o A pension from your job.
o Personal Income from savings, investments etc.
o Income if you work after retirement.

From your expenditure records and from your old bills you should be able to estimate your *spending* for the year. You will need to know how your expenditure varies from month to month — your gas bill, for example, is probably due in January, April, July and October but the bills may vary, April being the largest.

However you are paid — weekly or monthly — it is easiest to budget on that basis so that you can see how much money you've got at the beginning of the week or the month.
Your budget is based on:
o How much money comes in during that period.
o How much goes out during that period.

Keeping up to date

If your circumstances change — you move house or change jobs, for example — you'll need to draw up a new budget or, at least, modify the old one. But even if there's no change, you'll still need to keep your budget up to date. Don't forget to allow for expected inflation or the unexpected bill — roof repairs, for example.

So review and update your budget regularly — every three months, say. If you do this between now and the time you retire, not only will you have an accurate idea of how much it costs you to live, and the rate by which this increases, but you will be expert at gathering information (bills etc) that you need to work your budget.

Look at the example chart which illustrates one method of calculating your budget from month to month. In this example you enter the balance from the previous month at the top of the chart, your income and spending and calculate the totals. Work out the balance at the end of that month and carry it forward to the next month.

	Jan	Feb	March	April	May	June	July
Balance from previous month							
Income							
Total income							
Spending							
Regular lump sum							
Day to day							
Occasional lump sum							
Total							
Balance at end of month							

Pension matters

Your income in retirement will probably come from one or more pension schemes. This will almost certainly include the State Retirement Pension and any pension from your job.

At first glance the gap between your total salary and your total pension may look quite daunting. But then compare your net pension with your net salary. For most people the gap shrinks significantly.

And for the lower paid they may even be better off in retirement than at full-time work.

John and June are 64 and 59 years of age and living on John's wages as a handyman/gardener of £4,000 a year.

John retires in November 1982 at the age of 65 and receives from his employer a pension of half pay (£2,000 p.a.) plus the State Retirement Pension for a married couple of £2,732.60, giving them a total income of £4,732.60.

Of course John and June will have to pay a little tax on this but they will still be better off than when John was in full-time work.

Jim and Margaret are the same ages and live in similar circumstances. Jim earns £6,000 a year as a driver with a market garden and is also on a half pay pension. So Jim and Margaret will have a total of £3,000 plus £2,732.60 giving £5,732.60 which again will make them better off after tax because of the Age Allowance.

This is a tax allowance for which you may be eligible at retirement age. It means that a larger proportion of your income will be free of tax.

How do I qualify for the State Pension?

This is payable to you at 65 years of age (if male) and at 60 years of age (if female), on condition that:

o You have retired (i.e. given up full-time paid work altogether).
o You have paid sufficient contributions.
o You have reached pensionable age but are still working part-time and not earning more than is allowed under the earnings rule.

The basic amount from November 1982 is:

o £32.85 for a single person
o £52.55 for a married couple.

If in your case you have paid graduated pension contributions between 1961–1975, you will be entitled to an additional maximum amount of £2 a week. If your employer has not opted out of the State Pension Scheme which began in 1978 you may well qualify for an additional Earnings Related Pension. Social Security leaflets NP34 and NP31 from a post office or social security office will give you detailed information about this scheme.

If you are in doubt about your right to a State Pension or have any other concern about it, check at once with your social security office.

Do I have to claim my pension?
o Claiming your pension is your responsibility.
o The DHSS will normally send you, 3–4 months before pensionable age, a claim form to do this for your basic pension.
o If not, make inquiries at your local office because delay could mean a loss of benefit.
o You could be entitled to extra pension if you have dependants.

How will my pension be paid?
o Usually weekly in advance by order book at a post office of your choice. Each order slip is valid for three –

months (though in some circumstances requests for late payment might be considered). After 12 months delay you lose your money.
o Monthly or quarterly in arrears on a crossed order which can be paid into a bank at your request.
o At your overseas address, if you are going abroad for three months or more, providing you ask well in advance. However, if as a UK citizen you decide to live abroad then you will not get the increases paid to UK pensioners unless you live in the Common Market or in a country with whom we have an agreement.

o Direct to you, but at a reduced rate, if you are in hospital for longer than eight weeks.

What happens if I decide to go on working full-time?
o You will eventually receive a larger basic pension. This is called 'Deferred Retirement'. You could receive your basic pension plus a third more if you stay on in full-time work for five years beyond retirement age. As the rates of these benefits are subject to change your local social security office will refer you to their leaflet NP32. This is also available at post offices.

Is my pension taxed?
o Not if your State Pension is your sole income.
o Only if you have additional items of income then the total amount (including the State Pension) after Age Allowance will be subject to tax where applicable.

What if I'm a single person?
In principle the rules for receiving your pension are exactly the same. However, it is always worthwhile checking your own financial circumstances with the DHSS regulations. For example, if you are a single woman, you do not qualify for the Age Allowance until you are 65, even though you may already be in receipt of your State Retirement Pension.

What if I'm a married woman?
If you are a married woman there are two ways of qualifying for a State Pension:
o In your own right, if you are 60 and have paid sufficient contributions, when at work.
o Through your husband's contributions if he is 65, retired and has paid full contributions.
You cannot have both.

You may have worked but not have paid sufficient contributions to qualify either for a full pension or for one based on your husband's pension because he is not yet 65.

If you come into this category you will probably be wise to claim the graduated pension in your own name when you reach 60. This may be only a very small amount, but you may lose out if you wait for your husband to become 65. The DHSS are only allowed by law to pay any arrears due to you for a maximum of one year.

What if I'm divorced?
The circumstances for divorcees vary. All the facts about your entitlements are listed in the Social Security leaflet NP32A.

If you are a woman and have never worked during your married life you would still be able to claim your pension at 60, unless you re-married, based on your former husband's contribution record. This would continue even after the death of your former husband.

What if I'm a widow or widower?

If you are a widower aged 65 or over, your entitlements are quite straightforward, and are explained in Social Security leaflet NP32A.

If you are a widow and lost your husband before you had reached the age of 60, then you have quite important decisions to make when you are 60. You can choose to do one of the following three things:

o Claim Retirement Pension if you have retired from full-time work.
o Stay on Widow's Benefit until 65.
o Delay claiming either Widow's Benefit or Retirement Pension in order to qualify for a bigger pension at retirement or age 65.

If you were widowed after 60, retired or not, you can qualify for a Retirement Pension based on your late husband's contributions.

If a Retirement Pension had not already been claimed by either of you when your husband was alive, a Widow's Allowance will be paid for 26 weeks and then converted to a Retirement Pension calculated in the usual way.

Your circumstances may differ slightly from the examples given as guidelines so it is always sensible to check with the local social security office.

Can I have a Supplementary State Retirement Pension?

If your total resources, including your savings, still leave you in the low income group, then you can claim this supplement in addition to your State Retirement Pension.

The details of what is meant by low income are given on forms SB1 and SB8 which are available from social security offices or post offices. This supplement to your pension is not a charity and is always subject to any changes in your financial circumstances.

About one in four retired people already claim this supplement, and you have a right to make a claim if you qualify. Many people fail to claim either because they are not aware of their rights or mistakenly believe it is a charity.

Other pension schemes

Occupational pension. If your employer has contracted out of the State Additional Pension Scheme, then you will be entitled to the pension to which you have contributed during your period of service.

If your employer has not contracted out you are not likely to get a pension from that employer because you have been paying additional contributions to the state scheme.

There are of course non-contributory schemes, such as those operated by banks or the Civil Service for their employees.

All schemes must have rules and employees should have copies of them to help them to work out their pensions. Some employers produce explanatory booklets which give information in simple terms. So the first step is to obtain a copy of the rules.

Remember that a pension from your employer is deferred pay. You have earned it, whether it has come from a contributory or non-contributory scheme.

If your employer is providing a pension it is as much a part of your total remuneration as pay, sick pay, paid holidays, subsidised canteen, season ticket loans and any other benefit provided for the workforce.

You should know exactly what your entitlement is likely to be and what options are available to you under the scheme. Looking for the answers to the questions below will help.

It is a good idea, when such information is not regularly provided, to obtain the answers yourself from up to five years before you retire and update the information annually until you are due to leave.

Some questions to ask

Below is a series of questions. Having looked at them you should be able to produce the set of questions that fit your situation and know where to go to get the answers:

o Who is the person responsible for the pension scheme at your firm?
o What age is specified for retirement in your firm's pension scheme?
o When do you start getting pension payments?
o On what basis is the amount of your pension calculated?
o How is the qualifying period calculated?
o Is the wage/salary you are getting at retirement used as the basis of your pension?
o What fraction of your salary is used to calculate your pension?
o How do you calculate the amount of your pension?
o Are pensions increased annually?
o Is any increase guaranteed?
o What has been the average increase over the past five years?
o Does your pension benefit your widow/widower?
o Does your pension scheme make any provision for your children?
o Is it possible to make additional voluntary contributions to increase your pension?
o Is it possible to commute part of the pension, that is, give up part of your pension in return for an immediate tax-free lump sum?
o What happens to your pension in the case of a divorce, re-marriage or separation?
o What pension do you get if you retire early?
o Who will actually pay the pension?

Getting the answers

Approach:
o Your personnel department.
o Your pension fund office.
o The trustees or administrators of your pension scheme.
o Your trade union official.

Suppose you find it difficult to get the answers you need? Perhaps you are not asking the right person? Perhaps the answers are given in a way you find difficult to understand?

Don't be put off. Start finding out early enough to be able to make practical decisions before retirement. Be persistent — it's to your benefit in the long run. Be prepared to repeat your questions until you get answers that tell you what you need to know.

Remember it is possible to have a collection of pension payments from both State and private schemes.

Roger began working life as a journalist and now works as a freelance author. He is entitled to five pensions when he eventually lays down his pen.

Three of them are state pensions: the normal retirement pension, the old graduated pension and the new state earnings related pension.

Then there is a small pension due from a former employer who had a non-contributory scheme. His name still appears on their list of future pensioners although he will have left their

PERSONNEL
OFFICE

employ some 30 years by the time the pension is due for payment.

Finally there is a pension due to him from a private contributory scheme which he organised for himself through an insurance company.

He could easily forget that small pension from his former employer and it certainly will not be paid unless he applies for it and notifies his change of address to the company.

Personal pension plans

If you are self-employed, or if you are employed and do not belong to an employer's pension scheme, or for some reason you feel that your pension provision would otherwise be inadequate for your needs, it might be worthwhile for you to copy Roger's example and make some additional provision through a personal pension plan.

What are personal pension plans?

They are schemes run by insurance companies for individuals rather than for groups of employees.

While you're still working, you pay an insurance company premiums which are invested. The company pays you a regular income when you are 60, or from the date of your retirement until you die. Or you can take a tax-free lump sum and a lower pension.

For example, if you paid £1,000 a year from the age of 40, you might get a pension of £15,000 a year (after tax) at the age of 65. Or you could take a lump sum of £42,000 and a pension of £10,000.

Who's allowed to take one out?

All self-employed or those in jobs where they don't belong to any employers' pension schemes.

The main advantages

If you're a taxpayer, you can get tax relief on the payments you make up to certain limits.

Anyone outside company pension schemes can contribute a percentage to a personal pension plan.

The plans available are flexible and you don't have to stop working to start drawing your pension. It can start any time between certain ages (normally 60 to 75).

When should I start paying?

The earlier the better — starting just one year earlier could well increase the pension you get by over 10 per cent.

Do I have to pay regularly?

Not necessarily. With some plans, you can make one-off payments as and when you can afford to. With others, you agree to make regular payments each month or year — but even with these, you may be able to vary what you pay, miss out some payments or make extra ones.

What if I stop paying?

The payments already made will stay in the insurance company's fund, and you will get some pension from them when you retire.

What if I have the money from selling my business?

Putting your money into your business may be a good way to save for old age. But selling at the right time and price may not be easy — and your business could fall on hard times before then. There may also be capital gains tax to take into account.

There are many pension plans available. If you are considering taking one out, you should take advice from more than one source: your accountant, insurance broker or possibly bank manager.

The pensions seem enormous—any snags?

Yes — inflation. The examples quoted are based on interest rates in 1982 and growth in investment which look high in part, because of inflation. And if inflation averaged, say, 10 per cent over the 25 years you saved, the £15,000 pension quoted in the example would be worth only £1,380 at today's buying power in the first year of retirement — even less later on if inflation continued.

So you would need to aim for a much higher pension to protect yourself from inflation.

To get some idea of the rate of inflation visit the reference section of your library. Ask for the local newspaper file of 10 years ago and look up the prices of houses, cars and food. Look up old rent books and bills for rates.

Other sources of income

When you have worked out your pension income, think about all other monies you receive, for instance, from part time employment, interest on savings or from insurance policies. This counts towards your own liability to income tax. Remember, the sole fact that you have retired does not release you from paying tax.

Some state benefits

There are about 60 different cash benefits to help you in times of need. They are all summarised in a DHSS booklet called 'Which Benefit.' Here is a selection from those 60.

Medical benefits – free prescriptions for those retired. Simply fill in the back of the prescription form.

Low income welfare benefits

If your income is below a certain level (which depends on the size of your family, age of any children living at home and what you pay in rates and rent or mortgage interest) you qualify for:

o Free NHS dental treatment and glasses.
o Refund of fares for you (and your dependants) to go to an NHS hospital for treatment – including fares for an escort if necessary.

Help with heating costs

Supplementary pensioners qualify for more money if they are in poor health, live in inadequate housing, have difficulty in paying for their present heating, or are aged 70 or over.

Rate rebates, rent rebates, and allowances

Anyone who pays rates or rent may qualify for help. Whether you qualify – and how much help you get – depends on the size of your family and the amount you pay in rates or rent. In certain circumstances, you might do better to claim a State Supplementary Pension instead which allows for rent and rates. Your social security office should help you select the better option.

Goodwill

Supposing you do not qualify for a company pension – possibly because of insufficient service. Discuss the matter with your personnel officer or pension fund manager.

You may find that the company is prepared to make you a concessionary lump sum payment.

They may guarantee you holiday relief work. You may also be able to retain the privilege of staff discounts on purchases if applicable.

Remember to discuss these matters well before your leaving date.

Pensioners are eligible for a wide range of travel concessions

> **The Earnings Rule**
> **More misunderstanding and ill-will are caused by the Earnings Rule than by any other single aspect of pensions legislation.**
>
> **In November 1982 the rule stated: You may earn up to £57 per week and still draw a full State Retirement Pension.**
>
> **You lose 50p off your pension for each of the first £4 you earn over this amount (i.e. up to £61).**
>
> **You lose £1 off your pension for every £1 you earn over £61: in other words that's on a pound for pound basis.**
>
> **You lose your entire State Retirement Pension if you earn £92 or more.**
>
> **This does not apply after the age of 65 for women or 70 for men.**
>
> **Keep an eye on the Budget each year.**

Budget planning

Key information

For sorting out your money you will need a lot of information which is probably scattered in different places.

When budgeting, include things like car and house insurance, mortgage payments and so on. It will be easier to keep your budget up to date and to deal with any letters or problems if you keep a list of all the key information relevant to you and your family. Some of the things on the list may not involve weekly or regular payments but you may need to refer to them at some time—so keep all your information together.

Your records

Having records easily available can save time and trouble too when you need them quickly for dealing with the building society, bank, Post Office, insurance company, taxation and other offices. You may find it convenient to keep a note book or simple card index showing:

o Name and address of organisation.

o Telephone number.

o Amount and due date of periodic payment and method of payment i.e. current, deposit or savings accounts, standing order, direct debit, premium, subscription etc.

o Reference numbers, e.g. for mortgage, insurance policies, credit cards, loan accounts, tax code etc.

o Notes on, or photocopies of, all important documents deposited elsewhere, e.g. house deeds, wills.

Changes in your budget

There are two kinds of changes.

o The changes you feel you would like to make in the amount you spend and how you spend it in the years before you retire. These may include a choice to cut spending so you can save more as a conscious preparation for retirement or a decision to spend the sum you want to while you are still earning.

o The changes which are going to happen to you when you retire—the possible reduction in your income and changes in lifestyle.

Adjusting your budget

There is nothing like drawing up a budget to bring it home to you where you are spending more than you need or more than you can afford! This is probably why drawing up an honest budget is a hard thing to do. Look at the budget sheet in this topic. Fill in your present spending in the 'before retirement' column in as much detail as possible. Think about and changes you want to make at present. The topic should help if you want to re-arrange your spending. If you decide that you would like to cut your spending you may well be able to say straightaway

"I've been spending far too much on going to the hairdresser (or on the garden, or on cigarettes etc). I shall cut this by half." And if bigger items like food buying, or the car are costing you more than you realised, you could look at ways of buying food more cheaply, or at using alternative forms of transport.

Balancing your budget

If you are close to retirement you should be able to make an accurate forecast of income and spending and should then have a good idea of whether they will balance or not. Use the second column to fill in what your spending will be after retirement. This information will help you to plan ahead.

	Before retirement	After retirement
Income (Before tax)		
Employment		
Part-time employment		
Investments		
Pension(s)		
Any other source		
Total Income		
Expenditure		
Taxes		
Insurance		
National Insurance		
Pension scheme contributions		
House insurance (including contents)		
Life insurance		
Any other Insurance (except car)		
House and Living		
Rates (including water)		
Rent or Mortgage Repayments		
Heating and lighting		
Decoration, repairs		
Household requisites (washing powder, shoe polish, etc)		
Household equipment		
Furniture, carpets (repairs, renewal)		
Clothes (include dry cleaning, repairs)		
Telephone		
Garden		
Prescriptions		
Dentist		
Food and Drink		
At Home		
Away from home		
Pet food (include dog licence and vets)		
Transport		
Fares		
Car tax and insurance		
Car maintenance and running costs		
Recreation, Entertainment		
Papers, periodicals, books		
Hobbies, sports		
Club subscriptions		
Theatre, cinema, TV		
Classes, courses		
Holidays		
Personal spending		
Hairdresser, beauty parlour		
Cigarettes, tobacco, confectionery		
Football pools, etc		
Charities, donations		
Postage		
Total Expenditure		

Cutting back

But suppose you've been through your budget ruthlessly and you still consider that you need to cut down? You could try this exercise to see how much surplus or flexibility you can create in your budget.

To get a measure of how tight your budget is, rate your spending on each item from 0 to 4 according to how inconvenient it would be for you to cut your estimate back by 10%. Score: 0 = not at all inconvenient; 1 = slightly inconvenient; 2 = fairly inconvenient; 3 = inconvenient; 4 = very inconvenient.

You and your partner may not automatically agree — so you might like to do this exercise separately and negotiate an agreed conclusion. Cutting back by 10% may be very inconvenient (4) if:

o You feel you have already cut as far as you can.
o You cannot cut by 10% because the rate is fixed by someone else, e.g. car tax, mortgage.
o You cannot cut because you are committed for a certain time period, e.g. loan.
o You cannot substitute do-it-yourself for professional services.
o It would simply upset you a lot to cut back in certain areas.

Work out what the 10% cut backs on items you have rated 0 to 2 would raise in cash terms.

Make a note of any other cuts you think are possible without great inconvenience, particularly on items you rated 0 to 2. These cuts could be things you decide you can cut out altogether; or, things you have said you can cut back by 10% but could in fact cut further.

Comment

Are the cuts you want to make the same as those other members of the household want to make? Discussing these matters now might make for a happier retirement. Most people make an effort to keep spending roughly equal to income. The questions about cuts were intended to help you check whether you are spending unnecessarily, and to identify possible areas of flexibility or surplus in your budget.

Changes retirement will bring

Where the money goes

When you retire, your spending needs are likely to look rather different from now. It may help to think of the following areas of spending.

o **On the family** — your children will probably have left home, and be financially independent by the time you retire. On the other hand you may take on new responsibilities, elderly parents, or helping with grandchildren for example, which may cancel out any savings as far as your children are concerned.

o **Regular financial commitments** — you will probably be free of your mortgage by the time you retire. School fees too should be a thing of the past. So should payments into pension schemes.

o **Fewer work-related expenses** — for example, no more national insurance contributions, trade union dues, fares to and from work, meals at work and so on. You may also find less need to spend money on work clothes, or subscriptions to trade magazines. But don't forget to allow for any perks you get with your job, which on retirement you'll have to do without or pay for yourself: for instance free insurance and health cover, the use of a car, subsidised canteen or expense account.

o **Lifestyle** — it's likely that your lifestyle in your 60s won't be the same as the one that suited you in your 40s. You may want to spend more money on holidays and hobbies, less on entertaining.

o **Extra home expenses** — on heating the home for longer periods or paying for help with heavy housework, shopping or gardening.

o **Unpredictable, large expenses** — you may be faced with large bills which you can't pay. Your roof may need substantial repairs, you may want to replace your car, or your fence may deteriorate beyond repair. Some capital should be earmarked for unpredictable events — and you need to bear in mind the loss in income that occurs if you draw on savings.

Rearranging your spending

If your spending consistently exceeds your income, you will have to reduce it. But your problem is more likely to be a pattern of uneven spending contrasting with a regular income. If that is the case you need to look at ways of rearranging your spending.

Paying by instalments

Most of your large regular bills can be paid by instalments.

Rates. These can be paid by monthly instalments usually spread over 10 months. Contact your local authority — the address is on the rates bill. Pay by standing order through your bank, by post to the local authority or across the counter at the council offices.

Electricity and gas bills. The electricity and gas industries jointly have issued a Code of Practice for the payment of domestic gas and electricity bills. A copy of the code can be obtained from your electricity or gas showroom or by post from the regional or district office. You can pay your bills by:

o Regular budget payment schemes.
  An estimate is made of your annual bill for electricity or gas and you then pay in 12 monthly instalments through your bank or National Giro account.
o Savings stamps.
  These can be bought at your gas or electricity showroom. You can pay your bill with the appropriate stamps or with a combination of stamps and cash.
o Pay-as-you-go schemes.
  Under these you can make payments towards your quarterly bill whenever you wish. Ask at your local showroom for an application form to open an account.

Insurance. It is possible that your household and car insurance can be paid by monthly standing order at little or no extra cost.

TV licence. You can buy television savings stamps at all post offices. Some TV rental firms have schemes under which you pay for a licence with your rental payments.

Telephone bills. You can pay part or all of your bill by buying telephone stamps.

Season tickets. There is no British Rail system for paying for season tickets by instalment. You may be able to persuade your employer to give you a low-interest or no-interest loan to buy a quarterly or annual season ticket. You repay it in monthly instalments.

Bank budget accounts

Make enquiries at the major banks to see if they offer budget accounts. With a budget account, you add up all the bills you want to include in the scheme to get an estimate of the yearly total. Then the bank will have to agree your figures. You make out a monthly standing order for one-twelfth of the yearly amount (plus the charge the bank makes) and this is put into a special account. You then draw on this account to meet bills you have included in the scheme. Sometimes the account will be overdrawn, sometimes it will be in credit (banks are not keen on budget accounts permanently in the red). By the end of the year, the payments 'out' should just about equal the payments 'in' – you can make your own allowance for possible inflation if you want to.

The banks charge for a budget account and each bank has its own policy for charges, so find out how much it will cost before deciding to use this method.

Saving and spending for the future

There will be implications for your budget of large scale and possibly long term saving or spending.

o If you are worried about protecting your savings, consider taking advice to make sure you are getting the best possible financial returns.

o Before your retirement you may seriously consider dealing with large items of expense like repair or insulation to your home. The cost of getting the work done may well go up more quickly than the after tax return on your savings.

o Some people may consider buying a home if they do not already own one. Others may consider home extensions or moving to a more expensive property. If you are thinking of an investment along these lines do remember that there is no guarantee that the value of your investment will increase, but your overall expenses certainly will do. This may have the effect of leaving you with less spending money than you had budgeted for.

o You may want to check that your dependants wouldn't be left short when you die. Often an employer's pension scheme provides a widow's pension and possible lump sum too, on the death of an employee whether before or after retirement. However, you may consider it necessary to make further provision for your dependant if you feel that their total income after your death would not be sufficient for their needs.

o If you can choose whether or not to belong to your employer's scheme and feel that its benefits are poor, then check whether you would do better to go for a personal pension scheme. If you do this, of course, then your employer will not make any contribution to your chosen scheme.

Many people think of budgeting as being concerned with saving or spending this week, this month or even this year. Often decisions made now could have effects on your financial situation well into the future.

Friends and relations

How will retirement affect your relationships with your friends, your family and your relations?

Think about changes

In many ways the changes are likely to be very similar to those that happen when you move house to a new neighbourhood or change jobs. You'll be seeing less of some people you were accustomed to seeing every day. You'll see some new faces. You'll have the opportunity to break with some old routines and set up some new ones.

The activities which follow are designed to help you work out the pattern of your existing relationships with family and friends. It needs quite a lot of work to complete them fully, but having worked through them you should be in a better position to assess the possible effects of retirement on your own relationships with others. The example of Geoff Billings is used as a guide to filling in the activities. You may find it helpful to complete your own charts on a separate piece of paper.

Who do you know?

Write down the names of three people you know for each of these categories:
o People you see every day — for instance your partner or immediate family.
o People you see most days — for instance your workmates, or the neighbours.

o People you see about once a week — for instance at a club meeting, evening class, church and so on.
o People you see from time to time — for instance family or friends living some distance away.
o People you see occasionally — for instance family living abroad.

This is how Geoff drew up his list:

People I see every day
My wife Betty. My younger daughter Pam. The newsagent.

People I see most days
Vic, Ernie and John, at work.

People I see once a week
Joan and Henry Scott next door. Jim Bates who shares the allotment with me.

People I see from time to time
Angela and Tony, my daughter and son-in-law who live in Devon.
Stan Drake on the Trades Council.

People I see occasionally
Arnold and May Stratton, sister and brother-in-law who live over the other side of London. Joe Armitage, an old friend from army days.

What does this person mean to me
Complete the chart on the right.

For each person you have named, write the following scores next to their names:

o Score three points *each* time you have written their name against statements 1-3.

o Score two points *each* time you have written their name against statements 4-6.

o Score one point *each* time you have written their name against statements 7-9.

Add up the scores for each person and write the totals against the names on your first list of people you know.

A score of three points or less indicates that the person is an acquaintance with whom you have a fairly casual relationship. Conversation will tend to be limited to a hobby or work. It would be beyond the bounds of the relationship to discuss things like personal or financial problems.

A score of between three and nine indicates that the person is more valuable to you than just an acquaintance. You are confident that you could call on this person for help and advice. You know that they trust you enough to confide in you to the same extent.

A score of over nine indicates that the person is a partner, relative or particularly close friend. Their friendship and support is especially important.

Geoff scored as follows:	
Newsagent.	1
Next door neighbours.	1 each
Ernie and John.	1 each
Angela and Tony.	2 each
Jim Bates.	5
Stan Drake.	5
Vic.	5
Arnold and May.	6 each
Joe Armitage.	6
Pam.	12
Betty.	14

What does this person mean to me?

Using your own list and the chart below fill in the names of your friends and family against any statements that you think would apply to them. Here is the chart that Geoff filled in as an example:

		Your answers.	Geoff's answers.
1	I would want this person to be the first to know of important events in my own life.		Betty 3.
2	I would expect this person to talk to me first about important personal and private matters.		Betty 3. Pam 3.
3	I would expect this person to come to me first with important news.		Betty 3. Pam 3.
4	I would gladly give help and advice to this person if he/she had a problem.		Arnold 2 and Mary 2, Betty 2, Pam 2, Stan Drake 2, Jim Bates 2, Joe Armitage 2, Vic 2.
5	I would be happy to see this person drop by at my house.		Arnold 2 and May 2, Stan Drake 2, Jim Bates 2, Pam 2, Angela 2 & Tony 2, Joe Armitage 2.
6	I could talk to this person about personal and family matters.		Arnold 2 and May 2, Betty 2, Pam 2, Joe Armitage 2, Vic 2.
7	I pass the time of day with this person.		Newsagent 1, Joan 1 and Henry Scott 1 next door.
8	I know this person only through my job.		Vic 1, Stan Drake 1, Ernie 1, John 1.
9	I share a common interest with this person (e.g. tenants group, sport, etc.)		Betty 1, Jim Bates 1.

How often? How close?

Now, so that you can see the relationship between how often you see people and how close you are to them, fill in your friends and family on the chart below.

You can see from Geoff's chart that the people he is intimate with are his immediate family who live nearby — his wife Betty and his daughter Pam. He has a number of friends whom he sees less often and a few people who count as acquaintances. Geoff was surprised at first to see that he had classed his daughter Angela as an acquaintance. On thinking about it however it made sense to him. He usually only sees her once a year and no longer feels very close to her or her husband.

You may not feel very happy adding up points and working out the scores on your relationships. It may strike you as artificial to attach values of this sort to something as personal and sensitive as your relations with your family and friends. But it is precisely because it is such a sensitive area, that it is so hard sometimes to be objective.

The use of this points system can help you to stand back and take a detached look at the true nature of a relationship.

How often, How close?						
	Very close friends (Scores 9 or above).		Friends (Scores 4-9).		Acquaintances (Scores 1-3).	
	You	Geoff	You	Geoff	You	Geoff
People I see every day.		Betty, Pam.				Newsagent.
People I see most days.				Vic.		Eric, John.
People I see about once a week.				Jim Bates.		Next door neighbours
People I see from time to time.				Stan Drake.		Angela and Tony.
People I see occasionally.				Arnold and May. Joe Armitage.		

How will relationships change?
Retirement is bound to bring changes in the patterns of your relationships. On the following chart write in whether you expect to see your friends and family more often, about the same amount, or less often. Again we have filled in the chart for Geoff as an example.

You may find a fairly even spread across the chart. While you expect to see less of people in some categories — for instance work colleagues — you're likely to see more of people in other groups — perhaps family and social friends, or other members of sports and social clubs.

How close do you want to be?
The other change retirement may bring is in the balance of intimate relationships and casual acquaintances. Go over the chart again and put the score from the **What does this person mean to me** chart next to each name. Add up the scores from each of the three columns. A higher score in the **more often** column than in the **less often** column indicates that overall you'll have a greater commitment to personal relationships in retirement. A higher score in the **less often** column indicates that

you'll have less of a commitment. Is this how you want things? If not, can you think of ways of altering the balance between intimate and more casual relationships so that it is more to your liking?

For Geoff Billings, retirement is likely to be a time which brings small but not dramatic changes. The people he feels closest to — Betty his wife and Pam his daughter, — he is likely to see more of. Geoff also hopes to do more work on the allotment with Jim Bates who has also recently retired. He will be able to see significantly more of friends and family whom he was unable to see because of time and distance problems. In retirement he has the time to go and stay with them for short visits. The people he has less contact with are his work friends. Although they are not intimate friends there is likely to be a larger number of them and the kind of relationship they provide — the exchange of gossip, news, opinions and ideas — may be missed in retirement.

How will others feel?
Your own charts show the effects of retirement on relationships from your own point of view. But you also need to take account of the point of view of

others. Look back at the list of people you are expecting to see more of in retirement. For each of them think through the following list of questions. If you like you can write down your answers to them on a separate piece of paper.

o Do they have work commitments of their own?
o Are they retiring too and likely to have more time?
o Are they going to have to fit you into a busy schedule?
o Do they have dependants or family who make demands on their time?
o Do they have other leisure interests that occupy their time?
o Are they the sort of people you can drop in on casually or do you need to make arrangements first?
o Are you going to do things together or meet socially?

Thinking in advance about the effects retirement might have on your relationships with family and friends can be helpful, but even the best laid plans don't always work out as expected.

There follow two examples of how different people have planned their retirement and of how it has worked out for them in practice.

How will relationships change?

	I expect to see this person— more often.		I expect to see this person— about the same.		I expect to see this person— less often.	
	You	**Geoff**	**You**	**Geoff**	**You**	**Geoff**
People I see every day.		Betty 14, Pam 12.		News-agent 1.		
People I see most days.				Next door neigh-bours 1.		Vic 5, Ernie 1, John 1.
People I see about once a week.		Jim Bates 5.				
People I see from time to time.				Angela 2 and Tony 2.		Stan Drake 5.
People I see occasionally.		Joe 6, Arnold 6, and May 6.				
Total scores.		49		6		12

Mike: a gradual retirement

Mike Kilduff is a self-employed director of a small manufacturing company in the North of England. He is married with six children and will be passing the business on to one of his sons who is already in the firm. He plans to retire gradually from the business, and is currently working a four day week.

"I see it as a gradual withdrawal rather than a sudden termination of work — which I find very attractive from a financial point of view and it gives me a continuing interest."

Two of their children still live at home — one of their sons, James, who is working in the business, and their daughter Josephine who plans to marry this year.

Mike has a lot of outside interests. He likes gardening, is involved with the church, the bowls club, and a bridge group. He is also a governor of a local school.

He has discussed retirement with his wife, and he thinks that they have enough interests in common as well as individual interests to keep them happy. However he does say:

"My wife thinks that I shall be a bit of a nuisance around the house because I'm always doing things — she'll have no peace."

Mike's answers

This is what happened when Mike Kilduff worked through the activities. First of all he listed three names under each of the five categories.

People I see every day
Mary — my wife. James — my son. Josephine — my daughter.

People I see most days
David Macdonald, Nigel Harris and Susan Allen — work colleagues.

People I see once a week
Phil Hedges. Josephine Riley. John Maynard.

People I see from time to time
David — one of my sons, married with a family, living in the south. Jane — one of my daughters, recently married and living in the same area but currently very busy setting up home. Isobel Taylor — a member of the school governors committee.

People I see very occasionally
John Oliver — a school friend of Mary Kilduff's, a primary school teacher in the area. Bill and Joan — Mike's brother and his wife who live in Kent.

Mike Kilduff's final chart is shown below. As with Geoff Billing's example, he first of all works out of the score for each of his relationships, showing how important each of these people are to him, showing him exactly how close their relationship is. He then takes the names with these numbers and fills them into his final chart to show each of the following points:

o How frequently he sees each of them — using the headings down the left- hand side of the chart.
o How often he expects to see them after retirement — using the headings along the top of the chart.
o How much he expects his commitment to social relationships will change in retirement — by adding up the total scores in the vertical columns

Easing out

Mike Kilduff had planned his retirement very methodically. He had planned to ease gradually out of work routine. His contact with work colleagues would be slowly run down, rather than suddenly stopping. Mike didn't plan to extend his activities and interests in retirement. He felt he had enough already.

"I find that I'm slowing down — things take longer — I have enough interests already and I'm really looking forward to a bit more relaxation."

He is expecting to see more of some members of his family but less of others. He'll be able to visit David and Jane more often but will see less of Josephine who will be moving out of the house. He'll see about the same amount of James who will be taking over the family business. He plans to extend his leisure activities a bit. He wants to play golf and bowls more often in the summer, but is not planning to take on any more community work. He's going to retire as a school governor, and although he will still be active in the church he isn't planning to take on any more commitments than he already has. The thing he's most looking forward to in retirement is a bit more time to relax.

Mike's final chart

	I expect to see this person— more often.	I expect to see this person— about the same.	I expect to see this person— less often.
People I see every day.	Mary 18.	James 15.	Josephine 15.
People I see most days.			David McDonald 9. Nigel 3. Susan 3.
People I see about once a week.	Phil Hedges 5.	Josephine Riley 9.	John Maynard 3.
People I see from time to time.	David 9.		Isobel Taylor 3.
People I see occasionally.	John Oliver 5. Bill 9 and Joan 9.		
Total scores.	55	24	36

One year later

Mike Kilduff is enjoying his retirement but not finding much time to relax. The fact that he has lived in the same area all his life, has brought up a family there and has been an active member of the community has meant that people were quick to take advantage of any new found leisure time he had. Having been in business he was seen as the obvious choice as the bowls club treasurer. Despite his protests he found himself spending more time on church activities.

He started a lot of fairly long-term projects in the house — redecorating, changing the garden round and building a small greenhouse. It means that he was spending a lot of time about the house.

"I used to joke about getting under my wife's feet when I retired but it did become a bit of a problem — particularly the first winter when I was doing a lot of redecorating. We did have to talk that one through."

He saw more of his work colleagues than he had expected. This was partly because his son James was still involved and partly because he found he did miss their company. They also seemed to enjoy seeing him when he dropped in at the business. He did see more of his family — visiting them for short breaks — but less than he had anticipated since there seemed to be so much going on at home.

How did it work out?

For Mike Kilduff the changes retirement brought were not traumatic. His relationships with his family, friends and others were not drastically altered. He was able to withdraw gradually from his work, and even then kept up occasional contact with his colleagues there. The only possible problem area was his relationship with his wife. He had always devoted a lot of time to his work, so it took a while for her to adjust to him being around the house in the day time. Again, the gradual withdrawal from work helped but it was this relationship which he had marked down on the chart as meaning the most to him, that caused the most problems.

Marjorie: keeping continuity

Marjorie Hilton is a teacher. She is single and lives on her own. She has had a varied and interesting career and came into teaching when she was about 40. Not qualifying for a full pension she has decided to work until 65 for financial reasons. She nursed an invalid sister up until fifteen years ago when the sister died.

"I actually have very few relatives at all. I have a cousin Winifred who has a son, and my adopted daughter and her family."

Marjorie has lived in York for 30 years and has a lot of friends and acquaintances there.

"I have a lot of friends — I don't want to give the idea that I'm a poor lonely solitary type, because I'm not, I have quite a lot of friends in York and elsewhere."

She decided to stay in York after her retirement, though she had considered moving back to Lancashire where she came from originally.

"If you stay in the same place you are there as the person that you've always been and you've got the friends and activities you've always had. And so I've decided to stay here."

Her adopted daughter is now married with a young family but keeps in regular contact.

"I value that because of the contact with children, and with her because she's only 26 and it gets me involved with younger people. I also have a very nice young neighbour who also has two little children and I'm very happy to have contact with them."

Marjorie's answers

This is how Marjorie Hilton completed the activities. First she listed three names under each of the five categories, then, just as in Mike Kilduff's and Geoff Billings' examples, she wrote the names and their scores in the appropriate position on the chart.

People I see every day

There's only one — Mr. Jarvis — at the newsagents/corner shop.

People I see most days

Mrs. Roscoe — my next door neighbour. Mrs. Tanner — the school headmistress. Mr. Pym — I work with.

People I see about once a week

Elsie Simms — a friend I've known since I came here thirty years ago. Joanna — my adopted daughter, and her family. Mrs. Abrahams — a friend in the Business and Professional Womens Group.

People I see from time to time

Bill Johnston — local archaeology society. Sybil Althorp — local natural history group. Amy Peebles — a close friend I used to teach with.

People I see occasionally

Winifred — my cousin in Lancashire. She's slightly disabled so finds travelling a chore. She visits occasionally in the summer. George and Connie Watts — old school friends from Lancashire.

Continuity

Marjorie has set out to maintain the continuity of many of her relationships in retirement. She recognised that she had solid roots in the area and relationships that she valued. The chart shows that she expects to maintain most of her contacts at about the same level, while seeing less of her work colleagues and more of her close friends and the people she knows through special interests like natural history and archaeology.

One year later

Retirement came with a bit of a jolt for Marjorie Hilton. Within a month of finishing her work her cousin Winifred died. Being one of the few relatives she had she had to take a big part in clearing up her cousin's affairs and dealing with her property and possessions. She moved back to Lancashire for nearly a month while this was going on and even considered moving back there in her retirement.

She got over this initial upset, decided to stick by her original decision to stay in York and soon settled into a satisfying new routine.

"I enjoy being retired, I don't regret in any way not teaching. I'm interested in all sorts of natural history, in gardening — I have a garden and keep that going, and I'm interested in reading and books and that sort of thing."

One thing she did notice was the way other people responded to her as a retired person.

"So I thought I'd better find out if the pension I'm getting is correct. I went down to enquire about this at the Social Security and I was interviewed by a sweet young lady who came down to me and said 'There, there my dear, you don't need to worry, it's perfectly all right' and so on. And you know about a month before I'd been the head of a department, but it amused me, it didn't upset me, I saw it as humorous. But it happened, and I think for some old people, it's depressing."

Marjorie's expectations of retirement were also affected by her neighbours moving away from the area. It left a big gap in her day-to-day life and she had to change her plans to allow for it. She now visits her adopted daughter and her family more often and sometimes babysits for them.

How did it work out?

Marjorie Hilton had decided before her retirement that she wanted to stay in the same neighbourhood. The upheaval caused by the death of her cousin Winifred nearly upset this resolution, but in the end Marjorie realised that the people she valued most were those near the home she has made for herself in York.

Marjorie had to cope with more changes in retirement than she had expected. The first year wasn't easy for her, but she was able to cope with it and go on to enjoy her retirement.

These two examples show very different experiences of retirement. For Mike it was a question of slight adjustments to the plans he had made, while Marjorie had to adjust to the loss of two people who were important to her. Neither of their original plans worked out entirely as they expected, but they were both able to successfully adapt those plans to meet changing circumstances. Planning ahead *is* helpful but only if you're prepared to go back and change your plans to suit the changes going on around you.

Marjorie's final chart			
	I expect to see this person— more often.	I expect to see this person— about the same.	I expect to see this person— less often.
People I see every day.		Mr Jarvis 3.	
People I see most days.	Mrs Roscoe 9.		Mrs Tanner 3. Mr Pym 3.
People I see about once a week.	Elsie Simms 9.	Joanna 9.	Mrs Abrahams 5.
People I see from time to time.	Bill Johnston 3. Sybil Althorp 3.	Amy Peebles 9.	
People I see occasionally.		Winifred 9 Connie 9 & George 9	
Total scores	24	48	11

This is my life

Recent history is popular at the moment. Nostalgia is big business. Specialist shops which sell everyday objects from the 1920s and 1930s are springing up. Record companies are releasing records of bands and singers who were popular in the 1930s and 1940s. There is a great deal of interest in things with which you have had contact in your lifetime.

But for you, thinking about your past isn't just nostalgia. When you are moving into a new phase of your life, as you are when you retire, it can be useful to think about your past and pick out some pictures of yourself. You may surprise yourself by rediscovering things you had forgotten or discounted; things that present a clear and stable picture of yourself, a picture you can rely on in new situations.

Getting in the mood

Find yourself a half-day or, better still, a weekend and examine what you've got in your house or flat.

If you have a junk room or an attic, a garage or a chaotic upstairs cupboard, go through it, and find a collection of objects that come from different periods of your life. Try and choose a variety; some that have sentimental value; some that you've merely had a long time; some that you've been given and just not got round to getting rid of.

Now examine each object in turn.

Try and remember:
o How you came by it.
o Any disasters that have been associated with it.
o Whether you have ever lost it and if so how you felt.
o What other people have said about it.
o Whether you have ever considered parting with it.
o Shut your eyes and let a picture come into your mind of an event associated with it.

If you have a partner, share a house with someone or have a friend of long standing who spends a lot of time at your house, ask them what they recall of each of the objects.

Do they have the same feelings as you? Or is your memory and experience of each object strictly personal?

A valuable collection

Now re-sort and add to your collection so you have items that mean something to you from as many periods of your life as possible.

Jess's valuable collection was as follows:
o Photograph of father in the greenhouse at family home.
o Cameo brooch belonging to mother.
o Copper aeroplane brooch made out of a penny by brother when he was at art school.
o A school report.
o Nose from a glider from wartime job as an inspector.
o Ration card.
o Hairbrush, present from husband, second wedding anniversary.
o Lock of son's baby hair.

o Pegbag, made by daughter at primary school.
o Newspaper cuttings from local paper of son's and daughter's O level results.
o Fruit spoon, present from Silver Wedding anniversary.
o One centime piece, picked up off floor on holiday to France last year (first ever trip abroad!).

For each item in her collection Jess

managed to remember an event associated with it, though the act of acquiring the object was not always the important thing. For instance, she was given the cameo brooch on the death of her mother but its main association in her mind was that her mother had always worn it on a high collared blouse when Jess had been a small child.

Most of Jess's objects were connected with other people and were reminders of what they had meant to her. Only a few helped her to think about things she'd done herself.

"It's only when I sit down and really think about it that I begin to realise the value that I do place on my relationships with others. I suppose I've always been someone who gets the most out of life through what I do with and for other people."

So next, she reorganised her collection and added some things to it so that she had more objects which reminded her of work and interests she'd had, as well as the objects which reminded her of people.

Look at your own collection of objects again. How many of them are related to things you've done, achievements, relationships, places? What aspects of life have you placed value on?

Whatever they are, they are unlikely to change in your retirement. You take a set of values and priorities with you regardless of changing circumstances.

Photos and pictures

Lots of people have a collection of photos that record, sometimes rather eccentrically, the history of their lives. You might get the impression if you were an outsider to our society that people spend most of their lives on beaches playing cricket!

If you can, find a collection of photos and pictures that you have acquired over the years. Look at them carefully and see just how many of them help you remember an event.

How many of them are just vaguely familiar? For instance, you know you went to Clacton on holiday in 1935, but you can't really remember much about it.
How many people's names can you remember?
Can you work out who took each group photograph (there is usually one notable absentee with lots of group photos)?
Are there any periods in your life when few photographs were taken?

Can you remember why this should be?
When you look at the photographs in rough date order are there cases of people drifting in and out of your life? If there are, think about them, try and remember how important they were to you at that time, and when the last time was that you actually thought about them before you looked at the photographs again.

If there are gaps in your memory see if you can think of anyone who could help you remember.

Give yourself a present
One thing you might consider doing is to mark your retirement by giving yourself an organised photograph or memento album.

Or even more than that, give the members of your family photograph albums of their lives too. Even very old negatives can produce good prints.

Doing the album will be a way of sorting out events that you recall with pleasure.

The stories of your life

By now you might have already started finding reports and accounts of various parts of your life – birth certificate, school reports, old wage packets, correspondence about buying a house or a car, old letters, birthday cards, newspaper reports of births, marriage and deaths, church service cards, and so on. Most peoples' lives are documented in some way.

If you look at these documents you will probably find they present quite a strange account of your life. For instance since you are unlikely to have birth certificates or documents of any brothers or sisters they probably won't crop up in the documentation of your life very much. There are probably accounts of you at your place of work, or your medical record which present equally limited pictures of you.

Some different stories
Try playing around presenting different accounts of yourself and compare what you pick out from your life to emphasize on each occasion. Here are some ideas for writing accounts of different aspects of your life.

After you retire you decide to apply for a part-time job. It's entirely different from any job you've ever had so you need to emphasize other aspects of your life to make yourself appear suitable. Name such a job and write a job description.

An old friend of the same sex who you haven't seen from your school days writes out of the blue and asks you to fill in the details of the last 45 years.

A local newspaper is running a series on people coming up to retirement in which people describe their working life. You decide to write to them.

Your granddaughter has to collect an interview on life between the two wars. She asks you if you'll write something down about it.

If you've lived in the same area for many years write an account of the changes in it.

Imagine that after you retire you move somewhere completely new and meet your new neighbours for the first time.

They ask you to tell them about yourself.

Everyone selects bits and pieces of their history to recount in different situations. They won't always be the same – sometimes they might even seem at odds with different parts of your history. You might want on one occasion to emphasize your hard working and serious nature and on another your fun loving and frivolous nature.

So you have many different aspects to your personality, your skill and your knowledge. You can draw on all of these and use them in your retirement.

Thinking about these things will perhaps have helped you with your picture of yourself. But remember too that the sorts of things you've been looking at and thinking about can have some practical uses.

You could think about:
o Tracing your family tree.
o Writing up the story of your family in your local area.
o Using your collection of objects and photos to amuse your grandchildren.
o Using some of the material you've discovered at a local history class.
o Doing some research to fill in some of the blanks in your memory. Try your library, check newspaper cuttings.

Attitudes to work

Consider some of the experiences which may have helped to develop your present attitudes to work. Think about the job you do and about the importance to you of having a job.

Thinking out your responses in this way should help you when you leave your job and have to make decisions on adapting to retirement.

Your job

Your attitude to work involves not only your own approach to the job you do but also may be influenced by the fact that in society in general jobs tend to be seen as a way of evaluating people. How often, when you meet a new acquaintance after a long period do you ask "What are you doing these days?". If you know a person's job, even if he is a stranger you find yourself producing a rough identikit of his abilities.

Occupational identity is very strong. A job involves skills and expertise. It also provides a certain status. When people think about giving up work, there may be a fear that there will be no strong identity to replace the one that occupation has provided. And perhaps also that future status will not be so certain either.

So think now about what your job has provided you with. The chart on the right lists some statements about characteristics of jobs. Look at the list and tick which ones are not important, important and very important to you. Add any others not included that you feel have been important to you in your own job.

Peoples' attitudes to work are as various as the jobs they do. For some people who have had jobs that they feel are boring or monotonous, the important characteristics may have been income and friends, the job itself taking strictly second place. For others whose work has been absorbing the skills and expertise of the job itself may have been all important.

Look at those items you have ticked as important to you. They are all things which have affected the quality of your life. Giving them up will bring changes in your lifestyle. And it's worth exploring in some detail how you feel about this prospect.

A job provides:	Not important	Important	Very important
Income.			
Companionship with friends, colleagues, associates.			
Opportunities for social activities.			
Topics of conversation to take home.			
A readily recognisable public image, e.g. joiner, teacher, postman, bank manager.			
Roles, e.g. foreman, craftsman, supervisor, manager, organiser.			
Opportunities to learn new skills.			
Opportunities to develop expertise.			
Opportunities for challenge — competitiveness, meeting deadlines etc.			
Minor and sometimes major crises which call for decision-making.			
Opportunities for service to others.			
Opportunities for self-development.			
A regular routine.			
Discipline.			
Add others.			

Attitudes vary

Attitudes to jobs are as varied as the people who do them.

David was an ambitious go-getter: Brought up to believe that work is good for you, he believed that people didn't deserve what they had not worked for. In fact, if they didn't work they must be shiftless and lazy. He couldn't see a time when he wouldn't be working all out at something or other. Over the years, without realising, he had come close to being a 'workaholic'.

Joanna, since first she started nursing, had been totally absorbed by it. Most of the time she was unaware of how hard she worked. Living at the hospital meant she didn't have to worry about finding her own accommodation but it did mean she was always 'on hand'. Often her working hours spilled over into her leisure hours. While this was a nuisance at times, mostly she didn't give it a thought because her job seemed to give her so much of what she needed out of life — it was exactly how she wanted to spend her time. It was only as retirement approached that she wondered how she would fill the enormous gap that giving up work would leave. She would also have to find somewhere to live, something she had never had to do before. She kept promising herself to sit down and think it out, but other things always turned up, so she never did. Had she been asked, she would probably have agreed that work was her hobby.

Arthur had been at work since he was 14, had worked hard at a variety of routine jobs which he thought of as 'alright' as long as they brought in enough money to pay the bills. Ever since he could remember, though, he'd looked forward to Friday night. Somehow, he felt more 'himself' at the weekend. He was really glad to be giving up working for somebody else and have the chance to do the things he really wanted. For him, retirement couldn't come soon enough. With the business of earning a living out of the way 'for good and all', he could do all the things he liked best.

Jill, a housewife, had worked part-time, on and off, since the children went to school, usually managing to find something to fit in with the children's school hours. She liked getting away from the house for a while, the company did her good and she enjoyed having a little money she could call her own, even if it did usually end up with the housekeeping. Now that retirement age was near, she wasn't so sure whether she wanted to give up working. The real benefits for her had been meeting people and making new friends. She found, too, that being sympathetic, a good listener, and having experience of the ups and downs of family life the 'girls' would confide their troubles and ask her advice.

How do you feel about your job?

Most jobs have good and bad aspects. Now you have read the experiences of David, Joanna, Arthur and Jill how do you feel about your own job? On the chart over the page tick how you feel about your job. In considering the points listed, it might help you to think about what aspects of work you would be glad to leave behind, and which aspects you would try to retain when you no longer have a job.

David, Joanna, Arthur and Jill, all have different attitudes to their work. How about you?

How do you feel about your job?
Tick 'yes' or 'no'

	Yes	No
1 Are most of your waking hours spent at work?	☐	☐
2 Does your work-load spill over into your leisure time?	☐	☐
3 Do you have to work fixed hours?	☐	☐
4 Are you under pressure most of the time?	☐	☐
5 Is your work load decided by someone else?	☐	☐
6 Does your work physically exhaust you?	☐	☐
7 Are you 'underemployed', so that time drags?	☐	☐
8 Do you find your job dull and boring?	☐	☐
9 Do you feel you have skills and gifts which are not being used?	☐	☐
10 Will you be pleased to give up the job because you have no interest in it?	☐	☐
11 Have you learned new skills at work?	☐	☐
12 Do you think of your work almost as a hobby?	☐	☐
13 Has your work helped to bring out personal qualities you did not guess you had?	☐	☐

Add other views.

When you no longer have a job

Below are some questions that may help you explore how your attitudes to work will affect certain decisions to be taken about your retirement.

o If your job takes up most of your time now and you have little time for leisure, how will you spend it when all your time is free time?

o If someone else has usually fixed your working hours, are you able to allocate time to doing the things you want to do in the same organised way?

o If over-organisation is exactly what you want to escape from, have you decided how you can best enjoy your new opportunity to please yourself?

o If you have often had to work in conditions of competition and pressure, will you be pleased to be rid of them? Or have you become so accustomed to them that you need to find some substitute?

o If your work was just a dull, boring way of earning a living, will you, on retirement, take the opportunity to make life more interesting?

o Are there ways in which you can use or develop your skills and personal qualities? If you are not sure now, do you plan to find out?

o If the main value of working (apart from income) for you has been contact with other people, will you expect any changes in the number and kind of relationships you have with workmates and colleagues? Will you expect to make new friends among the retired?

o If your hobby is work, and you would find total leisure too difficult all at once, can you begin to put out 'feelers' for a part-time job, take late retirement, act as consultant, become self-employed and try to reduce your working hours gradually? Or, perhaps you will be able to find some voluntary work which will require the same skills, personal qualities and commitment?

o If you think you will be short of cash, are you making it known among all your contacts that you will be looking for part-time work?

You may well find that as yet you have no answers to some questions that are important to you. Remember that your plans for retirement can be filled out gradually and being aware of questions that *are* important to you is a good starting point for plans.

New Goals

For most people, the job ceases to hold top priority when the time to retire arrives. Instead, new goals present themselves — or have to be sought. These may involve making certain compromises.

This is what happened to David and Joanna, Arthur and Jill.

David had almost become a workaholic until he recognised his problem. He realised that he had lost contact with his family and had no real hobbies. Though there were some difficulties, he made efforts to be more involved with the family. He took up golf again and joined a chess club.

He had heard about the Employment Fellowship whose activities appealed to his interest in organisation and administration and knowledge of management. He decided to find out more with a view to using his business acumen and his capacity for hard work.

Joanna knew she would miss her busy, responsible and people-filled life. As she would no longer 'live in' she would have to make extra efforts to find a niche in the community and make new friends. She tried to replace some of the satisfactions of her job by joining the Red Cross. Rather reluctantly she went with a friend to a 'Painting for Pleasure' class at the local adult centre. She was surprised to find that she was quite good (and recalled that years ago, at school, she had won a set of pencils for art). She continues to learn how to play the guitar. Soon new friends as well as old will be popping into her flat.

Arthur had to reorganise his week so that the weekend would still have that 'special' feeling to it. Pleased to be rid of the work routine he decided to use his skills in his own interests. Thinking about some of the jobs he had done at home or with friends over the years he realised that he could turn his hand to quite a few things, bricklaying, flagging — he'd build his garage and repair next door's path with a friend — painting and decorating — he

and his wife always did their own — and gardening — he shared an allotment with his neighbour. He was going to help his married son modernise his kitchen and do a few jobs around his own place, and get some more practice in at bowls. At the back of his mind was the idea that if money was really short he could always do some part-time work as a handyman, though he hoped it would not be necessary. 'The wife' was pestering him to go to Spain while he still had some of his retirement money. In an unguarded moment he agreed to go with her to a class at the college to do six nights of Holiday Spanish. *"She says there's no writing, and no exams . . . well, it might be alright."*

Jill was dreading giving up her part-time work because she knew she needed lots of company. When the supervisor asked if she'd be willing to do an hour's voluntary work a week as a helper with a family contact line, she was delighted. Jill loved running her home but not the feeling of isolation that comes from being indoors all day. As an outgoing person she had soon made new friends and had the satisfaction of knowing she was helping others by drawing on her own life experience.

Your job and people

Before retirement, people often claim that what they worry about most is whether they can manage on a reduced income. Studies have shown, however, that many are even more concerned about the loss of contact with former workmates and colleagues. At work, you have a mixture of acquaintances:

o People you can pass the time of day with.
o People you work closely with who share the same skills and experience.
o People you can share confidences with (perhaps because you know they will never be too close).
o Close friends.

This variety can be much reduced after retirement unless you decide to do something about it. Look at the chart below and think about the importance of relationships at work. When you have ticked the answers appropriate to you, think about your current plans. Do they take into account the possible need to adjust relationships and to perhaps seek new ones?

	Yes	No
Will you miss your friends when you leave work?	☐	☐
Are a large number of your social activities connected in some way with work, e.g. membership of employees social/sports club, going to works' dances, celebrations etc.?	☐	☐
Are the people you meet at work the same people you meet in your leisure time?	☐	☐
Do you have friends who are not connected with your work?	☐	☐
If you travel as part of your job, does this limit your contact with neighbours and local friends?	☐	☐
Are your friendships affected by the fact that you are:		
o **A shift worker?**	☐	☐
o **Work unsocial hours?**	☐	☐
o **Work in an isolated situation?**	☐	☐

From work to leisure

Attitudes to leisure

"I'm interested in such a lot of things . . . old abbeys, archaeology, history — and I haven't much time for them."

"I shall probably have time to listen to my records."

"I see myself watching sport and fishing and doing the things — you know — you've missed all these years."

To some, leisure means the opportunity to relax, to rest, to sit back and do nothing. To others it means time for action and increased physical exercise. Some see leisure as a golden opportunity for creative output; others go in for self-improvement of all sorts and some are glad of the extra time to fit in overspill from work and beaver away at more of the same. The odds are that throughout adulthood you have tried a variety of these approaches to spare time.

However, if you look back at recent years you will probably be able to see that there is a broad pattern which typifies your own attitude to leisure. Since retirement offers a unique opportunity for you to use time exactly as you wish and to operate a wide range of choices, it might be a good idea to consider where you stand now. To be able to make any decisions on what to do with your leisure time you'll have to first work out just what your feelings are about leisure.

What does leisure mean to you?

Tick which answers apply to you

A reward for having done some work. ☐

Being able to choose freely what you will do next. ☐

Being 'at ease'—free from pressure and tension and the burden of 'I ought to' or 'I must'. ☐

Very precious—made up of brief periods to be savoured and not wasted. ☐

A time to do something which would contrast as much as possible with what you were doing at work. ☐

Rather frightening and to be avoided if at all possible. ☐

How do you spend your spare time now?

Think back over the last year and try and recall the whole spread of your leisure activities. Below are a list of questions which deal with a number of features of leisure. Look at them and fill in which of your own leisure activities apply to each question.

Which of your leisure activities:

Involve artistic or creative skills?

Do you find particularly relaxing?

Involve being with other people socially?

Involve helping others?

Get you out and about?

Exert you physically?

Involve getting a product i.e. garden produce, pottery?

Involve no one except you?

Involve real mental stimulation?

Involve watching, spectating?

How much leisure?

Look again at your list of current leisure activities and think about how much time they take up.

Edward a printer who is coming up to retirement drew up the timetable below to show how his leisure fitted into a typical working week. Look at Edward's timetable and use it to:

o Make a rough estimate of the extra numbers of hours of free time Edward will have when he retires.

o Look at his spare time activities
  – will they be sufficient to spread over the additional time he will have to fill in retirement?
  – will he need a wider variety of activities?

o Make a similar timetable for yourself and ask yourself the same questions.

You may be perfectly happy with your leisure timetable for retirement. But it is probably worth reviewing after a few months of retirement to see whether your calculations about spending your time were wholly realistic. You may find that activities you allocated more time to didn't really merit that much time or that you'd like to try something new.

Whatever your feelings about your timetable for leisure, two useful keywords to bear in mind are **time** and **variety.** Spending more time on current activities may in itself provide some interesting results. You may decide to become an 'expert' or to explore different aspects of activities that have previously been limited by time. Introducing more variety into your leisure pursuits can be exciting at the outset. Try new areas, you'll probably discard some, but even so they may put you on the track of others. If you keep on experimenting eventually you'll find a balance which is satisfying and probably get quite a lot of enjoyment from the false trails as well.

Leisure and people

What interests will you share with your partner, relative or friend you share your home with? Ask them to look back at your timetable and after discussion, write down the interests you agree you will share.

It is often a good idea if there are also some you do not share. This will allow for exchange of ideas and experiences, and also some time apart.

Looking beyond yourself

Many couples grow closer as the years go on and move into retirement in unison. Others may be unaware that they have grown apart and face retirement as 'intimate strangers'. This makes planning the future together both more difficult and even more necessary.

Relying solely upon your partner, closest friend or nearest relative for social contact can set up strains and tensions. If your leisure choices are broadly based they can offer opportunities both for developing your partnership (or relationship) and for widening your contacts. Think of the wide range of people work normally brings you into contact with. This variety will be much reduced after retirement unless you take steps to alter the situation.

Bear in mind that you can introduce some variety into the social side of your leisure activities if you take action to keep in touch with your own neighbourhood, involve yourself with the specific interests of your town or region or perhaps link yourself with national or even international developments through clubs and societies.

Are you alone?

Being alone is not the same as loneliness. Some hobbies call for the capacity to enjoy being alone. Often these are the ones that need powers of concentration (puzzle solving), manual or technical skills (craftwork) or creative gifts (artwork, craftwork, writing etc). Given a balanced use of leisure, reasonable concern for and interest in people, periods of solitude can enrich, refuel and add zest to your social life and activities.

Edward's working week			
	Morning	**Afternoon**	**Evening**
Mon Tues Wed Thurs Fri	Work	Work	**Visit Mother Darts Read paper/TV Social Club/Darts TV/Pub**
Sat Sun	DIY. Shop with wife Rest in/visit pub	**Allotment & Bowls Allotment & Bowls**	TV/Pub **Visit son's family or vice-versa**

Making leisure work

In this topic you will be asked to look at the kind of person you are, at some of the experiences that went to developing your present skills and interests and helped to form your present attitudes. You will be asked to think about your personal style in approaching people, situations and occupations.

A busy working life does not leave much time but if you plan to 'make leisure work', it would be useful to consider what 'makes you tick'.

School days

Complete the following sentences

At school . . .
I always envied people who were good at:

I recall a teacher saying I'd done really well in:

I recall my school friends thinking I was good at:

I was always very resentful when I was denied the opportunity to:

I was always totally bored by:

My parents insisted that I concentrate on:

If I had the chance I should have liked to look more deeply at:

I was very pleased when I did well at:

The lesson I looked forward most to was:

What made you tick?

Looking back — early days
Over a lifetime you will have collected skills, know-how and experience of all sorts. Each period of your life has probably seen the accumulation of new skills. At the same time areas you might once have been inclined towards may have been forgotten or not developed through lack of opportunity.

Schooldays may seem a far cry from planning retirement but you may have had some special interests or gifts then which you were unable to develop once you started work. You may have been obliged to concentrate on particular subjects and been forced to exclude other interests. Perhaps your choices in those days were made out of necessity or were those of other people and not yours at all.

The activity on the left helps you to think again about your schooldays. It's in the form of incomplete sentences and should help to start you off thinking about areas of activity you might now want to explore. If you are still in contact with people from your schooldays talk to them about what went on, it might help you remember more. Remember how you have changed and all you have learned since. What you once found difficult or boring might be just 'your cup of tea' now. The activity might remind you of situations you enjoyed and suggest occupations for retirement.

Your Citizens Advice Bureau or library service will help you to contact local societies.

. . . At work and in the services
At work, and remember to include work in the home, you will have collected all kinds of skills and knowledge. You take them so much for granted that you don't realise just how many skills you have. Some of these could come in handy in retirement activities, so it's worth going back over the things you've done, enjoyed, and been good at in the past.

Think of other people you know. Have they any skills that you admire or envy? A skill that you would like to have acquired? Perhaps you could learn that skill now?

Why not take up one or two of the occupations you think you might have shone at if you had had a real chance to try before. This might provide the sort of challenge that sometimes crops up at work but less often in retirement – unless *you* put it there.

Skills and gifts can usually be grouped. Often individuals have greater strengths in one group rather than another. Where do your strengths lie?

Size yourself up

Sometimes it is quite difficult to assess your own abilities accurately. It can be a good idea to ask the help of someone who knows you well and whose opinion you value.

The table below will help you to sort out the skills, gifts and preferences you have collected over a lifetime. It asks you to list your views against another opinion.

While you may just want to do the activity using the tables, they could also form the basis for real discussion between you and your partner.

After completing the table below you would have now identified:

o Skills and interests you have already.
o Skills and interests you might like to develop.
o Particular areas of high or poor performance.

Tables from "Decide for Yourself", Hobsons Press for CRAC, Cambridge.

Size yourself up.

	How do others see you?			How do you see yourself?		
	No gift for	Good at	Could develop	No gift for	Good at	Could develop
Sociable. Being with people, doing things in co-operation with others.						
Creative. Writing, drawing, drama, music, designing.						
Practical. Do it yourself, crafts.						
Helpful. Offering a service or companionship to others.						
Scientific. Enquiring into natural world, and the how and why of science and technology.						
Administrative. Organising & planning, committee work, being 'in charge' and getting things done.						
Physically active—sporting. Taking part in active sport activities.						
Literary. Writing, reading, going to the theatre.						
Mathematical. Book keeping, accountancy, computing.						

o Compare and discuss with your partner the differences that show up in the two columns.
o What interests that you now follow would you like to devote more time to?
o What new interest would you like to take up that would encourage any potential that either of you has noted?
o Ask your partner/close friend to complete the table for herself/himself.

All the time — your life-time to date in fact — you have spent selecting and rejecting experiences, striving to make good and coming to terms with what could or could not be, you have been adjusting to circumstances and developing as a person.

The closer you come to knowing what kind of person you have become, the more successful you are likely to be in making the kind of adjustments necessary after you have retired.

How have you developed as a person?

Whatever activitites you choose, personal style will affect the way you approach them.

Personal style Again, ask your partner or a friend to make an assessment too and tick which styles apply to you.						
	How do others see you?			How do you see yourself?		
	Moderately	Very	Exceptionally	Moderately	Very	Exceptionally
Active. **Always on the go, hard working, plenty of drive.**						
Conscientious. **Give attention to detail, take pride in work, concentrate closely.**						
Sensitive. **Aware of other people's feelings, do not like to hurt others.**						
Sociable. **Easy going, friendly, like to be with people, good humoured.**						
Co-operative. **Respond well to other people's suggestions, can fit in well with others.**						
Dominant. **Want to be out in front, take initiative, accept responsibility.**						
Resilient. **Overcome difficulties, can accept criticism, not easily upset or discouraged.**						
Self-sufficient. **Can stand on your own feet, resourceful.**						

Adjustment to leisure

How to get started

Thinking ahead before retirement gives you breathing space to adjust to an unaccustomed freedom of action. It gives you the stimulus to provide not merely for the six months or so after retirement – the honeymoon period – but to consider a plan of action that will keep the momentum going; that will keep you healthily stretched just a little beyond the too comfortable minimum; that will give a reasonable variety of short term interests and provide for longer term major interests; and one that will match your own personal style.

Preliminaries

o Try 'taster' sessions of possible new pastimes before committing yourself

o See whether you really have an aptitude for a new hobby or activity before buying new equipment, accessories or paying membership fees.

o If you decide to learn something entirely new, try to get 'over the hump' of the difficult and boring bits sometime before retirement. It is more enjoyable to apply a skill than to struggle to acquire it or to get dispirited when you are not very good at it.

o If you want to do some voluntary work, get some specialist advice first. Offer the minimum amount of time initially until you are sure about how much time you want to commit yourself to.

Finding out before retirement

Find out – from your Citizens Advice Bureau, Library, Town Hall, Adult Education Centre, College of Further Education, Community Centre:

o About the area you live in. Often the habit of taking an annual holiday 'away somewhere' leaves you unaware of all your home area has to offer.

o Where you could take up again some of the interests you had to drop because you were too busy.

o Where you can continue your education – this can mean all sorts of things from taking up crafts and hobbies as pastimes to commitment to a

serious course of study. You can polish up your skills, develop your gifts, keep in touch with new developments in this way. (Why not, for example, find out what is meant by 'the new maths', or how computers work?)

o Whether you could match up the skills, expertise or simply the goodwill you have to offer to the needs of others. Voluntary associations and your social services department will be glad to hear from you.

o What action groups there are in your area. You could offer organising ability, good ideas or just 'get up and go', if you feel there is something that needs to be done or changes to be made. You may see the need to start an action group of your own.

This is just a checklist to make suggestions. You need to explore any of these items that interest you in detail.

When you have decided what to do—consider the cost

Allocate, if you can, resources for:

o Occasional major treats, eg. holidays, celebrations.

o Chosen club membership for you and your partner.

o Fees for recreational, educational, social activities.

o Incidental expenses in connection with leisure, eg. travel, renewal of equipment etc.

Consider possible alternatives:

o It could be better to take a less expensive holiday and have sufficient 'movement money' for you and your partner to have a wider choice of activities throughout the year.

o Explore the range of subsidised or free activities available in your area. Most Town Halls have an information office or ask the Citizens Advice Bureau.

o Find out if there are any low cost self-help groups in your area through which you could enjoy hobbies and interests. If not, think of starting a self-help group of your own.

Attitudes to leisure affect the quality of life

Some people look forward with trepidation to all the extra leisure that retirement brings. It seems perverse then, to think of increased leisure as a problem when throughout your working life you've considered it so precious. How many Monday mornings have you wished you did not have to go to work? The feeling is familiar even to the most dedicated.

Constructive organisation of your leisure periods will help you avoid the anxiety that comes from the prospect of having too much time on your hands.

Retirement day

The last week at work is bound to come and so too, eventually, the day of retirement itself. This marks a very significant stage for you, the changeover into a new way of life. As with so many significant moments in life, retirement is frequently marked with some sort of ceremony or celebration. These sorts of celebrations can prove very useful in helping you and your family and friends to adjust to a new situation and new circumstances.

Have a look at the chart below. On it are listed a variety of different occasions, some sad, such as a funeral, some joyous, such as christening. Many of the ceremonies and celebrations listed are significant in a number of ways. A house-warming party, for example, as well as being a happy occasion and a good excuse for a general celebration, is a way of representing your commitment to a new place and a new set of people — though that doesn't, of course, mean that you have to leave the others behind!

So, fill in the chart below by taking these various occasions in turn and deciding just what you feel they represent.

A changing life

Important celebrations and occasions which mark significant events in peoples' lives often represent three different processes:

o Separating yourself from your previous lifestyle.
o Making the changeover.
o Getting into a new lifestyle.

By 'going public' at a party to celebrate the event, these three processes are acknowledged by everyone concerned. It makes the change in lifestyle quite clear.

Perhaps one such occasion with which most people are familiar is getting married. There are three stages:

o The engagement where the couple formally state their intention to marry. When they do this they are effectively saying they are no longer on the open 'marriage market'.

o The period of the engagement is a changeover time during which the couple are neither on the 'marriage market' nor are they married. Most people are either single or married. Engaged couples seem to be somewhere in between, trying to make preparations, adjust and face up to reality.

o Marriage, both the ceremony and the reception that follows may be seen as a process of moving into a new life, acquiring a new status. This is often marked by humour — when the bridegroom says "My wife and I . . ." and all the guests greet such a statement with howls of laughter.

The occasion

What it represents	Christening.	Confirmation.	Engagement party.	Coming of age.	Wedding.	Wedding anniversary.	Bar-mitzvah.	Retirement.	House warming.	Passing exams.	Funeral.
Joyous occasion.											
Solemn occasion.											
Sad occasion.											
Marks a new lifestyle.											
General celebration.											
Marks leaving old lifestyle.											
Marks a break with certain people.											
Marks a commitment to new people.											

A ceremony can be important for you in several ways:

o It can help you accept your new status as a reality. Everyone is there to acknowledge it.

o It can therefore also help other people to accept your new status, both the group you're leaving and the group you're joining.

o Quite often it can help you make this changeover by making you passive for a while, neither one thing or the other. This period has been likened to going through a door and not being in either one room or the other.

Separation

So how does all this apply to retirement?

There are many different customs. Some are fairly widespread. You may not have heard of others. Which ones apply at your place of work? Towards the date of retirement workers may:

o Attend pre-retirement courses, which are occasions which separate them from the rest of the workforce and their interests.

During the last few days they may:

o Leave the work task they usually do.

o Separate themselves from their own work friends and go round their place of work saying goodbye to people.

o Finally hand over responsibility for their job to a younger worker.

Separation from work brings gains and losses. But in both cases they mean change and thinking about them beforehand can be useful. So look at the following list and think what your answers might be:

Personal identity

How will you feel when you can no longer say "I am a carpenter/clerk etc?"

Social identity

How will you feel when people no longer assess your place in society on what you do?

Personal and social worth

Do you feel you will still be contributing something worthwhile to life when you stop work?

Status and self-respect

What sort of things will contribute to you respecting yourself after you stop work?

Self-achievement

What sense of achievement or satisfaction will you have when you no longer work?

Friends

Will you be separated from your friends when you no longer work?

Understanding time

How will you mark off the hours, days and weeks when you no longer have a work routine, clocking off time etc?

Diversion

Will you be able to divert yourself from your private worries and fears when you no longer work?

Finances

How will you organise your finances when you no longer work?

The last day of work

Like other celebrations that have been mentioned retirement day parties are often occasions of some emotion. They are occasions for enjoyment and for appreciation of the person at the centre of it all. However just as at a wedding where the bride's mother enjoys having a good cry, feelings can be mixed.

o It might be the first time that there has been such a public statement about your worth and value as an individual at work.

o It might be that it is at the retirement day party you really feel for the first time the impending absence of work in your life.

Get the best out of your retirement celebrations; come up with a few traditions of your own to set the feeling of having gone out with a bang rather than like a damp squib. And if you find it an emotional occasion, there's nothing wrong with that; people usually do feel emotional at important occasions in their lives.

Knowing what will happen

Check what sort of retirement parties are held where you work.

Below is a list of possible things to help the celebrations on. Tick the ones which are the custom at your place of work. Then tick which ones are most likely to give you pleasure, and finally any you feel anxious about.

Few people look forward to such events with either complete pleasure or complete dread. So it's rather a matter of making the most of the pleasurable aspects and playing down the anxieties.

Here are some of the sorts of issues you might feel most concerned about.

Giving a speech. This doesn't mean you've got to speak for three quarters of an hour without notes – remember what it's like to be on the receiving end!

If you feel confident about making a speech, think about how you can use the opportunity. Perhaps you would like to express how you have felt about work and in what ways you are looking forward to retirement.

If you're not so confident just find a couple of things to say.
o Thank you for the present. I feel sure I shall enjoy it.
o Thank you for the celebration, it was kind of you to organise it.

o I'd just like to say that although I have enjoyed working here, I'm now looking forward to the first day of my new life.

Being the subject of a speech. Enjoy it if you can and remember that the person giving the speech is expressing on behalf of *everyone* feelings about your value and worth (even if you suspect that the Managing Director doesn't know you from Adam!).

If you do find yourself worried about being the subject of a speech it's a matter of fixing your attention on the door on the other side of the room . . . or thinking about all the things you won't have to do tomorrow.

Mixing with people you don't know. Well you don't have to see them tomorrow, and you may never have to see them again.

So not much of consequence can happen, and everyone does mean you well.

Expense. It's worthwhile deciding in advance what you want to spend on celebrations, and making it clear from the start:

o Come along to the party. It's all on me.

o I'm game for a round of drinks. I can't afford much more. Us retirees you know, we have to watch the pennies!

o We'd like you to come out for a meal with us. I think it would cost you about £8 for a couple and Harry and I would like to treat you to a drink beforehand.

o I'm having a small celebration at home if you fancy bringing a bottle for when the drinks run out.

	Takes place	Gives pleasure	Causes anxiety
Break with usual patterns of work in the week up to retirement day.	☐	☐	☐
Have official party during office hours.	☐	☐	☐
Have an informal drink with work friends during work hours.	☐	☐	☐
Have a celebratory meal with friends outside work hours.	☐	☐	☐
Bring partner to farewell party.	☐	☐	☐
Receive a gift from the place of work.	☐	☐	☐
Be the subject of a speech.	☐	☐	☐
Give a speech.	☐	☐	☐
Be accompanied home by friends on final day.	☐	☐	☐
People other than your work friends invited to celebration.	☐	☐	☐

Look back at the list of retirement celebration events. Think about the ones which don't happen where you work, and about which ones of those you might enjoy.
Do you have any choice in the way the party is organised? Perhaps you could suggest including some of the things you enjoy. If you can suggest ideas that go down well you'll be doing a service to people retiring from where you work in the future.

The changeover and the new life

Retirement is different from many of the other events where something about your lifestyle changes.

The separation from the old life is definitely marked for most people. The changeover begins the day work is over and you start to move into your new life.

But how does society view a person of leisure?

Unfortunately there do not seem to be any clear expectations. In some ways this reflects the way retirement is regarded in our society. Older people have no automatic rights to prestige and esteem as they once did. They lose their work status but there are few events to help them gain a new and respected status. There's a danger they will get stuck betwixt and between, not a worker but not anything else either.

It hardly seems surprising that in a recent survey the most frequent piece of advice of those who had retired to those about to retire was 'plan ahead'. If society isn't going to help you to get into a new life, then you have to do it for yourself. The role of the retired person is therefore exactly what *you* choose to make it.

New territory

It may be that the sort of celebrations held where you work are limited to work associates and doesn't include your partner, family or outside friends at all. If that's the case then tell them about what happened and how you felt. Share it with them. The celebration was for you but what it represents affects other people's lives too.

But more than that, think about the new territory into which you are moving. Think about celebrating that movement with the people who inhabit that territory. Hold a 'new-life' party. Think

deliberately about a venue outside work. After all, that's where all your celebrating will be done in future.

Reasons for celebrating with family and friends

o It says you are looking forward to your new life.

o It allows them to join in some part of the celebrations if they are excluded from other parts of it.

o It stops the feeling of anti-climax at the end of work hours on the last day.

o It makes you feel your new life is something to value.

o It's a positive joyful act with which to start your retirement.

If any of these reasons appeal to you then *celebrate*.

Having a celebration in your own home or the local area can help establish you firmly in your new territory and help you lose that feeling of standing in a doorway between two rooms!

Making changes

The first few months after you retire is a time for testing out changes you want to make, pursuing those you feel excited about, consolidating those you feel comfortable about. The topics in this chapter are designed to help you work your way through the first novelty of retirement. They look at the implications of a change in lifestyle and consider the various choices you have to take in responsibility for your health. The topics on finances give particular emphasis to what actually being retired means for you and your money. Several topics give you an opportunity to consider adjustments to your social life after you've retired. And finally there's a chance to explore your initial ideas about how you'll spend your time. The time immediately after your retirement is a time of change. You can begin to act on your plan and get a feel for what being retired is like.

A new routine

Most of us spend much of our lives following a pretty tight routine — the routine called work. School prepares us for this life — with its timetable for lessons, dates for completing homework, an emphasis on being punctual, and so on. Working life continues this pattern by giving us set tasks to be completed by a particular time, or at a particular speed. Few of us are in a position to set our own deadlines or work at our own speed — until we retire. In retirement we are suddenly in the position of being able to say *"No, I don't think I'll do that today, I'd much rather do this"*, or even *"I don't enjoy doing this, so I think I'll just give it up"*.

For many people this is the great attraction of retirement — they see themselves sitting with their feet up reading the paper, taking things easy. Being in a position to determine a personal routine can be an important responsibility — and reading the paper can be boring if you do nothing else the whole day.

Routines *can* be repetitive and dull, but they can also give a valuable structure to the days and weeks and help us to do more of the things we would really like to do.

Work routines

John is a self-employed joiner. His routine changes constantly. Sometimes he will be working for himself doing small jobs for local householders, sometimes he will take time off to do jobs on his own house. His 'work' often spills over into his evenings and weekends, his leisure pursuits often spill over into his weekdays.

Nastasia works as an accounts clerk with a large company. She keeps regular hours, always working from 9–5 Monday to Friday and takes her coffee, lunch and tea breaks at the regular office times. She works under close supervision at the office and never takes work home.

Bill is a salesman with a large shoe manufacturing company. He covers an extensive patch in the north of England visiting retailers and taking their orders. He has to work out his own schedule and his own selling techniques. He works under little supervision and the only real test of his work-rate is the review of his sales figures.

Think about the day-to-day activities of these three people at work in terms of:
o The place they occur.
o The time they occupy.
o The people involved in them.

Now look at the chart and see how many of these aspects remain unchanged for each individual in their normal working lives. Against each name, there are boxes for each aspect of the working day. A heavily shaded box ■ shows that no changes occur, a lightly shaded box ▣ shows occasional change and an unshaded box □ shows frequent change. The example below shows that Nastasia has the steadiest routine.

What sort of routine are *you* accustomed to? Think about your own working life and fill in your own patterns of shades. The less frequently your routine changes the more dependent you are likely to be on a steady routine and the more attention you may need to devote to establishing a new routine in retirement. If you have grown used to variety you may need to plan ways of providing it after you have left work.

Roles

We all play many roles — parent, son, daughter, employee, club secretary etc — but before retirement, for many people the major role is likely to be determined by the job. This not only provides a ready made routine and gives a sense of purpose but, even if you don't care for the job much, often carries a certain status with it. The skills, expertise and personal qualities developed at work also colour the kind of reputation you have among colleagues.

Knowing the sort of job you do helps others to build an image of your 'role' in life even if they don't know a great deal about the actual work you do. To a large extent the job defines the person. When you retire your role is defined solely by you, by your efforts.

At work	John	Nastasia	Bill	You
The place				
The time				
The people				

In many peoples' eyes retirement is regarded purely as a 'play' role. You are invited to 'enjoy it' — no demands are made beyond this, no imposed routines or expectations. As a result it is often difficult for others to build an image of the role of a retired person. In fact, it may not even occur to them to do so.

What this means is that you'll have to try harder to find new purposes and strong new roles in life to make sure that your sense of personal value is not reduced or lost or that your sense of purpose is not replaced by feelings of apathy.

New routines

Bert Hardcastle was given a good send off when he left his job as a fitter. He got a cheque from the management, his workmates had a 'whip round' and bought him some new fishing tackle and took him and his wife to the 'Crown and Garter' for a night out. He announced that he was going to have a good rest and do nothing but what he felt like for a bit. "*I might go fishing for a week, or Elsie and me might take a holiday, or I might stop at home and watch telly all day if I feel like it. I don't know yet!*"

Rosemary Pringle, a teacher, was very moved by the number of parents who contributed to her retirement presentation. It was something she thought about often on the cruise she took immediately after leaving.

Both Bert and Rosemary felt they needed a honeymoon period immediately after retirement. They believed that they had earned a reward for a life-time's hard work — half a century for Bert and not much less for Rosemary. But they both recognised that holidays shouldn't go on forever.

Within a few weeks of returning from that trip Rosemary was moved to reconsider her role and routine, mainly as a result of coming up against the same question from everyone she met; "*What are you doing with yourself these days?*" She noticed that along with the genuine interest there was just a hint of condescension. Rosemary's "*I expect I'll keep myself pretty busy*" left her thinking hard about what exactly she would be keeping herself busy with.

Bert had had time for reflection on his fishing trips. Something of a 'philosopher' in his own way he came up with the following thoughts:

"*Last month it was 'Can you get them started on 100 gross steel coils, Bert — it's a rush order.'*
"*Last week it was 'Enjoy your retirement — have a good time'. Reminded me of our Sue telling her youngest to go off and play!*
"*Down at Bracegirdles they knew me as a skilled chargehand and what sort of chap I was. Who knows now?*
"*Well, I like to enjoy myself as much as the next man but I like a bit of purpose in life. Looks as though I'll have to organise myself a bit so that other folk besides the ones I worked with will see what skills I've got and what sort of chap I am. See where I fit in in the neighbourhood. I'll have to be up and doing.*"

Rosemary and Bert realised that in retirement they would have to make much more personal effort to maintain a satisfactory pattern of life — one that would include some variety, some challenges and some opportunities to keep old friends and meet new ones.

Now consider how the characteristics of *your* role at work may help you in your plans. Fill in the chart that follows. The examples of John, Nastasia and Bill are included to help you.

At Work

	Role	Purpose	Skills/abilities	Expertise	Personal Qualities
John	Self-employed joiner.	To be independent and build up a profitable business.	Manual skills.	Craftsmanship. Organisation.	Reliability. Honesty.
Nastasia	Clerk.	To do an efficient job.	Trained in book-keeping and accounts recording.	Quick with figures.	Painstaking. Accurate. Unflappable.
Bill	Salesman nationwide.	To become manager. To work independently. To have freedom of movement. To meet people.	Communication. Persuasive powers.	Knowledge of product and market. Capacity to meet sales targets.	Energetic Ambitions. Sense of humour. Well liked.
You					

Getting started

The satisfactions of life before retirement — the sense of having skills and know how that people often need and want, the recognition others are prepared to offer you, the security you get from friends and associates — can all be found in retirement.

The bonus is that once you have retired you have freedom of choice and the decisions are all yours.

Obviously there are a number of issues to consider when making these important decisions about planning for retirement. Here are some of the questions to be asked.

What sort of routine do you feel happy with?
What roles do you want to keep or develop?
In what ways can you retain a sense of purpose?
How can you use your skills and expertise in a new situation?
In what ways will any new situations allow you to express your personal qualities?

Bert and Rosemary were only momentarily put out by their initial experiences. In their own way they considered options for new roles and routines.

The chart on the right shows how they set about thinking of possible action to ensure that they had satisfying roles and routines in their retirement.

Look at their ideas then write down the issues that concern you and any action you can begin to take.

When making your plans think about the amount of time your activities will take up:

o Choosing a large number of activities may not necessarily fit your needs best.
o Fewer activities might take up more time in a more satisfying way.
o An absorbing interest which promises to be lifelong (for example, collecting china, cards, beer mats, Victoriana etc.) may, in fact, take up comparatively short periods of time.

Bert

Issues to consider	Action
o Will not be short of money but need to be more careful.	o Discuss new money arrangements with Elsie and spend two half days a week helping with shopping.
o Would like to keep in touch with my old trade.	o Offer voluntary services as a skilled man at local volunteer centre — one day a week or do odd jobs part-time for 'pocket money'.
o Like people — don't want to feel 'out of it' but can't afford to be at the club every night spending.	o Ask if there are any part-time jobs behind the bar at the club or other local pub. Work out a not too strenuous timetable for DIY and maintenance jobs at home.
	o Spend half a day a week with the grandchildren.

Rosemary

Issues to consider	Action
o Good organising ability and experience of committees. Having been a teacher I'm used to dealing with children.	o Get involved with local child welfare committees where my expertise will be valued and to which I would enjoy giving my time.
o Used to company at work — living alone could be isolating. Want to keep up with education in some way . . . keep my mind stimulated!	o Investigate possibilities of involvement with dramatic or literary discussion groups.
o Devotion to work and associated activity had left little time to develop domestic skills which attract me.	o Find out more about cookery, gardening and home maintenance by both reading and attending classes in adult education.
o Large garden. Cost of help in the garden now a luxury. I might have to give it up.	o Begin to grow veg and flowers for house.

You

Issues to consider	Action

A new identity

Many people make a poor adjustment to retirement at first because they feel deprived through no longer having a work role. However, once they no longer identify themselves as former workers lacking a role, but as retired people with the option of living a self-styled life, adjustment becomes easier. Rosemary can maintain a stronger sense of identity by saying *"I give some time to my committee work for children's welfare and look after my house and garden"*, than by saying *"I was a teacher."* Bert can describe his function as a volunteer helping the young unemployed with manual skills experience or as an active member of a pensioners' association.

Those whose jobs can become a hobby or vice-versa have even less difficult in retaining an identity. If someone says 'I'm a joiner' or 'I'm a sculptor' — he can go right on saying it after he retires.

Keeping going—an eye to the future

Making plans for retirement can be exciting: putting them into practice takes effort and persistence.

Coping with other peoples' attitudes may be something you did not expect to have to worry about. You may meet fixed ideas about the way retired people are 'supposed' to behave and these may be more relevant to your parents' generation than your own. Times have changed, yet attitudes do not always keep pace. Fifty and 60 year olds looking forward to retirement no longer expect either to feel or to be thought of as elderly the day after they leave work — or for some time to come.

This is what happened to Bert and Rosemary shortly after retirement.

Bert's experiences

Younger colleagues behave as though they thought that on his 65th birthday he had arrived at old age overnight.

He did not feel at all different when he had retired but he noticed that it was often suggested that he would — as though the experience of 'before' and

'after' would somehow change him as a person.

He knew it was well meant but it was irritating to find that after retiring people seemed to think he needed advice on almost everything.

Rosemary's experiences

Now she had left work she was in some way considered less important since she was no longer a professional working woman.

She did not feel less important — this view was being forced upon her.

Although she intended to be as independent and individualistic as ever, people tended to think that all the retired were alike.

Conclusions

Everyone makes their own conclusions but many people have expressed the following:

o Having spent a lifetime becoming more and more individual, by retirement every individual has developed a strong personal identity.

o The rate of ageing and its effects are as individual as any other process.

o When the constraints of working life have gone, there is opportunity to express the true nature of your individuality.

o Society's image of retirement is often out of date and the prejudice that sometimes arises can be challenged by individuals.

Planning for health

Most peoples' health improves after retirement. One research study came to the conclusion that retirement is associated with a substantial lowering in the incidence of serious illness. But retirement like other stages of life has its pros and cons, which can affect your health.

Each person reacts to retirement in a different way, but there are particular gains and losses mentioned by many people.

The healthy aspects of retirement are naturally the freedom to leave the harmful effects of work behind. Retirement is a time of opportunity during which your health can actually be improved, not just a time in which health hazards can be avoided.

You are probably clear in your own mind about those things which you have gained and lost on retiring from work. You may want to build into your life those things from which you feel you gained a lot at work. You may like to think of positive things you could do to your lifestyle to keep you feeling good mentally and physically. Diet and exercise are obviously two important considerations. The need to be occupied and stimulated mentally are equally important. Take a long look at yourself and decide to take action.

It may help you to draw up a health profile and fill in the results on the chart below.

You can add to the health profile in the space provided. Add items which are relevant to your own individual circumstances. If you are a swimmer for example you may wish to record how far you can swim.

Many people have tried to say exactly what health is. For your own purposes it's helpful to have something measurable you can refer to because it's easier to get an accurate picture than by just vaguely thinking *"I'm about as healthy as I was last year."*

Your health profile

Test	Your Result	Action
Weigh yourself. Strip off, look at yourself in a mirror and be honest. Are you very overweight, just right or too thin?		**Find out roughly what your weight should be. If you are over this weight, decide you will never be any heavier than you are at the time of your retirement. Weigh yourself at the same time every week and take action if your weight does increase by more than three pounds from your present weight.**
Count how many cigarettes you smoke on an average day.		**Decide you will never smoke any more cigarettes. Decide whether you would like to stop smoking.**
See how far you can walk in six minutes.		**Give yourself the six minute test every three months. If you stay reasonably fit and do not develop any disease you should be able to cover the same distance in six minutes for at least the next five years.**
Count how many times things have got you down in the last month.		**Do this count every three months and if you find things are frequently getting you down see if you can find a cause. If you can't find a cause do seek the advice of your doctor.**
Work out how much alcohol you consume in an average week.		**If this is more than you honestly think is good for your health, aim to cut down.**

Your personal health plan

You are now in a position to work out your own health plan for retirement. You may decide it's a good idea to plan to be at least as fit one year into retirement as the day you left work. This is to say, if you fill in your health profile again one year after you retire you wouldn't be any heavier, smoke any more etc.

You may decide that you are going to take more trouble over your health and be even more healthy than when you retired.

To carry out such decisions may require a plan of action. Again, just as your health profile pins down facts, your plan of action will be easier to follow if you decide to set targets you can measure.

Here is an example of Jack Allen's plan. Just before he retired Jack had a minor heart attack. On retirement he decides to develop a plan of action to improve his health and fitness. He makes the decision because he recalls with nostalgia the days when he was fit and he regrets no longer feeling particularly healthy. His doctor has also told him to keep fit, now he has retired he finds he is bored and tends to worry about his health.

Jack puts the following plan into action having discussed it with his doctor.

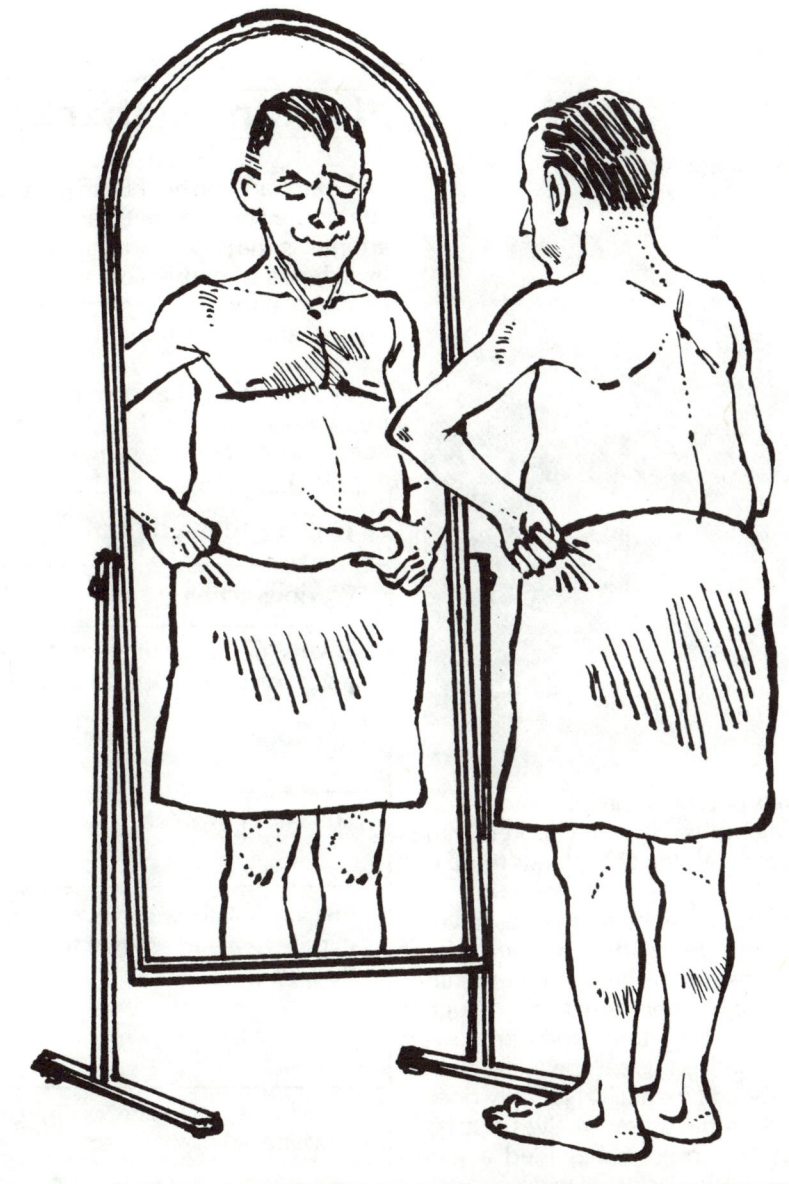

Jack Allen's health plan		
Short term goals over three months	**Action**	**Long term goals in the next year**
Lose a stone in weight.	Cut down on starch, sugar, fats. Introduce different foods into diet. Don't drink any more alcohol than I am now. Take care what I drink when I go out (no more than two pints on any social occasion? Drink halves?)	Lose a total of two stones in weight.
Get fitter.	Try a weekend walking holiday. Walk the dog twice a day (two miles in all). Exercise in the morning (check with doctor). Take up more active occupations. Help Joyce with house work. Get books out of library on carpentry.	Plan for a longer more ambitious holiday which involves plenty of activity. After I've started a few weeks of morning exercise see what else I could take up. Swimming? Take evening classes in carpentry and do a project at home.
Cut down to 10 cigarettes a day (from 15).	Only buy one packet every two days. Put only 10 in packet each day.	Stop smoking.

So Jack puts his health plan into action at the age of 65, having checked with his doctor that what he intends to do is OK.

Two years later he says he has never felt better. During the two years he divided the time into three-month periods for his short term goals, though he kept his long term goals in view. He has noticed great benefits both physically and mentally. Not only does the kitchen have new shelves but his interest in carpentry has filled a gap left by work. Jack's plan also gives him a different view of his health. Instead of sitting in an armchair worrying about his health he improves the way his body works and feels.

But there have been other benefits too. Jack's relationship with his wife Joyce has improved. Joyce had dreaded his retirement in some ways. She worried about having him in the house all day. Jack's health problems just before his retirement had been an added strain. Joyce was rather sarcastic about Jack's health plan when she first heard about it. She thought it was a bit of a joke, and didn't believe that any of his good intentions would last longer than a week. But she was proved wrong. And she was so impressed by the results, not the least of which were that Jack was more cheerful and their sex life improved, that she decided to work out a similar plan for herself.

Plans and setbacks

Joyce embarks on her health plan at the age of 62. She is diabetic and has mild arthritis. In the past she has also suffered from bouts of depression, which were probably at their worst during her menopause and when the last of her children left home.

Joyce draws up her own health profile, works out her health plan and keeps notes on her progress in her diary. Unfortunately at the age of 65 she is involved in a bad road accident and has to spend some time in hospital with a broken hip and fractured skull. Joyce has to revise her health plan, but does not abandon it. She cannot be as active as she was for the time being and has to give up a lot of the voluntary work that she has been doing.

Below are the revisions she makes to her health plan during her long convalescence. The extract shows how she revised the action part of her plan.

Joyce's revised plan

Previous action	Revised action
Take a long walk of at least five miles once a week with a friend.	Do more gardening. Think about getting a greenhouse, which would mean less stooping, and I could work there in the winter too.
Look after my feet.	Pay for a few sessions at the chiropodist.
Occasional dizzy spells. Get my eyes tested and arrange to see the doctor.	Find out from doctor if headaches are to be expected after the accident. Can I do anything apart from take painkillers? Check if relaxation exercises might help.
Do exercises 10 minutes night and morning.	Work out different exercises while I'm less mobile. Only five minutes at first. Find out about flexibility exercises, ie could I try swimming?
Cycle or walk to the hospital where I help out with the WRVS rather than taking the car.	Try to take a short walk each day. If I can get to the shops, Jack could meet me in the car.
Join pottery evening class.	Think about doing another evening class next year. Do more knitting and crochet in the evenings.
Make a serious attempt to give up smoking.	Had succeeded in giving up smoking but started again when I got home from hospital. Try to cut down to five a day and keep it at that level.
Keep weight down.	Watch weight more carefully since less active.

Plan of action

Draw up your own plan of action. First check your health profile and the items on it.

Write down what you ultimately intend to achieve, that is your long-term goals. Then decide what your immediate objectives will be over the next three months. Note down what action you are going to take over the coming weeks to reach those short term goals. At the same time think about what else you could do later to help you achieve your long term goals.

Notice that many of Jack's and Joyce's actions involve only small changes to their daily routine, for instance 10 minutes spent on exercise twice a day. If they had written down actions that involved sweeping changes right from the start they would probably have found them more difficult to keep up. Making small, gradual changes to your lifestyle over a period of time can have quite far reaching effects.

Take stock each month and note down any improvements or set backs. And if you do find that you have set backs see if you can revise your plan of action in small ways to help you overcome them. Again, small actions are more useful than big resolves to 'pull yourself together'!

Once you start taking action new possibilities open up. Occasionally you may find that you'll want to re-write your plan as your goals perhaps become more ambitious. As you get fitter you'll be able to set new goals. Also it might be a good idea to check your original health profile now and again. Reminding yourself how much you've acheived should give you plenty of encouragement.

Short term goals	Action	Long term goals

If you develop some illness, or have an accident, don't get disheartened and give up altogether—revise your plan like Joyce did. And remember that if there is a sudden alteration in your health do go and see your doctor.

Action for health

Two ways you can help yourself to health are by keeping as fit as you can and by eating sensibly. But what other action can you take to keep your body in as good a working condition as possible?

What do you need to do for yourself?

o You need to be aware of your body and its condition. It's good sense to know about your body.
o You need to take note of early warning signs related to your health that could mean something is wrong.
o You need to take some responsibility for your own health care. It is an issue which concerns *you*.

All of these really depend on having reliable information. It's easy to worry needlessly about your health if you have unreliable information. If you are interested in any of the issues raised then you should be able to get reliable information from:

o Your doctor.
o Health visitor.
o Health Education Council.
o Scottish Health Education Group.

This topic is a starting point for you to think about what sort of action to take over maintaining your health.

Use the section on each subject as a basis for deciding what information you want to seek, who might be able to help you and then in the space below each paragraph, write down any action to take.

Only a limited number of health issues are included. You may decide that other issues concern you too, for instance diabetes, back pain, prostate problems, high blood pressure. If you are worried about any of these things or any other health issue then you can use the same plan for acting upon them.

o Find out about them from a reliable source.
o Sort out what sort of responsibility you personally can take over them.
o Work out any action points.
o Keep a record of your action.

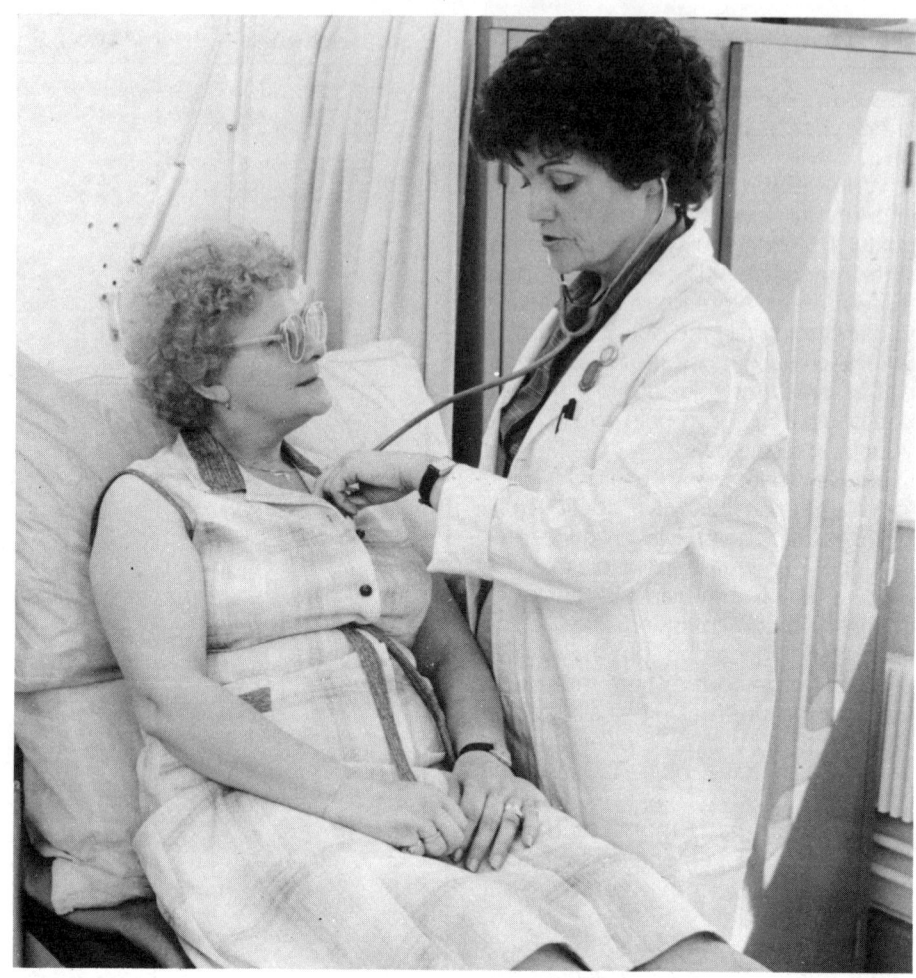

Eyes

Know your body
Some changes in the eyes occur as people get older because the lens of the eye becomes less elastic. Funnily enough, this means that people who are short sighted may experience an improvement in vision as they get older. But for many people their eyesight deteriorates a little with age.

Early warning signs
o If you have any sudden problems with your eyesight, see the optician even if you're not due for a check up.
o If your eyes become itchy or dry, don't treat it by yourself by putting in eyewashes but seek the advice of your doctor.

Take responsibility
Some suggestions:
o Check the quality of lighting in your home. Make sure you have enough lights. Get yourself a reading lamp for close work.
o See an optician every two years to have your eyes tested.
o Check benefits. If you need glasses or need to change your prescription for new lenses, financial help is available for older people who are in receipt of a supplementary pension for NHS glasses. (Get free dental treatment and glasses leaflet F11, from a social security office.)

Your action points

Skin

Know your body
Skin does get tougher as you get older. Cells on the surface appear drier because the glands which provide the oils of the skin do not work so efficiently. In addition, the elastic tissue underlying the skin changes and becomes less elastic. Your skin doesn't insulate you as well as it used to and you may feel the cold more.

Early warning signs
o If you notice any changes in your skin, like a small ulcer that's slow to heal, or if your skin becomes very dry, go and see your GP.

o If you develop red and itchy patches of skin anywhere on your body, draw it to the attention of your GP.

Take responsibility
Some suggestions:
o Treat your skin with care.
o Don't soak in the bath for long periods.
o Think about how much you wash out of habit and how much for cleanliness.
o Make the most of the sunshine but don't burn your skin.
o When you buy cosmetics don't take their rejuvenating qualities too seriously.

Your Action points

Bones and joints

Know your body
As you become older your bones become more brittle. If you have a fall, you are more likely to break a bone than 10 or 20 years ago. Over the years, normal wear and tear has its effect on the joints of our bodies. Older people often experience rheumatic aches and pains, not to be confused with some forms of arthritis — a disease which people of any age may get.

Early warning signs
If you have unexplained aches that last longer than a day, or aches more than once a week that aren't a result of heavy exercise, seek the advice of your doctor.

Take responsibility
Some suggestions:
o Aches and pains around your joints do not mean that you should restrict your movements. Without overdoing it some exercise is the best course of action.

o Diet is important too. There are many theories about the way certain foods are beneficial in the treatment of bone problems . . . ask your GP.

o He will also be able to prescribe drug treatment if he feels it is necessary.

o Many people also find that less orthodox forms of treatment like acupuncture and osteopathy are helpful.

o There are private physiotherapists but talk to your doctor who may be able to arrange NHS treatment.

Your action points

Ears

Know your body
As people get older they often experience some slight hearing loss. It is important to diagnose the cause of the hearing loss. It may simply be due to wax in the ears, or perhaps to some less treatable condition. But it is important to know the cause and not to assume that it is due to getting older.

Early warning signs
If you find you can't hear a conversation or the telephone bell seek help straight away from your doctor.

Take responsibility
Because the deaf are treated with little sympathy many people who sense they are losing their power of hearing try to deny it even to themselves.

Some suggestions:
o Some people whose hearing is not so good feel that they are being 'got at' by others. It is worthwhile asking your family and friends to speak clearly *at you*. For it is not only you but other people who need to adapt too. Their support is an important element.
o There are many services available to help people who do not have good hearing — lip-reading classes, hearing aids, special telephone bells, individual ear phones for TV and other gadgets.
o There are also agencies, for instance the Society for the Hard of Hearing.

Your action points

Bladder and bowels

Know your body.
The bladder muscles can become slacker as you get older and therefore you may find you have to empty your bladder more frequently. Bowels can become sluggish and constipation is sometimes a problem.

Early warning signs
Any changes that you notice, for example discoloured urine, pain on urinating, bouts of alternate diarrhoea and constipation, or bleeding or weight loss, should always be reported to your doctor.

Take responsibility
Some suggestions:
o If you find you have to empty your bladder more frequently, adapt your routine to take account of it. This does not indicate incontinence!
o Roughage — that is food like fruit, vegetables and brown bread — is an important ingredient in everyone's diet. It helps your digestive system to function healthily, try and eat plenty of it. It's better to alter your diet than to take laxatives. If you have to take laxatives don't do so for longer than 48 hours without seeking medical advice.

Your Action points

Feet

Know your body.
Problems with feet can arise at any age. Corns, bunions, warts, skin infections, ingrowing toe nails all cause problems and can be uncomfortable or painful. As people get older, conditions which affect the bones and ligaments of the foot can become distressing. Feet which have been mistreated for a long time eventually rebel.

Early warning signs
If you feel discomfort where your feet are concerned, seek help!

Consider going to a chiropodist if you can afford it. There is a shortage of chiropodists but be persistent in your search. Ensure you are dealing with an experienced and qualified person by choosing a state registered chiropodist who will have the letters SR.Ch after his or her name.

Take responsibility
People with diabetes or arterial diseases have to be particularly careful about their feet and should be advised by their doctor on the best way to look after them.

Your action points

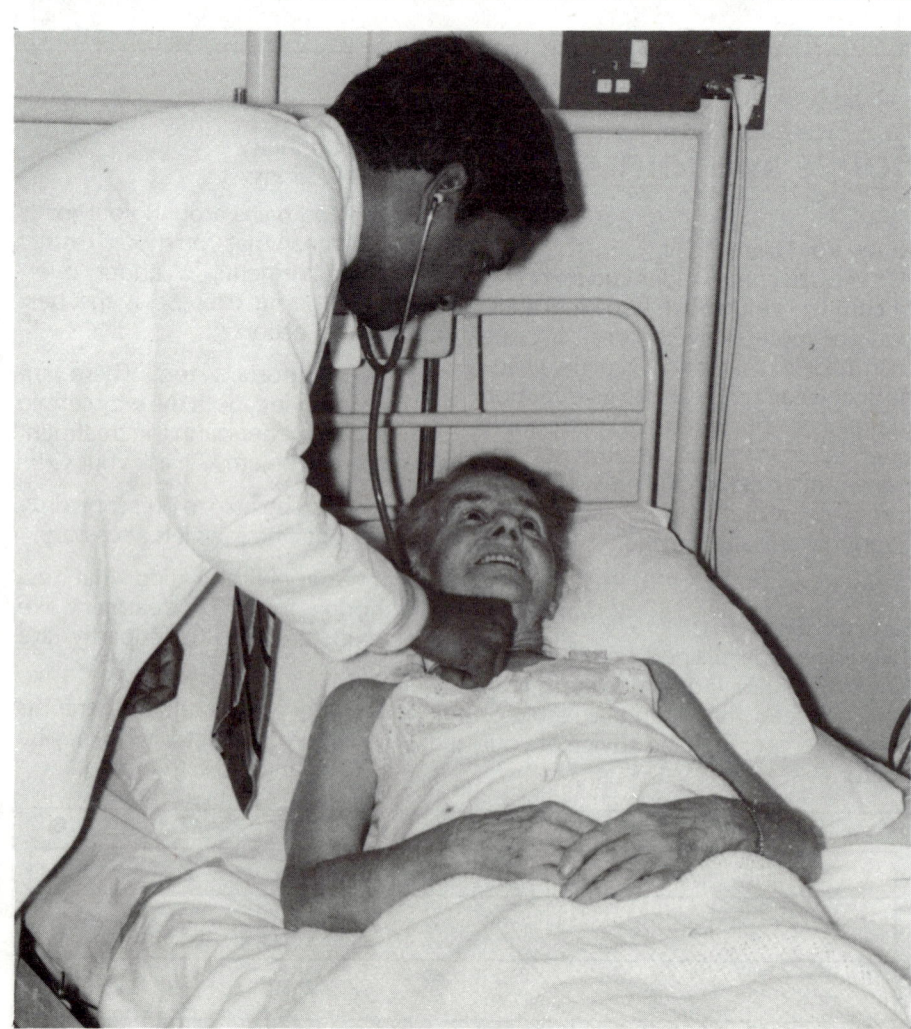

Action calendar

You will probably find it useful to keep an action calendar for your health.

Write down on it your action for health over the course of one year. Keep reminder dates for your own health action i.e. breast examination. Note down dates for check ups and appointments with your doctor and other professionals. This topic has dealt with a limited number of areas which can form the basis for your action calendar.

However there will probably be areas that are of particular concern to you that you will also wish to record your action on.

Checks
For women:
Breast examination
Breast cancer is the most common form of cancer in women. Even so, 94% of women will never have it. If you find a lump or any other abnormality in one of your breasts, the chances that it will be cancer are small—but don't delay—*go to the GP at once*. Remember cancer is curable and the chance of a cure is better the earlier the disease is found. You owe it to yourself to put doubts out of your mind or get the earliest possible treatment if something is wrong. Do a regular check on your breasts. Start now, whatever your age, and keep a firm date each month to examine your breasts (you will probably find it easier if you have a particular day in mind, say the first of each month or if you still have periods, the last day of your period).
You can get a leaflet on breast examination from your doctor or the Health Education Council.
Cervical smear
   The Department of Health recommends that women under 65 should have a cervical smear test every five years.

Food for thought

A healthy well-balanced diet is important in retirement. If you have managed to keep fit and healthy up to the time you retire then you are probably the best one to judge what is in your best interests. For those who do not feel so confident, here are some suggestions.

Control your weight

Being overweight or underweight can cause health problems. There is a tendency to put on weight as you grow older. Women tend to do so more than men.

Being overweight often leads to high blood pressure and diabetes in adult life. Arthritic joints like knees and hips are made worse if they have a lot of weight to carry about. Being overweight forces the heart to work harder and also aggravates the breathing problems due to bronchitis and other chest

infections. Overweight people are also at greater risk in surgery and their bone fractures are more difficult to treat. Reducing weight can improve your state of health.

Some people grow thinner as they grow older. Broadly speaking slim people live longer and are able to get about more easily because their joints do not have to carry excess weight. A

sudden, inexplicable weight loss however should always be investigated.

A poor appetite may make it difficult to ensure that the body gets sufficient nutrients to function efficiently. Few people want to live a long time without benefiting from the extra years. You need not worry too much providing a *balanced* diet is eaten. Problems only arise from too narrow a range of foods.

Daily nutrition needs for the over 60's

Milk — not less than ½ pint (includes cooking and hot drinks).

Meat, fish, cheese, eggs, poultry, beans and other pulses — one of these at each of two of the day's meals.

Fruit — Citrus fruits e.g. oranges, grapefruit, lemons, and blackcurrants when available.

Vegetables—Potatoes, say, and at least one other root or green vegetables or salad.

Bread and cereals — Bread, preferably wholemeal, rice, pasta, breakfast cereals

Fluid — 4–5 pints (all drinks)

Need nutritious food be expensive?

A well balanced diet need not cost a lot
The following is an example of a 'least cost' diet to satisfy the nutrient needs of the average person:

Margarine	71g (2.8 ozs)
Potatoes	111g (4.4 ozs)
Carrots	3g (0.12 ozs)
Frozen orange juice	43g (1.7 ozs)
White bread	318g (12.7 ozs)
All-bran	129g (5.16 ozs)

The total cost is about 50p per day. (1982 prices)
No one would seriously suggest that this would be an agreeable daily diet for any length of time but it is reassuring to know that the simplest of low cost foods if selected from a range of the major food groups, can provide a healthy diet.

Watch what you eat and drink

o Fats are the most concentrated source of calories (twice the calories of proteins or carbohydrates.) Be careful of obvious fats like butter, margarine, oils and cooking fats. Hidden fats are also found in cakes, pastries, biscuits, meat products, such as sausages, fatty cuts of meat, cheese, chocolate and peanuts.

o Sugars provide no nutrients only calories so they should be avoided. If you have a sweet tooth use artificial sweeteners in drinks. Fruit is a sweet substitute for puddings. Apples and oranges can add a sweet taste to vegetable salads and casseroles of meat or poultry.

o Alcohol provides almost twice as many calories as fats do. Sweet wines, sherries or vermouth and beer are particularly rich in calories. So are the tonic water, lemonade and cola drinks that go with spirits. Use low calorie drink mixers instead. An occasional alcoholic drink makes you feel better about life and can sharpen your appetite if you are feeling jaded. Too much alcohol presents obvious problems but also it may become a substitute for food and so unbalance the diet (in which case vitamin supplements may be needed).

o Strict routines can be boring however ideal they are. There will be times when you feel you want to break the rules: you may find them being broken for you. The human body is flexible enough to be able to cope with the occasional extra input of sugar, fat or alcohol: it is the continual abuse that does the damage.

Eat more fibre

There are a dozen or so different kinds of fibres, all with different roles to play. Cereal foods, fruit and vegetables are all important while bran is good in relieving constipation and may help some forms of diarrhoea. A balanced high fibre diet is rich in starch and vegetable protein and has less fat, sugar and animal protein.

How much is enough?

You are probably having enough fibre if you have regular, bulky, bowel motions.

High fibre foods

Fruit.
Fresh vegetables.
Cereals made from whole grain e.g. muesli, bran.
Brown rice.
Whole meal pasta.
Bread or cakes made with whole meal flour.
Nuts.

Whenever possible eat the skins and peel on vegetables and fruit.

Eat a balanced and varied diet

Make sure you are getting all the vitamins and minerals you need for good health.

As you get older it is harder for your body to absorb all the vitamins and minerals it needs. This makes it particularly important to have a good, plentiful supply from your food. Vitamins and minerals used to be known as 'protective factors' because of the role they play in building up resistance to disease. Long term use of medicines can increase the body's need for vitamins. For example, taking aspirin as a pain killer for long periods of time causes a small amount of bleeding in the gut. This way iron is lost and anaemia may be the result.

Aim to have fruit or vegetables at each meal or snack.

Wholemeal bread and wholegrain cereals are also good sources of vitamins and minerals. Maintain a good balance by having a *variety* of foods especially when you find you are eating less.

Vitamin and mineral supplements can be a helpful boost to your reserves if you have been ill but they should be looked on as a temporary measure unless prescribed by your doctor. Apart from the risk of overdosing (high doses of some vitamins can be very dangerous) supplements are no substitute for foods.

Take more exercise

This is probably the most effective way of protecting yourself from heart disease in later life. Exercise is also a good way of controlling weight. As you get older your metabolic rate — the rate at which you use energy for just keeping alive — slows down. This is partly due to the muscles getting smaller because they are used less. This tends to make it harder to slim as you get older. It is therefore particularly important to combine exercise with eating less in any slimming effort.

If you are underweight, exercise can help to build up muscle and improve appetite. It lifts the spirits too.

Exercise is putting joints and muscles through a full range of movements. Exercising regularly is important in keeping you supple, maintaining your strength and staying power. The great thing about exercise is that it improves your general, physical and mental health.

o Start any exercise session with mobility exercises.

o Move on to muscle strengthening exercises.

o If an exercise routine bores you, try jogging, swimming, cycling or a team game of your choice paced to suit your fitness level.

Thinking of making some changes?

Here's what four recently retired people did.

Mary and Jim are married. Mary did not need to be concerned about her weight but knew she could improve her general health by joining in Jim's effort to control his weight and cut down on sugar and fats. Her efforts to serve less animal fat led to a new interest for both of them in some vegetarian dishes and they often substitute fruit for sweets and puddings. She found too that her tendency to constipation occurred less and less. They both decided to walk more and went swimming together once a week. Jim also planned to start cycling again.

Sylvia is a single woman. She cut down her spending on food but tried to bring variety into her new low cost budget. Vegetables, fruit and salad in season helped her to achieve her target. When they became more expensive she found interesting ways of using pasta, rice, beans and pulses.

Bert is a widower. He joined a class 'Cooking for Men' at his local adult centre and became more confident in his own abilities in the kitchen. He learned a good deal about the nutritional values of food too. He reckons the exercise he gets in the garden growing his own vegetables keeps him fit, gives a real edge to his appetite and makes cooking for one really worthwhile.

Fill in the box below to show the changes you think you need to make. Mary's and Jim's, Sylvia's and Bert's decisions are included to help you.

	You	Mary (Married)	Jim	Sylvia (Single)	Bert (Widowed)
1 Control your weight.			✓		
2 Eat more fibre.		✓			
3 Eat a balanced and varied diet.				✓	✓
4 Take more exercise.		✓	✓		

Making changes

If you need to make some changes to achieve your particular goals you may find that this is not always easy to do. There is often a wide gap between what you feel would be good to try and what you continue to do either because habit is hard to break or because others set up difficulties for you. Suppose you want to change. Here are the things to think about.

Your own attitudes

Be clear about your present attitudes to food Do any of the following apply to you?

I prefer the kind of food I got used to as a child.
I see food as a kind of reward for hard work.
Sometimes I eat more than usual as a consolation when I'm feeling down.
I don't care what I eat.
I am not too sure about the nutritional values of the food I eat.
Others (add your own).

_____

_____

_____

Childhood patterns of eating were probably fine at a time of life when your energy output was at its highest. Do you need the same number of calories now? If your eating habits are haphazard, perhaps you could improve your health by taking a hard look at the quality and variety of your diet.

Attitudes of other people

You may or may not be lucky enough to have always had a balanced varied diet and to have been able to match your intake with your body's requirements, you may never have been overweight. On the other hand events may have overtaken you. Your life may have become more sedentary and you may still be eating the same amount as when you were more physically active. You may want to make changes and your family or whoever you live with do not. Custom may dictate your behaviour. Have you experienced any of the following customs?

o Buying rounds in the pub means I sometimes drink more than I planned to.
o When friends press drinks on me it's hard to refuse – they'd be offended.
o When someone cooks my favourite meal it's hard to disappoint them just because I have altered my eating habits.
o If someone gives me chocolates as a present it would be ungrateful not to eat them.

A brief explanation of the changes you are making should make the situation easier to deal with next time. Talking things over and making your changes gradually will help if you want to avoid resentment in others.

Meals are important social occasions for bringing people together. And so if you are instituting changes in your eating patterns you need to remember that occasionally at least the value of having a meal, say, with friends may outweigh the fact that you won't be able to control your food intake.

Your goals

Write down a list of the changes you need to make to improve your diet and the ways you can achieve your goal. Some suggestions to start you off are given below.

Changes I need to make	How
Cut down on alcohol (too many calories).	Call at pub early evening once a week only.
Eat less sugar (too many calories, no nutritional value).	Gradually cut down on cakes biscuits and only one spoon of sugar in tea until I can drop it altogether.
Eat more fibre (good for general health).	Make sandwiches with wholemeal bread, eat more vegetables and fruit.
Add more of your own.	

Keeping fit

How can you help yourself to better health after retirement? One of the best things that contributes to good health is activity.

Active living

There are three requirements that go to make up successful day to day active living:

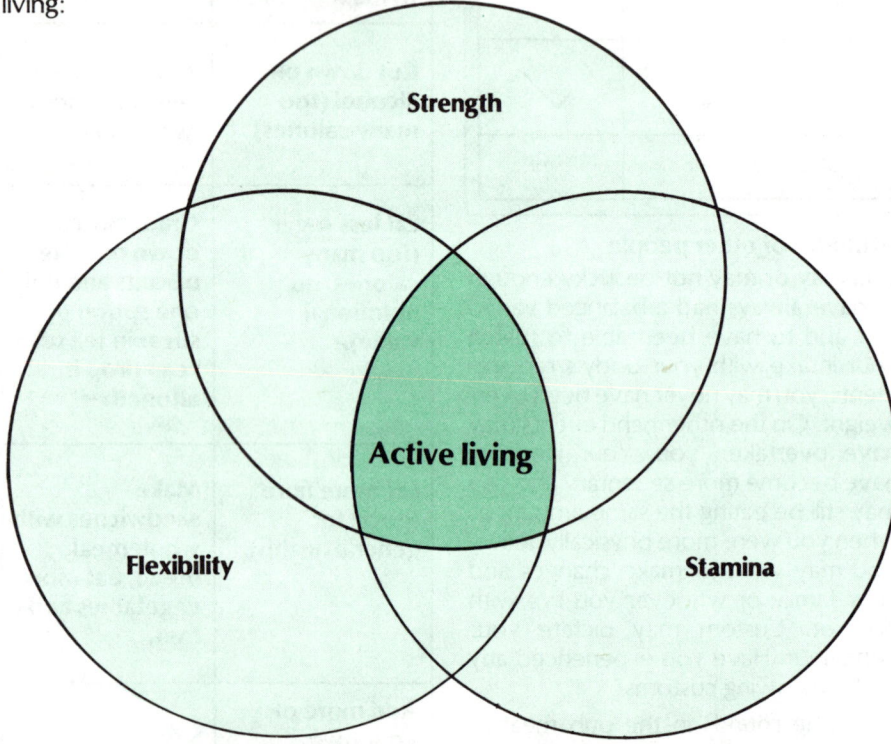

But what are flexibility, stamina and strength, and how can you make sure that they are part of your daily life?

Flexibility
Flexibility is being able to bend and stretch and twist and turn. Day to day living is much improved if you have a full range of movement in all your joints.

Here are a number of day to day activities. If you have flexibility then you will be able to do them all.

Zip up the back fastener to your dress.
Cut your toenails.
Scrub your back.
Brush your hair thoroughly.
Reach the dust on top of the wardrobe.
Bend to get a packet of soap powder from under the sink.
Examine the exhaust pipe under a car.
Reach to open a high window.
Get up from a low chair.
Step down easily from a bus or train.

Just think about the problems of getting the more essential of these activities done if you don't have flexibility — inconvenience certainly but for some of them it would also mean risk of injury. Or think about an occasion in the past when you walked too far and were unable to bend your knees the following day.

Flexibility can be maintained, even restored, by daily practising a full range of joint movements very gently.

Stamina
If you have the capacity for rhythmic exercise and can sustain it, then you have good stamina.

Day to day living is helped if you are able to increase and keep up new levels of activity. You *can* increase your maximum capacity for exercise. Moderate exercise can be taken for longer periods without fatigue. That means you can do everyday tasks more easily.

If they leave you less exhausted you'll feel better about doing them.

Do any of these everyday tasks make you tired?
Making the beds.
Cleaning the floor.
Cleaning the windows.
Mowing the lawn.
Weeding and hoeing.
Cleaning the car.
Washing by hand.
Painting and decorating.
Using a dustpan and brush.
Walking to the shop (say ½ mile).
Carrying the shopping home.

They all demand stamina and flexibility.

Stamina can be increased by doing a little more. People who are noticeably out of condition are the ones who see the benefits sooner.

Select one or two of your everyday chores, or look back at the list. How long do they take?

Next time you do the same task, try doing it a little faster. Make a bit more effort. Try and get yourself a little breathless doing it. If you do get a little breathless, it means you're trying harder. By gradually stepping up your level your maximum capacity for activity will improve.

You should soon start to see the benefits, and feel less and less tired when you do the same activity.

> **If you have *any* doubts whatsoever about doing more activity see your doctor before you start.**

Take a walk
Measure the route for a walk you enjoy, say a round trip of two miles. Over a period of six weeks do the walk as often as you can, once a day if possible. Time yourself. Keep a note of conditions — walking into a wind requires more effort than walking with it behind you. Write down your best time for each week.

If taking walks is not something you tend to do then you might decide instead to test yourself in other ways.

Keep a list of physical activity that makes you breathless. Do that activity again, test yourself, by putting in a bit more effort.

Take a walk:
Fill in your times on this chart.

Week	Time	Conditions
1		
2		
3		
4		
5		
6		

> For most young people, walking on the flat at three miles an hour is gentle exercise. It wouldn't make them tired.
>
> The older you get, the nearer your maximum capacity this activity would be if you don't make efforts to improve your activity level.
>
> Recent research done with a group of retired people following a forty minutes a week exercise programme produced excellent results: increased flexibility, strength and stamina.

Strength

Muscle strength is something you want to be able to rely upon. You want to know that you can get out of a low easy chair. This means having the leg strength to straighten your knees and win the battle against gravity.

It's an insurance policy as well. If one muscle gives way, all the others need to be strong enough to provide extra support.

The stability and reliability of your joints depend upon the strength of the muscles acting around the joint. For example, your knee might well let you down, if all the supporting muscles are weak. Not only would this weakness increase the risk of injury but would reduce your capacity to pull out some extra strength when needed.

Balance too, depends upon muscle strength and this becomes important to watch as you get older if accidents are to be avoided.

So you need muscle strength for good co-ordination in routine daily activities but especially at those times when you need to make an extra effort like:

o Having to run at the last minute for a bus or train.
o Trying to keep your balance when the tube or train brakes or suddenly lurches.
o Having to walk up several flights of stairs when the lift breaks down.
o Lifting and carrying in the garden or doing strenuous DIY jobs.

o Taking longer than usual walks at weekends or on holiday.
o Being involved in competitive sport. If this has been your interest all your life, why give up on retirement? Just take more time and do it with people of your own fitness level.

The sort of gentle exercise you do for sufficient joint mobility to maintain the full range of active movements is not alone enough to maintain muscle strength. Stamina is not enough either.

What you need to do is to work your muscles hard for repeated short periods of time.

You need a variety of exercises for various muscles. Amazingly powerful arms won't help the trunk at all.

It's worthwhile getting a special exercise book for helping you work out some activities to develop your muscle strength.

> If you feel you would like to be more active check out some of the following questions and answers. The questions represent some of the doubts that people commonly express.
>
> **"If I do attempt to do exercise, will it be painful?"**
>
> It may well be when you start. We all know that if you go on a long walk when you are unaccustomed to it you will have stiff legs the following day.
>
> If you stick at it and step up your level of activity the pain becomes less as you start to do more and muscles become more exercised. Most peoples' level of activity is so low that simply walking as an exercise would be enough to count as training for activity.
>
> **"Older people wear out their joints, don't they, if they do too much exercise?"**
>
> It's important to exercise your joints. If the muscles surrounding your joints are well exercised it helps to keep them more stable and less prone to strains and sprains. Also if you're exercising your joints the lubricant which keeps friction down is stimulated, and so protects your joints from damage.
>
> The amount of exercise to keep your joints mobile is actually very small, and just going through the full range of movement possible for that joint seems enough.
>
> **"Will it matter if I stop all the activity and exercise occasionally?"**
>
> Within a week of stopping regular exercise you will notice some deterioration in general fitness. Just think about times in your life when you've had to stay in bed for days or weeks!
>
> Now even after patients have had quite major operations they are encouraged to do some form of activity two or three days after the operation.

Here are a few examples of mobility exercises
Mobility exercises should be done at an unhurried, relaxed tempo. Increased range should be coaxed, not forced. Breathing should be free and easy, to fit the rhythm of the movement. About 10 or 12 repetitions are enough for each exercise, and there is no need to increase this number or the speed of the movement. Progress is achieved by gently increasing the range of the movement or, when you are mobile, by maintaining this level of flexibility.

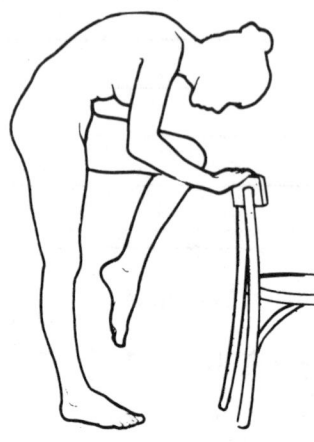

1 Arm swinging

Feet wide astride, arms hanging loosely by your sides. Raise both arms forward, upwards, backwards and sideways, in a circular motion, brushing your ears with your arms as you go past. ◄

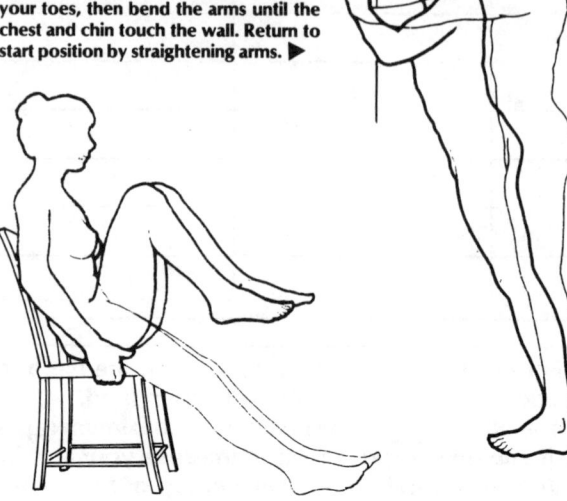

6 Wall press-up

Stand with hands on wall 12" apart at shoulder height, arms straight. Stand on your toes, then bend the arms until the chest and chin touch the wall. Return to start position by straightening arms. ►

2 Side bends

Feet wide apart, hands on hips. Bend first to the left and then to the right, keeping the head at right angles to the trunk. ▼

3 Trunk, knee and ▲ hip bends

Stand 18" behind the back of a chair, with hands resting lightly on the back. Raise the left knee and bring the forehead down to meet it. Repeat with the right knee. Do not rush. This must be a long, strong movement.
NB When you are used to this exercise, you can dispense with the chair and work from the standing postion. The supporting leg can be bent.

4 Alternate ankle reach

Feet wide apart, both palms on the front of the upper left thigh. Relax the trunk forward as you slide both hands down the front of the left leg. Return to the upright position then repeat on the right. (NB THOSE SUFFERING FROM MILD BACK TROUBLE MUST NOT PASS THE KNEES WITH THE HANDS). ▼

7 Abdominal exercise

This exercise, which will flatten your tummy muscles, is very worthwhile, but again the abdominal muscles can be strained if you start too enthusiatically.
Sit on the front part of the chair, legs straight, heels on the floor. Lean back and grip the sides of the seat for support. Bend the knees and bring the fronts of the thighs up to squeeze gently against the body. You can do the same exercise with the legs held straight.

8 Leg exercise ►

As you do a squat, you will soon become aware of weakness in the legs. This is because unfit adults seldom bend their knees beyond the range needed to climb stairs or sit in a low chair.
Stand 18" behind a chair, with your hands on the back. Lower the body into a squat, keeping the feet flat on the floor (ladies may stand on their toes at this point). Straighten both legs and come up on the toes, then return to the squat position. You can dispense with the chair and place hands on hips.

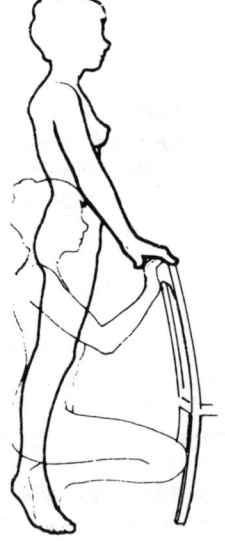

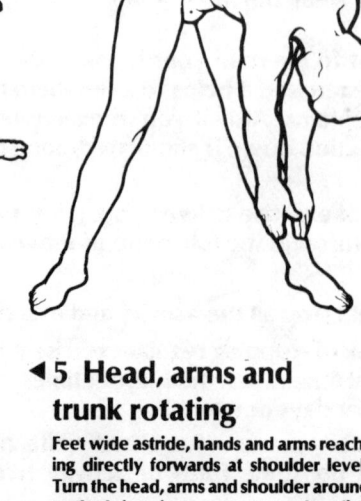

◄ 5 Head, arms and trunk rotating

Feet wide astride, hands and arms reaching directly forwards at shoulder level. Turn the head, arms and shoulder around to the left as far as you can go, bending the right arm across the chest, then repeat the movement to the right. Keep the hips and legs still throughout.

9 Running on the spot ►

Stand with arms loosely by the sides and gently run on the spot. Do not begin by raising the knees high, but aim to get them higher as you progress. Start with a very short time—say 30 seconds, and gradually build up.

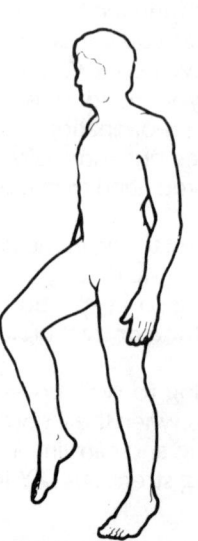

There is no need to do these exercises naked. Loose indoor clothes will do. The diagrams are drawn naked to show exact body positions.

Illustrations reproduced by kind permission of the Health Education Council.

Action now

One of the problems some people have about deciding to step up their activity and exercise is the worry that other people will think they are odd.

If you are worried about feeling odd then you may have to develop into a secret exerciser! Or perhaps you can find like-minded people so you can all be in it together.

Below are various activities. They all demand slightly more from you than simply following a day to day routine.

Yoga

Yoga can help you relax and increase muscle strength.

Pick from the following the option which appeals to you most:
- Go to a yoga class. ☐
- Buy a yoga book/cassette and teach yourself. ☐
- Go to a specialist club where you can join a class of older people. ☐
- Get some friends interested and start your own group. ☐

Walking

One of the best forms of exercise for strength, stamina and flexibility.

Pick from the following the option which appeals to you most:
- Join a rambling club. ☐
- Join a senior rambling club. ☐
- Step up your own walking activity. ☐
- Try and develop social activities where you and friends together do more walking. ☐

Keep Fit

Again this is a great help for strength, stamina and flexibility.

Pick from the following the option which appeals to you most:
- Find a club or association for older people which has keep fit classes. ☐
- Go to a general local authority keep fit class. ☐
- Buy a book and develop your own keep fit regime. ☐
- Go to a gymnasium and have private tuition. ☐

Swimming

Swimming is a valuable form of exercise which helps you develop strength, stamina and flexibility. It's particularly suitable for older people because the water carries the body's weight, cushions sudden movement and there are no undue stresses on bones which may be brittle. Warm water is also relaxing!

It's never too late to learn to swim, so don't dismiss it because you've never learned.

Pick from the following the option which appeals to you most:
- Go to general sessions of the local swimming baths. ☐
- Find a bath that has special sessions for older people. ☐
- Find a local club or association for older people that organises outings to swimming baths. ☐
- Find a local authority adult education class in swimming. ☐
- Find a local authority adult education class for older swimmers. ☐

Here are the basic categories into which the options for tackling these activities fell.

o Joining a class or group who are not defined by age.
o Locating a class or group of like minded people in your own age group.
o Developing an interest with a group of friends and doing the activity together.
o Deciding to pursue your chosen activity privately.

Whichever way you think is best for you is probably the one that's going to work.

Being able to choose the way you are more active takes into account the fact that you want the activity to be fun as well as beneficial. As you do more activity you may find you'd like to change your style. Even if you start off a secret exerciser you may decide later to enjoy the more social side of being active. So it's worth remembering that many forms of activity, bowls, walking, old time dancing, adventure holidays and so on do cater for a pleasant social life as well as healthy exercise!

Less likelihood of heart attack.
Lower incidence of coronary disease.

Slows down deterioration in physical abilities which may otherwise occur after 60 years of age.

Eases the effect of chronic disease e.g. of heart, lung, muscles.

Activity & exercise

Reduces risk of hypothermia in the elderly.

With mild hypertension (high blood pressure) exercise is believed by many to be generally helpful.
But exercise is no substitute for drug treatment of this condition.

Makes you feel and be more lively.

Savings & investments

Everyone hopes to have sufficient financial security to enjoy retirement. Even if your income has been small you may have been saving regularly to help to make this possible and you will want to make sure your nest-egg does not lose its value.

Even if you have not managed to save up any cash you could still find you are worth a fair amount. Over the years most people collect together a surprising number of possessions some of which might turn out to have been good investments. You may find that retirement does not reduce your income as much as you thought and would like to make best use of your unexpected surplus however small. You may find yourself with an ex gratia payment from a generous employer or a lump sum as part of your pension.

It's not easy to decide the best investment for your money. Investing is a very individual matter. Inflation, interest rates, tax regulations, exchange rates are all constantly changing. So watch regularly for Budget alterations and other changes which might affect the facts given here.

Planning your savings

There is little point salting away your money in savings that are not easy to withdraw if you are likely to need them to pay regular bills.

When you have worked out your basic budget and know how much is available for saving then decide whether you have enough to spread over the short term (easily available) the medium term (four to 10 years) or the longer term.

Broadly speaking, the longer you leave your investment, the higher the return, but it would be unwise to 'lock up' all your money like this. Your personal situation might alter and you might need some of your capital quickly. Interest rates alter and you might regret not being able to move your money about to take advantage of better terms.

If you don't pay tax at all, don't make investments where tax is deducted at source, like building societies, because you will not be able to claim back the amount paid or you will have the inconvenience of making a claim for repayment — as with local authority bonds.

If you are a taxpayer, it would be better to choose some investment that paid you interest free of tax or if you are likely to fall into the higher rate, go for capital gain.

Some questions to ask yourself

o Over what period of time do I want to go on saving?
o Have I enough cash available to meet my recurring expenditure after tying-up the money I would like to invest?
o Have I worked out the benefits to me of choosing between short, medium and long term saving?
o What choices do I have that will help me either to reduce the amount of tax I have to pay or to avoid having to pay tax at all?

Life expectation figures		
If you are:	**You can expect to live to**	
	Male	**Female**
50 } 55	76	80
56 } 60	76 78	81
61 } 65	79	82
66 } 70	79 81	84

So your plans should attempt to cover 15-25 years.

Before investing shop around

Ask for advice from more than one source. You could try the following:
Money Advice Centres — these offer unbiased advice free.
Citizens Advice Bureaux — you can find out here whether there is a Money Advice Centre in your area. Most CAB's have an accountant on their staff.
Most banks offer finance planning advice. In addition to the Manager's services some set aside a special day each week when customers can request a confidential appointment for these discussions with an investment adviser.
Insurance companies.
Insurance brokers.
Accountants.
Investments Consultants.

It is up to *you* to compare the costs and benefits of as wide a range of options as you can.

Remember

When you invest successfully you can expect *one* of two things to happen:
o Your capital will grow.
o You will get interest on your capital.

You cannot expect both with certainty. No one can offer capital growth and guaranteed interest rates and only the Government can offer inflation proofing.

The following investment income is taxable at source from:

Building societies (never reclaimable by non-tax payer). Interest is payable free of tax, persons not liable cannot reclaim tax from the Inland Revenue. If paying tax at higher rates of investment income surcharge ask your tax officer's advice.

Dividends and interests from:
Company securities.
Local authority bonds.
Unit trusts.

{ **If you do not pay tax or pay at reduced rate claim a rebate.**

Investment income from the following is not taxable at source:

National Savings Certificates.
Trustees Savings Bank.
Clearing banks.

National Giro Bank.
National Savings Bank.

Be flexible. Keep an eye on your investments. Keep informed and be prepared to move your money around. Many newspapers and magazines now offer financial information features aimed at the small saver as well as the better-off. The retired are particularly well catered for.

Radio and TV money programmes too will keep you abreast of changes that might affect you.

Some examples

Joe Fielding, 60, has always put his savings in a Post Office (National Savings Ordinary) account which was currently (1982) earning 5% interest. He had never had to pay tax on these savings before but now found he was liable because he had more than £1,400 saved. It was only when he picked up a few leaflets in the Post Office that he realised he could be using his money in a variety of other ways.

There were the National Savings Bank Investment Account, (13% interest, taxable), National Savings Certificates 24th issue Index-linked, Save-As-You-Earn Savings (taxfree) designed to protect the buying power in line with price levels and Index-linked National Savings Certificates (taxfree).

As he was on the point of retiring and would be getting a small lump sum, he decided to buy some index-linked National Savings Certificates as a hedge against inflation. He also decided to make sure of the £4 bonus on each £100 after five years and noted that the index-linked increase would, itself, also be index-linked. (Even in the unlikely event of inflation reducing to zero, Joe would never get less than his original investment.)

He also decided to look into the rates offered by some companies for Insurance Bonds as a risk-free lump sum investment offering a guaranteed income. Joe still kept some money in an ordinary account for his day-to-day money needs and emergencies. His other medium-term investments would give him a good return and maximum security.

Joe's boss, a director of the firm, had also taken a maximum investment of £5,000 in Index-Linked Certificates and did the same for his wife because they were free from investment income surcharge and capital gains tax.

Sylvia Jones, 58, was anxious to provide adequately for her old age as she lived alone. She wondered if it would be a good idea to take out an annuity but was rather vague as to what this meant. She knew nothing about investing money and wasn't keen to seek professional advice in case she didn't understand it. Instead she went to her Citizens Advice Bureau who put her in touch with a local Money Advice Centre. Here, free of charge, she found

out what she wanted to know. She was satisfied that it would be unwise to tie up her capital in this way until she was at least 70 years old.

Meanwhile, she would study the kind of interest rates that were being offered by different insurance companies so she could with confidence choose the best buy when the time came.

James Sterne, 62, envied his well heeled neighbour who was able to employ an accountant to advise on his financial affairs. James had to plan his own. He had a fair income and even when necessary expenditure had been met he had still had a reasonable sum for investing.

He decided to keep some of it in his bank deposit account to meet unexpected bills, holidays and the like. Then he bought some insurance-linked building society bonds and some government gilt edged, index-linked stock and kept the local authority bonds he had inherited. All these he considered 'safe'.

As medium term investments carrying some risks, he wanted a 'flutter' on the Stock Exchange. He realised that as a small investor with limited expertise he would be better off buying Unit Trust Shares which gave him access to stocks and shares while leaving their management to skilled specialists. These and a modest purchase of some government dated stock gave him the added interest of involvement as he was determined to watch carefully the movement of interest rates so that he could gauge the time to sell.

He further invested a sum in growth bonds as a gamble — this was money he was prepared to lose on if they did not do well and there was always the chance of some capital gain.

Brian Merchant, 55, had recently changed jobs after a short period of redundancy. His occupational pension had suffered as a result. After considering the alternative ways of saving towards his retirement, he decided to negotiate with his employer to see if he could increase his contributions (sometimes possible up to 15% of salary March 1982). He saw this as a good investment which would reduce his tax now and give him the option of tax free commutation of a larger pension on retirement.

What are you worth?

It could be more than you think
Some possessions are likely to increase in value because they are rare, very old, or excellent of their kind. Others may acquire a temporary increase in value as a result of fashion demands. Most collections will appeal to someone. Some possessions will be depreciating and you might as well sell them if you are short of cash.

Possessions	Value £	Tick if likely to go on increasing in value
House		
Antiques		
Pictures		
Silver		
Jewellery		
Collections		
Coins		
Stamps		
Books		
Furniture		
'Bygones'		
Car		
Caravan		
Boat		
Motorbike		
Bicycle		
Pedigree pets		
Racing pigeons		
Others		
Total £		

Look at the items you have ticked. Unless you are particularly in need of ready cash it would probably be better to retain these as growing investments.

Among the items you have *not* ticked as being likely to increase in value there may be some to which you are not particularly attached and don't wish to pass on to any descendants. You could then sell these for the best available price and invest the cash to increase your income.

o Items of interest which are not truly antiques are often saleable at surprisingly high prices if a demand arises and so it is useful to keep an eye on local flea-markets, auctions, antique and bygone shops and notice changing prices and fashions.

o Over the last 25 years, a house has been one of the best investments you could have. The market is more static now (1982) but property remains a good investment.

o Boats and caravans no longer depreciate in value quite as much as they once did, though this may change.

o Collections of china, coins, stamps, card series may be worth valuation for insurance purposes though it depends on their condition and rarity. Remember though that the value put on your possessions will not always be the same as the price you could sell at. This is particularly true of jewellery. The larger auction houses can often provide free valuations of what an item could fetch on the open market.

What is the best investment

It is not always easy to decide the best way to invest your money and much depends upon how much you have at your disposal and what you want it to do for you. The small saver can protect his money by choosing from the 'low risk' group; others should carefully consider what risk they can afford to take.

High risk

Planned returns less predictable. Results range from good to disastrous. Only use money you can afford to gamble with. Suitable for those with larger incomes.

Stocks and shares—not for the amateur.
Management and property bonds.
Government stocks—undated.
Growth bonds.
Gold and Silver—subject to change.

Medium risk

Much depends on skills and management of spread of choices. *Timing* your buying and selling very important.

Unit and investment trusts managed by specialists—spread your risk over the market. A way into the equity market for the small investor.
Unit Linked Savings Plans—a variety to choose from.
Government Gilt-edged, Index Linked stocks—fixed at 2% over prevailing rate of inflation up to 1988.
Government Stocks—dated.
Home Reversions—the later the better.
Annuities—best returns at 70/75 years of age, buy when interest rates are high.
Insurance Bonds.

Low risk

You can protect your capital from inflation i.e. protect its buying power or receive interest. Government backed investments will do both. Good for smaller savings e.g. Savings Certificates and indexed gilts.

Local government loans—have to wait for them to mature, shop around for interest rates.
National Savings Certificates (24th issue)—index-linked. Interest is 10.56% tax free over 5 years. Best return after 5 years.
Building societies—Ordinary Share Account: pays interest. Subscription Shares: higher rates of interest if you continue over agreed number of years. Term Shares: you deposit lump sum for agreed period—higher rates of interest. If you do not pay tax do not invest here as tax paid by the society is not reclaimable.
British Savings Bonds (5 years): good for non tax payers.
Insurance companies—shop around to compare wide variety of endowment schemes.
Bond shares—life assurance linked to building societies etc.
National Savings Bank Investment Account—13% interest (1982), good for non tax payers.
Trustee Savings Bank—similar to National Savings Bank.
Banks—Current Accounts: some pay interest, most don't. Deposit Accounts: pay interest but watch movement. Investment and Bonus Savings Accounts: shop around for best buys.
National Savings Bank Ordinary Account—first £70 interest tax free, ie. you can have up to £1,400 before paying tax, 5% interest per year.
S.A.Y.E. Scheme—Index-linked, you save regular monthly amounts over 5 years. If left for further 2 years higher interest guaranteed. Good hedge against inflation. Tax free.

More income from your investments
Check that your investments are working as well for you as they can. You should be looking for investments that stand a chance of maintaining their buying power, either through an increasing income as time passes, or through capital growth with the possibility of withdrawing regular amounts to use as income. Only indexed gilts do both, but these have a very low starting income and you must hold them until maturity to get the guaranteed benefit.

What are your plans?
Decisions about saving and investing are very personal. It is well worthwhile, though, making sure your choices are informed ones. Find out as much as you can before committing yourself, especially if your money will be tied-up for a number of years.

After balancing your budget, think about the following:

o What are your needs:
  – To retain the buying power of your money during retirement?
  – To use your cash for investment income?
  – To increase your capital?

o How much of this do you need to have available for emergencies?

o How much is left for saving and investing?

o How much will your proposed investment cost?

o How easy (or otherwise) will it be to convert your chosen investments into cash?

o How much risk is involved? How much risk can you afford?

o Have you considered the effects of taxation and inflation upon your investments?

o How much will your investments yield?

o Have you considered alternatives?

o Have you discussed your plans with your spouse/dependants?

Change is continual in finance – this will affect you, however small your savings. Watch for changes in interest rates and tax regulations. Be prepared to move your money about if you can get a better return. It is your money. Look after it.

Making a will
You don't have to be rich to think of making a will. Whatever your circumstances you would be concerned about any dependants you may have. You may in any case be worth a good deal more than you think. In a period of inflation for example the value of property has risen sharply. Ownership of even the most modest style of house means you are worth over £20,000. Savings, maturing insurance policies added to this make a significant sum. Even if there is little to leave, a good deal of confusion or distress can be avoided if you first make your wishes clear.

Joe Fielding's affairs were uncomplicated. He did not own his house and as he was childless he wanted his wife to have everything, except the racing pigeons and greyhound he wanted to give to his life long friend Fred.

Joe's wife was also anxious that her niece should have the bits of antique china her Aunt Alice had left her. They bought two printed will forms from a stationer and each made out wills in favour of the other with the exception of the bequest each wanted to make. Each will was then signed by two witnesses who were present when the wills were drawn up. Neither of these was Fred or the niece, as a witness is not allowed to benefit from a will. They told their niece and Joe's wife's sister where the wills were going to be kept.

Both Sylvia Jones and James Sterne whose affairs were more complex decided to use a solicitor to draw up wills. To reduce expenses Sylvia appointed her niece and nephew, some ten years her junior, as executors – to arrange the distribution of her property after death. With their knowledge she then deposited her will in the bank. James appointed his firm of solicitors (better than naming a particular solicitor, who might have died before him) as executors.

If there is a will

Regardless of what the will says, your wife or husband can claim a third of everything you leave, except land and houses. Your children can claim a further third between them.

If there are no children, your wife or husband can claim a half share instead of a third. Similarly, if there is no widow or widower, your children can claim a half share.

A will isn't necessarily the last word. You can of course state that you wish to disinherit your wife, husband, mistress or children. However you cannot guarantee that your wishes will be carried out. There are a number of instances where claims may be upheld regardless of any provision you may have made in your will.

Provision for dependants

Anyone who was dependent on you immediately before your death may have a claim on what you leave — whether or not there's a will. So may a former wife who hasn't remarried. The costs for fighting a claim are likely to be paid out of your estate.

Family arrangement

The people who benefit under a will (or intestacy) can, within two years, get together and redistribute what they've been left. They can also disclaim legacies. Any capital transfer tax bill will be based on the final arrangement. They will need legal advice.

Joint tenancy

If a couple own a house on a joint tenancy, the death of one of them will mean that his or her share will automatically go to the other — no matter what the will (if there is one) says.

If you don't make a will

It may well involve a good deal of time and possibly money finding out whether or not a will exists. Then the law will decide who should inherit your *estate* (money, property, possessions). For this it is necessary to apply for a grant of Letters of Administration. These, by law, are applied for by the surviving spouse, children, grand children, parents, brothers and sisters, in that order. Your estate might end up being administered by the very person you would have least liked to do it.

Estimate whether your estate would be liable for capital transfer tax	£ (value)
Money, property, valuables.	
House.	
Contents.	
Valuables (jewellery, plate, etc).	
Car.	
Money (bank, building society etc).	
Shares, investments.	
Proceeds of life insurance.	
Things you part own (house, boat etc).	
Others.	
	Total A
Money owed by you (mortgage, HP, etc).	
Anything you are leaving to spouse.	
Gifts to charities (up to £200,000)	
or political parties (up to £100,000).	
	Total B
Subtract B from A	**C**

If the figure which comes out at C is more than £50,000, or comes to more than £50,000 when you include any non-exempt gifts made during your lifetime, then you may be liable for Capital Transfer Tax. Ask an accountant, solicitor or bank manager for advice.

Wills and tax

Everything that passes to a surviving spouse either during your lifetime or after death is exempt from capital transfer tax.

Other exempt gifts:
o Regular gifts (over, say three years or more) gifts made out of your income.
o Gifts of up to £250 each in any tax year to any number of people.
o Wedding gifts (up to a maximum of £5,000).
o Gifts of up to £3,000 in any tax year not exempt for any other reason.

Keep a hold on common sense

Don't assume that the biggest tax saving is always the best solution. Planning for capital transfer tax won't make you any richer: all it means is that more of your property goes to other people, and less to the taxman. In the rush to save tax for others, don't forget your own financial security. Think very hard before making yourself technically dependent on your children. And remember that old age can be expensive. Don't give away your money or your property if you might need it later.

Income tax

You may be surprised to know that your income in retirement, including your pension, is subject to Income Tax. The amount of tax, if any at all, can alter your views on how to organise your money in retirement.

Your tax position is unlikely to be identical to that of anyone else. If in doubt, arrange to visit your local tax office, who can send for your papers if they do not normally hold them, or PAYE inquiry office. This is always better than comparing your case with that of a friend.

The tax year in which you retire brings many financial changes and it is important to inform your tax office as early as possible of alterations in your circumstances.

After retirement your affairs may be dealt with at a different tax office. But you can always make inquiries at your local office. The address can be found under 'Inland Revenue' in the telephone book.

If you take a part-time job it is your responsibility to let the tax office know, not your employer's, even if you think you are not likely to be taxed.

To assess for yourself what tax you are liable to pay, you have first to work out your taxable income. This is your total income for the year ending 5th April — the Inland Revenue take each financial year to begin on 6th April and end the following 5th April — less any allowances for which you are eligible.

Calculating your taxable income

Pensions

Few pensions are free of tax. The State Retirement Pension is taxable, though tax is not deducted before it is paid. If the State Pension is all the income you receive you won't have to pay any tax because the pension comes to less than the Age Allowance.

However, if your State Pension added to any other taxable income you get, such as a pension from your former employer or investment income, comes to more than your outgoings and allowances, there will be some tax to pay. It's worth noting that if you get a pension from your former employer, then under PAYE system, you may find that the tax due on the whole of your income is deducted from that sum.

Age allowance

A man (or his wife) who is 65 or over before the end of the tax year, whether or not they have retired, can claim Age Allowance instead of the allowance for an ordinary single person or married man. Age Allowance is higher than the ordinary Personal Allowance. For the 1982–83 tax year full Age Allowance is £2,070 for a single person, £3,295 for a married man.

A single woman of 60–64 years does not qualify for Age Allowance. If her income is sufficient to attract tax she will qualify for the normal single person allowances.

If her State Pension is her only income she would be below this threshold and would not therefore have to pay tax.

Age Allowance is not a payment due to you: it is a tax allowance. It is not given automatically, so if you think you qualify, get in touch with your tax office and give them details of your income and date of birth.

If your total income is more than £6,700 for the 82/83 tax year you will not get the full Allowance. The Allowance will be reduced by £2 for every £3 your total income exceeds £6,700. But, it will not be reduced below the ordinary Personal Allowance.

Married women's pensions

If you are a married woman, a pension for which you qualify on your own contributions counts as your own earned income. This means that your husband can claim your earned income allowance on it. For the 1982/83 tax year, up to £1,565 of your earnings (including any pension you earned in your own right) is tax free.

If you get a pension based on your husband's contributions, it normally counts as your husband's income, and wife's earned income allowance cannot be set against it. Although you may be entitled to a pension of your own you can choose to get a pension based on your husband's contributions because this is higher. But when totalling your earnings you are entitled to assess your individual pension calculated on your own contributions.

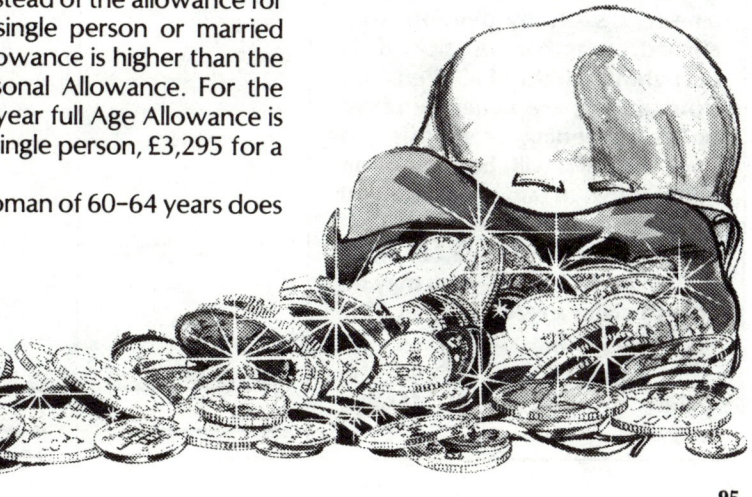

To check your total income from taxable pensions you may find it helpful to fill in this table.

Taxable pensions The following pensions are taxable and normally count as earned income:	Tick here if you will get this pension and fill in amount (if known).		For married couples where wife is taxed separately. Tick here if your wife will get this pension and fill in amount (if known).	
	Tick	Amount	Tick	Amount
State Retirement Pension Including any graduated pension and invalidity allowance if paid with retirement pension. (NB — If paid with invalidity pension — not taxable).	☐	☐	☐	☐
Non-contributory State Retirement Pension	☐	☐	☐	☐
Self-employed pension provided you got tax relief on the payments you made into the personal pension scheme (if you didn't get any tax relief, the pension counts as investment income).	☐	☐	☐	☐
Partnership retirement annuity Provided you retire through old age or ill health, and the income from the annuity comes to no more than half your average yearly share of the profits in the best 3 years of the last 7 years during which you were involved virtually full-time in the partnership (anything over this counts as investment income).	☐	☐	☐	☐
Pensions from abroad You are normally liable for tax on nine-tenths of any pension from abroad, whether or not it is brought into the UK. Pensions from abroad are generally taxed on a preceeding year basis—so your tax bill will be based on nine-tenths of any pension you got from abroad during the previous tax year. Ask your tax office for leaflet IR25. (NB — you may be able to claim a credit if foreign tax has been paid).	☐	☐	☐	☐
	YOU £		**WIFE** £	
Total income from taxable pensions.	☐		☐	

Tax-free pensions and benefits

The most important tax-free pensions for the retired are Supplementary Benefit and War Widows' Pensions.

In addition to these benefits you don't have to pay tax on the following:

Grants for improving or insulating your home.

Rate rebates, rent rebates and allowances.

Tax free social security benefits (disablement pensions paid for war injuries, annuity and pension additions for some gallantry awards, industrial injuries, war disablement pensions, mobility allowance, compensatory pensions paid to policemen and firemen etc.).

Luncheon vouchers up to 15p a day.

Gifts from generous relatives.

'Ex gratia' retirement payments from employer.

Certain earnings from working abroad.

Proceeds from SAYE, National Savings Certificates, Ulster Savings Certificates, Premium Bonds and final bonus from British Savings Bonds.

Income from family income life insurance policy.

Strike and unemployment pay from a trade union.

Betting winnings, lottery prizes.

First £70 interest from ordinary account with National Savings Bank.

Redundancy payments not exceeding £25,000.

Proceeds from Life Insurance Policies (regular premium).

Unemployment Benefit and Sickness Benefit is taxable income. Supplementary Benefit is not. Tax will not be taken from your benefit when it is paid to you but you will not be able to claim a tax refund while you are claiming benefit. Ask for leaflet IR 41 (Tax Office).

Don't forget, if you go back to full-time employment or take up part-time work you will find that certain expenses are allowable against tax. These can include tools, trade union subs, work clothing and certain travel expenses.

Earned income

If you have a job after you retire your combined income (from the job, your pension, and investments) may make you liable for tax. Your employer will usually deduct the tax that's due under the PAYE system. The tax deducted under PAYE will cover any which has still to be paid on your investment income and on your State Pension, as well as the tax due on your earnings alone.

It may look to you as if you are losing too much from your pay-packet in tax, but if the tax due on the other parts of your income is not collected under PAYE, you have to pay up in a lump sum at the end of each year.

Investment income

Your investments provide another source of income on which you may be liable to pay tax.

In some cases the tax will be deducted by the companies who hold your investment (i.e. at source), but with others it is your responsibility.

Investment income is taxable at source from the following:

o Dividends and interest from company shares and debentures.
o Local authority bonds.
o Gilt-edged securities.
o Building society accounts.

Investment income is *not* taxable at source from the following:

o Trustee Savings Bank
o Clearing Banks
o National Giro Bank
o National Savings Bank (£70 exemption in ordinary account)
o British Savings Bank (subject to Tax/Tax-free bonus after five years)
o Government securities on the National Savings Bank Register.

Investment income surcharge

People with large amounts of investment income have to pay a special tax called Investment Income Surcharge. After the first £5,500 of investment income, tax will be at 15%. If the total investment exceeds £12,800 you may be liable to higher rates. Check the amounts at each Budget.

When you come to fill in the form at the end of the topic, you will find you are asked to summarise all your investment income showing the full amount *before tax.* Even where tax is deducted at source you must still fill in the gross income you receive. At the foot of that form there is a section in which you can then state the total amount of tax you have already paid. You will then be able to work out the balance outstanding, if any. All companies that deduct tax at source will send you a record of your gross income and the amount deducted. You should retain these.

Of course, when dealing with an investment where tax is deducted at source, such as local authority bonds, if you find you are not, in fact, liable to pay tax on your income you can claim the money back. There is, though, a single and most important exception to this rule; it is worth considering this in detail.

Building societies

Any interest you receive from a building society is generally described as 'tax-free'. But, what you are in fact receiving is a portion of the total income from your investment after an amount, equivalent to the basic tax-rate, has already been deducted. This tax is *never* recoverable.

If you do not pay tax then you shouldn't invest in a building society. You can get a higher return from other investments, where you can get a refund.

This rather complicated and important subject is dealt with in detail in the leaflet 'Income Tax and Age Allowance' (IR4A). Ask for it at your local tax office.

Any other income

You have to declare to the Inland Revenue any money you receive from other sources such as letting. You will need to look carefully at the notes on your Tax Return Form to see if you have any income in this category.

You will now have all the information you need for calculating your taxable income. Before moving on to complete the form with your own details here are two examples of people assessing their tax positions.

Patrick and Mary Murphy decided to work out how much tax they will have to pay. First they checked the list of pensions. They are both of retirement age, though Mary works a few hours a week.

These figures are for the 1981/82 tax year, when £5,900 was the top income for Age Allowance.

Patrick and Mary had a bad moment when they found that their income went over the £5,900 mark, but then realised that they could subtract £40 for their interest payments on their mortgage, bringing their income down to £5,872. Mary reckons that with any luck the limit will have changed by the time they finish paying off their mortgage in five years' time.

So, their taxable income amounts to:

	£
Income	5,912
Outgoings and allowances	4,310
Taxable	1,602

Tax at 30% on £1,602 is £480.60.

Patrick and Mary dug out their P60s from their various employers. These forms record how much tax you have paid.

They were relieved to find that they had paid slightly more tax than they had actually needed to. So, they can look forward to a small rebate.

The Murphy tax position

Income

	£
Patrick's State Retirement Pension	2,462
Patrick's pension from Westons Furniture Limited, his former employer.	1,800
Mary's pension from Belfast Textiles Limited, her former employer.	800
Mary's part-time earnings at the corner shop	820
Interest from the Murphy TSB investment account	30
Total	**5,912**

Outgoings and allowances

	£
Mortgage payment — of which £40 is interest	40
Age allowance (for married man)	2,895
Wife's earned income allowance (maximum allowance to be set against Mary's pension and part-time earnings).	1,375
	4,310

P60 Certificate of pay and tax deducted

Employer's full name and address

Do not destroy

Tax District and reference

Year to 5 April

19

Employee's National Insurance number

Employee's surname (in BLOCK CAPITALS)

Works no. etc.

First two forenames

Final tax code

Total for year

Pay	Tax deducted	Previous employment		This employment	
£	£	Pay £	Tax deducted £	Pay £	Tax deducted or refunded "R" indicates refund £

National Insurance contributions in this employment

Contribution Table letter	Total of Employee's and Employer's Contributions payable 1a	Employee's Contributions payable 1b	Employee's Contributions at Contracted-out rate included in column 1b 1c	Employee's Widows and Orphans/life insurance contributions in this employment	Holiday pay paid but not included in pay above	Week 53 payment indicator
	£	£	£			
	£	£	£			
	£	£	£		£	
	£	£	£	£		

I/We certify that the particulars given above include the total amount of pay for income tax purposes (including overtime, bonus, commission etc.) paid to you by me/us in the year shown above and the total tax deducted by me/us (less any refunds) in that year.

TO THE EMPLOYEE
Keep this certificate. It will help you to check any Notice of Assessment which the Tax Office may send you in due course. A duplicate form P60 cannot be supplied.

P60

George and Dorothy Buchanan wanted to check on the amount of tax they are paying — they suspected that they were not paying quite as much as they should be and decided to work out how much they might have to pay. Again the figures used are for 1980/81.

When George and Dorothy checked their P60s from their former employers they found that they were paying only about £750 in tax, so they needed to put £90 aside to cover a demand from the taxman for these arrears.

If you receive a justified amount for the payment of tax arrears remember that the tax inspector will usually arrange payment by instalments.

Now you have seen what the Murphys and the Buchanans did, fill in the form and estimate your own tax. This form is designed for married couples — this is because of the way in which the tax system operates. Single people of either sex, should refer to 'husband' throughout.

If you are paying maintenance to a former wife much of this will not be applicable and you will need to get advice from your local tax office.
Remember:

o Age Allowance. This will be reduced by £2 for every £3 the total income exceeds £6,700 to the point where the ordinary Personal Allowance operates i.e. £7,975 (married) £7,456 (single).

o Investment Income. Fill in gross amounts even where tax is deducted at source. In 'D' at the foot of the form include the amount deducted, also any tax already paid under PAYE on earnings or pensions. With building society income remember for the purposes of this form, interest must be 'grossed-up' i.e. divided by 0.7. Include the balance, i.e. tax paid, in 'D'.

o Many people are misled by the attractive but dangerous comment 'Tax-Free'. The advertisers know this only too well and play on it for all they're worth. Proceed on the assumption that *all income* apart from some social security benefit *is taxable*.

Income

	£
George's State Retirement Pension	1,284
Dorothy's State Retirement Pension — she has an adequate record of contributions under the new Home Responsibilities Protection Scheme, despite having been at home for the last couple of years looking after George's elderly mother.	1,284
George's pension from Tartan Accessories Limited, his former employers	2,012
Dorothy's pension from her teaching post at St Catriona's Day School for Girls	1,830
Total investment income from their deposit account at Bank of Scotland and loan made to George's cousin to start his own souvenir shop	190
Total	**6,600**

Outgoings and allowances

	£
Age allowance for married couple (reduced by ⅔ on the main amount by which its total income exceeds £5,900)	2,429
Wife's earned income allowance (maximum allowance to be set against Dorothy's pension)	1,375
Total	**3,804**
George's and Dorothy's taxable incomes (Take 'B' from 'A')	2,796
Tax payable at 30%	838.80

Estimating your tax

Income for tax year (in pounds, ignoring any pence).

Taxable pensions.	Paid to husband	☐
	Paid to wife	☐
Earned income from (part-time) job (less pension contributions).	Paid to husband	☐
	Paid to wife	☐
Investment income (gross amounts before tax of interest, dividends, unit trust distributions).	Paid to husband	☐
	Paid to wife	☐
Any other income (enter 'before-tax' amounts).	Paid to husband	☐
	Paid to wife	☐
	Fill in Total 'A'	☐

Your outgoings and allowances for tax year (in pounds, ignoring any pence).

Allowable expenses in (part-time) employment, paid out of earnings. These include tools, Trade Union subs, duty clothing allowances, certain subscriptions and certain travel expenses — see Tax Return Notes included with your Tax Return Form from the Inspector of Taxes.	By husband	☐
	By wife	☐
Interest which qualifies for tax relief (including mortgage but not option mortgages). Check what you're paying with lender.	By husband	☐
	By wife	☐
Age Allowance.	Single	☐
	Married	☐
Wife's earned income allowance (though see notes about married women's pensions).		☐
Other allowances (e.g. blind persons).		☐
Covenants.		☐
	Fill in Total 'B'	☐

To find your taxable income.

Write in your Total 'A'	☐
Write in your Total 'B'	☐
Subtract 'B' from 'A' to get taxable income	☐

What tax are you liable for?

Work out tax at 30% on Taxable income 'C'	☐

If you or your wife have worked during the last financial year use your P60 forms to add up how much tax you or your wife have already paid under PAYE (if any) on your (part-time) earnings and/or pensions.

How much tax have you already paid 'D'	☐

Also include any tax deducted at source on investment income.

Compare the amounts at C and D.

Do you owe tax?

If the figure in 'C' is greater than the figure in 'D' then you owe tax and will have to pay it — but you can adjust the balance for any tax overpaid or underpaid in previous years. Make an appointment with your local Tax Office to discuss it.

Making changes

What will affect the income tax you pay?

If you have decided that you want to increase your retirement income by working part-time or letting off part of your house think carefully how it would affect your tax position. Is the extra income likely to take you over the total income limit, so that your Age Allowance will be reduced?

If so, you may find that the extra income means you will pay quite a lot more tax. Is it worth it? If in any doubt, make an appointment with your local tax office to get help with working out possible increases in taxation.

Tax refunds

Don't forget that when you stop earning, you start getting a pension(s) and possibly Age Allowance so a new set of balances starts operating.

Many people seem to expect that they will have overpaid tax and will be entitled to a refund when they retire. This can only happen if you have already paid more tax on your earnings and pension(s) up to April 6th than you should. So don't expect a windfall from the taxman!

Gains on life insurance policies

Supposing you invested £2,000 in a single-premium life insurance policy two years ago. Now that you've retired, you'd like to cash in about £1,000 of it. The decision is yours, but you may be adding to your tax problems, especially if you're getting Age Allowance. Although any taxable gain you make when you cash in this type of life insurance policy is free of basic rate tax, it is counted as part of your investment income for the year. And increasing your income can mean you get less Age Allowance so pay more tax.

You're allowed to cash in one-twentieth of the total premiums you've paid to date for each year that you've held the policy without it altering your tax position. If you cash in any more than this amount, it's counted as gain for that year and liable to tax — even if, really, it's just the return of the money you invested.

Here is an example of the sum of £2,000 being invested for two years. With an allowance of one-twentieth available for each year the total non-taxable amount comes to £200.

	£
Total investment	2,000 ×
Years held 2 @ 1/20 allowance	1/10
	200

So, cashing in £1,000 of your investment would lead to a taxable 'gain' of £800.

	£
Total withdrawal	1,000
Allowance	200
Taxable Gain	800

The figure of £800 would be added to your total income for the year and could reduce your Age Allowance dramatically.

If you cash in the whole policy only the profit you have made, if any, on your investment would be added to your income. Otherwise, cashing in more than you are allowed against tax in any one year can lead to a big increase in your total income and therefore your tax bill.

Generous relatives

If your son plans to give you a regular £20 a month this is not subject to tax.

There's no income tax to pay on gifts. But if your income is too low for you to pay tax anyway and you do not receive Supplementary Benefit, it may be better for your son to give you the money under a deed of covenant. Because of the special tax rules for deeds of covenant he could get tax relief himself, and every £100 you end up with will cost him only £70.

But be wary if you're getting Supplementary Benefit, or any other Social Security benefit which is affected by your income. Covenant payments count as income, so may reduce your benefit.

Claiming tax back

If you have any money in unit trusts, shares, local authority loans or similar investments you will receive a tax voucher when you receive your annual dividends. These tax credits cover the tax you would have to pay on this income if you were a basic rate taxpayer.

If you regularly have to claim tax back, ask for special claim form (R40) instead of the normal kind of Tax Return. It may save you a lot of trouble. Arrangements can be made for repayment of tax by instalments through the year. Ask the taxman.

Paying tax at higher rates?

If, after retirement you still pay tax at a top rate of 50 per cent, then it would make sense to invest the maximum amount allowed in tax-free investments such as National Savings Certificates.

Alternatively you could invest your money for capital gain (e.g. in unit trusts aiming at capital growth) rather than for high income. You could sell some of your investments to provide income.

The first £5,000 of net capital gains you make on assets sold in the 1982-83 tax year are free of tax. Anything over £5,000 is taxed at 30 per cent — tax will be substantially lower than higher rate tax plus any investment income surcharge.

See the Inland Revenue Tax Return Guide P1 (Ins) (1982) for notes on exemptions and relief, bringing losses forward and decisions on whether total proceeds exceed £5,000 or total net gains exceed £3,000.

The Budget

Taxation, of course, is as much subject to change as any other government policy. The information in the topic is based upon the Budget of March 1982. As a result of government legislation changes may arise. Try and keep abreast of these where they might affect you.

This topic has attempted to offer guidelines only and it should help to give you confidence to work out your tax position where it is within a normal range. Your local tax office will be able to answer your individual tax queries.

You can either write them a letter outlining your problem and giving as much information as you are able, or make an appointment to visit your tax office and discuss the matter.

o Think about the details you are likely to need to put your case clearly.
o Put the information together beforehand in an organised way, i.e. finding bills, account reference numbers, official forms like P45 and P60, list income and outgoings (the topic activities will help you here).
o Jot down the major points to refresh your memory.
o Give tax references (notice of coding, tax return details) or the name and address of your last employer.
o Keep a dated copy.

Your changing budget

After retirement, when you have made your planned adjustments to your changed financial situation it might be tempting to think your budget will tick-over satisfactorily without much attention. But change is inescapable and usually brings the unexpected.

Need for constant review

The changes you could easily forecast for the early days of retirement may not be the ones that most affect your income as the years go by. Frequent review of your affairs will help you to feel more confident about dealing with problems that arise out of unexpected changes.

What changes?

Day to day

There may be day to day changes which call for immediate decisions. For example, if your income is less than it was but you seem to be spending more on food you may decide to eat less, or cut expenditure on something else because you prefer to spend what money you have on the food you are used to.

Your income may be more than you expected leaving you to choose, say, between using your spare cash on more frequent holiday breaks or increased short term savings.

Larger scale

Larger scale changes are likely to be more disturbing. Some longer term planning may be necessary too. Inflation has been with us for some time. Since it is impossible to predict what will happen in the future, it is always a good idea to be flexible enough to make short and longer term adjustments.

o Rents and rates tend to rise not fall. Standing charges (for gas and electricity for example) may increase more than you could have foreseen. Falling interest rates could reduce your expected investment income.
o You may be unexpectedly faced with storm damage that means a major roof maintenance job. Floods may ruin carpets and furniture you thought would last a lifetime. Do remember to check insurance policies on your house and contents.

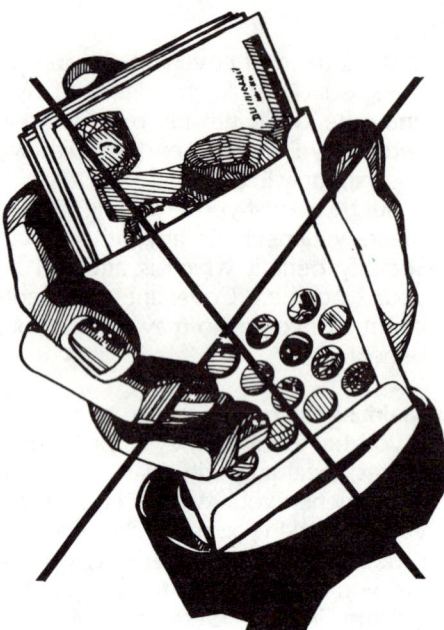

Adjustment to change

Think about a whole range of circumstances that might call for some adjustments to *your* budget. Look at the charts Day to Day Budgeting and Larger Scale Budgeting.

They show:

o Items that are fixed – you have no choice
o Items about which you have some choice

Now look at your own current budget and mark with an 'F' those items that are fixed – i.e. whatever income or expenditure you have little or no say about.

Mark with a 'C' those items you can choose to change.

Day to day budgeting	
Choice (C)	**Fixed (F)**

Income:
    Part-time work.
    Letting premises.
    Savings and investments.
	Income:
	    Pension (s).
	    State benefits.

Expenditure:
    Food.
    Hobbies and interests.
    Holidays and travel.
    Clothes.
    Car/motorbike.
    Minor repairs/decorating.
    Telephone.
    TV.
    Insurance.
	Expenditure:
	    Rent.
	    Rates.
	    Heating and lighting.
	    Mortgage repayments.
	    Taxes.

Larger scale budgeting	
Choice (C)	**Fixed (F)**

Income:
    Pension lump sums.
    Legacies.
    Maturing insurance policies.
    Pools and other wins.
    Investment income—
    longer term.
    House sale.
	Expenditure:
	    Major repairs.
	    Major replacements.

External influences
Here is a checklist to remind you of some possible external influences.

Taxation P.A.Y.E., V.A.T.
Interest rates.
Local rates.
Water rates.
Fuel Prices.
Inflation/retail price Index.
Concessions for retired.
Social service benefits.
Changes in the law.

Check this list to see if recent changes give you clues to the kind of alterations you need to make in your budget. For instance if the retail price index comes down rapidly the money you invested in index-linked certificates might do better elsewhere. You might also decide that since you were spending a little less day to day you could afford to spend more on hobbies and interests. If the reverse was the case you might have to look for ways of cutting down your spending.

Budget changes
Make sure everyone at home is involved in making any choices whether they are about cutting down or spending. If you can't agree you could try scoring each possibility to see which choices are most acceptable. Use a scale between nought to four where nought is the least and four the most popular. Here is an example of what one family did, the Harpers.

The Harpers
Arthur hated decorating. He knew that the carpet was getting shabby but he thought it more important to save for a rainy day. Elsie thought that if they had a cheaper holiday this year and bought a carpet in the sales, they could have the house decorated and still save a bit. Mrs Murphy, Elsie's mother, thought Arthur should do his own decorating and voted for the new stair carpet as she was afraid that if it become more worn she might trip and fall. However, she felt she shouldn't be too dogmatic. The table shows how they decided to have the decorating done professionally.

Letting everyone have their say will ensure that all the possibilities for spending or cutting down on spending are explored and the final decision is likely to be more acceptable.

Possibilities	More savings	More on holidays	Have house decorated professionally	New carpet for stairs and landing
Arthur Harper	3	0	4	2
Elsie Harper	2	4	4	3
Mrs Murphy (Elsie's mother)	1	1	0	2
Totals	6	5	8	7

The Stirlings

James and Maggie had married late, and had retired before their youngest children, still living in the family home, had finished their studies. They had not managed to save as much as they would have liked. The old house had been fine for the five of them but when the twins left home Maggie suddenly began to find the effort of keeping a large and frequently empty place tiring and unrewarding. James wondered whether it was sensible to go on paying out the increasing bills for heating and lighting. They decided to jot down their ideas and discuss them:

o Carry on and see how long they could keep going.

o Sell the house, buy a smaller, cheaper house with garden. Invest the cash difference and reduce outgoings on rates, heating etc.

o Sell the house and buy a flat or bungalow. Likely to cost a lot for a reasonably sized flat or bungalow.

o Sell the house and rent a flat. Invest cash difference. Use some to buy new modern furniture.

o Take in tenants. Some expenditure needed to create bed-sits. Would provide some income. Need not sell furniture.

o Divide house into two flats and live in ground floor flat. Considerable expenditure but regular additional income. No need to sell furniture. More privacy than with bed-sits.

The question was raised with the children but they did not want James' and Maggie's decision influenced by their needs.

So, James and Maggie looked into the costs of dividing the house into bed sits or two flats. They got details on fair rents, the effect upon the rateable value of their house and the amount of tax they might now have to pay. They then worked out what they would need to raise as a loan from the bank to add to some of their savings.

As neither of them really wanted to leave their home this seemed the best solution for them. They would cut down on outgoings and when their bank loan was repaid would have additional income. The option of moving remained. Had they not considered it important to do a frequent review of their budget they might have gone on eating into their savings until a crisis.

Maggie's Problems

House too big for two.

Would find it hard to leave so many memories.

Not enough room for children to come and stay in a smaller place. They may stop coming.

The furniture is too big for a small house or flat.

James' Problems

Rising costs, rates, heating and lighting. Crazy to spend as much for two as for five. May need to start using savings eventually.

Maggie always busy and looking tired.

I've invested a lot of expense and time in the garden. Home produce important to me.

Mrs Shapiro

Mrs Shapiro needed to cut her outgoings firstly because she wanted to save a little each month towards Christmas, when her family came and she likes to give them all presents and secondly because her old washing machine needed replacing. She considered going to the launderette, but it is too far. So, she needed to make a regular saving of about £6 a month towards the Christmas food and presents, and she wanted about £250 for an automatic washer. Credit or hire purchase she thought too expensive.

She decided to make a list of her outgoings to see what she could do without, or at least cut down upon, and how difficult in each case she thought it would be. Having eliminated from her budget essential items that could not be altered such as rent, insurance, food etc, she gave everything a score of one to four taking one to stand for something that was easy to reduce or forego. The score of four she gave to such items as her Railcard or the rental and licence of her TV that were very important to her; and, because these were fixed costs and could not be cut down upon, she would have to go without them altogether which she was very reluctant to do.

Mrs Shapiro ignored the items that scored three and four for the time being and concentrated on the ones and twos. She decided to sell her piano since her hands have gone rather stiff and rheumatic. She was delighted to hear that she should get £150 to £200

for it and that would finance most of the washing machine as well as saving on tuning costs.

Then she turned to the other items on the list. The sub to the Ouse and Nene Canal Society was only £2 a year and she decided to retain this, as she enjoys walking along the banks of the canal and appreciates the Society's efforts to keep the canal clean.

The question of eating out was tricky. She met her sister regularly and her sister likes a meal out. But the restaurant was getting dearer all the time and Mrs Shapiro wasn't that keen on restaurant food anyway. She resolved to cut spending here by 50% with the option of cutting down further after discussing it with her sister. Batteries for the cassette recorder could be eliminated entirely if she could get a gadget to plug the recorder into the mains. This would cost her £1.20, she discovered. She also decided to cut down on sweets and chocolates. Now she adds up the results of her possible savings.

Saving per year

No piano tuning	20	(+ capital of £150–£200)
Less eating out	12	
No more batteries	5	(though she had to pay £1.20 and will consume a little more electricity.)
Fewer sweets and chocolates	4	
	£41	

So she has saved a little more than half what she needs for her Christmas fund, and found most of what she needs for the washing machine. She looks at the other items on her list. Window cleaning is dear. Perhaps she could have it done every other month, rather than every month, saving £9. The grandfather clock has cost a lot in repairs this year. If it goes wrong again, she decided she will give it to her son — who will get it anyway when she dies. She considered cutting down on stamps and stationery but keeping in touch with friends is too important to give it up.

Her savings are now:	Saving
No more clock repairs	25
Less window cleaning	9
	£34

This gives her the money that she needs for her Christmas Fund, but she still had £50 to £100 to find for the washing machine. She decided to look around and see whether she could get a new twin tub for the money available to her, or a second hand automatic with a guarantee.

Mrs Shapiro's Budget	How much it costs this year	Score to cut
Piano tuning	£20	1
Window cleaning	£18	3
Subscription to Ouse and Nene Canal Society	£2	2
Repairs to grandfather clock	£25	3
Eating out (meals when she meets her sister in town)	£18	2
Batteries for cassette recorder	£5	1
Stamps and stationery	£12	3
Sweets and chocolates	£15	2
Railcard	£10	4
TV licence	£46	4
TV rental	£96	4

Other considerations

Do you need to increase your income?

You could consider:

o Taking a part time job.
o Deferring your retirement.
o Working from home as an out worker or self employed.
o Taking tenants into your home.
o Selling your house and moving to a smaller house or flat.

Remember though, increasing your income by these means may affect your right to various state benefits – supplementary pension, rate and rent rebates, low income welfare benefits for example. You will also need to balance up the extra income and your desire to work against the possible loss of benefits and extra tax.

If you are able to defer your retirement, that is go on working full time after the official age, you do not draw your retirement pension or pay National Insurance contributions (but your employer will). You do get a higher state pension when you draw it and have the right to draw your pension after five years should you go on working.

If you are working at home keep a detailed account of all income and expenditure. Forward this to the tax office with your tax return. Remember you pay tax only on your profits not on total income. If you charge against wear and tear of your property this could attract a rates increase.

Perhaps you do not want to work in retirement or it isn't possible. There may not be any work available or you may not be fit enough. You should make sure that:

o You are getting all available state and other retirement benefits.
o That any savings and investments are placed to your best advantage. You should expect to move them about from time to time. Radio and TV money programmes and family finance columns in the press will keep you informed.

Should you pay off the building society mortgage?

This is something which could make a big difference to your budget. It is a question that faces many people at the time of retirement especially those who receive a tax free lump sum. You might want to pay off your building society mortgage:

o Just to get rid of a debt—because you dislike being in debt.
o To increase spending money.
o To seek a financial advantage.

FOR paying off
o Monthly instalments available for spending or re-investing.
o If you have retired early with a lump sum, paying off your mortgage leaves former instalments as increased spending money to tide you over until you become entitled to the State Pension.

AGAINST paying off
o More tax to pay—no longer relief on mortage interest.
o When inflation is high you are repaying with pounds that have depreciated in value i.e. it costs less. You could put the capital you would have repaid the mortgage within index-linked savings.
o You cannot reinstate a loan with tax relief unless you buy another house.

Work out the best financial advantage for you. It is worth reviewing this annually.

Interest payable to building society (not capital). £	Interest payable to you if amount payable invested. £
Deduct tax relief. £	
Total	Total

National budget changes

What the Chancellor of the Exchequer has to say in his Budget Speech is often of particular importance to pensioners. Check the reports in the papers and see what he says about it.

1 **Income tax and age allowances**
If your income is to keep up with inflation these allowances should be increased. If they are allowed to remain the same or decreased then you are, in effect, paying more tax.

2 **Age allowance limit**
The limit up to which the age allowance applies in full may be altered. This will especially affect pensioners whose total incomes are over £6,700 (1982/83).

3 **Amount of pension increase (if any!)**
There are usually increases in the State Pension and other social security benefits which will come into operation the following November. These may balance other tax changes.

4 **Taxes on various goods**
There may be changes in taxes on drink, tobacco, petrol, TV licences and other things, all of which will affect your outgoings.

Aim to update your personal budget in April to keep up with these changes.

(or then Japhet) of pub...
house Japhet) of pub...
washing linen, dirty or
otherwise.
Three months have
passed since Spring
Grove, encouraged by
Charterhouse, b,d
£7,500,000 for fellow
washerfolk St. George's
Laundries. Little has been
heard of them since.
The offer was some-
thing of a formality, anyway, like the apologetic
letters you get when
laundries misplace your
shirt. Spring Grove al-
ready had acceptances
representing 53 per cent.
of St George's.

Grove were
much. A few S
shareholders
same, their
helped push S
shares down
bid, to 71p.
They now
per cent.,
nothing for
fits already
merger, or
mies of pu
plimentary
together.
Last Ma
pulled off
when th
laundry
British
(British
Hotels)
deal. C
BTH in
tract,
adjustn
for lau
service

Quantum leap

They described the
acquistion as a quantum
leap forward, and left it
at that. Some St George's
shareholders gratefully
took cash instead of
shares, feeling that Spring

TEXTILES

lTex ...191
Mohir ..48
ulmr&L ..18
xpt Int ...18
arr-V ....
CawDawff
CoatsPtg ..60
Corah N ..56
Courtlds .77
Dawson .128
Illngwth 'A'
          13
          26—
Lister ....
NottMtg 184—
Nova 82
SEET 61
Tern-Con 43—
Tootal ...31
YoughiC 5

TOBACCOS

Bats ...478+
Imps ....97+
Rothmns ..98+

TRUSTS

Alliance 317+
AA Sec .136
BrArrow ..38
B Assets ..98—
Fleming M
          59—
          136
Globe ...143
Hill Phip 143
KitchT ..120
LondonT ..70
Penrsus .276
R.I.T. ...360
Robeco .442+
T.R.CofL 88
T.R.I.G. 77—
T.R.T.I. 101
Wood HI ††
†† Dealings suspended
a Ex-rights issue
Ev-dividend
xc Ex-capitalisation issue

UNIT TRUSTS

ABBEY UNIT *66·8	Tech *24·1
Gen	UnivEner *45·3
ALLIED	**CHIEFTAIN** 26·3
Cap Tst *53·9	Amer *32·9
Equity 29·2	Far East 35·1
GovtSec 63·5	High *24·2
Gwth&Inc 97·0	**CONFEDATN LIFE**
High Inc *70·4	Gwth 83·7
High Yld *31·2	**CRESCENT** 37·
Int 25·1	Amer *59·
Japan 59·3	Res 49·
MetMin 87·4	HighDs 75·
O'seas 58·4	Int *59·
Pacific 30·2	**EQUITY & LA**
Recovery 80·2	Equity&Law 101
SecsofAm 62·5	**FRIENDS PRO**
SmallerCo's 81·0	Dist 76
do. 2nd	**G AND A**
ARBUTHNOT	G&A *10
Cap 35·0	**GARTMORE**
Comm 57·1	Amer *10
EastInt 40·5	Brit
High Inc *35·7	Comm
N.Amer 37·3	FarEast
Pref 22·1	HighInc
ARCHWAY	Inc
Fund 118·9	Int
BARCLAYS	**GUARDIA**
Amer 35·9	Guardhll
Aust 65·3	**HENDERS**
Extra 32·6	Aust
GwthAcc 77·6	Cap
Trustee 180·3	Euro
Cap *97·9	Fin&ITU
Fin 98·0	HighInc
Gen 47·7	Inc&Ass
Inc *123·9	Int
500 *110·7	N.Amer
Prof 57·6	HILL SA
	68·9	Brit
		Cap

Looking after your investments

Most people have investments of some
kind, especially those who have
received lump sums on retirement, or
redundancy payments or maybe a
pools or premium bond win.

Why not make an annual review?
Check the list on the right.

If you decide that it is worth while
changing your investments then act on
your judgement. It costs nothing to
change investments in building societies
or National Savings, bank deposits but
with stocks and shares you will have
charges to meet.

Also remember to review other
kinds of investment, for instance,
annuities, house income plans,
investment type life insurances, occupational pensions, personal pension
schemes, Premium Bonds and property
and valuables.

Investment review

Fixed capital investments
(no risk of losing the capital you put in
but the amount of income can vary)

	Income Last year	This year
Bank deposit accounts.		
Building Society accounts.		
Certain life insurance investment bonds.		
SAYE (Save as you earn) scheme.		
Monthly income account.		
Finance company deposits.		
Local authority loans.		
National Savings Bank (NSB) and Trustee Savings Bank (TSB) accounts.		
National Savings Certificates.		

Fixed income investments
(the value of your capital may vary but
the rate of income you get is fixed)

	Income £	Capital Gain	Loss
British Government stocks.			
Local authority stocks and yearling bonds.			
Company debentures.			

Index-linked investments
(the value of your capital is linked to the retail
price index and so maintains its buying power)

	Length of Term	Date bonus accrued
Index linked National Savings Certificates.		
S.A.Y.E.		
Indexed gilts.		

Shares, Unit trusts, bonds etc
(most risky as both the value of your capital
and any income you get can vary)

Last year	This year

Any other investments

	Income Last year	This year

Family and friends

Now you've got more time. It's yours to use as you choose. The first few months of retirement bring opportunities to see far more of some people than you have for a long time. On the other hand it may mean spending less time with those who have been friends for many years.

In everyday relationships when trying to work out the level of social activity in your life it breaks down into three areas:

O The amount before retirement.
O The amount after retirement.
O The amount you really want.

If you're feeling uncomfortable about the amount of contact you have with relations, friends and neighbours now you have retired then probably you haven't yet achieved the level of social activity you really prefer. Of course, this balance can take a bit of achieving. For some people it presents no problem but others find it doesn't just come overnight.

George and Carol Pettifer

George retired seven months ago. They now find that their children expect them for frequent weekends. As far as they can see this is because their children feel that it would be a nice way for George and Carol to spend their time.

They enjoy seeing their children and grand-children but don't like the amount of travelling. George and Carol live in Leeds and spend two weekends in four either in Birmingham or Bangor. They're also spending a great deal of money on travelling.

Bob Smithson

In the past all he has had to do to keep most of his friendships in good repair was to get out of bed and go to work. His job provided him with friends. Since retirement it comes as a shock to realise that although many of his friends live quite close by, he never seems to see them.

Now he has to have a reason to go and visit, or call back at his old workplace. He is not the sort of person to push himself. He tends to think things like *"Do they want to see me? They've got their own lives."* All the same he wishes he did have a reason to visit — he misses the company.

In both cases the balance hasn't quite been achieved yet. Neither the Pettifers nor Bob Smithson have really sorted out the amount of social activity they feel happy about.

Getting a balance

Think about some of your contacts and try and choose a variety: immediate family friends, acquaintances, work friends, family friends of long standing. Make a list of them and then ask yourself these questions about each of them.

How often do I see this person now?
Where do I generally see this person?
Now that I've retired do I find myself talking about different things to this person?
Am I expected to do more for this person now?
Now I've retired do I feel closer to this person?
Now that I've retired do I enjoy seeing this person?
Do I now feel that I have a lot in common with this person?

Do you see people often enough or too often? Perhaps you expected when you retired that neighbours would drop in more often to see you than they do? Or may be you are thrown together with some people more than you'd like, neighbours popping in at all hours? Where do you meet work friends now that you are no longer at work, and what do you talk to them about? Is there more than the bond of work to hold you together?

Bob Smithson's plan

Think back to Bob Smithson. His work friends had always been the centre of his social life and he decided that he didn't see enough of them now, although he didn't want to go back to his place of work to maintain the contacts.

So what Bob did was think about the questions on the list and decide on a plan which would involve a definite arrangement.

The action that Bob decided to take was to arrange on a regular basis to see his friends socially by supporting the works darts team.

Darts gave him and his friends an interest in common outside work. He could still find out if George Brent had had his operation and whether Betty the boss's secretary had left. But at the same time not all the conversation was about work. He found he heard enough to keep him happy, but not so much as to make him feel left out.

Deciding on your plan

You may feel perfectly happy about the level of social activity in your life. But whatever your feelings you may want to make some changes. The first step is to decide upon a proper plan of action for instigating those changes.

You may think that dreaming up a plan of action sounds odd and calculating and that relationships and friendships just happen naturally. Waiting for things to happen naturally is fine but they may take a long time. Are you prepared to wait that long? And, of course, they may never happen at all.

Retirement is a good time for making changes in your life. You've already made one major move in leaving work and this can gear you up so that other changes are easier to make.

It does take courage to make changes — sometimes it's easier to let things slide however unsatisfactory they may seem. But a little effort can produce some very worthwhile results.

What do you want to do?

The first type of action you may decide upon is to make definite arrangements to see someone. If you tend to be lazy like Bob Smithson this is a good way of helping yourself to avoid 'not bothering'. And of course everyone knows where they stand too. Also if you're feeling overrun then arranging to see someone on Friday may discourage them from calling to see you on Tuesday, Wednesday and Thursday too.

George and Carol seem to have got into a situation where they've committed themselves rather more than they are happy about. It's no one's fault but it has rapidly become a routine. If you're in a position like George and Carol of doing too much you could start by thinking what your ideal would be. Try writing it down.

George and Carol decided they didn't want to travel lengthy distances every other weekend, or spend as much money on their expeditions.

Their idea was:

"We'd be happy to go and see our daughter in Birmingham about every couple of months, and our son in Bangor about the same. That would work out as being away for a weekend about once a month rather than once a fortnight. We'd also like to see them a bit more at our house."

But George and Carol are anxious about putting their ideal into operation yet. As Carol says it's much more difficult than it seems.

They have thought *what* they want to do but they haven't thought *how* they want to do it.

How do you want to do it?

The main obstacle George and Carol have in deciding how to put their ideal into action is their fear of offending the family. They don't want their family to get the wrong idea. They don't want them to think that any decision of George and Carols' to see them less often reflects a change in their feelings towards them.

What they decided to do was break up the routine. They began to accept occasional social invitations in their own area on weekends when they would normally be expected to be staying with their children. They talked over with their children different ideas about how from time to time the entire family could meet up somewhere for outings. They also suggested having their grandchildren over to stay with them occasionally during half terms and holidays.

They made a deliberate decision not to tackle things head on by bringing up the essential issues of the time and money involved and the general wear and tear of all the travelling.

As George says *"I don't want the kids to start worrying about us being short of money or getting old. Because although I reckon it would tax anyone what we've been doing for the last few months, the children would be bound to read things into it."*

Ethel Woodcock had a different sort of problem. She retired this year at 60, she's single and very involved in her local community. Her niece has a job and three small children and asked Ethel if she would do some childminding if there was an emergency. The emergencies seem to be more and more frequent and Ethel reached the stage of either having to do something about the situation with her niece or give up some of her local community commitments.

Because Ethel is no longer working her niece sees her as having vast amounts of free time. This of course

isn't a correct assessment of the situation. Although Ethel likes to feel she is wanted she is not happy about feeling used.

Ethel's first move was to refuse to baby sit on one occasion because she had already arranged to do something else.

After this she started to give her niece a clearer picture of what she did day to day, writing all her engagements on the kitchen calendar which was easily visible and talking about what she did.

"I'm really pleased that things have gone so well since I've retired. I never seem to have a minute to spare, just listen to this — my average week . . .!"

Fortunately these hints worked. But Ethel had also worked out a further plan. This was to talk to her niece about her childminding problems and to take some time to help her find other facilities in the area.

Ethel successfully managed to adjust the relationship. She continued to do some baby sitting on a more limited basis. She hadn't wanted to end it altogether — she did value her relationship both with her niece and with the children.

Relationships are about mutual support and companionship, emotionally, practically and physically too. Bob needed to think about companionship, George and Carol were concerned about the emotional aspects of their relationships with their children. Ethel was giving practical support.

Each made practical alterations in managing relationships that were already important to them, and tried to clear matters up so everyone knew where they were.

o Making definite arrangements can mean everyone knows where they stand.
o Sometimes people fear to offend in relationships. Consider the pros and cons of coming out in the open with your problem or grievance. Clearing the air can work wonders.
o Many people are more comfortable dropping hints rather than making bald statements, especially if they are worried about offending.

What is important is to work out *what* you want to do and work out a way of *how* you are going to do it that is satisfactory for everyone.

110

Rediscovering

Some people find themselves moving nearer to their family when they retire. **Dick Graham** retired earlier this year. He had been a widower for five years and during that time his social life revolved mainly around friends at work. When he retired his older brother Bill and his wife Dora invited him to stay with them in Wales. Bill is eight years older than Dick and the two had never been very close.

Dick enjoyed his stay. Both brothers had been in the construction industry and they found they had plenty to talk about, particularly Bill's new house and its deficiences. They don't see each other that often even now but find they look forward to their meetings. For Dick going to Wales acts both as a brief holiday and also a chance for a good talk, and for the first time that eight year gap between them has not been important.

Bill has suggested Dick might like to move up but Dick has decided not to do this for the time being. He enjoys the new found contact but finds it's nice as it is at the moment. To move might mean decreasing the enjoyment. In a few years time of course Dick may change his mind.

Molly and Laura are two sisters of 62 and 60 who still do not get on well, though they seem to have decided to spend their future together rather than apart. They have nothing in common except their ages, the fact that they are both single and both see themselves as loners. The only other thing that holds them together is a united front against a large number of cousins.

Their interests are different. Laura is

active and restless. She has travelled widely, worked in a number of interesting jobs and is currently a member of many organisations and classes. Molly is the passive, stay at home type. She has held the same job all her adult life, lived all her life up until her retirement in the house in which she was born and has few outside interests.

The two now spend a lot of time together, visiting each others' flats at opposite ends of the town. They still have their independence and have their own interests, though they find that their similar life situations and needs draw them together.

Laura the younger sister provides several reasons:

"A sister is more to you than anyone else. We are different but I understand Molly — she takes a lot of understanding — and we don't quarrel. We've got more sense than to quarrel. We are closer now than when we were young. Then we each had our own friends being two years apart. We mean more to each other now. You gain more sense with age."

Both Molly and Laura are rather withdrawn and self sufficient. Their friendships are few and not very close and it seems natural that they now turn to a relationship which is already established rather than working on new ones.

The opportunity to develop family ties to suit changing circumstances depends of course on availability of relatives. Dick Graham and Molly and Laura were presented with such opportunities but some people feel their family relationships are fixed and offer no possibilities for development.

Making more contact with people you know involves several things:
o The need to be aware of each other's lifestyle and make allowances.
o Discussing the sorts of adjustments that might be good for the relationship.
o Being aware that things can be sticky for a while when you are getting to know people better.
o Deciding to try and do something if things go badly, talking about the problem, making different arrangements, and having the will to move apart if it seems better for all concerned.

Close relationships

Of course the closest relationships that most people have is with the person they live with. When you retire there will be adjustments to make partly because your routine will have changed. It's worth thinking about the time you spend together and apart and how changes in your routine may affect other relationships of the person you're living with.

Try jotting down what your partner does in a typical week. Ask yourself *"What would he or she be doing if I was at work?"* And ask your partner to write down their activities for the week.

At the end of the week ask your partner to tell you what he or she would have done differently if you hadn't been there. This should help you get some idea about your partner's general routine, jobs and social commitments. In the chart on the right are Cliff and Vera Jessups' accounts of a week's activities.

Day	Cliff	Vera
Mon	am—Vera normally goes and sees Mrs Frederick at the housing association. pm—She's gone to town and will meet Mary her school friend.	am—I didn't go and visit Mrs Frederick because I was going out in the afternoon to see Mary but I try and see her every week.
Tues	She's gone to the sales today, but I think she normally stays in on Tuesdays.	I couldn't resist going to the sales although Tuesday is usually housework and seeing Doris from next door.
Wed	am—We spent the morning in the garden and Doris from next door came round and had a cup of coffee with us. Had lunch together. I think Doris and Vera usually have a bite at mid-day together about twice a week but she didn't stay today. pm—Vera went to her dress making class.	am—Saw Doris today, she came over this morning but didn't stay for lunch. pm—Went dressmaking and dropped in to see Mrs Frederick afterwards.
Thur	am—We went to visit the grandchildren. I know Vera always does this Thursday mornings. Stayed at our daughter's for lunch, I don't think Vera does that very often. pm—Vera walked down to the shops and stopped to have a cup of coffee with one of her friends but I think that was a chance meeting.	am—Went to visit grandchildren. Stayed and had lunch. It's a bit more of an occasion now Cliff's around more. pm—Went down to the shops and bumped into Elsie. Stayed and had a cup of coffee.
Fri	It was nice today so we went out for the day. I think usually Vera would go to the Stroke Club to help but I don't think she does it every week.	Went to Formby for the day. I missed the Stroke Club—I feel a bit bad about that so I must make sure to go next week.

There does not seem to be much disagreement here apart from a little misunderstanding about how important the Stroke Club was to Vera.

Talk to the person you live with about their social commitments on the average week. If your partner feels some regret at having to alter social events, perhaps you could work out together a list of social activities your partner is committed to and work out your own routine in order not to intrude on these.

Retirement brings opportunities to spend more time together. At the same time you are bound to become aware that the person you live with also has other commitments and relationships that are part of the pattern of his or her life. You may each want to continue to do things independently as well as doing more as partners.

Helping out

There is a tendency today to think about retirement as a time for receiving. After a lifetime's work, it's tempting to think about resting from all the exertion and discipline of working for others. Retirement is a time for freedom to please yourself and enjoy the dignity and respect which society owes to you after a lifetime of work.

One woman, Anne Forster, felt strongly that being on the receiving end was not all that she wanted in retirement. She was so angry that she wrote to The *Times* about it:

*Pensioners are being got at. We must prepare to do battle and maintain our independence and preserve our attractive personalities . . . now I am haunted by the fear that if I cannot dispel the assumption that I am a senior citizen, the following events may reasonably occur. (i) I shall have a gang of young thugs sent to my home to paint my kitchen instead of going to prison; (ii) I shall have patients from my local mental hospital drafted to dig my garden; (iii) I may be forced to go to suitable entertainments, drink tea and wear a paper hat; (iv) I may receive vast boxes of assorted food to which I feel I am not entitled. We pensioners are in a terrifying position. We are **recipients** . . . hands off please. I am in charge of my life.*

Receiving

She puts her point over in strong terms and you may not agree with any or all of what she is saying. She suggests that once you are seen as an elderly person you are seen as being in need of gifts or charity which it may be very difficult for you to refuse socially. This acceptance of gifts may make you feel that an imbalance has been forced on you that you are powerless to redress.

You may yourself have come across this idea that retired people should be in receipt of those things which the rest of society considers they need.

But there are different ways of looking at retirement. And you may not choose to take the 'sit back and enjoy it' view. There is nothing magical about the act of retiring which makes you into a different person.

Giving

Here are some activities that you may have been involved in recently. They are all about doing things for other people. Note down the last occasion when you did any of them and add more of your own activities:

Activity	Last occasion I did this
Baby sitting.	
Selling raffle tickets.	
Watering a neighbour's garden.	
Mending a fuse for someone else.	
Helping to run a jumble sale.	
Driving a neighbour to the station to catch a train.	
Collecting someone's pension.	
Fetching shopping for someone.	
Phoning the doctor for a sick neighbour/friend.	
Being a committee member of a local society, club or group.	

Now look at your list of activities and think about them in terms of giving and receiving. You will see they are all about giving. Is there anything which you could not do again, or carry on with, when you are retired?

Of course you can enjoy the good things about being retired, feeling free to do what *you* want each day, taking advantage of the various concessions, travel, hairdressing, whatever is going, but at the same time you can carry on being involved in the giving side of things as well. This can have many advantages.

o For some retired people it can improve an image of themselves which may have been damaged after they stopped full time paid employment.

o It can also help to combat the ideas which Anne Forster in her letter found so offensive and limiting, and shift the balance away from always being at the receiving end towards being involved in giving.

o For society too there are many advantages. People gain from the energies and skills of retired men and women, energies and skills which would otherwise be wasted.

Your activities could involve your own family, friends, neighbours or people at work. What they share in common is that, almost certainly, you were not paid for doing these jobs. You volunteered, you offered, you helped out where and when you were needed.

Many people restrict their giving to family and friends. They feel a reluctance to get involved outside this circle. If they go any further than this they fear being put upon, not being able to back out of the giving, being asked to do more than they are able.

So think now about your own experiences of helping out.

Three volunteers—you, you and you

During the war years, the saying was 'Never volunteer'. People in the forces, particularly, felt if they did step forward they might find themselves walking into something they didn't care for at all.

In the war as is usually the case in a time of crisis people were usually willing to give help to complete strangers because people close to them were being helped in the same way by others. Generally people were expected to help and did so unstintingly.

Think back to the Second World War years. What happened to you and your family? Suddenly there were many unexpected crises and services were stretched in all sorts of ways. Everyone now talks about the way people helped each other in crises. For instance, taking in neighbours or friends who had been bombed out, inviting distant relatives to 'come to us' away from the dangers of blitz bombing, collecting salvage paper, helping out with emergency services, organising life in the shelters, helping people with official forms and papers, cooking meals for people who were bombed out.

Wartime was a time of crisis, emergency and dislocation. It tends to stand out in people's memories. Thinking back can you remember ways in which people responded to difficulties and helped one another? Can you remember times when you needed help or were asked to help? How did you feel about it then?

. . . and now?

There's always the feeling that voluntary work can simply be used to keep people off the streets or to cut down on paid work rather than create jobs. And of course there is the quite understandable view that the welfare state was set up so that collectively, society would pay for the services and support which many people need in order to enjoy a full life. We all pay taxes and social insur-

ance so that we can feel secure at all stages of life and in all situations of need — this means the provision by the state of clinics, hospitals, schools, personal services and the people to staff them. Many of these provisions, though they originated in voluntary action, are now an established part of public expenditure.

In addition over many years people have not been attracted to volunteering or helping out because it tends to carry a rather high minded do-gooding image, one that is associated with charity, soup kitchens and lady bountiful.

Pros and cons

It's up to you whether you decide to extend your helping-out beyond family and friends. When you are making your mind up it's worthwhile thinking about the pros and cons.

Reasons against:

You won't enjoy it.

You'll get exploited.

You'll get too involved and won't be able to get out of it.

You won't be thanked.

Reasons for:

It helps you make new contacts and relationships.

You can put skills and spare time to good use.

It can help you to feel valued.

It gives you a way of taking part in things that you consider worthwhile.

It makes you feel involved.

Helping

What sorts of occasions arise where helping out is a possibility?

Volunteering help, giving and receiving may be a response to a crisis as in the war years, or in the case of bereavement, an accident or some kind of natural disaster. But it can also be a part of friendships, neighbourliness or the simple recognition of need in someone else's life. Perhaps you have had, or someone close to you has had, a particularly bad experience. It could be a burglary, divorce, a road accident. Often when help is needed it isn't sought. People who are emotionally upset may not be able to ask. Nevertheless you can possibly recall a feeling that you wanted to help even if you didn't do anything about it. There may also be times when you want to give help or get involved because you feel something is wrong or could do with changing.

Some quite well established voluntary efforts like toy libraries, Samaritans, Victims Support, Women's Aid, Claimants Union started in this way and so have many pressure groups and campaigns up and down the country.

Think back and see if you can find examples from your own life of ways in which you may have helped out, or wanted to help.

MAKING CHANGES

In the chart below you are asked to think about helping out. John Brown's thoughts on the matter have been filled in to give you an idea, read them and then fill in your own examples. It doesn't matter which part of your life you draw on — yesterday or years ago.

	John Brown What happened	John Brown The outcome	You What happened	You The outcome
An occasion you wanted to help.	My neighbour's husband died suddenly —she had to cope with bills and children as well as fixing the house. It was obvious she was finding this hard.	Not long after this our grandchildren came to stay. They seemed to get on well with the neighbour's children. Now her children come to us sometimes and we babysit for her. Last time I showed her how to fix her washing machine.		
An occasion when you felt strongly about something.	I was annoyed when I saw that our local bus service was being cut back.	I wasn't sure who to complain to so I didn't do anything about it. But I'm still annoyed.		
An occasion when you could see the need for something which you could do.	One of my workmates is a bachelor —his mother lives in the country and wanted to come and stay with him but she is too frail to travel on her own.	I could easily have offered to drive her in my car, but I did not like to offer. In the end he ordered a taxi but I know it cost him a lot of money.		
An occasion when you were asked to help.	Someone at the pub told me about a history group which was getting ready to publish a little book of local memories of our town. I've been in the print all my working life so they asked me if I could show them how to lay it out.	I would have liked to have helped—but I was a bit busy about that time. I thought it might be taking on too much, but it sounded interesting though.		
An occasion when you were asked to help but didn't see the need.	My daughter told me that her friend's husband had been knocking her about again. She asked me if I would help the woman move out while he was away on business.	I told her no. I felt I shouldn't get involved. When she landed up in hospital a few months later I wished I had helped her after all.		

114

Giving assistance John Brown	Knowledge	Skills	Sympathy	Interest	Conviction
Coping after a crisis.	✓	✓	✓		
Loss of service.				✓	✓
The 'one-off' offer to help.		✓	✓		
Working in a community group.	✓	✓		✓	
You					

Giving Assistance

The chart below sets out for you various aspects of assistance that John Brown could have given in four situations. Look at it and then see if you can work out the different aspects of assistance you might give using the examples you have already chosen.

If you look at John Brown's examples in terms of their wider implications for him and his friends, neighbours and community it may be possible to draw out some similarities with the examples from your own life.

In the case of his widowed neighbour and his workmate there could easily have been some paid professional worker who could have helped. But also in both cases the help that was needed — babysitting, house maintenance, driving — was the sort of help anyone could offer. It is also the kind of help which, though not dramatic, can make a great deal of difference to the quality of someone's life.

In the case of the bus service and local history group, John Brown would have had to have found out a bit more about the area he lived in and the bus service. In both cases he might have found himself learning new skills, coping with new situations and perhaps feeling more a part of what went on around him.

Getting involved

Of course it's true that while they are at work or bringing up a family many people find they have very little time left for helping out or getting involved with groups or projects. But it's something you may have more time for in retirement.

In reading through this topic you have probably realised that you have had some considerable experience of helping out in your life. There's no need to limit the helping and being helped to family and friends. You can widen your scope now you have more time and may well find it rewarding. Widening your scope may mean getting involved with what is commonly called 'voluntary work'. If the name puts you off ignore it and just think of it as helping out — lending a hand where it's needed — but stretching a bit farther than you have previously.

Working as a hobby

These quotes are taken from people involved in a good neighbouring scheme organised through a volunteer centre. They illustrate the kind of reasons people give for becoming involved with volunteer work and the satisfaction they receive.

"It's not self satisfaction. It's the feeling of doing something with one's life."

"At least I can feel I did something with my life apart from the housework."

"It's another form of contact."

"We all want to be needed. It's a biological need."

"I don't like the word 'do gooder'. It gives me a great deal of pleasure."

"I don't like to think of my skills being wasted when I can use them to help others."

If you feel you would like to get involved in some way but are not sure how to go about it or what would suit you, the rest of this topic may be of help.

Starting out

A good way of discovering the range of activities in your area is to go to a volunteer centre. They act rather like a job centre in matching peoples' skills and preferences to available activities.

Most large towns will have a volunteer centre listed in the telephone directory.

Many areas will have an employment fellowship centre. These centres are linked to The Employment Fellowship, a national charity experienced in providing activities for the retired and elderly. Also nationally there is REACH – Retired Executives Action Clearing House. Your local Citizens Advice Bureau will be able to advise you on these and other organisations in the area.

Having made your initial contact you may be given an appointment for an interview, or you may be interviewed on the spot if you call in. From then on the whole process may seem familiar, rather like an interview for full-time work.

The interview

At the interview you will be asked about your background, interests and preferences.

There may seem to be a lot of bureaucracy and paper work at this stage but all the information given will be confidential and only the organiser will have access to it, so there is no need to worry.

There is a reason for these formalities. It is as well for you to be aware from the outset that what you will be getting involved in will mean commitment and serious consideration. And, it helps if the organiser knows you well enough to ensure that your interests and skills can be used where they are needed most.

On the right is a copy of the kind of record which a Volunteer Centre would keep for each volunteer. Fill the form in to help you work out what you want to do.

As you can see, the questions divide up roughly into two main groups:

o **Type of involvement**
The sort of work you prefer.
Your special skills and interest.
Any voluntary work experience you may have.

o **Amount of involvement**
The time you have available.
How often you are available.
What other family commitments you may have.

lb

Fuller Volunteer Interview Form & Record Sheet
CONFIDENTIAL

Date . . . .
Interviewed by . . . .

Mr/Mrs/Miss

Name

Address

Telephone   Home   Work

Age

Family commitments
(if any)

Time available   Frequency

Occupation(s)

Voluntary work
experience
(if any)
past and present

Transport and Escort
(circle appropriately)

use of car/driver but no car/non-driver
available to drive/regularly/occasionally/in emergency
available to escort/regularly/occasionally/in emergency

Work Preference (circle first choice and tick others)
1. elderly, mentally handicapped, mentally ill, physically handicapped, children, families.
2. babysitting, befriending, escorting, gardening, granny sitting, odd jobs, shopping/errands, transporting with car, wheelchair pushing, holiday play projects, club/groups/residential homes.
OTHER (please specify)

In addition to the above, are you interested in working with other volunteers on specific projects? YES/NO

Special skills or Interests (circle first choice and tick others)

			Others
Animals	Driving	Listening	Repairing
Babycare	Gardening	Organising	Talking
Church	Hairdressing	Painting	Typing
activities	Languages	Reading	
Cooking			

Name and Addresses of two referees
1.   2.

Where did you hear about us?

Type of involvement

Much depends not only on what the particular volunteer organiser has to offer but also, on what you want to do. At a volunteer centre, the range of activities can be immense. Requests for help may come directly from individuals, or they may be referred by organisations or professional workers in, for example, the social services or education departments.

During the interview you may hear of things which are new to you but which seem interesting and attractive. The interview helps you to discover what is available but also it may result in you finding that you have more to offer than you had realised.

Amount of involvement

Work out how much spare time you think you will have and don't promise too much at first. Many organisations are desperate for help. It is not fair on you or the group if you offer more than you can manage and then have to drop out. It may sound a little formal but a contract or a written agreement describing your job can be a great help, particularly if you feel like changing later on.

Going straight to a particular service

You may be sure about the type of job you want. If this is the case you can by-pass the volunteer centre and inquire directly to the organisation you have in mind. Most hospitals and probation departments have someone whose special interest is the organisation of volunteers. The same may be true for your social services or education department. The formalities will be the same as at the volunteer centre.

Training

For most voluntary activities no special training is needed, though you will need to draw heavily on your own experience of dealing with the full range of situations.

However, some types of work do need some specific training.

For bereavement counselling, adult literacy, work with the Samaritans or for the victims of crime, you will be expected to attend training sessions. In some areas, the probation and after-care service will also provide a short training programme. The sessions are usually on a weekly basis and will aim to

familiarise you with appropriate resources. You will also be taught how to listen and cope with emotional stress.

Apart from these specific training programmes, most volunteer centres run weekend or evening meetings at which you can learn ways of becoming a sympathetic and careful helper. For example, there may be sessions when volunteers can become more aware of what it means to be blind or confined to a wheelchair.

Checklist for better volunteering

Here are some hints which should help you to get the most out of volunteering and enable you to make a useful contribution.

o Draw up a chart of skills, preferences, time and experience, use this as a way of assessing how appropriate a voluntary job is likely to be to you.

o Be clear about what you think you can offer — this means saying firmly what you will *not* do.

o Ask as many questions as you feel like about the place you are going to be working in and the people you will meet.

o Go back to your volunteer organiser, if you have one, soon after you have started; he or she will like to know how you are getting on.

o If you feel you have taken on too much — then say so.

o If you want a change — or more to do — say so.

o If there are allowances for travel (or for lunch) then do claim these. You may not need them — but others may. Not claiming makes it harder for them to draw their necessary expenses.

o Talk to other volunteers. Your organiser may put on social evenings or day-time events when you can all get to know one another. Meeting other people through volunteering is a way of widening your social circle — it can also be a way of picking up useful advice and help.

For many people there are few problems with volunteering. But occasionally people feel unhappy about what they've taken on. Problems however *can* be sorted out, as the following examples show.

Flo Robinson

Flo retired about a year ago. She has always liked children and enjoys reading and feels that her job as a secretary to a local authority transport manager called for a great deal of patience and tact.

When she went to her volunteer workers' centre she said she would be interested in helping children who find reading a problem. She was pleased when she heard that her local education authority wanted volunteers who would be prepared to teach children at their homes. She is fit and active and doesn't mind getting out and about and was glad to find that her fares would be paid, in her area there was no free transport for pensioners. But Flo found that the job was not what she expected. The scheme was organised by someone in the education department that she never met; and it turned out that the children had far more problems than simply not being able to read. She also found that too much of her time was taken up in travelling and she found this was tiring. Flo gave up the scheme.

What went wrong for Flo?

During the interview with the volunteer centre Flo had given information about the skills and experience she possessed and would like to use, her own preferences on the sort of work she would like to be involved in and the time she had available.

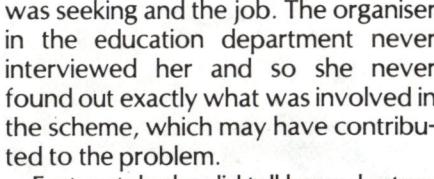

The following chart summarises the information she gave at the interview.

Skills	Patience, tact.
Preferences	Children, reading.
Time	2 hours a day, 2 days a week.
Experience	Secretarial work.

The job Flo was given required specialised skills. Patience and tact were not enough in this situation, nor was her own liking for children and for reading sufficient.

The job involved a long bus ride to get there and back so by the time she had completed the round trip she was not only exhausted but most of the day had gone. This wasn't the two hours a day involvement she had been looking for.

Her secretarial experience in no way helped her to deal with the sort of problems she was now faced with. She felt helpless and out of her depth.

The outcome

In Flo's case there was a mismatch between the kind of involvement she was seeking and the job. The organiser in the education department never interviewed her and so she never found out exactly what was involved in the scheme, which may have contributed to the problem.

Fortunately she did tell her volunteer organiser about her problems. A few weeks later she began working with a group who ran a toy library for mentally and physically handicapped children. She mainly plays with the children or reads stories while their mums and dads have a cup of tea and a chat in peace.

The toy library is open only one afternoon a week, which she finds enough at present. But in the autumn she may feel like doing a little more, so she's thinking about offering to be the group's librarian.

Bill Jobbings

Bill is partially sighted and widowed. He lives with his married daughter, but he finds the days rather long while the family is out at work. When he visited the volunteers' co-ordinator he wondered what he could offer apart from friendship and a sense of humour. During the interview it emerged that he was very fond of playing the piano and had in the past often played at concert parties.

The co-ordinator suggested he went along to an old peoples' home and played some tunes a couple of afternoons a week. Bill liked this idea and felt he could manage the journey by bus. At first, things seemed to be going reasonably well, but, after a while, he began to feel that he was becoming part of the wallpaper — he couldn't really detect any strong interest in his playing. Things came to a head in his fourth week when one of the more vocal residents asked him if he'd come to do his practice. He felt this was too much and he didn't go, back again.

What went wrong for Bill?

This is Bill's chart, summarising the information he gave at the interview with the volunteer centre.

Skills	Sense of humour, play piano.
Preferences	Working with other people.
Time	One or two days a week.
Experience	Have played the piano at concert parties.

Bill was able to use his skill at playing the piano but was unable to make the personal contact he wanted with the people at the home. This was partly because nobody had prepared the way or introduced him at the home, and partly because he had no experience of dealing with this type of audience.

In other ways the job suited Bill very well. It didn't involve any more time than he wanted to spend, it involved working with other people, and it involved playing the piano. With just a little more thought by the organisers Bill could probably have been quite happy at the home.

The outcome

Bill never did go back to the organiser, but when two of his friends from the local pub found out about his piano playing they got him to do a short session on the pub piano. After that somebody else in the pub whose mother lived in a sheltered housing scheme asked him if he'd like to play there occasionally. With his confidence restored Bill was soon a regular visitor at the sheltered housing scheme and learned quickly how to involve his audience in the music and singing.

Working for money

Many retired people consider at some point about taking up a job again. The reasons range from shortage of money or missing friends at work, to simply being bored at home.

It is an important decision to make — for one thing it is to some extent a decision to put off retirement proper.

The first activity in this topic asks you to think carefully about the *reasons* why you might want to take up work in retirement. If you decide that you do, the rest of the topic examines the *strategies* you could then adopt in seeking paid employment, and at some of the possible implications of working in retirement.

Activity 1

Use your skill for yourself

Can you use your professional expertise in one of the following:	I am able	There is likely to be a demand
Consultancy.		
Partnership/group advisory service.		
Lectures/training sessions/counselling.		
Absentee coverage on an occasional basis.		
Other work done at home e.g. finance, accounts, costing.		

Can you use your practical expertise in one of the following:	I am able	There is likely to be a demand
Manual.		
Craft.		
Technical.		
Artistic.		
Domestic.		
Clinical.		

Remember it pays to do some market research.
You could try some of the following:

o Do some checking up on the area you have chosen to work in and find out if others are already offering the service or expertise you want to offer.
o If the market is already satisfied either look at a new area or consider how you can make your service different or complementary to what already exists.
o If you are offering something new, advertise 'on spec' in local newspapers and shops to test local response.
o If you want to develop on a larger scale consult the nearest Small Firms Information service centre provided by the Department of Industry.

Planning to be Self-Employed?
Ask at your local D.H.S.S. office for the following leaflets:
N.P.18 National Insurance Guides
N.I.41 for the self-employed
N.I.27A Guidance for self-employed people with small earnings

Activity 2

Look for new ideas

While some employers may believe that in some occupations ability declines with age and that older workers are less adaptable to change, it is comforting to note that in fact employers often prefer older workers as employees because:

o They recognise their qualities of loyalty, reliability and good standards of work.
o They value judgement acquired with experience.
o They can usually depend upon their good time-keeping habits.
o They know the retired are not looking for promotion.
o They are usually available to work flexible hours.

So, if you want employment in retirement make sure you are looking in the right place and be persistent. But do beware of the occasional employer who may exploit – offering low pay and bad conditions.

Places to look for part-time work

Have you tried the following:

o Job Centres will advise you of part-time work and do not mind how often you remind them that you are still available (telephone if you prefer this to calling).

o Local newspapers.
o Local newsagents 'notice boards'.
o Your former firm.
o Your friends and neighbours – if asked they will keep a look out. Most part-time work is discovered by word of mouth.

o An employment fellowship centre (schemes run by retired people which provide employment in workshops and centres for the retired). If there isn't one in your area, perhaps you and your friends could start one. The employment fellowship will help you get started. Ask your local Citizens Advice Bureau for their nearest address.

o Buretire U.K. Ltd – an organisation affiliated to the Employment Fellowship which sponsors part-time employment opportunities for the

Here are some ideas to start you off. Fill in the chart.	I am willing to do	There is likely to be demand for
Electoral Roll (clerical).		
Routine clerical work (industry and business).		
Agents (pools, promoters).		
Book keeping.		
Occasional retail sellers.		
Distributors (leaflets).		
Lollipop men/women.		
Exhibition work and sales promotion.		
Gardeners.		
Caretakers.		
Home help.		
Cashiers.		
Jobbing repair work.		
Typing.		
Machining.		

retired and disabled. It covers all occupations.

If there is no Buretire Service in your area, here is another opportunity for self help. Contact the Development Manager for advice on getting started.

o Professional journals.
o A number of small commercial employment agencies cater exclusively for redundant and early retired experienced executives and also for the retired with specialised skills e.g. accountancy, technical writing, translating etc.

In times of economic depression, part-time jobs are not easy to find. However, local conditions are constantly changing and there are often opportunities open to the retired which may not attract other groups of would-be workers. Be prepared to seek out opportunities. Census figures show that within one to two years after statutory retirement a significant number of people seek work.

Why work in retirement? The following reasons are often given. Read them through and tick those appropriate to you.	Tick	Comments
1. I must have more money to meet expenses.		
2. I would like a little extra 'movement' money for treats and luxuries.		
3. I realised I could use my hobby to make money.		
4. I want to go on using my skills and I might as well get paid for it.		
5. I like the companionship at work.		
6. I've always wanted to work for myself but just couldn't make the break before. I can now.		
7. I know I'll miss work too much to give it up altogether.		
8. I like my job and I'd jump at the chance to carry on.		
9. Having a job gives my life some purpose.		
10. Doing a job keeps me well and active.		
11. This offer came up so I accepted without thinking much about it.		
12. My partner/former employer/former customers/friends keep on suggesting it.		
13. I don't know what to do with all the extra time at home.		
14. It's the only way I can get out from under my partner's feet.		
15. My partner is still working so I thought I should carry on.		

If you have ticked any of the statements numbered 1–4, ask yourself: **Where do your priorities lie?**
If they are largely concerned with the earning power a job would yield, think for a moment whether you are prepared to forfeit other interests and leisure time to that particular priority.

If you have ticked any of the statements numbered 5–10, ask yourself: **Do you have positive feelings about keeping on?**
If you have ticks in this group, your feelings about continuing work in retirement are positive ones. It will help your decision making if you sort out the motives that lie behind your choices. For example, if you have ticked "like companionship at work", is this because you think you will be able to adjust to the loss of those companions by finding new ones in a part-time job? Is this right for you or are you simply shelving a difficulty for a later date when you will still be looking for ways of replacing work mates?

Now write in your comments.

If you have ticked any of the statements numbered 11–15 ask yourself: **Have you really thought enough about working in retirement?**
These are really vague reasons for carrying on working. It might, for example, be a good idea to give your partner some breathing space from time to time but is this the best reason for restricting your own retirement? Think hard about your motivation and then fill in the comments section.

Strategies

If you are quite sure you want to look for work in retirement the next thing to consider is the type of work you would prefer, and the strategies you could use to obtain it. The chart below describes the choices that need to be made.

Choosing to carry on working for your present employer doing the same job will have very different implications from taking an entirely new job, or a different job with the same employer. The activities which follow look more closely at the options open to you if you choose to take a different job in retirement.

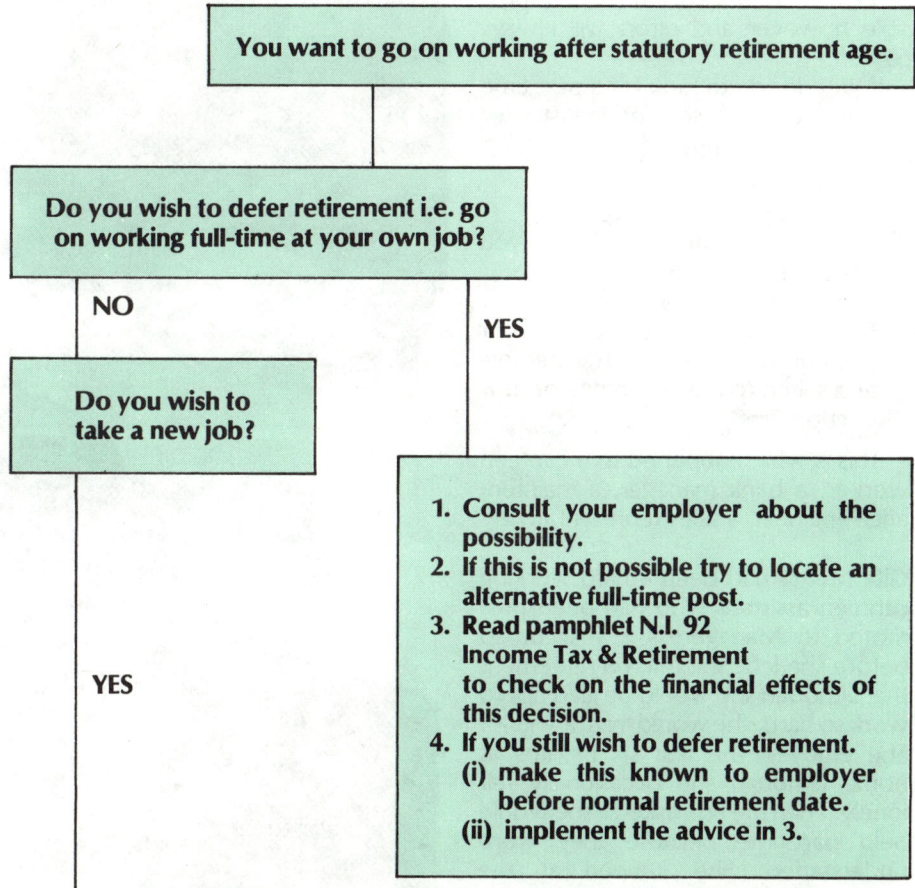

If you've decided from the diagram that you do want to do part-time work, then there are several different areas that you may want to explore.

Use your skills for yourself
You may feel you have skills you'd like to use as a self-employed. Perhaps these are professional skills from past work experience, or perhaps they are practical skills either from work or interests that you've had during your life. If you want to explore ideas about using your skills in this way the Activity 1 will help.

Look for new ideas
You may not be particularly concerned to use skills you already have. If it's just a job you're looking for (and remember any job will bring new skills), the Activity 2 should help by presenting you with some ideas.
Once you've done Activity 2 though, try Activity 3 as well which should help you think about some of the implications of being employed in new circumstances.

Use your skills for others
You may prefer to be an employee. This might be at your present place of work or at another employer's. If you are presented with the posibility of doing a different sort of job at your present place of work it's worth thinking about any problems you might have. On the other hand, going to a different employer could present it's own problems. Activity 3 should help you to explore these ideas.

Activity 3

Use your skills for others

It's as well to realise that at present (1982) the likelihood of being requested to stay on in a job beyond retirement age is remote. The same applies to the possibility of being able to secure alternative employment in the same skill or profession as before. It is never impossible however and effort will always pay off.

If you decide to look for a part-time job in the same sort of industry or profession, be prepared to:

o Be adaptable.
o Accept a change in status.
o Be paid lower rates of pay than you have been accustomed to.
o Work unsocial hours.
o Be flexible enough to see that your present skills may be transferable and suited to a whole range of new occupations.

This is what happened to a canteen worker, a bank manager, a maintenance engineer, a sales representative.

Gita Mehta had been a hard working canteen assistant who had been promoted to Manageress a year or so before she left. She felt, on retirement that although she would be glad not to work so hard, she would miss 'the girls'. She enjoyed the first six months at home although she occasionally felt lonely. Then the firm asked if she would help part-time because they were understaffed. She jumped at the chance.

Bill Norton, formerly a bank manager, decided to work part-time until his wife, a teacher, had retired. While the bank was willing to employ him as an occasional relief manager he decided he wanted a change. Within a short time of retiring the Job Centre offered him a part-time job as a book-keeper at a glass company. He considered this but eventually decided to take the job as a cost clerk at the leisure centre which had been advertised in the local paper.

George Grey, a maintenance engineer, nursed a sick wife up to and immediately after his retirement. Her death left him at a loss and he went

back to his firm to see if they could offer him anything 'just to fill the time'. He almost said 'no' when they suggested he help out the supervisor with the training of apprentices for a few hours a week. He thought he would not have the patience but finds he enjoys it.

Barry Stuart, a sales representative, found he was restless after retirement. His pension from his former job was very small and he needed some extra income. Although he could have found some work in selling, his wife begged him to try something that would not

involve so much travel. A friend of his recommended him for a part-time job as warehouseman with one of his former customers.

The chart opposite lists a number of problems that can arise for people returning to work either at their original work place or at a new occupation. Using the information given on Gita, Bill, George and Barry, put a tick on the chart to indicate which of the problems *might* arise for each of them. Then work through the chart again indicating which of the problems might apply to you.

Might this be a problem?	For Gita	For Bill	For George	For Barry	For You
Adjusting to being an 'ordinary' helper along side workers who knew them as 'the boss'.					
Not being able to make decisions they believe should be made.					
Not being asked for advice when they think they could give it.					
Being bored by routine tasks.					
Working in an environment not accustomed to.					
Adjusting to having a different status.					
Having less freedom and mobility on the job.					
Working alongside younger employees.					
Noticing that former systems had been discarded and copying with any new ones.					
Being under-estimated by new workers who didn't know them, before.					
Working at jobs they were unaccustomed to.					

Conditions of employment

However you find a job, whether a chance offer comes up or you have to seek out an opportunity for yourself, think about the sort of conditions you want.

To help yourself think about this, it might be a good idea to draw up a list of the sort of conditions you are prepared to accept. You can measure this against any opportunities that come your way.

Here are some questions you might ask yourself to provide the information you need to work out your list of the conditions of employment acceptable to you.

How many hours a week are you prepared to spend on work?
Is it important which times of the day or week you are prepared to spend on work? For instance are there times in the week when you are not able or willing to work? How many of your other tasks or interests are tied to specific times of a week?
Would you be prepared to do irregular hours, seasonal work, weekend work?
How far are you prepared to travel to work?
How much time are you prepared to spend travelling to a job?
How much money are you prepared to spend on fares, petrol, lunches and so on?
Are you prepared to do mentally demanding work?
Are you prepared to accept a down grading of your income bracket?
Are you prepared to accept a down-grading of your status at work?

James Cairns had been retired for two years when the possibility of some part-time work book-keeping with a local firm came up. He found the idea quite attractive. The firm seemed reasonably flexible over arrangements so he sat down to work out what ideally his conditions would be.

Some things James was definite about. He was sure he didn't want weekend work and did want to work for someone else. Some things he had no strong views on, for instance he wasn't bothered about the money, or about time of day.

Have a look at James' list (below) as a guide to drawing up one of your own. Use it to help you weigh up any job opportunities you have.

A flexible list of course will probably give you more opportunities. The more specific you are and the longer your list of conditions the longer you may have to wait. And if you find that none of the opportunities you get measure up to your list of conditions it might be worthwhile asking yourself again *"Do I really want a part-time job? — Am I prepared to make the proper effort required?"*

Once you start part-time work, keep your list of conditions and if you run into difficulties, check out the various items on your list. For instance have the hours of the job expanded beyond what you wanted? Is it more demanding than you can cope with? Are out of pocket expenses more than you anticipated?

In this way you will be more able to gain the full benefits of any work you take on.

James Cairns' list of conditions

- 20 hours a week, maximum.
- Monday-Friday (no weekend work).
- Mornings *or* afternoons (would prefer not to work on Wednesday afternoons, it would clash with my volunteer work at the hospital).
- I'm not prepared to work irregular hours.
- Don't mind about fares, lunches etc as long as I break even.
- Do want to work for someone else.
- Don't want anything too demanding (my wife used to complain I was obsessed with work, so I don't want to bring problems home with me).

Out and about

This topic looks at three people, a married couple living in Manchester and a woman living alone in Edinburgh, who came to discover that there is more to the areas they live in than they had supposed. Reading these case studies and working through the activities may help you in thinking about your own approach to getting out and about in your own neighbourhood.

How well do you know the area you live in? You may have lived in the same neighbourhood all your life and still not know much about it.

Perhaps you have always commuted to work and gone away a lot at weekends. Perhaps you have recently moved to a new area. Some people seem to be able to move into a new area and soon know everybody and everything going on. Others can live in the same house for years and hardly know their next door neighbours.

Getting to know your own area can be rewarding in itself but can also help you to make new acquaintances and branch out into different activities as well.

Mildred — places, people and activities

Mildred is 67. She moved to Edinburgh with her husband seven years ago when they both retired, to be near their son and his family. Within a year of moving, their son was offered a promotion which involved working in Libya and his whole family moved out there. Eighteen months later, her husband died and Mildred found herself on her own in a city she still felt was not her home. Financially she was quite comfortably off. She kept her car but still found very little to fill her time. She still had a few friends from before her husband's death but found it awkward seeing them now because it was too strong a reminder for all concerned that he was no longer alive. She found she could go from one day to the next without speaking to anyone, except for a few words with shop assistants.

On one of his leaves from Libya, her son presented her with a boisterous young red setter. She suspected it had been bought for the family and they had found it rather too much of a handful and passed it on to her. She did find that exercising it got her out of the house more than before and she enjoyed the walks across Bruntsfield Links and the Meadows, sometimes even as far as Holyrood Park. She had always felt a bit self-conscious ambling about on her own but with a dog she felt more purposeful and it was surprisingly easy to stop and have a chat with other dog owners or passers by.

It was from one of these conversations that she found out about the dog training classes being held locally and since she found the red setter difficult to control, she went along to them. The only other owner of a red setter at the class was Sybil and they soon became friends. Sybil had always lived in that area of Edinburgh, had been a teacher and was also widowed. She was very active in the Cockburn Association, an organisation to save historic buildings from being demolished to make way for redevelopments. Mildred had developed a strong affection for the area on her walks through it with her dog. She felt sympathetic towards the aims of the Association and soon joined it to become an enthusiastic member. Before long, she was writing letters to the local papers and to her M.P. and petitioning the council whenever it looked as though the planners were going to condemn another perfectly good tenement building. This involvement with local politics brought her into contact with a local pensioners association group, of which she became an active member. Her interest in local architecture led her to join an evening class run by the University extra mural department on Edinburgh's architectural heritage. It was through Mildred talking to other members of the class, that they discovered a common enthusiasm for playing bridge and organised a bridge circle meeting about once a week in each other's homes.

Making a start

At this point Mildred wrote down a short list of her activities as they stood one year ago. She then organised a branching chart to indicate how her involvement with places, people and activities had developed in the last year. Her chart shows how after the initial step of going to dog training classes she was able to branch out into other activities.

1 year ago

Go to dog training classes once a week.
Go shopping.
Drop in to see Sybil.
Daily walk with the dog.

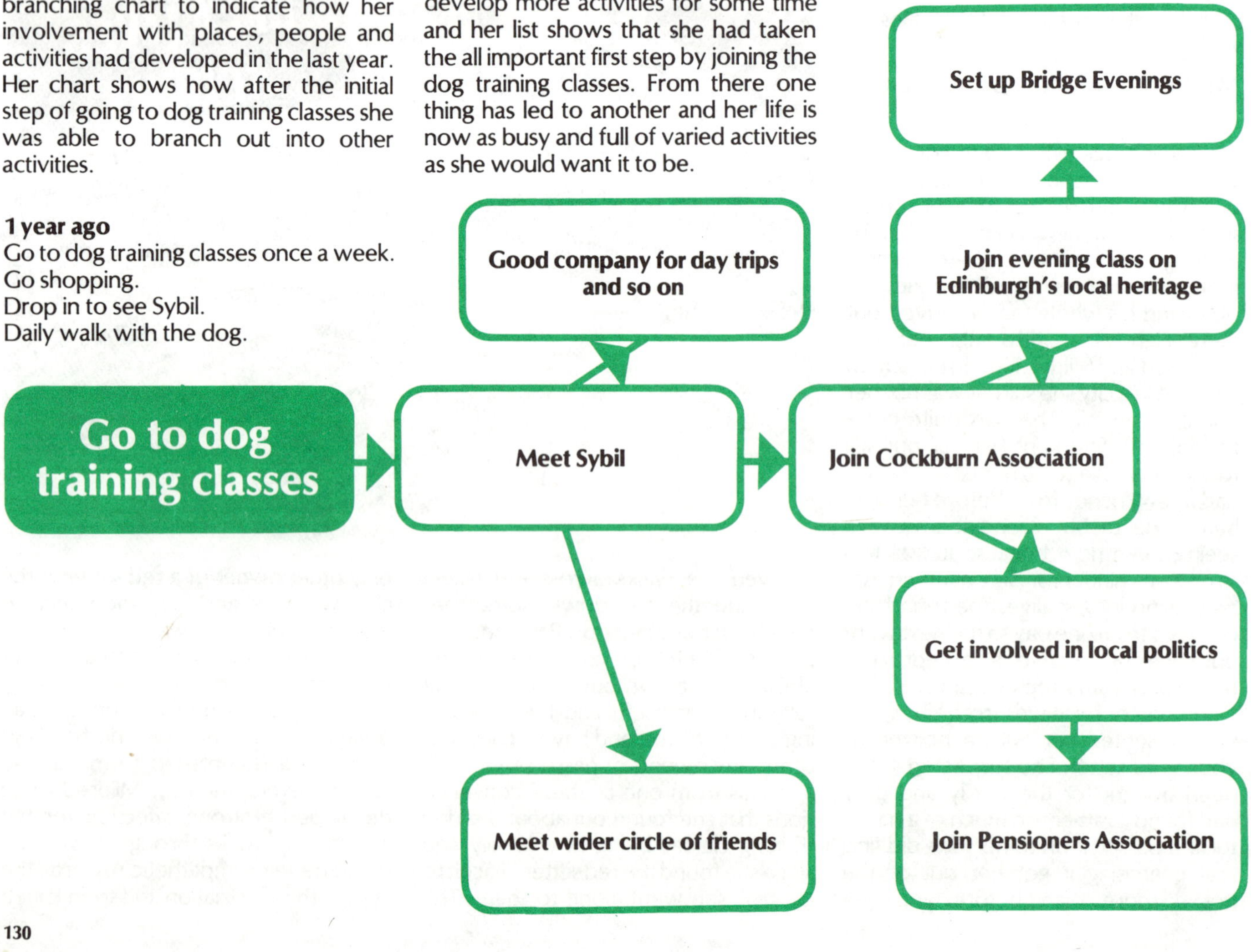

It's easy for Mildred to say after the event 'one thing just led to another'. But remember that she had to put a lot of her own energy into following things up and making things happen for herself at each stage of the chart.

Mildred's range of activities has increased quite significantly over the past year. She had been anxious to develop more activities for some time and her list shows that she had taken the all important first step by joining the dog training classes. From there one thing has led to another and her life is now as busy and full of varied activities as she would want it to be.

Go to dog training classes → Meet Sybil → Join Cockburn Association

Meet Sybil → Good company for day trips and so on

Meet Sybil → Meet wider circle of friends

Join Cockburn Association → Join evening class on Edinburgh's local heritage

Join evening class on Edinburgh's local heritage → Set up Bridge Evenings

Join Cockburn Association → Get involved in local politics

Get involved in local politics → Join Pensioners Association

Mildred's chart shows a gradual development of activities in a fairly controlled way. She rarely goes into a new activity without knowing something about it or somebody involved in it.

The evening bridge session is a new activity for her. It is the first session of something that she hopes will become a regular event. But the people are familiar to her as they are friends from the University evening class. And of course she is perfectly familiar with the place since it is her own home.

Attending a meeting of the local pensioners association is not an entirely new experience: she has been to two other official meetings but she still feels she doesn't know the ropes very well. Visiting her friend Sybil is entirely familiar to her. Sometimes they take the dogs out for a walk together. Also, it gives Mildred the chance to chat about Cockburn Association matters or catch up on news of a local planning development. They are planning a day trip to Anstruther in the car which will introduce a new element.

None of the new events in Mildred's life are entirely unfamiliar to her. She has found from experience that it's very hard to start on something entirely new, but it's much easier to branch out from activities she is already involved in. So when she does try something new she takes care that at least some of the elements of the event, the places, the people or the activity, are to some degree familiar to her.

So, next she makes up a list to assess this degree of familiarity of things she will be doing over the next fortnight or so.

o Evening bridge session. The first one is at my house.
o Attend a social evening of members of the pensioners association at the house of one of the members.
o Daily walk with the dog over Bruntsfield Links and the Meadows.
o Make a day-trip in the car, with Sybil, to the Fisheries Museum at Anstruther.
o Attend a meeting of the local Pensioners Association.
o Drop in to see Sybil.
o Take a bus down to the High Street to have a look at some properties the council are proposing to sell for private development.

She then looked at all these events and broke down each one into its component parts: places, people and activities. Look at the chart that shows this.

With the aid of this chart she was able to assess the degree of her familiarity with each of these component parts. By looking at the events broken down in this way she could see which balance she was happiest with and perhaps this would lead her to seeking a comparable balance for any new events she might become involved with in the future.

Mildred was happiest with a reasonably high degree of familiarity overall. So, in the future if she was for example planning to go to a residential weekend course on architecture she might try and persuade Sybil to go with her. This would enable her to maintain the balance with which she is most comfortable. Other people might feel perfectly happy about a higher proportion than Mildred of unfamiliar components.

Event			What Mildred did
Place	**Activity**	**People**	o Broke down each event into its individual components of people, places and activity.
My house.	**Evening Bridge session.**	**Friends from the evening class.**	o Looked at each event and assessed which of the three components were very familiar, which were familiar and which were unfamiliar.
A house in Nicholson St.	**Meeting of the Pensioners Assoc.**	**Other member.**	o To help clarify this to herself she shaded very familiar components green, familiar components light green and unfamiliar components she left white.
Bruntsfield Links and the Meadows.	**Walking the dog.**	**Other dog owners.**	o Try and do a familiarity chart for yourself.
Anstruther.	**Day trip in the car.**	**Sybil.**	
House in Marchmont.	**Pensioners Assoc. social evening.**	**Other members.**	
Sybil's house.	**Drop in to see Sybil.**	**Sybil.**	
High Street.	**Bus trip to look at property threatened with re-development.**	**On my own.**	

Patrick and Theresa — places, people and activities

Patrick and Theresa are both 65. They have two daughters, one working in London, the other lives nearby and has a young family. Patrick has lived in the same part of Manchester all his life. He worked in an office at the nearby hospital for 35 years before his retirement just under a year ago.

Patrick likes a steady routine. When he was working at the hospital he always took the same bus to work and the same bus home again. Several years ago he used to do some overtime and go for the occasional pint and a game of darts with his office friends after work, but he gave that up.

He just wasn't interested in always having something to do and somewhere to go in an evening when all he wanted to do was put his feet up and watch the television. At weekends he would generally tend the garden, play bowls at the local park or watch television. He and Theresa didn't often go out in the evenings but they did have friends among their neighbours, many of whom they had known for years, and they sometimes visited each others' houses. They saw their daughter and her family at least once a week.

Before Patrick left work they suggested to him that it would be a big help to have a man of his experience as a voluntary helper at the hospital, so he agreed to do two afternoons a week. But when he did retire he still found he had a lot of time on his hands, and although he was an enthusiastic television viewer the novelty of being able to watch it any time during the day soon wore off.

It was Theresa who one day suggested that they go to the museum not having actually been in it since she was a child. Here they noticed a poster advertising a free tour of a local historic building which was only ½ mile from where they lived. They made inquiries about it at the education section in the library and came away with a lot of leaflets on other services the museum provided. Patrick was surprised to find there was so much of historical interest in the area he lived in, that he had never known about.

He became particularly interested in industrial buildings and quite informed

on which were the best tours to go on, and the most interesting talks to attend. Talking to other people at these events he learned about a whole range of activities going on in Manchester that he never knew existed — and most of them free.

From that first step they branched out into a wide range of activities and

events which brought great variety and interest to their first year of retirement.

On some weekdays they do free guided tours of the Manchester town hall. Patrick had only ever been in a few times in his life. He now drops in whenever he's in town to have a look at their 'What's on this month' noticeboard and pick up the free leaflets giving information on local entertainments, activities and services.

They took a day trip to the coast through the 'Breakaway' club advertised in the Altrincham and Sale Guardian. You don't have to join the club, if you read the paper you are automatically a member.

They went on a special day of 'Activities for the over 50s', run by the local leisure centre. It only cost them 50p each. They met some people there who shared the same interests. Patrick has now joined the indoor bowls club at the leisure centre and they both do relaxation and yoga classes.

They also found out about a retirement group that meets locally and gets in a lot of interesting speakers. They've had demonstrations and talks from the Gas Board and the Electricity Board on the most economic use of fuel, on cooking for one or two, and a cooking demonstration after which they were able to eat the results.

They discovered that the amateur dramatics group at the theatre in Altrincham gave free entry to pensioners into their dress rehearsals. They enjoyed going along to these more than they

had ever enjoyed going along to the theatre. It was a more relaxed atmosphere and the cast were really interested to know what they thought of the production.

Neither of them has paid full price for a hair cut since they found out, through the retirement group, that one of the Further Education Colleges has a hairdressing department and is pleased to have volunteers to practise on. It's much more fun than going to the proper hairdresser.

It was through this contact with the college that some of the members of their retirement group were able to join in with a college day trip to the House of Commons.

They got to know so many local people over the year that they were called in to help organise the annual Carnival Week. They put in a lot of work during June but had great fun and made many new friends.

Although Patrick and Theresa had lived in the same district of the same city for most of their lives they had never had the time or the inclination to explore it thoroughly. They knew certain parts of the area well, and they knew a few of the people who lived there well. But in retirement they were able to explore much more widely and take more of an interest in what was on offer in their area. They scanned the local papers for any local events, they went into libraries, sports centres, museums and colleges to find out what was going on, and they were prepared to try anything or go anywhere so long as it sounded interesting and didn't cost too much. They found there was a lot more going on than they had ever suspected.

Patrick and Theresa drew up this branching chart to show how their activities grew over the first year of retirement.

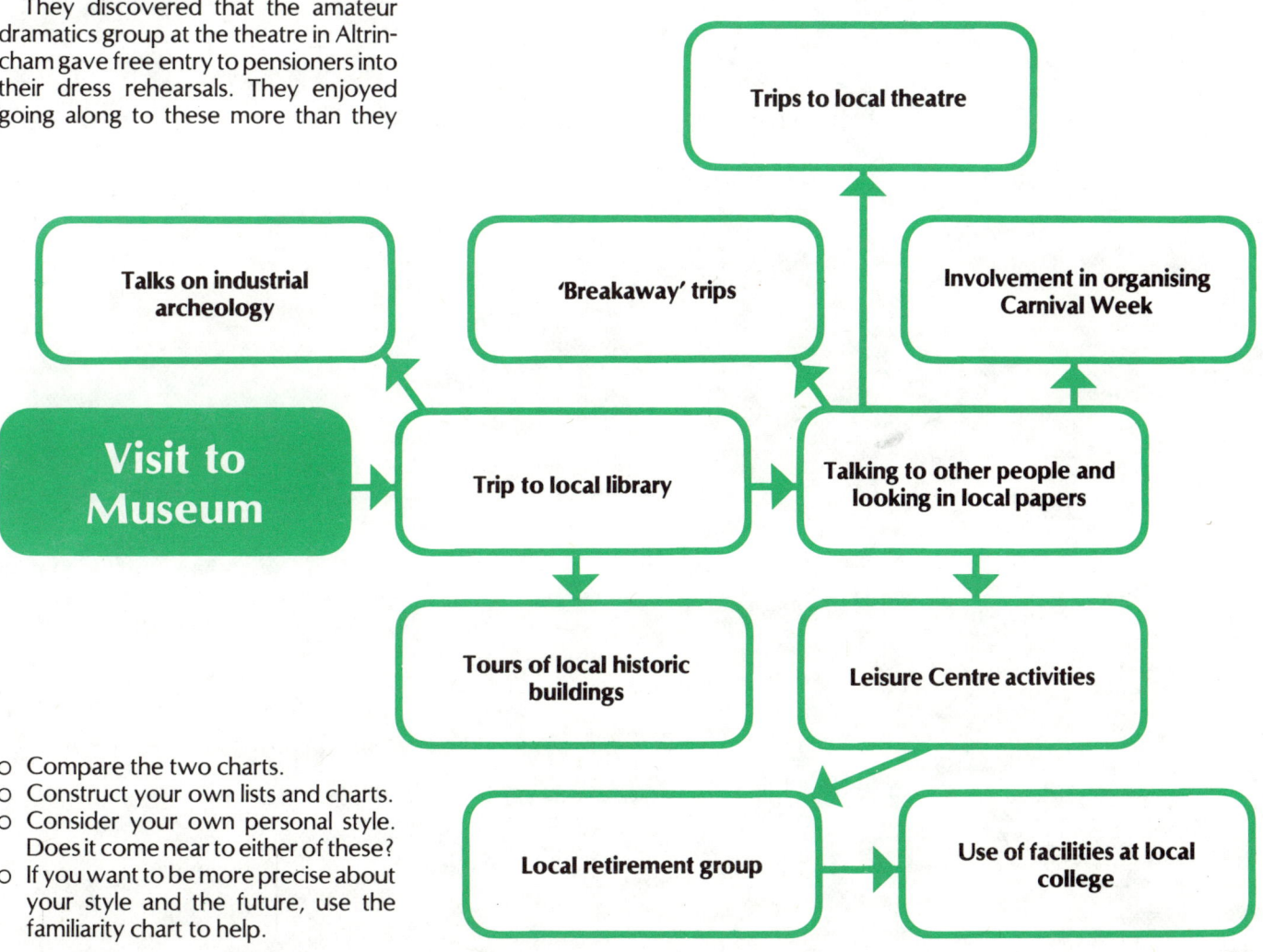

o Compare the two charts.
o Construct your own lists and charts.
o Consider your own personal style. Does it come near to either of these?
o If you want to be more precise about your style and the future, use the familiarity chart to help.

Taking opportunities

After the first novelty of retirement and the changes that it involves there comes the chance to reflect that other changes continue to happen in your life. The topics in this chapter are designed to help you re-evaluate and think about taking new opportunities, putting the stamp on your life you want it to have. You are asked to look at the sort of variety of experience you inject into your everyday life. The health topics deal with responsibility for health care after initial health plans have been made in retirement. The finance topics deal with issues that crop up for everyone: how your handling of money affects the quality of your life and transport and living arrangements. The topics on your social life are about taking action more than making adjustments. Several topics help you explore your view of yourself after you've retired and other people's views too. Finally a number of topics take a look at learning and how it continues through life.

A new lifestyle

The 'honeymoon' period of retirement is usually self centred. Your major satisfactions at this time lie in simply pleasing yourself. All the best holidays, though, come to an end: it is largely because you have to put a time limit on them that they gain 'edge' and add zest to life.

You may decide to keep occupied by doing all the jobs around the house that you never had time for when you were working. But when the house is in apple pie order — what then?

Routine, Ritual and Drama

The 'honeymoon' period is one of the most critical periods of retirement. Unless there is a deliberate time limit on this phase disenchantment will set in and it may then become increasingly difficult to make the necessary adjustments. At work, the daily routine of getting up at a particular time, taking the same journey to the factory, office or shop, time-keeping and dealing with the day's workload, sets up patterns which even if boring provide a dependable, background to daily life.

While at work, people often find themselves involved in small rituals. You rely upon them without being aware of the fact that they generate a sense of security, mark events bringing order and method to what has to be done.

There are few jobs that do not provide dramatic moments which, however we feel about them at the time, add zest to life.

Working life

In these lists to the right are a number of components that contribute to the routines, rituals and dramas of working life. Read through them and tick which ones have been elements in your life. Having looked through the charts you will see just how many of these activities give some colour to everyday life.

It might be useful if you consider the part these three aspects play in your life. Some serve to divide up parts of the day; some to give you a break from work; others help to give a timetable to weeks, months and years.

Typical routines and rituals

Early rising. ☐

Getting ready for work. ☐

Early morning or evening dog walk. ☐

Preparing sandwiches. ☐

Feeding pets. ☐

Quick breath of fresh air at lunch time. ☐

Leaving house tidy. ☐

Gardening. ☐

Speedy breakfast (or substitute). ☐

Buying morning paper. ☐

Pass the time of day with neighbours/fellow commuters. ☐

Clocking on and off. ☐

Plant-watering. ☐

Tea/coffee/smoke breaks. ☐

Getting on with the job within a time schedule. ☐

Asking for advice. ☐

Giving advice. ☐

Having a joke with work fellows. ☐

Calling at the local. ☐

Journey home. ☐

Buying evening paper. ☐

Working overtime. ☐

Looking forward to evening meal and relaxation. ☐

Evening visit to pub. ☐

Watching T.V. ☐

Listening to the news. ☐

Going to church regularly. ☐

Lunchtime visits to pub with work mates. ☐

Works dances, socials, annual outings. ☐

Going to the club. ☐

Making plans for bank holidays. ☐

Making plans for weekends. ☐

Workshop or office celebrations e.g. Christmas, birthdays, apprentice awards, weddings, anniversaries, retirements. ☐

Attending committee meetings and performing at them. ☐

Making speeches. ☐

Planning the working day. ☐

'Fun' events e.g. initiation of apprentices, 'send-offs' for young marrieds, trips, betting syndicates. ☐

Typical dramas

Decision making and problem solving. ☐

Tension arising from likely outcome of decisions. ☐

Confiding in workmates
—about personal affairs
—or about work matters. ☐

Trying to achieve objectives. ☐

Meeting production targets. ☐

Meeting sales targets. ☐

Conflicts with colleagues. ☐

Dealing with crises. ☐

Pressures of overwork. ☐

Having to do unwelcome shift work. ☐

Worries about too little work. ☐

Fear of redundancy. ☐

Negotiating conditions. ☐

Adjusting to re-organisation. ☐

Adjusting to new management. ☐

Adjusting to new technology. ☐

Inspection of products. ☐

Inspection of work. ☐

Dramatic moments may be no more than brief spells of worry or tension, or they may be big emotional experiences, helping you cope with your worries and tension. Often they set the adrenalin flowing and involve bursts of energy, providing a change in pace from the routines and rituals that are distinctive because of their regularity.

How do *you* think of routine and ritual?

You may feel that routine is boring, likely to restrict your freedom, little more than a mindless habit. Perhaps you value routine because it provides order and security. You may see rituals either as too conventional and obsessive or as an agreeable aspect of life. It is not always easy to see the difference. Sometimes routines turn into small rituals (such as always having a traditional Sunday dinner) sometimes into more important ritual ceremonies (like retirement day, silver wedding anniversaries).

Below, together with some examples, are some of the purposes that routines, rituals and dramas can serve both in domestic life and publicly. Look at them and add any examples from your own life that you think contribute to the purposes outlined.

The list shows that such events can provide pace, depth and variety in your life and it is equally necessary after retirement to maintain these elements.

However small scale, an element of drama will not only always be present but is necessary to stimulate everyday life. A retirement that, in attempting to avoid the stresses, strains and crises of work, puts up no challenges to take their place is a dull prospect.

Perhaps you associate drama with stress, strain, worry or friction. Nevertheless, for some people the more 'dramatic' moments in life, even the painful ones, are the moments when they feel really alive.

Do you remember your wartime experiences — army battles, 'dog fights' in the air, dodging the 'U' boats in convoy. Or, as a civilian, do you recall the whine of the V2 or incendiary bombs, rushing to air raid shelters, putting out fires, helping the injured and many more. All these experiences drew out a camaraderie and exceptional strength

---

Routine and rituals can:

Help you to get a clearer idea about your emotions
(Retirement day presentations).

_____

Give a sense of security
(Locking up at night, regular budgeting).

_____

Give a feeling of fulfilment
(Getting the house and garden to rights, always having a pet and caring for it).

_____

Confirm your attitudes
(Weddings, christenings, family gatherings).

_____

Mark the passage of time—daily, monthly, quarterly, annual events
(Holidays, spring cleaning, birthday parties, anniversaries).

_____

Generate atmosphere (Family and other celebrations, entertaining).

_____

Make public statements about values and attitudes held
(Local fêtes, observances of membership of clubs and organisations).

_____

Make public statements about status
(Being appointed to an office—chairman, social secretary, club fixtures organiser).

_____

Strengthen ties
(Family gatherings, regular visiting of friends and family).

_____

Strengthen beliefs
(Religious rituals, attending public parades).

_____

Reinforce order and custom
(Armistice Day, coronations, offering cups of tea in a crisis).

_____

Provide symbols for remembrance
(Birthday rituals, Remembrance Day ceremonies).

_____

Solemnise behaviour and decisions
(Dressing the part for funerals and celebrations of all sorts. Wearing the uniform of national groups at public ceremonies).

_____

Reduce conflict
(Kiss and make up, shake hands).

_____

from ordinary people. They made them value living a good deal more too with smaller dramas. You feel you are making some impact on life if you have met a crisis coolly or if you've become committed to an activity meeting a real need.

Of course, not all the drama that occurs in peoples' lives is a result of facing up to crises. Quite often people inject some drama into day to day life to make a change.

Here are some examples.

For fun, spend a week doing what your partner usually does and ask your partner to do the same.

Try a total change of menus.

Do something unconventional, unexpected, uncharacteristic.

Help with neighbourhood schemes, street parties. If they've never happened before, suggest them.

You could, perhaps, take a part in volunteer services. This can cover a wide range of activities. You could take an interest in one parent families, be a substitute grandparent, offer needy neighbours transport to hospital.

Membership of organisations, social service, social activities, church, clubs, action groups will 'extend' you in all sorts of ways. Some examples are given below.

To summarise, accepting drama in your life involves you in:

The unexpected.	Playing a part (different roles).
Letting yourself go.	Being noticed.
A wider variety of experiences.	Seeing life in a new perspective.
The possibility of meeting more people.	Decision making.
	Ordering or organising events.
Getting to know people more closely.	Solving problems.
Unusual experiences.	Setting up goals and trying to achieve them.
Taking a lead.	Finding new challenges.
Feeling a wide range of emotions like fear, joy, excitement, exhilaration, shock, relief.	Comic events.
	Tragic events.

Some points to consider

The rituals of working life cease with the job

It is easy to allow this to contribute to a sense of loss after the honeymoon period is over. It is just as easy to build up alternative patterns to enrich retirement. The 'pay off' is that in retirement, you can choose to enrich your retirement either with new routines and rituals or by keeping those you most valued when you were at work. The process of making these transfers can make life even fuller than it was before. Much of the 'dramatic' element of working life relates to role and status but in retirement it is still possible to:

o Seek challenges through new occupations, tasks and hobbies that stretch your capacities.

○ Set targets by improving or learning new skills taking on new responsibilities (limited by *you*) which extend you and help you to go on developing your personality.

○ Seek acceptable conflicts by becoming involved in public concerns e.g. local and national politics, action groups etc.

Consider the emotional spin-off. Everyone is glad to reduce tension and

pressure but everyone feels more fulfilled when responding well to challenge. In retirement you can set your own limits but don't 'chicken out'.

○ The people who are less happy in retirement complain of boredom and loneliness.

○ The rate of change (of technology, of values, attitudes, customs) is accelerating. Why not be involved. Be flexible. Try to keep abreast of the times and be part of them. To opt out is to become a 'has been'.

○ There is fun to be had from some

eccentricity. It can add an extra dimension to a humdrum existence.

After retirement
Look back at your selection of choices of routine, rituals and dramas before retirement. How many of these have you carried over into retirement. They are natural components of everyday living and help to 'texture' it giving it more 'body' and richness. After retirement the quality and mix will no doubt change over time but 'texturing' is something you can do all your life.

All in the mind

In the same way that work affects your physical health, so it affects your mental health.

Work—ups and downs

Put a tick on the list against the things you feel may have been the harmful aspects of your job and probably not good for your mental health.

Boredom.	☐
Stress due to difficulty in coping with the work.	☐
Conflict with colleagues.	☐
Conflict with clients and customers.	☐
Feelings of failure to achieve something.	☐
Doing a job you weren't happy with.	☐
Strain of travelling to work.	☐
Anxiety over job security.	☐

At some stage of your working life you may have experienced all of these. If you were unlucky enough to experience more than one of these harmful aspects of work over a long period, then retirement is probably a great relief.

The disadvantages of work are clear but what about the advantages? Some people would say that there were no aspects of their work which were helpful to their mental health but this is rarely so.

In the list below put a tick against those things which you feel were positive aspects of your job and probably good for your mental health.

Being creative or productive.	☐
Rewards from getting work done.	☐
Relationships with colleagues.	☐
Stimulation.	☐
Sense of value as a person.	☐
Independence and having a role outside the home.	☐
Promotion.	☐

There are good and bad effects on all of us whatever job we do. You may not even have been aware of the beneficial aspects of work until you retired and recognised them now that they are absent. Sometimes this loss can make people feel low.

Think how often you went to work feeling depressed and felt better by lunchtime. Usually at work you don't have time to think about what was worrying you in the morning. Some of your colleagues may have been close friends with whom you could discuss your problems. You had a chance to let off steam with them.

Widening your social group

When an area of contact with people i.e. your place of work, is no longer there, you may need to make an effort to replace these contacts.

Think of a typical day recently spent at home. Write down all the people you spoke to on that day and a few details of what you talked about.

Peter Lomax did this exercise for a typical day.
Postman — weather.
Wife — shopping that needed doing.
Neighbour — about the chap down the road who keeps lighting bonfires.
Milkman — holidays.
Daughter — (phone call) about coming to tea on Sunday.
Barmaid and Ted — (at pub) the Budget.
Wife — (sitting in the garden) about daughter's money problems.
Neighbours — general chat while playing whist.

One of the advantages of a wide social circle is that we can talk about different things. Mrs Lomax has heard her husband's political views many times and disagrees with them. But Ted at the pub and Peter enjoy putting the nation to rights together. Peter and his wife can talk about their daughter's money problems but he wouldn't want to talk about these to Ted.

If you feel, from your own list, that you don't have a wide enough social circle then consider ways in which you would widen it. Think about hobbies, outings, seeing more relatives, adult education, voluntary work, clubs, societies, seeing people from work more.

Any of these activities will involve you being among other people. They will give you opportunities for making new friends, keeping up with old ones. You'll feel happier with yourself and your life and have less time to feel low.

Leave work.

More time.	**Loss of work friends felt keenly.**
↓	↓
Use leisure to get out and take on new activities.	**Feel isolated and fed up.**
↓	↓
Meet people.	**Make no effort to go out.**
↓	↓
New social circle.	**No opportunities for meeting people.**
↓	↓
Feel good.	**Feel miserable.**

Feeling miserable

If you are feeling miserable it's nothing to be ashamed of. Everybody does at some stage. It doesn't mean you are mentally ill.

The question is, however, just how severe does depression and anxiety need to be before it can be considered a mental illness? This is difficult to answer because it depends so much upon the individual, his social situation and the views of his doctor.

Roger Barasel moved to a seaside town which he and his wife had visited for years on holiday. The move was made some two months after his retirement. Although they didn't know many people in the town, they still decided to settle there.

Unfortunately Roger's wife died shortly after the move to the town and he became depressed. He went to see his new doctor for help to cope with his grief. He was diagnosed as having severe depression and received treatment. However, if he had been in another social setting, he might not have had to go to his doctor at all. If, for example, he had stayed on in the town in which he and his wife had lived for 30 years, the town in which he had brothers and sisters, then he might well have been able

to cope with the grief without any need for medical help.

One person may go to their doctor complaining of depression and receive drug treatment; another might encounter a GP who spends more time talking to the patient in the hope that he could be helped to cope without the need for drugs. Often psychotropic drugs, as mood affecting drugs are known, are prescribed only for a short period to ride the patient over a bad patch in his life.

Roger Barasel had his drugs gradually reduced six months after his visit to the doctor. Certainly, it isn't the case that once you start taking drugs like these, you will be on them for life. No doctor wants his patients on drugs longer than necessary.

Some people say pessimistically that mental illness cannot be cured. But there are treatments for mental illness and in many cases people are completely cured — after their treatment they return to their normal state of mind.

Warning signs
One major difficulty in helping people with mental health problems is that the affected person may not realise that he or she is in difficulty. Sometimes a depressed or anxious person may struggle on for too long without seeking help from the services which are available.

Depression
Depression isn't something you have to put up with. If someone is depressed but not willing to discuss that depression with other people, how strongly should you encourage them to do so?

It is difficult to give firm guidelines but there are certain signs which suggest that the depression is of sufficient severity to require help.
o Self neglect, that is failure to keep up appearance or house or garden to previous standards.
o Avoidance of friends through becoming housebound.
o Failure to eat.
o Inability to discuss any subject without the depression coming into the person's mind and therefore the conversation.
o Marked increase in alcohol consumption.
o Unwillingness to take decisions.
o Sleep disturbance.
o A suggestion that the person is going to commit suicide.

On this last point, while it is true that many people who talk about ending their lives do not actually do so, it is also true that people who do make an attempt to take their lives often tell other people of their intention beforehand.

So if a friend says "I sometimes just feel like doing away with myself" or something similar that depression should be taken seriously. The doctor should be contacted immediately.

Hidden anxiety
Once people start feeling anxious, whatever the original cause, a vicious circle builds up. Being anxious we become more aware of minor aches and pains and that makes us feel more anxious. We feel upset and find it difficult to listen properly. Then we may misunderstand what other people say and become anxious about that too.

Sometimes people feel tense, nervous and worried but do not themselves recognise that they are in an anxiety state. Even when the anxiety is expressed openly the person may not realise how severe their anxiety has become and that they need medical help. It may also pass undetected by their friends and by their doctor. However there are certain signs which indicate the possibility of problems.

o Obsession with one particular anxiety. A continual fear of cancer — this type of anxiety about a single subject becomes all pervading in the mind of the affected person and is called a phobia.
o Hypochondria — constant complaining about minor symptoms.
o Frequently imagining catastrophes.
o Constantly panicking about having to cope with problems.
o Overreacting to any bad experience. It's normal to be afraid of going to a certain place if you were attacked and robbed there, abnormal to refuse to leave the house again.
o Unusual inability to sleep.
o Increased consumption of alcohol.

Of course, many perfectly well adjusted people may exhibit some of these traits to a degree all their lives. Some people may just not be interested in their appearance or what they eat. Many older people have difficulty in sleeping; as you get older you may find you need less sleep anyway. And we all know people who are forever going on about their various ailments, real or imaginary.

But if these ways of behaving are a departure from the way a person normally behaves it suggests that something may be wrong. If you note these signs in a friend or relative and they strike you as unusual or extreme in some way for that person then it raises the possibility that they are suffering from depression or anxiety.

Mental illness —misconceptions

There are many different stories about mental health and illness. Some of them are not very helpful to a sensible approach to the issue. Check your own views by filling in the chart below.

How did you score? The true statements are 1, 3, 4, 8, 13.

You may be surprised that statements 1 and 13 which seem to express quite opposing views of mental illness, can both be true.

Look at these statements and put a tick in the appropriate column.

	Agree	Disagree
1. Some mental illnesses are an abnormality of mind which is completely different from the normal state (like a broken leg is different from a normal leg.)		
2. Mental illness is hereditary.		
3. Women are more likely than men to suffer mental breakdowns.		
4. During the war years there were fewer mental breakdowns among people in Britain.		
5. People who can't cope and have breakdowns are weak-minded.		
6. There is more stress and tension in society nowadays than when I was young.		
7. The older you get, the more likely you are to worry and get depressed.		
8. There are certain 'crisis' points in everyone's life (like divorce, loss of job, death of a close relative) when the strain can be too great.		
9. There's no real treatment for mental illness.		
10. There's a stigma attached to being mentally ill in the way there isn't if you're physically ill.		
11. Your personality changes as you get older—you're more likely to have sudden changes of mood.		
12. Once you start taking tranquillisers or anti-depressants you're on them for life.		
13. Mental illness is just an exaggeration of the normal condition of mind in the same way that obesity is an exaggeration of the normal physical state.		

The fact is it depends on which type of mental illness we are discussing. For example, schizophrenia is an abnormality which is as different from normality as a fracture is from a normal healthy bone.

It seems that some qualitative change takes place in the mind of the affected person and that his or her mind is completely different from the normal state. However, many other conditions that are also called mental illness are not so different from normal. The two most common diagnoses made are depression and anxiety and these forms of mental illness are in almost every one, exaggerations of the normal states.

Statement 10 about the stigma attached to mental illness has been true at times in the past, but fortunately attitudes are now changing. This kind of illness can cover a wide range of psychological states.

Statement 6 about the degree of stress and tension in society is something of a trick question in that there's no right or wrong answer. It's difficult to measure stresses in society and even more difficult to compare people in different historical periods.

There are many popular views about mental illness which research has shown not to be true. For example the statement that mental illness is hereditary cannot be proven because in most cases of mental illness social factors are so important. Even if a father with a tendency to bouts of depression has a daughter who suffers in a similar way, it could be argued that this is a result of her social conditioning.

Research has shown that no change in mental outlook, in mood or personality occurs as a result of the ageing process. Some people believe that as they get older they will naturally retire from society. Others think that people become more cantankerous and resistant to new ideas as they become older. These are quite popular beliefs yet no consistent pattern of change in mental attitudes can be laid solely at the door of ageing.

Depression or anxiety is nothing to be ashamed of. It isn't a sign of weakness but it is a sign that you or maybe someone you know needs time and perhaps a little help from others to adjust to their present lifestyle.

In sickness and health

This topic looks at getting the best out of medical services. Doctors, health visitors, district nurses, pharmacists, dentists and chiropodists are there to help you maintain your health and to help you deal with any problems.

Along the top of the chart below is a list of professionals who look after your health. Think about the last time you visited each of them. Tick which of the feelings listed on the left hand side of the chart correspond with how you felt at the time of the visit?

o If you've put a tick in row 1, it's worth thinking about why that particular visit was a success. It may help you to understand why you are not so happy with other visits and how to change things.

o If you put ticks in rows 2, 4, 5 or 7, you may not have given the professional sufficient information about yourself. Many people feel nervous when they have to explain themselves to 'an expert'. The important thing is to put your own point of view clearly, so that the professional has sufficient information to be able to help.

o If you put ticks in rows 3 or 10, it may be that you went, in the first instance, to the wrong professional. Sometimes it's necessary to go through more than one professional, but often a bit of checking up beforehand can avoid wasting your time.

o If you put a tick in rows 6, 8 or 9 it may be that there was a failure in communication. This could have been through the exchange of information being unsatisfactory. Or, perhaps you felt that the professional was not giving you the time and attention necessary to make communication effective.

The two main reasons for an unsatisfactory visit to any health professional can be summarized as:

o Going to the wrong professional.
o A failure of communication between you and the professional.

This is what is dealt with in the rest of this topic: who to go to and when, and how to communicate effectively with them when you get there.

Your Feelings	Doctor	Health Visitor	District Nurse	Pharmacist	Dentist	Chiropodist	Others
1. I was very happy with the visit.							
2. I had such a difficult time getting to see this person that I wasn't in the right state of mind for the meeting.							
3. I wasn't sure this was the right person to deal with my problem.							
4. I didn't have time to say everything I wanted to.							
5. I felt tongue-tied.							
6. I couldn't understand what was being said to me.							
7. I felt as if I was making a mountain out of a molehill.							
8. We didn't seem to agree what the problem was.							
9. I felt this person was unsympathetic towards me.							
10. Having seen this person I was passed on to somebody else and I wasn't sure why.							

Who to go to and when

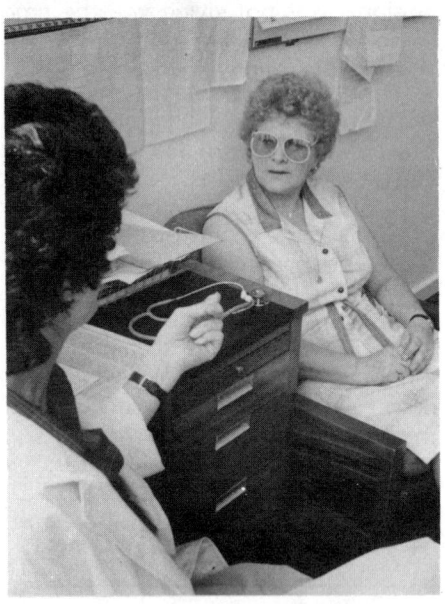

The doctor

Most people turn first of all to their doctor if worried about their health.

Many people worry about wasting a doctor's time with trivial complaints.

'Should I go and see the doctor or will it clear up on its own?'

'There's so many people more ill than I am — will I be wasting his time?'

If you're not sure whether to take action about a complaint, do go and see the doctor:
o If it's unusual or persistent;
o If you've asked among your friends and they advise taking some action;
o If it continues after a few days of 'wait and see';
o If your pharmacist advises it.

If it turns out to be nothing serious, then everybody's happy and you haven't wasted his time because he has put your mind at rest.

Facts about general practice

You will have noticed great changes in general practice in your lifetime. Most doctors now work in group practices or health centres. They usually have receptionists, often secretaries and nurses as well. There is less home visiting from some practices; deputising services are used by many doctors at nights and weekends — so you may be visited by a doctor you have never seen before.

There have also been changes in medical education. Most general practitioners, particularly the younger ones, know the special needs of groups of patients like the elderly, children, or people with handicaps. Some doctors are interested in the health problems of elderly people (and some, it must be admitted, are not!).

You may have been registered with a doctor in your area for several years. If you have moved to a new area, you can get a list of all the G.P.s in your locality from a post office — or failing that, from the offices of the Family Practitioner Committee — the address will be in the telephone book.

It's a good idea, if you have a choice of doctors, to ask around in the neighbourhood. If a friend recommends a doctor that he gets along with, it's likely that you will too. If you live in a rural area, you will probably have no choice of practice.

It may be helpful to be aware of the following when dealing with a general practice:
o Patients who are registered with a doctor in a group practice can see any of the doctors, not just the one they are registered with.
o If you request a home visit, your doctor has to come out to see you.
o The Community Health Council can deal with complaints and suggestions from the public about the hospital sector, or about general practice.
o A patient can change doctors at any time by going to another practice and asking to register with a doctor there. You don't have to give a reason for making the change and your record cards will be sent on.
o If a doctor's list is full, or your house is a long way from the surgery, a doctor may not agree to register you.
o The Family Practitioner Committee is obliged to find a doctor for any patient who cannot find his own doctor.

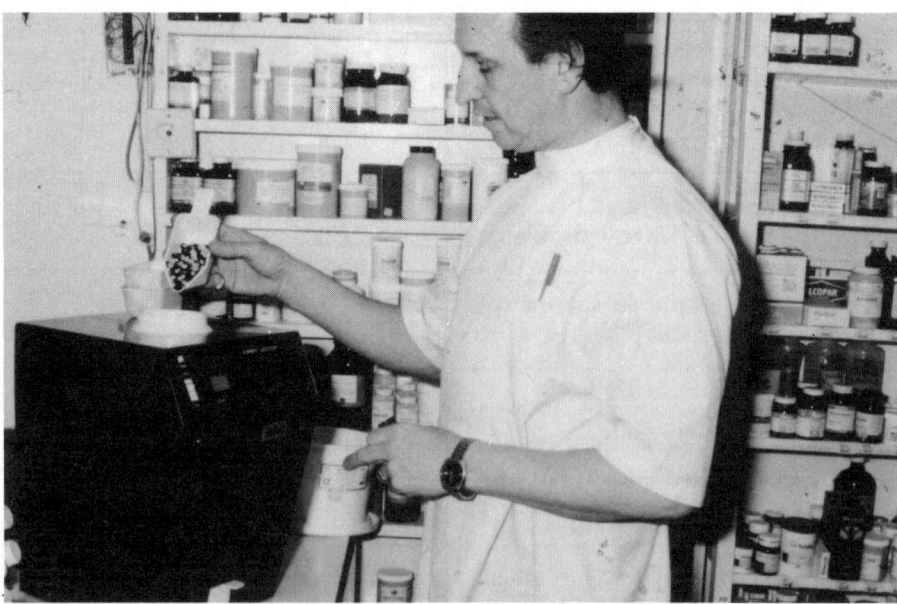

The pharmacist

Most consultations end with the patient leaving the surgery with a prescription. When you take a prescription to the pharmacist, he must write the name of the medicine on the container and the date that he dispenses it. Usually the dosage instructions are written on the label too. If not, ask the pharmacist. You can check with him too, about anything you're unsure about, or anything the doctor told you about your treatment which you've forgotten.

You can discuss with the pharmacist any problems you have taking your medicines. For example, some drugs come in tablet form or liquid form. If you find it difficult to take tablets, you can ask to have the medicine as a liquid. But your pharmacist cannot change the prescription your doctor has written out — he will refer you back to your doctor if that is necessary.

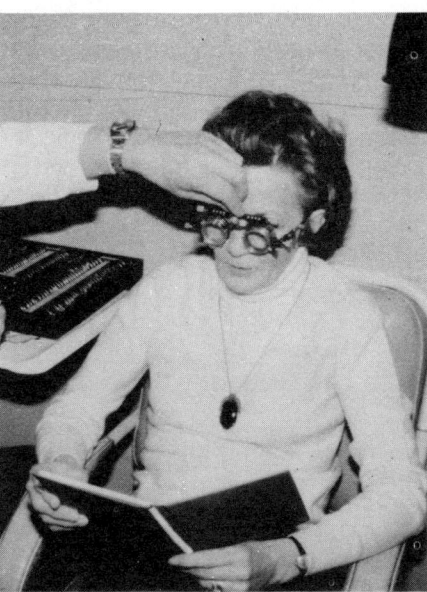

o Problems which you may be having with a disabled elderly relative.
o Problems you have because you, or your spouse, are disabled.
o Advice about social security and housing problems.
o Family problems, such as a disagreement with a daughter-in-law about the way in which she is bringing up your grandchildren.

The health visitor can give you advice and information directly, or refer you on to the appropriate source.

The health visitor

The health visitor is a qualified nurse, who has taken an extra year of training after working in hospital. This training concentrates on the prevention of disease and the health visitor is well prepared to promote preventive ideas in the community. Most of her work is with the mothers of young children, because preventive medicine starts in childhood. Yet increasingly health visitors are practising preventive medicine in older age groups.

Health visitors work in the community, outside hospitals. They work in teams with ten or fifteen health visitors covering a town or part of a city of a country area. Each health visitor works with a group of general practitioners. If there is a group practice of three general practitioners, one health visitor will work most of her time with them, while another health visitor might be working with two 'single handed' general practitioners.

The health visitor works *with* general practitioners not *for* them. This is an important distinction because it means that you can approach the health visitor directly. You can simply phone, or call in at the surgery or health centre, and say you would like to speak to the health visitor and be told how to contact her. Subjects which can be discussed with the health visitor are:

o Aspects of preventive medicine, like stopping smoking, weight control and the benefits of exercise.

The district nurse

The district nurse has taken special training in home nursing, usually after working in hospital. She is assisted in her work by nursing auxiliaries who help with straightforward tasks, such as bathing, leaving the nurse free to concentrate on more difficult problems. Most of her work is with people who are suffering from chronic disease, but she is also able to help the relatives of someone acutely ill, and give them advice on how best to cope.

It is the district nurse who would deal with the arrangements for a chronically ill person coming out of hospital.

The district nurse works with the general practitioner in the same way that the health visitor does. She works with him and not for him and she can, therefore, be approached directly, without having spoken to the general practitioner.

Ophthalmic optician

The ophthalmic optician is qualified to examine your eyes, test your eyesight and supply lenses where appropriate. Appointments can be made without a doctor's referral. The National Health Service allows everyone to have at least one free examination every year, and if more are clinically necessary, these too are free.

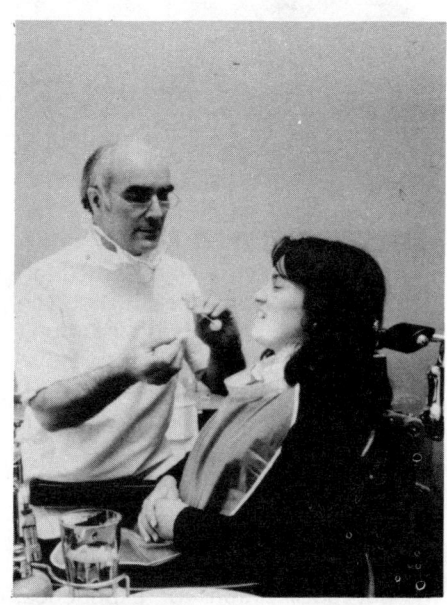

The dentist

Registration with a dentist is not the same as with a G.P. Each new course of treatment is a new contract between dentist and patient. If you want to be treated as a N.H.S. patient, you may need to shop around a bit to find a dentist willing to treat you on those terms.

The only way to be sure that the dentist will not charge you private fees is to sign the N.H.S. contract form, which requires the N.H.S. number, before treatment starts. If you have difficulty finding a dentist to treat you as an N.H.S. patient, contact the Family Practitioner Committee, or the District Dental Officer.

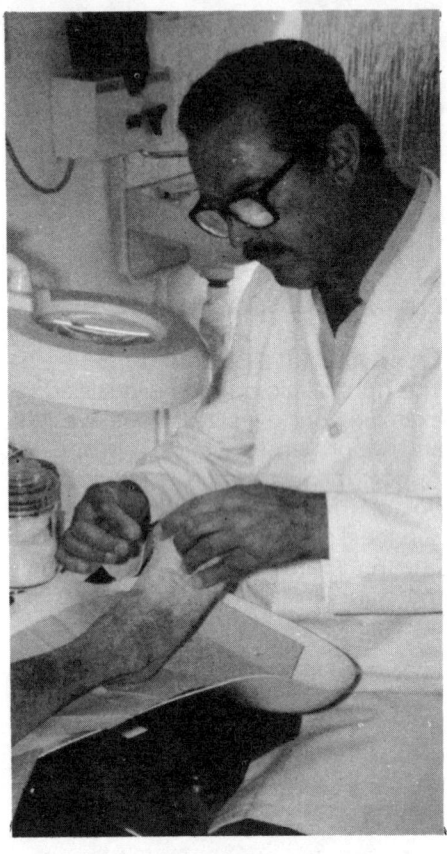

The chiropodist

Anyone can apply for chiropody treatment on the National Health. You can go direct to the chiropodist, you don't have to be referred by a doctor. However, there is likely to be a waiting list, particularly if the treatment required is only for simple foot care.

Private chiropodists are listed in the Yellow Pages. They are worth checking up on whenever possible because chiropodists are still allowed to practice without qualifications or experience. One way of ensuring that you are dealing with a qualified chiropodist is to choose a State Registered Chiropodist who will have the letters S.R.Ch. after his name. This not only ensures that the chiropodist is trained, but also that he is insured to cover the cost of legal action should he cause any damage.

Talking to professionals

Talking to the professionals who are trained to help look after our health can be a daunting experience. They *are* busy people and many people are anxious not to 'waste the doctor's time'. Added to this, many people feel uneasy at having to give honest and often detailed, accounts of things they regard as personal to a virtual stranger. However, few health professionals have the time to investigate for themselves exactly what a patient's problem may be. They rely on the patient to tell them what the problem is, and also to tell them when the recommended treatment is not working, or is in any way unsatisfactory. So it is essential to communicate effectively with health professionals, and to be persistent when necessary.

Here are some of the problems encountered by people dealing with health professionals. How many of them have you experienced?

"I feel there's not enough time to say all the things I want – and there's always a queue of people behind me waiting to go in."

"A doctor is a difficult person to talk to – like a solicitor. You feel you don't know the right language, the jargon."

"Sometimes I feel embarrassed and can't think how to put it into words."

"There have been times when the doctor's put me off. He's glossed over what I wanted to say and before I know it, I'm outside the surgery."

"You feel that the doctor is someone up there – above you, and it makes you feel uneasy."

"When I get in there, I can't remember all the things I wanted to say. You feel silly bringing out a piece of paper with a list on it."

"It's difficult to ask a health visitor questions. You feel you should just tell her what's wrong and let her do all the talking."

"Sometimes you tell her something you're worried about and she seems to ignore it and go on to something else."

"I've asked a doctor questions, and instead of answering me, he says things like 'It's nothing to worry about'."

The professionals' point of view

Professionals, too, can have problems when talking to their clients. Consider the following remarks:

"Sometimes you know there's something troubling a patient and whatever you say or do, you just can't get them to open up and talk about it."

"Some clients don't stop talking – they don't let you get a word in edgeways."

"It's difficult sometimes to get through to patients – to explain things in a way they understand. You know sometimes they are not really listening or understanding or won't remember what you've said when they get home."

"Some clients won't be told anything. They think they know all the answers and won't listen to you. You wonder why they bother to come."

"There are people who ask for things – demand them – when they are not appropriate or necessary."

As always there's two sides to take into consideration.

It's worth improving your ability to talk to health professionals if you do feel you have problems because then your relationship with them will be better and your meetings more worthwhile.

Getting the most from health professionals

If you feel dissatisfied after talking to a health professional, try and work out why you feel this way. And then decide to act differently next time. Here are some suggestions on how you might improve things when you next go along.

o Think about what you want to say before you go to the appointment. Even say it out loud if that helps. Or write it down if that helps.

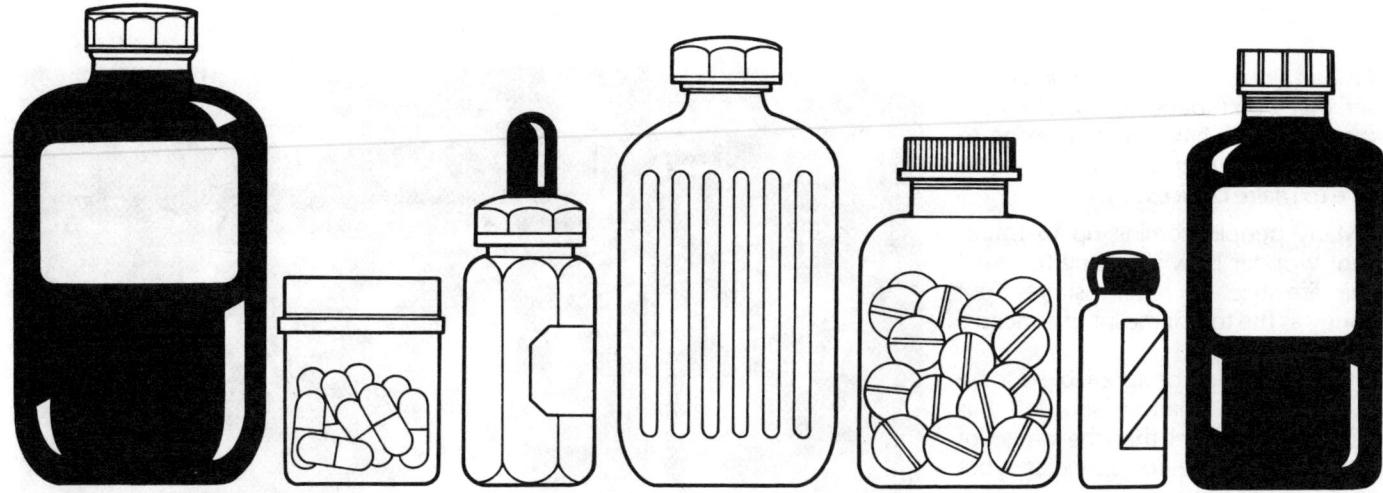

o Say what is worrying you most, *first*. Don't leave it until you are getting up to go.

o If you find the subject embarrassing – remember, professionals are almost impossible to shock.

o If you think that your problem will take a long time, ask for a longer appointment so that you won't be rushed.

o A lot of people find difficulty in expressing themselves. If this is true for you why not admit it straight away. Say something like, 'I do find it difficult to explain things and say what I feel'. The professional will then be alerted and may listen more carefully.

o Don't be put off if there's something you want to say. Be assertive. That doesn't mean be aggressive but it does mean being determined to say what you want to say.

o Rephrase the problem in another way, or keep referring back to it, if you don't get a satisfactory explanation to a question.

o Professionals can be bad at giving their patients information. And some people don't want information. If you're one of the people that does, then ask for it. And ask again if you don't understand, or if you are not given a complete answer.

The most satisfactory consultation between a professional and his patient is one where the patient presents his problem, the professional brings his expertise to bear upon it and together they work out some kind of solution.

Complaints
If you are unhappy about any of the health services provided by the National Health Service you should discuss the matter first of all with the local Community Health Council. These are listed in the telephone directory.

Looking after yourself
There are areas where you are in a position to take direct responsibility for your health.

The human body is not the same as a piece of machinery, like a car or a washing machine, which wears out more quickly the more it is used. The efficient working of our bodies and minds does not wear out because of regular use. Rather the opposite, their efficiency drops when they are *not* regularly used.

So, obviously keeping fit and having a sensible diet are mainstays of health.

However, there may be times when you are ill and here are some guidelines for a sensible approach to any treatment you may need to have:

o Be informed.
Make sure you know something about the drugs you take – how they will act, what they are supposed to do (in case they don't), if there are any side effects to look out for, or other drugs, alcohol, or foods that should not be taken with the medicine you've been prescribed.

o Treat medicines with care: never take a larger dose than is directed on the package.

o Ask the advice of the pharmacist about any drug if you are unsure about something.

o Never treat any symptoms for longer than a week without consulting your doctor.

o If you're already taking medicines prescribed by a doctor, check with the pharmacist before you buy any others over the counter. Some drugs interact with each other and can have unpleasant effects.

o Don't keep any medicines longer than a year. Most lose their effectiveness after this date. Destroy them rather than put them in the dustbin, animals and children get into all kinds of places.

o A lot of medicines that you buy over the counter won't actually do you any harm, but they are not likely to do you any good either. For instance, many cold remedies, just contain aspirin and a few other ingredients. You might just as well take a couple of aspirin with a drink of lemon and honey you make yourself.

o Shop around generally. Look at what a packet of tablets actually contains. Often you can pay double the price for some 'brand name' tablets which are exactly the same as the half-price equivalent. You are just paying for the name. Ask your pharmacist's advice.

Thinking it through
Having worked through this topic, look back at the activity chart recording recent visits to health professionals. If you were in the same situation again:
o Would you visit a health professional?
o Would you visit the same one?
o Would you approach the meeting any differently?
o How would you go about it?

Changing standards

"I mean you've got to face up to the fact that you'll have to change your standards. You have to start saying to yourself it's either . . . . . or . . . . You have to make choices."

Many people coming up to retirement wonder how it's going to affect their life-style. A recent survey put money as the top of the list of concerns about retirement.

You may make the agreeable discovery that your financial situation has improved and feel that the range of choices you have for spending your money is opening up.

Or you might think 'less money fewer options'. But do you have to restrict your options? Do you have to change your standards? And does this mean lowering them?

Whatever your financial situation is now, thinking about the choices open to you can help you decide what you do value.

Feast or famine?

Most people do see retirement as a time when they are going to have to assess their priorities about how they spend their money. They may have to cut out some things, do less of others, choose between alternatives.

One man who retired five years ago said this:

"I decided I would have to make a choice between keeping the car or the telephone. I couldn't afford to have both. I decided to choose the telephone because actually it made me feel less isolated. If I felt under the weather I could phone people for help. Whereas with a car I didn't have that sort of life-line."

Most peoples' lives contain episodes where they find they are having to make financial choices, leading to possibly giving things up or cutting them down.

Here is a list of occasions when you might have felt that your finances weren't adequate to cope. Look at it and choose any items that did apply to you. The questions following the list may help you think about these occasions.

o Starting first on a low income.
o Getting married.
o Buying first home.
o Having young children.
o Becoming unemployed or ill.
o Paying for wedding of child.
o Paying maintenance on divorce.
o Contributing towards keep and help for elderly parent.
o First setting up in business.
o Emigrating.

Try and remember what you did about money on each occasion.

Did you budget in advance and decide on a deliberate spending plan?

Did you work out how much one of your luxuries cost you over the course of a few months and cut it out?

Did you work out how much several of your luxuries cost in the course of a few months and cut each of them down?

Did you cut down generally on household expenditure?

Did you work out particular areas of household expenditure where there was some leeway for cutting down and economise in those areas?

Did you sell something?

Did you take out a loan of some sort?

Did you decide that someone in the household should get an extra job of some sort?

Did you just muddle through?

It's unpleasant being faced with financial problems but there are lots of ways that people choose to cope with them. Looking back at the list, you may have chosen different ways to cope with different events. You might not think you could have made different choices.

Arthur and Muriel Brady recall Arthur getting a job when he was demobbed after the war.

"The wages were not too brilliant and we didn't have very much of anything really. All our furniture had been destroyed in the blitz. We moved up to Birmingham where we didn't know anyone and didn't have any family there. We rented a furnished room so we didn't have to make any immediate capital outlay. We worked out our budget to the last detail and agreed that I would give up having a pint if Muriel would give up smoking — which meant we could eat at least! But eventually we got to the stage where we couldn't cut down any further. We'd already stopped having any luxuries at all and we were down to bare necessities. What do you do when you can't cut down any further? When things got really bad, we sold a diamond brooch which had belonged to my grandmother — that is something I've always regretted. Looking back on it I think I'd rather have borrowed money."

Choices and attitudes

"Those things that I do continue to do, I want to do on the same scale as I've been doing them before."

Is this you? Or is this more likely to be your attitude?

"I think you just have to be prepared to drop your standards and accept that things aren't as rosy as they might be." These are statements which sum up feelings about being under financial pressure. You may agree with these views or have others of your own.

Look at all the statements on this page. Make out your own list of times when you didn't have the finances to cope with your situation. See if you can remember *your* feelings on each occasion.

"I think that tightening your belt slightly on everything is the way to do it — maintain the same range."

"When it comes to a period of financial strain, many things you've been paying

for, just fall by the wayside naturally so you don't really feel as though you have choices to make."

"Even if you're forced to make choices, you've got to give yourself a little leeway and be kind to yourself over a few little treats."

"I do mind cutting things out, I'd rather borrow money, because I'm sure it will all sort itself out in the end."

The attitudes that come up in these statements seem to cover two distinct types of feelings:

o Feelings that you can have some control over by the way you make your choices.

o Feelings that generally things are out of your control and that accepting the situation is the only thing you can do.

How do the feelings you wrote down line up with these?

However you have felt about managing your income in your life, there are usually choices to be made and you still have choices in retirement.

Occasion	How I Felt

What sort of choices?

How you make your financial choices has got a lot to do with what sort of person you are as well as your resources.

Below are a list of things which may at the moment be part of your life.

They have been chosen for two reasons:

1 People's attitudes towards them differ. Some people may consider them necessities; some consider them luxuries and some see them as unnecessary.
2 All are considered by *some* people at least, to enhance the quality of life. Though certainly none of them is necessary for survival itself.

o By the side of the list are three headings. 'This is necessary', 'this is a luxury', 'this is unnecessary.'

o Look at the list and for each item put a tick under the heading which you think best describes your own attitude to that item.

o If you have difficulties in deciding whether you think something is, say, necessary or a luxury put a tick in the middle between those two headings.

If you have a partner then it's a good idea to think about possible changes in expenditure together. Compare your views.

Check whether you actually are involved with any things that are on the right of your list – *Unnecessary.*

Your first choice has been made, you can cut out what is completely unnecessary without problems. If you do feel a bit uncomfortable about the thought of cutting these things out, then check again. Have you put a tick in the correct column?

When you've decided, work out the total cost per year to you of the 'unnecessary' items on the list and note the figure down.

By this point you may have some cash in hand.

Next look at your necessary column and again work out the cost per year of each of the items on it.

Necessary items

Item	Cost
	£
	£
	£
	£
	£
	£
	£
	£

If you give up any of these things then you may well feel that you are lowering your standards.

But it may well be that the cash you have in hand from your *unnecessary* column, still leaves you feeling the pinch when it comes to paying for necessary items.

Is there any way you could alter your approach to *necessary* items?

	This is necessary	This is a luxury	This is unnecessary
Entertaining people.			
Car.			
Telephone.			
Major holiday.			
Weekend breaks.			
Resources for hobbies.			
Colour TV.			
Black and white TV.			
Radio.			
Record player/tape recorder.			
Cigarettes.			
Drinks.			
Plenty of new clothes.			
Visits to the cinema and theatre.			
Membership of clubs.			

If you find your finances have improved it's worth looking at the chart to help you think about your ideas about luxuries.
Will you want more of the same?
Or would you like to branch out and give yourself some new luxuries.
And does having improved finances alter your view of things that you used to think were unnecessary?

Options

If you do feel the need to reduce your expenditure in some way there are no absolute approaches, no 'right' or 'wrong' methods. Here are two possible approaches 'cutting down' or 'alternatives'.

Cutting down

If you don't want to forego certain things, you don't want to have to go without either a car or a telephone, can you find ways of, at least, reducing the amounts spent on them?

Could you try any of the following?
o Entertain people more simply or less often.
o Buy a smaller car, or do fewer miles.
o Make fewer telephone calls.
o Smoke fewer cigarettes.
o Drink less.
o Visit the cinema and theatre less often.
o Take out occasional membership of clubs.

Alternatives

On the other hand you might prefer to do without certain things altogether in order to maintain standards elsewhere.

You could find you've made more funds available for yourself by choosing:
A major holiday or weekend breaks.
A colour television or a black and white television.
Cigarettes or drinks.
Visits to the theatre and cinema or resources for hobbies.
After all very possibly for you a holiday is a holiday whether it takes place in Ibiza or Llangollen. And a television is a television whatever the colours.

Look at the chart below. It contains the same items and areas of expenditure as the chart on the previous page. Consider each item in turn and decide what approach you could adopt which will eventually give you the savings you need.

Ask yourself, is this something that you wish to maintain regardless of the cost? Or, is there room for you to reduce your spending to an extent without losing out altogether?

In the column headed **your decision** write down by each item whether you wish to 'maintain' 'cut down' upon or 'go without' it. Next, fill in the amount you currently spend on that item annually. If you plan to reduce or cut out entirely your spending fill in the **changed spending** and **savings** columns. Add up your totals and see if you've managed to save the amount you require.

Remember though, it's difficult to make any of these changes in isolation. Other people may share these goods or experiences with you. Changes need to be discussed and agreed upon.

Totally free choice over what to buy and how to spend money is granted to few people. Having to make choices doesn't necessarily mean having to lower standards. But it does mean establishing priorities.

When you reach the end of a chain of decision-making about giving something up or having less of something — if you find you feel *real* regret, then do think again, because it's those sorts of decisions that may make you feel you *are* lowering standards.

Your options	Your decision	Current spending	Changed spending	Savings
Entertaining people.				
Car.				
Telephone.				
Major holiday.				
Weekend breaks.				
Resources for hobbies.				
Colour TV.				
Black and white TV.				
Radio.				
Record player/tape recorder.				
Cigarettes.				
Drinks.				
Plenty of new clothes.				
Visits to cinema and theatre.				
Membership of clubs.				

Getting about

In this topic you are asked to think about your travelling needs — the journeys that you make, the means of transport that you use — and to consider the changes that will come with retirement.

In order to think about any changes you might make to your transport you first need to think about how you use it.

So think about your *weekly* needs for transport. Does retiring mean these needs alter in any way?

Fill in the chart below adding any other journeys you make and compare your needs before and after retirement.

Weekly needs before retirement Journeys	How many times a week?	How is journey made?	Weekly needs after retirement Journeys	How many times a week?	How is journey made?
Work			**Part-time work.**		
Travelling to and from work.			Travelling to and from work.		
Travelling in the course of work.			Travelling in the course of work.		
	———			———	
Shopping			**Shopping**		
Travelling to local shops.			Travelling to local shops.		
Travelling to distant shops.			Travelling to distant shops.		
	———			———	
Leisure			**Leisure**		
Travelling to pub/club.			Travelling to pub/club.		
Travelling to cinema/theatre.			Travelling to cinema/theatre.		
Travelling to evening class.			Travelling to evening class.		
Travelling to library.			Travelling to library.		
Travelling to allotment.			Travelling to allotment.		
Travelling to hobbies.			Travelling to hobbies.		
Travelling to sport.			Travelling to sports.		
Travelling to voluntary work.			Travelling to voluntary work.		
	———			———	
Social and domestic			**Social and domestic**		
Visiting friends and relatives.			Visiting friends and relatives.		
Giving lifts.			Giving lifts.		
Going to the doctor.			Going to the doctor.		
Other			**Other**		

Totals

Now think about journeys that you make less regularly, say over the course of a year. These could include holidays, weekend breaks, visiting friends and relatives who live some distance away. List the journeys on the chart below and again compare before and after retirement.

How satisfied are you?

It makes budgetary sense to have transport arrangements that are economical and of course it makes common sense if the arrangements are convenient!

Is the way you get around suitable for your current circumstances? Will you be able to adapt to your new requirements? What would the effect be if:

o You changed the way you used public transport facilities?

o There were alterations in public transport facilities?

o You changed your means of transport from car to bus/train or from bus/train to car?

o You changed something about the style of your chosen means of transport (smaller/bigger/newer/older car)?

Public transport

If you use public transport to get around has it met your changing needs adequately?

o You'll probably find that concessionary fares schemes operate in your area. And there are certainly a number of schemes which British Rail operates that provide favourable rates for the retired. There are often conditions to these various schemes — travelling at particular times of the day or the week for instance. How do such conditions suit you? Can you conveniently

Occasional needs before retirement Journeys	How many times a year?	How is journey made?	Occasional needs after retirement Journeys	How many times a year?	How is journey made?
Holidays			Holidays		
Weekend breaks			Weekend breaks		
Relatives and friends			Relatives and friends		
Others			Others		

arrange your activities requiring transport, in order to get the best out of these schemes? If you can't then you will be paying a higher cost for your transport.

o How would an alteration of bus or train services in your area affect your convenience? If services were reduced could you again alter your activities?

o If you think public transport services could be more effective in your area, have you thought about campaigning for better services?

If you find that public transport services don't satisfy all your transport needs, have you considered trying to work out a scheme with friends or neighbours where you share costs on someone else's car paying them your share of petrol and overheads?

This is an arrangement that could work particularly well if you have mutual interests. In a few areas there are now agencies at which you can be put in touch with people who want to do some car sharing.

Or of course you may want to consider the costs and benefits of having a car.

Changing the means of transport

It's difficult to work out comparative costs for a year's journeys by different means of transport. However you could look at some of the journeys you make now and compare the costs of what you do now with other means of transport.

Grace Faulkner used to drive to the office where she worked. It was a daily round trip of some 30 miles and it was a very awkward journey by public transport. However, after she retired she found she was making far less use of the car.

The only journeys she needed to make regularly now were visiting her sisters, who lived in the same town, and doing the weekly shopping.

She compared the cost of travelling to her sister's by car and bus. She found that the bus fare, using her concession-

ary tokens, is currently 34p single, 68p return. The petrol for her Mini costs her 50p for the same journey. When she added on even a small fraction of the costs of tax, insurance and depreciation of her car which she reckoned as at least £9 a week, she saw that taking the bus was clearly cheaper. It did mean visiting her sister at off peak times of the day but this didn't seem to be inconvenient.

She found many of the other journeys she made regularly since retiring would be much cheaper by public transport, although some of them would certainly not be as easy as the journey to her sister's. She was some distance from the shops for example and did not imagine she would enjoy carrying a week's shopping on and off the bus.

She checked the cost of a taxi to bring her back from the shops. She also looked into the costs on less regular journeys such as going on holiday, taking a taxi to the station and travelling by train. Overall, she found that these means of transport still proved to be

cheaper than keeping the Mini. She realised also that possible repair costs and the rises in insurance premiums and car tax, had been worrying her, so Grace made the decision to give up the Mini.

Grace Faulkner's findings highlight some of the costs of having a car. On the other hand if you are using public transport at the moment but are thinking about the possibility of buying a car you might want also to think about the benefits.

o You aren't tied to particular times, or to having to make connections.

o It's easy to carry things around; luggage, shopping and so on.

o You're probably less subjected to the elements.

o You're not susceptible to alterations in public transport facilities.

o You can get off the beaten track and go to places that are awkward to get to by public transport.

Look back at the charts transport needs and consider how convenient some of your journeys would be if you did decide to buy a car.

Cars

You might find that having a car has proved to be absolutely the best form of transport for you and you couldn't really consider any alternative. None the less, you might be wondering if the particular car you currently drive is the best suited to your needs.

If you don't have a car and you're considering buying one then look at this section too. You need to look at costs as well as convenience.

For most people making their minds up about a car is a matter of balancing cost against convenience. For some though, the actual enjoyment of the car itself is the major factor. If a car does a lot more for you than get you from A to B, if it's the joy of your life then you may be prepared to put up with perhaps more inconvenience and higher costs than many people!

Learning to drive

For many people retirement offers a chance to learn how to drive. It's a useful skill to have, if one partner is ill or unable to drive any longer. It is much more convenient for the other to be able to drive. Living in the country or going on holiday, more than one driver in the family can mean a great ease up of pressure.

Remember that once you pass 60, you often need to have regular medical examinations to get car insurance.

Mr Singh lives near Grace Faulkner with access to the same facilities. He decided he cannot manage without a car, since the journeys to visit other members of his family would be too difficult without one. But he has also decided that he wants to cut down on some of the costs. He decided to buy a smaller car and to go to car maintenance classes so he can do his own routine servicing.

What do you want from a car? Look at the following checklist.

o It needs to be the right size for my current needs.
o Its layout needs to suit me − (number of doors, size of boot, hatch back etc).
o It needs to be economical to run (petrol/oil).
o It needs to be economical to maintain (servicing, replacement parts etc).
o It needs to be comfortable (ride, noise, seats, etc).

If you've got a car already how many items on the checklist apply to it? If very few then it's a good idea to find a suitable substitute.

Choosing a car

You will want to get as much information as you can about any models of car that you are interested in.

There are four main areas to examine.

Technical information about the car

Body type and size, number of doors, boot size, engine size, type of suspension, miles per gallon, acceleration.

In-service information

Reliability, ride, handling, steering, braking, ease of parking, running costs, ease of maintenance, ease of getting in and out, noise level.

Personal feelings

Its style, comfort, image, safety, flexibility etc.

The table on the right shows where to obtain such information.

Potential costs

The information you find will help you work out potential costs.

Mr Singh worked out the actual outgoings (excluding repayments) he would probably incur in keeping the Mini he intended to buy on the road for a year. Here are his calculations (1982 prices).

Car tax.	£80
Insurance.	£70
Repair costs/MOT.	£100
Petrol/oil.	£320
Tyres/exhaust parts.	£60
Car maintenance classes.	£10
TOTAL	**£640**

This is the bare list of basic essential costs for you to consider. If you do not intend to do any servicing yourself, for example, then you need to add this on. You could use it as a check against any car you are considering buying.

You also need to think about initial outlay. If you have a car, how much could you sell it for?

How much can you afford for a different car first of all, paying cash then, if possible, with a loan?

If taking out a loan you need to add the repayments including interest on to your annual outgoings until it is repaid.

Transport is an important consideration. The solution you work out for *your* needs may affect both your budget and the way you live. It's worth thinking about getting the best out of it.

Print sources	Technical information	In-service information	Personal information	Comments
Manufacturers leaflets	●			May only give 'good' features, difficult to sort through when short listing.
Government leaflets	●			Usually give technical specifications. Give information related to the law regarding buying and driving a car.
Advertisements	●		●	May only give good features and may give very little hard information, may influence personal taste.
Car magazines in general	●	●	●	Usually good on technical information. The expert opinion may not be objective. Comparative tests may not be carried out under strict conditions. The personal opinions of the reviewer may be biased.
Motoring Which?	●	●	●	Reliable in-service information based on experts and on large numbers of owners. Comparative tests carried out under strict controls. Personal opinions stated as such.
Motoring Which? annual car buying guide	●	●	●	Annual summary of tests and owners experience and prices.
Technical handbooks	●			Give details of how to maintain and overhaul particular models. Produced by manufacturers and others.
Car salesman	●			Treat information with caution. Best to ask for specific technical information and conditions of sale.
Car mechanic	●	●		May have good knowledge of a limited range of cars.
Other owners		●	●	Useful source of in-service information.
Friends who know about cars	●	●	●	Beware of strongly held personal opinions.
AA or RAC	●	●		Will inspect used cars and provide detailed report on technical and in-service information and expert opinion.
Consumer Advice Centre	●	●		Have technical and in-service information on cars, and usually copies of *Motoring Which?* Will help you define your personal needs.
Don't forget: Your own personal preferences and experience			●	Do not overlook these when you are carrying out decision making exercises. They should have an important influence.
Your direct inspection of car		●	●	Especially important when buying secondhand. Important for rating personal features such as comfort etc. Have checklist prepared in advance.

Where to live

This topic asks you to think about where you live, whether you are satisfied and, if not, what you can do about it.

Retirement gives many people who have felt tied an opportunity to move. It's also a time when they can think about just how suitable their home is for their requirements.

It can be complicated to unravel your needs and make realistic plans. Your ideas about where to live may have been as vague as a general feeling that you would like a change, or as certain as knowing where you want to go and what sort of house you want.

Here are some statements which express ideas about where to live. Tick any which apply to you and add your own.

Some of the statements are much more definite than others (1, 4, 7 and 8) and if you ticked any of those, obviously, your own views are currently positive. If you ticked any of the other statements, it's probably worthwhile to try a few ideas out for size and then see whether you can produce a firm statement about what you want to do.

If you are completely satisfied about where you live, then all you need to bear in mind is whether you might want to make any changes in the future. Keep an eye open for the sort of accommodation available in your area, any housing schemes you think might suit you at a later stage, ways you might possibly want to alter your home later and so on.

1. I'm satisfied with everything about where I live. ☐
2. I like my house but it doesn't meet my needs anymore. ☐
3. I'm happy about the area I live in but not my house. ☐
4. I like where I am but I can no longer afford to stay here. ☐
5. I don't like this area, I'd like somewhere pleasanter. ☐
6. The area has changed and it no longer appeals to me. ☐
7. I'd like a complete change. ☐
8. I've seen somewhere I really want to move to. ☐
9. I'd like to move but I don't think I can make the effort. ☐

Staying and improving

If you are happy about the area in which you live but not so happy with your house, then you could consider alterations.

If you want to make alterations and you own your own house, then local authorities give grants up to certain amounts for:

o Improvements such as damp courses, dry-rot proofing, hot and cold water.
o Basic amenities (intermediate grant) such as bathroom, W.C.
o Insulation.
o Repairs (this is not so common).

Check with your local environmental health department about grants. To get a grant you need to be a freeholder of the house, or have a lease with at least five years to run and you have to agree that the house will remain your only or main residence for the next five years.

If grants are not available, you may be able to get a maturity loan from your local council. In this case, the capital need not be repaid until after the death of the borrower, when it is recovered from his estate.

Other improvements
If you see disadvantages to your house then make a list of things that have irritated or annoyed you.

Here are some that people frequently complain about. You may have others. Think how much it would cost to rectify them.

You may find that the outlay is more than you're prepared to pay. But giving a face lift to your home can work wonders for how you feel about it. So pick out the unsatisfactory items on your list, cost them carefully and check your budget to see if you could make some realistic savings over the next few months, or year, that would allow you to get them sorted out.

Disadvantage	To rectify £
Poor lighting.	
Poor heating.	
Inconvenient kitchen units.	
Poor insulation.	
Not enough electrical sockets.	
Decoration you don't like.	
Badly hung doors.	
Garden difficult to maintain.	
Dangerous footpaths.	
Poorly lagged plumbing.	

Moving

If you don't think you would be happy whatever you did to your house, or you are unhappy with the area, then moving is obviously something for you to consider.

In the next exercise, you are asked to do two things:

1. Think about what are, to you, the most important considerations about somewhere to live.
2. Think about what does and does not satisfy you about where you live.

Look at the statements in the chart on the right and give each item a score: 4 if it's very important, 3 if it's important, 2 if it's fairly important, 1 if it's not very important and 0 if it's not important at all.

When you have filled in this chart, having decided on the importance to you of these considerations, move on to fill in the next chart, to show how satisfied you are on each count.

Your home	Importance
Laid out as you want it.	
Decorated to your taste.	
Easy to run.	
Easy to heat.	
Garden the right size.	
Garage.	
Can afford rent / rates / mortgage repayments.	

Your area	Importance
The neighbourhood.	
Shops.	
Local health services.	
Access to family.	
Access to friends.	
Access to entertainments.	
Access to services (i.e., garages, public transport, plumbing etc.)	
Access to suitable informal activities (hobbies, clubs etc.)	

Now fill in the following chart — putting the items from the previous list in order of importance and under the headings showing whether you are satisfied with them or not.

If looking at this chart you find the total score for *satisfied* is greater than *not satisfied,* then the balance seems to be to stay and perhaps think about what, if anything, you can do about items that you've scored as important but you're not satisfied with.

Still think you'd like to move even though you're 'satisfied'?

Go through your scoring again.

Are you sure you've given everything an appropriate score?

You can use this chart as a shopping list — it summarises your most important considerations for moving and what you want to move to.

Importance	Satisfied	Not satisfied
Scores 4		
Scores 3		
Scores 2		
Scores 1		
Scores 0		
Total		

Value of house in Walsall.	£21,000
Rates per annum.	£200
Current travelling costs low — family nearby, holiday twice a year.	£250
Current telephone bill — not much higher than rental.	£80
Current heating costs (solid fuel and gas fires) per annum.	£300

Value of house in Ilkley.	£20,000
Rates per annum.	£210
Possible travelling costs higher.	£600
Telephone bill may be higher because of distance of family.	£160
Possible heating costs estimated from similar house.	£300

Costs and benefits

Before you go on to compare the merits of various places you could live, it's a good idea to have a serious think both about the full consequences of a move on your budget and on other aspects of your life.

To help you, here is how one person worked out possible changes to his budget and some of the other implications of a move.

Tom Owen lives in Walsall in the West Midlands. He has often thought of moving and he and his wife always fancied the idea of Yorkshire. While on holiday in Ilkley this year, he saw a small house that really appealed and decided to work out approximately how much the move would end up costing him.

So, he compiled a list with some examples of regular lump-sum spending to make a direct comparison between the two houses.

Look at his lists above. You'll see, first of all, that Tom stands to make £1,000 profit from his own house but he realises that this would soon be swallowed up by moving expenses, solicitors fees and buying new furniture. He calculates that his fuel and heating costs would work out about the same, as would his rates. But he feels there would be an appreciable increase in his travelling and telephone costs.

This extra expense would be incurred as a result of maintaining contact with people in Walsall . . . and he begins to wonder whether perhaps a rural village, near Walsall, might serve his purposes as well. Hammerwich or Burntwood perhaps? Both are rural but are near to Walsall and, therefore, to family and friends.

The 'Ilkley exercise' as Tom called it, was his first attempt at working out some of the consequences of moving. He found that it had more uses than just thinking about money. He became clearer on the importance he placed on convenient facilities and on being near family and friends.

Choosing between houses

Even when you've decided you'd like to move, it can be difficult to sort out the merits of one place against another.

To make your decision you have to work out exactly what your requirements are and how well they are catered for. Already in this topic you have been asked to assess on a scale of 0–4 the relative importance to you of various attributes of any house and area that you would live in. Now, using a scale of 0–4 again you can also score the extent to which a particular place fulfils each of your requirements.

If you then multiply one by the other — your requirements and the degree to which they are satisfied — it will give you an overall total which you can then use in assessing the relative merits of any two places.

For example, Tom Owen was looking at two houses in a small village outside Walsall. It was fairly important to him that the house was decorated to his taste, so he had scored this requirement at 2. Both the houses were reasonably well decorated; he felt the standard of decoration rated 2. In multiplying these figures together he found the houses to be of equal merit in this respect.

He then considered their gardens. This attribute really wasn't very important to him, he had merely scored it as 1. He looked at the first house and found that it had a neat, compact garden that would be perfectly easy for him to manage; he scored this as 4. The other garden, however, was really rather large and overgrown and, it was clear, it would require a fair amount of work to maintain, so he only gave this a score of 2.

In this way, as is shown in the lists below, he considered in turn the various attributes of the houses and the degree to which his requirements were satisfied in each case until he arrived at an overall total for each house from which their relative merits were clearly evident.

To assist your choice between different places you could try this method, using a long list of items both concerning the house itself and the area and facilities.

House 1			
Home	Importance	Standard	Total
Laid out as I want it	3 ×	4	12
Decorated to my taste	2 ×	2	4
Easy to run	3 ×	3	9
Garden the right size	1 ×	4	4
Garage	3 ×	3	9
Can/afford rent/rates, mortgage	4 ×	4	16
Overall total			54

House 2			
Home	Importance	Standard	Total
Laid out as I want it	3 ×	1	3
Decorated to my taste	2 ×	2	4
Easy to run	3 ×	2	6
Garden the right size	1 ×	4	4
Garage	3 ×	0	3
Can afford rent/rates, mortgage	4 ×	4	16
Overall total			36

Things to think about

The last section of this topic raises some other issues you might want to think about.

A place in the country
If you've lived in a town all your life you may find the idea of retiring to the country extremely alluring. The country is beautiful — but quiet! Bus services may not be regular — certainly not what you would have been used to in town.

The peace and quiet of rural isolation may be a little more extreme than you'd bargained for — it could take friends and relatives quite a while before they finally get round to coming out and visiting your new house.

Maybe you'd always wanted to do more gardening. Certainly moving to the country could provide you with this opportunity but do remember that maintaining a large garden takes a lot of time and effort.

And do look carefully if you come across the rose covered cottage of your dreams. It may have dry rot, a leaking roof and no damp course!

Perhaps a coastal resort was more to your thinking. Well, don't expect it to be the same as those two glorious weeks in July — a wet seaside, off-season, can be a most depressing sight!

Parts of the country, particularly certain seaside resorts, have a high concentration of older people. This can put a strain on the health services. It can also mean you won't find very many people, apart from older people, to mix with.

More money matters

Mortgages
Most people aim to have paid off their mortgage by the time they retire and those who haven't are often attracted by the idea of not having any mortgage payments to make after retirement. However, before you consider spending all, or a large proportion of your savings, or the lump sum you get on retirement, on paying off your mortgage, consider whether your pension is high enough to make the tax relief on mortgage interest beneficial.

If your income is over a certain level,

you could also consider changing to an option mortgage (you pay a lower rate of interest and forego entitlements to tax relief on mortgage interest).

Lease
You may not have been able to choose to buy the freehold of your property. While you will usually be able to have your lease extended when it expires, the new lease may be more expensive. Remember that selling property with a short lease to run may be difficult.

Rate rebate
Remember that once you have retired, your income may drop to the level which makes you eligible for a rate rebate. Get a leaflet from your council offices, CAB or housing advice centre. All owner occupiers are entitled to claim, also tenants (private or council) and sub-tenants on both furnished and unfurnished property.

Supplementary pension
If you are over pensionable age, retired from full time work and have an income which is below the statutory weekly minimum, you can apply for a supplementary pension. You will be asked to give information about your mortgage and rent payments but the value of the house you live in will be ignored. The supplementary pension, if awarded, will be the difference between your current income and what is called the scale rate fixed by the government, plus an amount for rent and maybe special expenses. The 'rent' for an owner occupier, covers the rates, mortgage interest and ground rent (feu duty in

Scotland) plus something for repairs and insurance. Should you be getting this supplementary pension, you wouldn't normally get a rate or rent rebate as well. 'Repairs' are only day to day maintenance — you get exceptional needs payment for unforeseen major disasters.

Tenants
You may decide to get extra income during your retirement by letting off part of your house. But remember that the income from tenants counts as earnings and may reduce the amount of State Pension you are entitled to. Be sure to make a thorough check on the legal position before taking on tenants — leaflets and advice should be available from your CAB or housing advice centre. If you have bought a retirement home before retiring and let it, the 1974 rent act will ensure that you can get possession if you can satisfy a court that you have retired from full time work and need the house as a home. You should make sure that your tenant has written notification, when the tenancy is granted, that you are planning to retire there at a certain time and will need possession.

There are now schemes whereby older people, living in houses too large for their needs, can make their property over to a charity — Help the Aged for instance — and in return, are given part of the house to live in, rent and rates free. The house will be re-modelled to provide accommodation for a number of others and the original owners have no worry about maintenance and insurance.

New friends

Retirement gives you an opportunity to spend time with old friends. Some established relationships are certainly going to increase in importance to you.

But it can cut you off from some opportunities for making friends — particularly in the workplace. However, retirement does provide opportunities for developing new interests and new areas of common experience.

So what changes?

The following study shows the variety of relationships that one person had at the time of her retirement and how the pattern changed afterwards.

Shonagh McLagon had worked in catering since leaving school at 14. She worked her way up to be a director of a small restaurant of her own. At this time she was nursing a sick husband at home and found her time entirely occupied with her husband and the restaurant.

Several years after his death the restaurant ran into financial difficulties and she was forced to sell it. So at the age of 60 she took a job doing the canteen accounts at a local factory, which she enjoyed enormously.

"The job was entirely different for me . . . it's the company, it was lovely. It's the fact that somebody expected me every morning . . . when you get up you have the feeling of 'right, I've got to do this and that' . . . now on the other hand I have to mark what day it is."

Shonagh had to retire at the age of 65 owing to company policy, but has been several times to cover when others were on holiday. She still misses work, mainly for the company it brought her.

"It's very quiet, especially when you're used to people. Apart from my daughter coming, if I didn't go out I wouldn't speak to anybody else. I've never been used to neighbouring because I've always been in business. It's a different life."

She became a member of the Soroptimists whilst running her restaurant business and has been on the executive and a president of the local branch. She has started a rota of afternoon meetings for retired members that takes place once a month at each other's houses. She is also a member of the local committee for a sheltered housing scheme but such activities don't often involve her during daytime.

In each box in the chart Shonagh wrote down the names of people she had contact with before her retirement. Then she put a star by each person she no longer saw afterwards.

The chart shows a concentration of personal contacts of adults roughly in Shonagh's own age range. When she retired she lost all her contacts with work but has not replaced them.

"The most disappointing thing to me is that I can't work — that would solve all problems, boredom, everything, just something to do".

	Age 0–12	13–20	21–45	46–65	66–80	81+
Family	Jeremy (grandson)		Wendy (daughter)			Uncle Paul (husband's uncle)
Friends				Mrs Appleby Miss Jensen Miss Sinclair (Soroptimists)		
Acquaintances		David (Next door neighbour)	David's parents	Mrs Wright (Abbeyfield Homes)		
Colleagues (at work)		Jenny Lewis* Daylene Berry*	Mr Mahon* Jeff Davies*	Mrs Broadbank* Mr Pritchard* Mr Dobson* Mrs Steward*		

Changes in relationships

Now fill in your chart. In each box write down the name of each person you knew before your retirement. Then put a star by the name of each person you no longer see, or, if you haven't retired, no longer expect to see after retirement.

Now look at your chart and think about the changes in your relationships that retirement brings.

o Will you be seeing more of older or younger people in retirement?
o Will you be seeing people in all of the age group categories or in just one or two of them?
o Will you be seeing people in each of the categories **family, friends, acquaintances** and **colleagues** or in just one or two of them?

Are you happy with the picture that you've drawn up of your relationships after retirement?

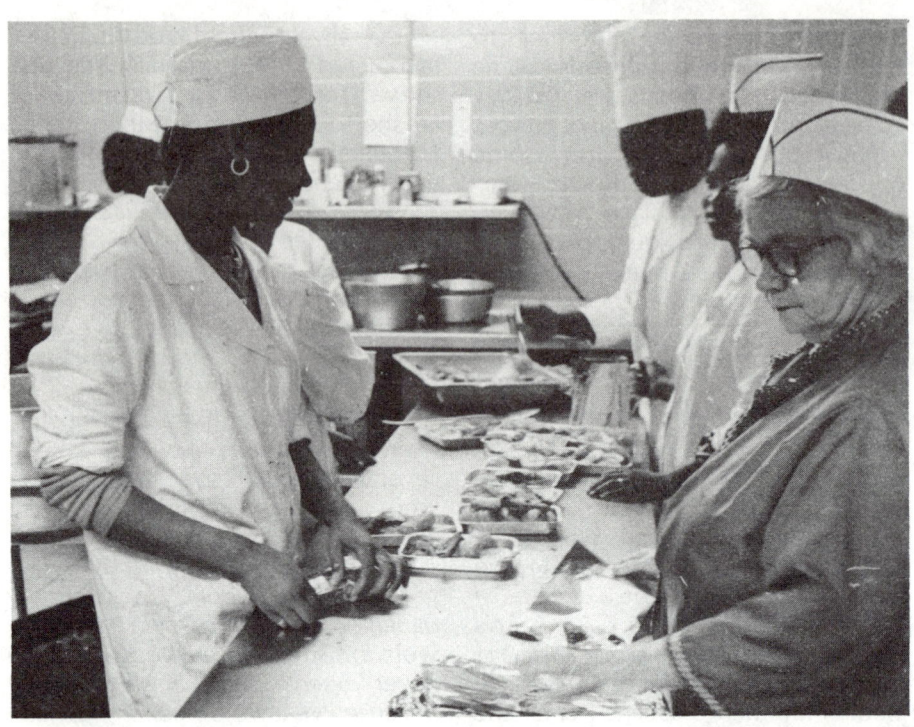

	Age 0–12	13–20	21–45	46–65	66–80	81+
Family						
Friends						
Acquaintances						
Colleagues (at work)						

Relationships are important

Whether we belong to a close-knit family group and see each other every day or live on an isolated croft in Scotland, and see only one person every two weeks, relationships are part of our lives. Everybody looks for a variety of things in relationships and each one may fulfil different needs. Here are some things people can get out of their relationships with others.

Identity The opinion we form about ourselves is partly based on what other people say and think about us. Work provides one setting for this — 'a sound worker', 'the boss'. In the family you may be father or mother, and also 'the brainy one' or, 'the black sheep'. Among friends you may be a 'a joker', 'a gardener' or 'the serious one'.

Emotional support Most people look to family or close friends for emotional support whether in a major crisis or just for a chat about day-to-day concerns. The important thing is that they are

people who really care what happens to you and vice versa, even though sometimes you may disagree.

Practical support You can help a neighbour build a fence or carry home their shopping without feeling any strong emotional attachment to them. But it's an important part of any relationships, and another way of giving and receiving affection.

If you look back at your chart and the people named on it you can probably see roughly how support is exchanged in your relationships.

Perhaps in looking at your chart you might think that what you really need is some new relationships.

Read the next section and think about how you might go about meeting new people. In thinking about what makes a new relationship tick, you might also be able to give an extra boost to those you already have.

Making new friends

The first steps to a new friendship may take a bit of courage. You are on new ground, perhaps feeling a bit exposed. Because you don't know someone you may misunderstand what they say or do, feel you might put your foot in it. But remember it's the same for everyone.

First impressions can be very important. But they can sometimes be misleading too! Here is an example taken from the newsletter of a social club which aims to help people in search of friendship.

Mrs. Jamieson and Mrs. Delderfield met for the first time in a group gathering at a restaurant. Mrs. Jamieson talked freely about one of her interests, a local charity, a subject in which Mrs. Delderfield had no interest at all.

To Mrs. Jamieson, the fact that Mrs. Delderfield was quiet and 'very well dressed' put her off. She thought she was stand-offish. Neither woman made any attempt to contact the other socially.

A few months later the two women met again at the restaurant and being the only two there were forced into conversation. Mrs. Jamieson found that Mrs. Delderfield had been a professional dressmaker which explained a lot about her being well dressed. And Mrs. Delderfield found that Mrs. Jamieson was actually rather shy and admitted to gabbling away when she was unsure of herself.

As they talked they found that they did have several interests in common including singing in local choirs. They agreed to meet again and struck up a friendship.

Think about some first impressions of people you formed in the past. Have you ever had a similar experience to Mrs. Jamieson and Mrs. Delderfield?

Friendships do strike up naturally but it can help if you exploit opportunities to meet new people. If you consider how you have made various friendships in your life you'll probably find they have arisen:

o Through work/the forces/school.
o Through activities and hobbies you've taken up.
o Through neighbourhood proximity.
o Through friends or relatives.

medicine, history etc. **Box 4/6**.

LIVELY loving humorous widow, interest antiques, history, maybe living abroad, seeks refined gent, affection reciprocated. **Box 3/6**.

WEST AVON widow attractive educated brunette, wishes correspond initally personable intelligent lonely gentleman, 55-63, car owner, friendship, outings, photo. **Box 25/6**.

WIDOWER 55 seeks companionship of lady for outings. country lover, professional gardener no ties, happy disposition, nr. London. **Box 47/6**.

LADY 54 active seeks friendship. sincere gent, travel country swimming, gardening, theatre, must be non smoker. Knowsley. **Box 44/6**.

INTERESTING lady 52, divorced, South Glos, varied interests seeks friendship with man between 50 and 0. **Box 45/6**.

GIANTS widow 65 refined smart sense of humour, kind, sincere realises happiness is sharing seeks sincere genuine gentleman. **Box 3/6**.

LOOKING for gentleman no ties, dham area, to share friendship, usic, outdoor life. I am a semi-ired nurse. Widow, Happy. **Box /6**.

CHRISTCHURCH Luxury ngalow, sep. D. room. 2 D. beds, acent golf course, vacant ssession, g.c.h. £38,000 Phone king 81590. **Box 41/6**.

car, owner, likes cooking gardening, country life, intelligent, conversation hopes to meet an educated widower divorcee with sense of humour genuinely solvent for friendship, possibly marriage, photo please, Hereford. **Box 32/6**.

BERKS Gent, working class 59 yrs 5'4" tall seeks lady for friendship, possible marriage, any area, photo appreciated and retired. **Box 37/6**.

WIDOWER 64 London area, seeks slim attractive lady 5ft 3ins to 5ft 6ins for friendship outings own home and car. **Box 35/6**.

LADY Cheshire 57 seeks gent non smoker, car owner, for holidays, dancing, genuine friendship, good cook, homeloving will move. **Box 36/6**.

WARWICKSHIRE widow 59, seeks friendship 5ft 10" **Box 34/6**.

BERKS Lady divorced 54, wishes to meet gentleman of similar age business gentleman preferred view to friendship. **Box 33/6**.

WEST Midlands widow seeks genuine male to share and care, widower 58 to 65, over 5'7". Why not find companionship widowers. **Box 30/6**.

WANTED "A man for all seasons" by lonely widow, mid 60s for friendship, car owner pref. like music, East Suffolk. Cancerian. **Box 20/6**.

WIDOW young 59 seeks male for friendship hope to move to Toronto Aug. is there a certain someone somewhere (

start new ho
agree relation
ties, 52 living i

ARTISTIC lad
interests music
arts, travel, see
anywhere, car
friendship po
caring relations

LADY 55 tal
walking, home,
seeks gent 58-68
nature, lasting
Box 39/6.

LADY late 50s
5'1" attractive
homely, varied
moved to Carlisle

EASY going
English divorcee, (
smoker, needs t
love of a good
naughty but nice
equilibrium. Reti
presently Berks bu
possibly abroad.
yours. Can you
exchanged, returne

GENTLEMAN s
retired, separated,
meet smart attracti
plus, willing to shar
life, for our mutu
happiness. Sha
Genuine. Photo a
returned. Bristol —
South. **Box 22/6**.

GENT 55 requires
willing to buy F & F o
21/6.

o Through common concerns (eg. children).
o Through clubs and social events.

All these have provided you with opportunities to pursue friendships. They all place you in contact with others. How many chance acquaintances have you met who have turned into friends? If you feel it would be a dividend to make new friends then in your choice of activities, interests and lifestyle, you could well bear this in mind: the choice of solitary pursuits is not easily going to put you in the path of other people.

So think about some of the activities you have chosen to do and the area you live in.

For an established interest could you attend a different club/ society/adult education centre?

If you are interested in lone pursuits such as stamp-collecting or bird-watching there are frequently societies which can bring together fellow enthusiasts.

Is there a post retirement club at your place of work?

Is there a residents association or interest group in your neighbourhood? This could give you a wide circle of acquaintances in your area.

Would you be prepared to join a committee or working group for a club or society you are involved in? This could put you in contact with a wider group and perhaps more people from other branches of that club.

If you look back at the list of ways people acquire friends you'll see that each of them gives you a starting point – something that you have in common outside yourselves that you can talk about. You may proceed by trial and error after that but then you can always fall back onto the common ground, which is reassuring.

Meeting new people

People differ over the ease with which they can manage meeting new people. For some, former memories of discomfort in unfamiliar company can be off-putting. If you are inclined to feel like this then it may be worthwhile thinking about what it is that makes you feel uncomfortable.

Remember too that other people you meet may have similar feelings. Recognising them in yourself may help you recognise them in others. Here are some things that may make you uncomfortable. Add any of your own that you have experienced.

o Feeling shy.
o Not knowing what to talk about.
o Being embarrassed by silences in the conversation.
o Being afraid of making a social blunder.
o Not being able to get a word in edgeways.
o Not knowing how to finish a conversation off.

_____

_____

_____

_____

Here are some suggested ways of overcoming any discomfort you might feel in unfamiliar company. They can help others feel at ease and that should help you feel more at ease yourself.

o Use the other person's name rather than just saying 'you'.

o Ask the other person's point of view, and give attention to what he or she says.

o Share those of your own experiences which seem to be similar to the other person's.

o Try and expand your replies beyond just 'yes' or 'no'. It's difficult to keep a conversation going in these circumstances.

o If someone is very shy don't fix him or her with a penetrating stare or be over attentive if other people are present.

o Invite someone he or she knows to join in your conversation.

If you haven't been meeting many new people recently you may have forgotten the sorts of feelings that can be aroused. Taking opportunities to form new relationships can mean that you do expose yourself and sometimes face the possibility of rejection. But, on the positive side it could lead to new and rewarding friendships.

Gentleman, 67 . . . . .

Some people take the step of advertising in a newspaper or magazine in order to seek new relationships. Whether you see this as a real possibility for you or not, try writing a three line advertisement of yourself. How would you sum up your strong points and unique characteristics? Remind yourself of your own value and the contributions that you as an individual make to your existing relationships. These characteristics are going to be present in new relationships.

Finally look again at the chart that you filled in on the changes in your relationships. Would you like to alter it? The way it looks now says something about your life. Thinking about altering it, is thinking about altering your life.

Getting involved

Involvement in your community can mean anything from starting a national charity to playing in a pub darts team. The differences between these activities are the sort of rewards you could expect from the activity, and the sort of commitment the activity would demand. Community involvement *can* be as demanding as a full-time paid job, or it can be simply a leisure activity to provide a little recreation.

Reasons for involvement

To help you think about the sort of community involvement that might interest you read through this list on the right of reasons that have been given by other people. Then tick the boxes to record how far you agree or disagree with each statement. Bill Sutcliffe whose case is looked at in more detail below is filled in as an example.

Bill Sutcliffe is just coming up to retirement age. He worked all his life running a small hardware shop and now he looks forward to taking things easy. He has a grown up family and many friends as well as a number of hobbies. Ten years ago Bill had a heart attack and has had to change his lifestyle. Both he and his wife were shocked by the incident and both were grateful for the help given by the British Heart Foundation. Now Bill wants to spend time in working as a volunteer for the Foundation. His response to the questions shows that he has marked statement 6 as a top priority, and that he is also in agreement with statements 4 and 8. He does not agree with any of the other statements.

Implications of the choices

Which of the 9 statements did you agree with most strongly?
o Were you thinking of a particular activity when you agreed with this statement?
o Are you still involved with this activity?
o Would you like to be involved in an activity that gave this sort of reward?
o Can you think of any activities available to you at the moment that might give you that sort of reward?

Reasons for involvement	You				Bill Sutcliffe			
	Agree strongly	Agree	Disagree	Disagree strongly	Agree strongly	Agree	Disagree	Disagree strongly
1. "I want to be able to use the skills and experience I have already."	☐	☐	☐	☐	☐	☐	☑	☐
2. "I want to have a status other than simply 'retired'."	☐	☐	☐	☐	☐	☐	☑	☐
3. "I want to keep in touch with things and maintain contact with people who are younger or older than myself."	☐	☐	☐	☐	☐	☐	☑	☐
4. "I want the companionship of working with others."	☐	☐	☐	☐	☐	☑	☐	☐
5. "I want to fill in some time."	☐	☐	☐	☐	☐	☐	☑	☐
6. "I want to help others."	☐	☐	☐	☐	☑	☐	☐	☐
7. "I want to remain fit and active mentally and physically."	☐	☐	☐	☐	☐	☐	☑	☐
8. "I want to try out a new experience."	☐	☐	☐	☐	☐	☑	☐	☐
9. "I want to work for a specific policy change."	☐	☐	☐	☐	☐	☐	☐	☑

You may already have an activity in mind that suits your own interests and you will probably be able to find an organisation that promotes this activity. If no such organisation exists you might consider setting one up.

Look at these examples of people who have become involved with organisations or self-help groups. With each of the examples look at the chart on this page and think how they might have completed it.

Mr Rice

"I've met a lot of different people in the Tooting Action for Pensioners Group and made a lot of contacts. There is a kind of friendship that exists in this group that is really extraordinary."

Pensioners' action groups are many and various. Most are local organisations campaigning for better conditions for pensioners in the area — bus services, refuse collection, access to public swimming baths, upkeep of local parks, welfare benefits, and so on. The group will usually be represented on local government committees. This allows it to keep all its members informed of any policies that may affect them and to exercise power through the votes of their representatives. If this is not enough, members can be mobilized to gather petitions or publicly demonstrate to make their point of view heard.

In the example above it's interesting that Mr Rice stresses the social advantages of the group — *"There's people to talk to who have similar interests and experience to your own, and there's a sense that if you do have a real grievance you have the power to do something about it, through the group."*

Miss Cuthbertson

"It doesn't matter what government is in power, no-one seems to get down to the nitty gritty of helping the poorest pensioner."

"I joined the local branch of the National Federation of Old Age Pensions Associations, hoping to influence policy. It's hard — you get so strung up."

The National Federation of Old Age Pensions Associations is also a self-help group — but it is a national organisation aimed at improving the living standards of retired people by bringing about changes in national policy on issues of major importance.

One of the most important of these is the campaign for a bigger State Pension for those who don't get an occupational pension.

"There's a stigma attached to Supplementary Pension — you're a second class citizen — young people can at least hope to improve their situation and get off Supplementary Benefit."

As well as the local branch of the National Federation Miss Cuthbertson is involved with a local pensioners' group and frequently petitions MPs on issues she feels are being overlooked.

"Ministers just repeat what's in the leaflets and all we get is what civil servants say they can afford . . . we've written to ministers about 'A Happier Old Age' and the Supplementary Benefit Review . . . I certainly feel our message is beginning to get through."

Sam Stanton

"It was my mate George who first got me to go down to the amateur dramatics society. He's very keen on theatre and that, and he knew I was good with electrics, so he got me to organise the lighting for one of their productions. I thought at the time I'd do it just the once as a favour, now I seem to spend most of my evenings there and a few weekends as well. I get that wrapped up in it I don't notice the time go."

Sam Stanton didn't set out to join a group at all. He had absolutely no interest in the theatre or in amateur dramatics but he was prepared to lend his skills as an electrician. To his own surprise he became increasingly absorbed in the technical problems of lighting a theatre production. He enjoyed the appreciation and the company of the other members of the society, and found himself happily spending time here.

Toxic waste protest

Action groups from Shelfield, Walsall Wood and Aldridge recently staged an angry demonstration to voice their fears about the dumping of toxic waste in the area.

The 200-strong group marched down Stubbers Green Road waving banners and shouting slogans.

Councillor Ray Burford, Chairman of Walsall Council's Environmental Health Committee, who has been involved in the campaign from the start, said that the council would continue to lend its full support to the fight against toxic waste dumping.

He said: "Now we have to gain the help and support of central government to put an end once and for all to the vile practices of firms producing toxic waste.

Jessie Wilde

"They've been dumping toxic waste in the underground mine workings at Stubbers Green half a mile away from us. The whole area is undermined by earlier workings so we're now living over an underground lake of toxic waste. Many people have been affected by sickness and nausea. School children have had to be sent home from school. When the wind is in a certain direction local people have to walk round with handkerchiefs over their mouths and noses. Permission for dumping was granted by the government so an action group has been formed to get them to change their minds."

The Walsall Wood Action Group is an example of a local community united in the face of a common threat. A petition has been signed by a large number of local residents, there have been public meetings, and action committees have been set up. Local councillors have been drawn in, and the Walsall Council Environmental Health Committee has been active in the campaign from the beginning. Pressure is being put on national government to put a stop to the dumping of the toxic waste.

Joe Daraldean

"I don't want to be 'helped out' by well-meaning do-gooders, I'm too independently minded for that. But there's the odd job about the house — like cleaning windows — that I can't tackle on my own. This skills exchange scheme put me in touch with Pamela — she's only in her 30s so it's no problem for her to do odd jobs like cleaning the windows, and in return I give her advice on this allotment she's just taken on."

'Skills exchanges' or 'link projects' are usually set up by a central organisation which puts in touch those who need a service or would like to acquire a skill, with those who can provide it. Age Concern were active in launching one such link scheme in Darlington in 1977. In this scheme everyone who 'borrowed' a service from the scheme had to 'pay back', by doing a job for someone else. Each person joining the scheme was given a list of what skills were available and two tokens. Each token entitled a member to one hour's work from the scheme.

After receiving two hours' work the member had to earn more tokens by helping someone else in the scheme.

Mrs Sinclair

"When they abolished the concessionary bus fares for pensioners, I was so angry that I wrote to the local paper to complain. I got so many letters of support that we had a meeting and decided to collect a petition. In two weeks we had 10,000 names and we took the whole lot to the Town Hall and dumped it on the steps. They weren't very pleased, but we got our concessionary fare back again."

Mrs Sinclair's petition to the local authority is an example of a one-off self-help scheme or pressure group. It brought people together over one particular issue — in this case changing the authority's policy on public transport. This type of group usually disbands as soon as its purpose has been achieved. Its members may have no more in common than a desire to see cheaper bus fares for pensioners.

On the other hand as they work together to achieve cheaper bus fares they may discover other issues they feel the same about and other policies that can be changed with a little group pressure.

What they got out of it

All of the examples given here involve an investment of time and energy. It may only be attending one meeting a year, or almost full-time work.

Mrs Sinclair's petition to the Town Hall is an example of a community project that requires a fairly short burst of activity, but a full-time commitment over that time. Setting up any kind of group activity — whether it's a rambling club or a political pressure group — is bound to involve a considerable amount of time and energy. On the other hand the rewards can be very high — the support and companionship from others who feel the same way, and the satisfaction of a common objective.

Joe Daraldean's involvement with the skills exchange is an example of a community activity which involves little time or commitment. There is no regular arrangement between Joe and Pamela, but each knows they can call on the other if they need a hand. From Joe's point of view it's convenient to be able to get some help in the house every now and again, and he rather enjoys giving advice on gardens and allotments.

Community involvement can occupy as little or as much of your time and energy as you choose. You may also find that the terms on which you first become involved will change with the passage of time — often in ways you least expect. These two examples show how Mr Rice and Miss Cuthbertson changed their opinions about what they valued in community involvement over two years.

Mr Rice

In the exercise at the beginning of this topic Mr Rice indicated that he was in strong agreement with these statements:

o "*I want to keep in touch with things and maintain contact with people who are younger or older than myself.*"
o "*I want to fill in some time.*"

Mr Rice joined the group initially for social reasons. He found that he missed the companionship at work, he was bored, and thought that the local pensioners action group might help him to meet other people in a similar position. After a few months in the group Mr Rice worked through the activity for a second time. He again indicated that he was in strong agreement with the statements above, but he also marked strong agreement with these statements:

o "*I want to have a status other than simply 'retired'.*"
o "*I want to help others.*"
o "*I want to try out a new experience.*"

The companionship is still the benefit he values most, but he has now become involved in the more practical work of the group.

Miss Cuthbertson

When she first joined the National Federation of Old Age Pensions Associations Miss Cuthbertson marked down strong agreement with this statement:

o "*I want to work for a specific policy change.*"

She also marked agreement with these statements:

o "*I want to help others.*"
o "*I want to remain fit and active mentally and physically.*"

Looking at the exercise again, having worked with the organisation for a few months she still held these views but she was also able to mark agreement with these statements:

o "*I want to keep in touch with things and maintain contact with people who are younger or older than myself.*"
o "*I want the companionship of working with others.*"

Her political aims had been in no way softened, but she felt that she valued the companionship of other members more than she had expected.

How are you involved?

The examples given illustrate a handful of individual cases, but there is no limit on the different ways people can be involved in their community, and the rewards they can get. Talking to the local shopkeeper, supporting a football team, writing a letter to the paper, are all examples of participating in the community.

Degrees of involvement
o What sort of involvement do you have in your own community? Make a list of examples.
o Which of the examples given in this topic correspond most closely with your own examples?
o Look at the list of reasons for involvement at the beginning of this topic. Which of them relates most closely to the examples in your list of activities in the community?

Community groups
The examples in this topic give only a taste of the variety of groups which operate in this country. This summary may give an idea of the range of groups.

o A community group can be as informal as a few people agreeing to meet for a cup of tea and a chat, to share an enthusiasm for model railways, or to share an allotment.
o It can be a group of people who come together to change one particular policy. At a local level this might mean the residents on a housing estate getting together to persuade the council that improvements to their homes are necessary. At a national level it can be organisations like Save The Whale or the Campaign for Nuclear Disarmament.
o National organisations like Age Concern or the Pre-School Playgroups Association began life as small self-help groups. They were started by individuals who felt that they spoke for a much larger number of people in the country as a whole, and that their voice should be heard at a national level. The fact that they were right is shown by the strength and size of both these organisations today.
o All the political parties in this country began as small groups of people who had ideas on how the country should be run, and felt that there were others who saw things the same way as they did.

And finally . . .
It's worth remembering that as a pensioner you join an increasingly large proportion of the population.

There are about 9 million pensioners in the United Kingdom which is about one third of the voting population. Dr Eric Midwinter, the Director of the Centre for Policy on Ageing — an advisory body to the government — has no doubts about how pensioners should use that power. He has recently stated: *". . . if the elderly are convinced — and it is a big "if" — that they have a political case to make and that they are genuinely prepared to face the problems involved in so doing, then they would be well advised to be realistic about it and not play around the edges. In the politest and most diplomatic sense, they would need to threaten — and make sure the threat is a realistic one — through the whole gamut of the rally, the protest meeting, the petition, the demonstration, the lobbying of councillors and MPs, but ultimately the cross on the ballot paper. They must say to a candidate on a ward, 'Fine, here we are, this is our policy, we have 1,500 votes in this ward promised to you if you deliver, if you don't we're voting for the other bloke! It's the vote eventually which will count."*

Images of ageing

"...then there is the undoubtedly well-meant but casual address by hospital staff who find it easier to call a patient 'Dad' than find out his own name; the jocular familiarity (so near the borderline of impatient contempt) of bus conductors; the lumping together of their pensioners by some personnel officers as 'old folk'."

Of course not all hospital staff, bus conductors or personnel officers are like that. But by the time you reach the age of retirement you will have met someone who will have dealt with you in terms of your age alone and not thought about you as a person.

It's easy to label people by age. It's something many people do. At the same time people's ideas about youth and age tend to alter as they themselves grow older.

Can you recall how your views on the 'prime of life' have altered throughout your life? Or how you thought of grandparents when you were a child and how you think about them now?

Youth and age

Think about the point in life when you personally would label someone as old and mark it on the scale.

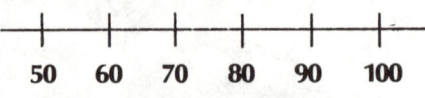

50 60 70 80 90 100

Next try and find someone from each decade of life.

Ask them each to name three people, one young, one middle aged and one old. Ask them to tell you the ages of these three people or if they don't know to guess the ages of the people they have mentioned.

Talk to them about the three people they've chosen. Ask why they see each of them as being young, middle aged or old.

Then fill in the chart to help you to compare the results. Put in any words used to describe the age of the person they were talking about.

You may have found that people you spoke to at the younger end of the age range had far more definite ideas about whom they thought of as old. Perhaps as we get older we get a more flexible idea about what old age is!

You may have found also that people mentioned looks, activity, health or a whole range of other things apart from age itself to describe youthfulness, middle age or old age.

The idea of age and old age is like shifting sand. Footballers may be old at 33, prime ministers young at 50. Occasionally you can hear of someone being called 'young' right into old age. You hear stories of solicitors aged 76 being 'young Mr. Davies'—old Mr. Davies, being 97 and living on the south coast or even dead.

You too may be seen differently by people of various ages. Coming to terms with the fact that you may be seen as old by some people though is not the same as accepting age as the main label people use to deal with you.

The age group of the people I talked to	Someone they thought young and their characteristics	Age	Someone they thought middle aged and their characteristics	Age	Someone they thought old and their characteristics	Age
0–10						
11–20						
21–30						
31–40						
41–50						
51–60						
61–70						
71–80						
81–90						
91–						

"It's in the paper so it must be true..."

Look through a week's editions of newspapers and magazines that you normally take. Or go to your library and examine a wider range than your usual reading matter.

Newspapers and magazines as well as the radio and TV often associate people of certain ages with certain activities or lifestyles. They put a 'label' on them on the basis of their age alone.

So it's worth looking at them because it may help you in your thoughts about how being older is seen in our society.

Look at the news stories in local papers. Ask yourself are the ages of the people in any particular story relevant? Take the following for instance:

> Two elderly women drivers were involved in the first car accident of the winter last Friday. Mrs. Grace Jones aged 59 and Mrs. Vera Briggs aged 65 collided on black ice on a country lane outside Frinton on Sea. Mrs. Jones received facial cuts and bruises, Mrs. Briggs a sprained shoulder.

Two messages come out of this story. One is that black ice was responsible. But apparently age was also important. Black ice could cause any car to skid. It could equally have been Tony Smith aged 17 and Chris Phillips aged 19. Presumably then the story would have been interpreted as the folly of youth rather than the infirmity of age!

Look at some of the stories in the national dailies. Look at stories about politicians, judges, actors, entertainers. How often do the ages of political leaders see the light of day? How often would we think it relevant to be told the age of any of these people?

Next, try looking at the advertisements. You might want to concentrate on magazines or Sunday colour supplements for this. Try and assess the ages of people shown in the advertisement pictures.

On the right are a list of items. Note down roughly the ages of the models, if you find an advertisement for any of the products.

	Age		Age
Bed linen		Clothes	
Cavity insulation		Household goods	
Breakfast cereals		Double glazing	
Deodorant		Bedtime drinks	
Washing powder		Make-up	
Stereo systems		Insurance	

You may well have found that insurance, double glazing, annuity schemes, bedtime drinks are often sold using older models. Perhaps one reason for this is that an older person and the product they are advertising are associated in people's minds with feelings of security and stability; they're cosy and safe.

Things which are advertised as being fast, for fun and to increase attractiveness are frequently sold using younger models.

Television

If you have a television, watch the advertisements one evening and see if your investigations from newspapers are borne out.

How many newscasters, programme presenters, are older people?

How many plays feature older people?

How many situation comedies feature older people?

You might even want to work out what proportion of time on the air older people get.

You may have discovered that young and middle aged people far outweigh the elderly on TV programmes. Of course you can't tell the age of people on the radio — perhaps that has more than its fair share of older people!

Also if you look at the few programmes that do have older actors, you may feel that they only play certain sorts of roles. Older people may be seen as forgetful, belligerent, confused, perhaps even foolish.

So as you watch plays or comedies on the TV see if you can spot the way elderly people have been typecast.

Here are some thinking points. You may not agree with them. Now that 1 in 6 of the population is eligible for a retirement pension:

o There ought to be more elderly people on TV.
o There ought to be more programmes for older people . . . after all their tastes *might* be different from the rest of the population.
o There ought to be more plays and comedies that represent elderly people the way that they really are and not just how other people imagine them to be.

How others see you

You may think that the way newspapers and magazines view older people has got nothing to do with you. But just stop for a moment and think back over the past few weeks to any occasions when you think people have acted towards you in a certain way because of your age.

Here are some examples to help you think about such occasions:

o You run for the bus. The bus conductor helps you on and guides you to a nearby seat.
o You retired six months ago and in town on Monday you met some old work associates. They say *"Well you haven't changed at all"* and you think *"I don't know what they expect to have happened to me in the course of six months!"*
o You go to a new hairdressers and the receptionist says *"Oh you'll be wanting the concessionary rate"*.
o You're sitting in the pub. A teenager jostles your elbow and says *"Sorry Grandad"*.
o You decide to have a lie-in one morning. About 11.00 o'clock your young next door neighbour rings the door-bell and wants to know if you're all right.

o The young assistant where you work finds out you're 60 and spends the rest of the week offering to reach to high shelves for you.
o The woman on the bacon counter at the supermarket starts talking about pensions and points out the cheapest cut of bacon.
o You are in your car and are overtaken by a group of youths who flash their lights and pull in sharply in front of you.
o You offer to help your daughter with some furniture removing and she looks doubtful.
o It's a family party and you are having a good time dancing and generally acting rather merrily. Your niece says *"I hope I'm still lively when I'm your age"*.

The examples show a number of attitudes:

o The main pointer of how to behave towards someone is their age.
o Older people are seen as in need of help, concessions or concern.
o Impatience with age.
o Being older means being infirm.

Now consider the occasions that you have thought up. Are any of these attitudes apparent in behaviour towards you? Which ideas concern you most? And what if anything can you do if you don't like the way you are treated?

Some of the occasions mentioned above you may not find upsetting. Or you may feel that since no offence is meant most of the time then you shouldn't take it. On the other hand you may feel you'd like to respond even if you aren't offended purely to make it clear that age is not a bar to activity.

Passing remarks about your age can be annoying whether condescending or not. You might feel more in control if you think about what responses you could make and how you make them.

If you really do get cross you could consider the pay-offs of responding sharply. Letting off steam can sometimes work wonders. On the other hand you could end up by finding yourself in a verbal battle. You'll already know whether you're the sort of person who can take on verbal battles. And if you are then it's probably just a question of adding age to your subjects for heated discussion.

If you don't feel that being aggressive is going to help then perhaps you could consider answering in kind: giving as good as you get. Or perhaps you could reply by dealing with some issue other than age.

Look back at the list of attitudes again. Pick out the passing remarks and statements and think about what you might say for each example. Then think about how you would actually feel if you did say it!

Consider this example again. You're sitting in a pub and a teenager jostles your elbow and says *"Sorry Grandad."*
What would your response be:

o Make a sharp reply *"I'm rather pleased I'm not your Grandad."*

o Reply in kind *"That's OK sonny."*

o Change the subject *"Don't worry. It's really crowded in here tonight."*

Impatience with age and unfair remarks about it can also be galling.

One possible response if people start tutting and sighing as you fumble for change at the supermarket is to widen the discussion. Make some remark about the construction of modern purses, or mention how your daughter spilled all the contents of her purse on the floor at the supermarket.

You could try varying these two responses and see what happens.

o Where you take age head on and actually respond in kind with a gentle reminder that everyone has an age of some kind.

o Where you concentrate on an issue other than age.

"But I don't want to be helped across the road."

Perhaps more difficult than the passing remark is the situation where you find yourself the recipient of help when you don't want it, or your status as a receiver of help is dwelt upon.

One formidable lady when seeking her senior citizens travel ticket in London was told:

"Oh yes it's the concessionary ticket you'll be wanting".

Whereupon she replied *"It is not a concession. It is my right!"*

What would you have said to the ticket clerk or the hairdresser who talked of concessions? There's nothing wrong with concessions but you may not want to feel like a receiver of charity. Well intended offers of help that nevertheless go against the grain are probably the most difficult of all the images of ageing to deal with. Perhaps you could accept gracefully but counter the offer with an alternative offer of help of your own?

When you don't want or need help you need to distinguish between people who are being:

o Genuinely kind.
o Thoughtless.
o Hurtful.

Think about offers of help you have received and try and work out whether the lines are crossed between you and your helper. Perhaps the helper has not really seen you as someone of independence with organisational abilities of your own.

See if you can work out whether you need to find a way:

o To say no without offending.
o To re-educate the helper.
o To show someone that the way they are offering help is hurtful to you.

By looking at the way that others see us, and how and why retired people are often seen as old and dependent when they are neither, it's possible to begin to work out what sort of response is most suitable for what situations. There are many different responses — being amused, annoyed, interested but not really concerned or deciding to try and change the image that others have of the retired and of yourself in particular. Images can be made and broken. They are not fixed or rigid though sometimes they may seem so. The choice of what to do is up to the individual.

Men and women

People are often labelled as having certain social characteristics because of their sex. For both sexes there are occupations and ways of behaving that are generally considered acceptable. If you behave in an unconventional manner you may make other people feel anxious. You may become a threat to them, perhaps challenging their own behaviour and occupations.

Breaking out

People learn from society how men and women are expected to behave and what they are supposed to be able to do. When you retire you are taking on a new life and you have an opportunity to do things differently.

This is worth thinking about for two reasons.

o Breaking out of the limitations both you and others have imposed on your life can enable you to perhaps get a different perspective about things.

o One day you may need skills that you don't have at the moment — skills that are associated with the other sex.

The great cooking debate

Pete Allen is 67. He retired two years ago and has gradually become more interested in the idea of learning to cook. He likes his food, enjoys organising a sequence of doing things efficiently and he also likes something tangible from his efforts.

He is thinking of going to adult education cookery classes. But there seems to be a certain amount of opposition!

His wife, Cassie, got rather offended and asked him whether her cooking was no longer good enough for him.

His son, Eddy, asked why he didn't spend a bit more time in the garden instead, which would save Eddy the bother of having to help him.

His grandson, little Eddy, said he could have done cookery classes at school but had decided it was too girlish.

When Pete mentioned it to his friends, mainly ex-work mates, they said they thought he was going soft and teased him.

There were no adult education cookery courses specifically for men, and a neighbour told him that she'd been to one two years ago where there were 16 women and one man.

So Pete was faced by people who were putting pressure on him for different reasons:

o His wife felt her own position to be threatened.

o It was more convenient to his son in this case, that he kept to his traditional male role.

o It didn't line up with his grandson's idea of what men should do. Pete's friends felt the same way and so did his neighbour.

o He was also faced with the prospect of finding himself the only man in a cookery class which might make him feel odd.

No one could blame him if he gave up on the idea. It takes courage to resist such pressures from other people. Unless Pete got to grips with some of the pressures he would always have numerous excuses for giving up.

So what could he do?

Talking to Cassie

o He could point out that it would be useful if he could cook in case Cassie was ill or went away to her sister's . . . that is, he could turn the discussion round to talk about how sensible it is to have the knowledge to be able to cope in an emergency.

o He could specialise, doing the sort of cookery Cassie isn't interested in like Indian or Chinese. He can then cook the occasional unusual dish to give Cassie a break.

Talking to Eddy

o He could discuss a new gardening plan with Eddy that involved everyone in less work.

o He could see if it wouldn't be possible for him to do more gardening; perhaps growing vegetables to fit in with his cooking ambitions.

Talking to little Eddy

o He could ask little Eddy just what he would do if he had to fend for himself — whether a diet of cheese sandwiches would be satisfactory.

o He could talk to little Eddy about his camping holidays and how he felt about having cooked meals for himself and his friends.

Talking to friends and neighbours

o He could just avoid bringing the subject up any more.

o He could invite his friends round once he had started cookery classes and demonstrate his new skills with his delicious meals.

Odd man out?

o He could ask the local education authority if they would consider putting on a class for men.

o He could ask around if he could find any like minded individuals who would like to do the same class.

o He could ask himself what reason does he really have for feeling odd, anyway. And who cares what anybody else thinks.

"I wonder how you cook lobster . . . . and what should you eat with it?"

"I can't see what's wrong with fish fingers for tonight."

The daily round

Here is a list of everyday household activities which are often associated with one sex rather than the other.

Tick which sex as a general rule you see being associated with each activity.

	Women	Men
Mending electrical appliances.		
Washing.		
Household maintenance.		
Sewing.		
Ironing.		
Carpentry.		
Car maintenance.		
Washing up.		
Household cleaning.		
Painting and decorating.		
Dealing with bills/bank etc.		
Arranging to get repairs done by servicemen.		

Swapping over

Now think about a skilled activity which you have always associated with the opposite sex and never tried . . . something that you think might be useful and fun.

If no activity readily springs to mind, try going through the prospectus of your local adult education centre.

Note down those classes which you immediately dismiss as not being for you. If your first thought is that they are for *men* or for *women,* stop and ask yourself why you should react in this way.

Is it just because you have always associated that subject with one sex or the other? Is it because they hold no interest for *you?* Would you be put off because you have never done anything like that before? Do you think you would be embarrassed if you were the only man or women in the class?

Having thought of a skill you might like to acquire think about whether you would be faced with the same sorts of reactions as Pete Allen.

○ Who if anyone might feel threatened about you taking up this activity?
○ Who might have fairly strong feelings about it not being the sort of thing that men or that women do?
○ Who might feel you should be spending your time doing more sensible things?

If your answers to these questions are your 'partner', 'family' or 'close friends' perhaps you should talk to them and see how they actually do feel. Sometimes you may worry that people would disapprove only to find out after talking it over that this isn't the case. Other times, if they aren't happy with the idea you may be able to talk them round to your way of thinking.

Could you marshal your arguments like Pete Allen did as to why it would be fun and helpful to take up this activity?

Breaking out of your ideas about the sorts of skills men and women have can be exciting. But the sorts of things discussed so far don't affect day to day living that much. However, thinking about men's and women's jobs within the home is a different matter.

Now look at your ticks again. Would you have ticked the columns in the same way if you had have been describing activities in *your own household?*

If there is a lot of agreement between your general idea of associations and what actually goes on in your house then it's likely that you do use fairly traditional ways of deciding who does what.

Of course you can divide up jobs in the house between people in a way that has nothing to do with whether they are male or female.

There are different styles of organising jobs.

○ One person has total responsibility for a particular activity.
○ One person acts as boss, the others act as labourers.
○ Whoever happens to be around has a go at doing a particular activity.
○ There is joint involvement over an activity and each person contributes equal skills.
○ For some activities it may be that no one has the skills, so outside help is sought.

Making changes

Talk to your partner or the person you share your home with and work out which of the styles listed on the previous page are used for each of the activities in your household. If you look through these styles of doing day to day household activities you will probably see that the first two fit closely with the traditional ideas about men's work and women's work.

Now think about how easily you could apply any of the styles that you don't use. Would you like to try them?

Write down any difficulties you imagine might occur if you did change styles. Ask your partner to do the same. For instance if one of you takes total responsibility for a particular activity has the other partner the skills to take it over if you did change?

Write down any benefits that you and your partner think could be derived from changing styles. Perhaps you should give it a try as an experiment.

Reactions to changing

Here are some possible reactions that changes in household styles might provoke.

o I found when I had entire responsibility for the household bills I felt rather nervous. I had never had to do this in the whole of my life and felt I couldn't learn it fast enough. I lacked confidence.

o I found that when I was put in the situation of being the labourer, pasting the wallpaper and standing at the bottom of the ladder, I felt very resentful.

o I felt very good about having total command over the painting and decorating and that I could do everything to my own ridiculously high standards.

o We found when we were exercising joint control about household cleaning that it took much longer and discussions about how thorough the cleaning was to be and how often it should take place got quite heated but we worked out an agreement and felt much happier with the results.

o We found when neither of us had total responsibility for doing the washing that nothing very much got done.

o We felt a bit ashamed about not being able to lay the tiles in the bathroom. So this time we decided to have a go together rather than pay someone else to do it.

Rearranging your thoughts about skills, sharing responsibility and organisation can have a good many long ranging effects on daily household tasks and also bring about some exciting and entertaining possibilities.

Attractiveness

Your personality is coloured by what it means to be a man or a woman. From an early age you will have learned what is regarded as the 'correct' behaviour for your sex and what sort of behaviour to expect from the opposite sex. This awareness of your sex is something that remains with you for the whole of your life.

Unfortunately the society that we live in can give rise to opinions that there is something ridiculous about older people being concerned with their image as men or women.

Being attractive

Of course we do talk about people being personally attractive without referring to their sex. We talk about people who have an attractive manner or an attractive personality. Describing someone in this way puts them in a favourable light.

Below are words which are generally linked with describing attractiveness. Some are associated more with one sex than the other.

Put a circle around the words you would feel uncomfortable about using if you were describing a 70 year old woman and then underline the words you would feel uncomfortable about using if you were describing a 70 year old man.

Pretty	Fragile
Personable	Lovely
Beautiful	Graceful
Delicate	Elegant
Gentle	Charming
Tender	Lively
Flirtatious	Sweet
Handsome	Pleasant
Good looking	Striking

Now think about if you were describing a 25 year old man or woman. Would you feel uncomfortable about using the words marked?

There is no reason why all the words should not be used to describe people of any age. But many words which are used to expand the idea of attractiveness are often associated with youth.

If you think you could use any of the words to describe someone of any age then you probably have an open view of what attractiveness is. The same applies if you felt many of them could refer to men or women.

Now think about some friends of about your own age or older. If you had to describe their attractive features, both the physical, and in terms of personality, how would you go about it? What sort of words would you choose to use?

The words you use will probably depend on your own views about how being older relates to being attractive.

Do any of the following statements come close to your own views?
o Feeling attractive is something which doesn't stop when you stop being young.
o As long as you carry on behaving in the same way as you behaved when you were young then you're likely to carry on feeling attractive.
o Feeling attractive is about being young. I'm no longer young and therefore I'm no longer bothered about being attractive.

The first view is a broad definition of attractiveness. Being alive is being attractive. The other two views accept that being young is being attractive.

Now look at those statements again. And instead of just the word 'attractive', use the phrase 'sexually attractive'. Did it make you feel differently about any of the statements? Part of what people generally accept as attractiveness is sexual attractiveness. Are your views about that different from your views about attractiveness generally?

Thinking again

When you retire, new friends and different activities can mean you are seen as a stranger again — what you do, say and look like will all be up for assessment. And you too will be making the same sorts of assessments of others.

So it's worth re-examining your ideas of what attractiveness means to you — in its widest sense of what makes people attractive and then in its narrower sense of what makes people sexually attractive.

When you meet new people you find some more attractive than others. Finding someone attractive is a feeling that can happen to you at any time — it's in no way foolish or inappropriate, whatever your age.

o It can stimulate your own feelings of being attractive.
o It can make you feel excited that something new is on the horizon.
o It can bring out a side in you that has perhaps been submerged for some time.

For some people suddenly finding others attractive can sometimes be a threatening feeling.

o They may feel that if they show they are attracted they might be misunderstood.
o They may feel that other people they know will misunderstand and perhaps be jealous.
o They may feel if they do anything about it they will set off a train of events they can't control.

Sometimes you lose those feelings of enjoyment at meeting new people or your concern with being attractive because you go through a period of your life when such feelings aren't being used, when everything becomes routine and you aren't meeting new people. When you're suddenly in a situation of being seen in a fresh light by new people you may need to re-learn attractiveness.

Part of this process is learning to accept or cope with other people's attitudes and part of it is reminding yourself of how your own attitudes towards yourself encourage other people to be attracted by you.

Personal appearance

You can get a clear picture of how people see themselves by looking at their personal appearance.

Think about changes to your personal appearance in the past 10 years. Have you changed your hairstyle?
Have you changed the sorts of clothes you wear?
Have you changed the colours of the clothes you wear?
Have you changed the sorts of shoes you wear?

If you're a woman have you changed the type of make-up you wear?

Do you think that the general picture of you is 'older' now than it was 10 years ago?

Have you made deliberate decisions to change your appearance during this time? Have you taken interest in fashions and followed them?

Have you paid attention to what other people, perhaps friends and relatives have said about your appearance?

Here are two reports of changes:

Daisy Linford
"Ten years ago I was dyeing my hair brown. It was naturally quite grey but I thought it made me look younger to keep my hair coloured. I felt I didn't want to look dowdy. So I carried on with this great rigmarole. Last year I decided it had to stop. It was too time consuming and expensive. I had the brown cut out and discovered my hair was bright white! I bought two new dresses for my holidays, one bright pink, one bright blue. They looked terrific. Now I wear bright cheerful colours all the time and feel that I look more attractive than I have done for years."

Tony Hall
"After a lifetime of wearing overalls everyday, I felt a bit like a spare part in decent clothes day in day out. I decided I'd buy some denim jeans like everyone has nowadays. The first time my son saw them he asked me why I didn't wear smarter trousers. And my wife refused to go out with me in them and told me I ought to act my age. So I'm afraid I've given in and it's back to the cavalry twill though I thought the denims looked nice and I felt happy in them."

How much does your personal appearance depend on what other people want you to look like?
How often do you buy clothes that make *you* feel good?
Do you think of clothes as a way of expressing yourself?
How long is it since you've bought an item of clothing that was different for you?
How much do you 'dress for your age'?

How you dress can be an outward expression of how you feel about yourself. Dressing so *you* think you look nice can say to other people 'Here I am, I'm attractive and I dress accordingly'.

Being clear that you want to be attractive to other people can bring to the surface some of the ideas that you have about yourself as a man or a woman, how you behave in that respect and how other people want you to behave.

Sex and attractiveness

How you express yourself as a member of your sex and feel about sex in general is called sexuality. And one of the problems about thinking about sexuality is that it is frequently regarded as just that — a problem!

There is a lot of pressure on people to think that sex and conscious feelings about one's sexual existence are only for the young.

If you don't express interest in sex and feel that your present existence is satisfactory, then that's fine. You don't have a problem. Although it's worthwhile reminding yourself that other people may have different views.

But if you feel dissatisfied with how you are able to express your sexuality or, other people's perception of it, then you might find it useful to think about some of the following points:

o There are lots of Victorian views about sex around even now — that it shouldn't be fun, that there are consequences to suffer. If you and your partner don't have to worry about pregnancy, you are in the fortunate position that the only consequence of your sexual relations is enjoyment.

o Newspapers, magazines and TV all equate attractiveness and sex with being young. Everyone is subjected to this sort of approach day in, day out. No wonder some people start to believe it. Do you?

o Many people have difficulty in imagining that their own parents ever have any sex life. Perhaps you brought your own children up without ever talking much about sex. They could just be embarrassed about any expression of sexuality. Being scathing about it is a way of coping with embarrassment.

o Sex is still very much connected in many people's minds with being involved in a partnership. Being part of a couple is seen as being a normal state of affairs. Of course, if you're single sexuality is just as much a part of your life. It's not irrelevant.

Your life

It may help you to think about attractiveness by thinking more about your own life. The following questions may help you. Some of them are about your own attitudes and reactions, some about other people's.

o Do you feel less attractive than normal when you are with young people?

o Do you ever see young people enjoying their sexuality and feel that that sort of enjoyment has nothing to do with you?

o Do you feel uncomfortable if someone flirts with you?

o Do you feel annoyed if other people expect you to behave 'old'?

o Do you enjoy it when other people find you attractive?

o Do you get cross if people make jokes or put you down for behaving like an attractive man or woman?

o Do your family, relatives and friends let you know what they think is appropriate behaviour for you?

Having thought about these questions, particularly if the first three have struck a chord, perhaps you feel you would like to change some of your own attitudes. Perhaps, however, your views are that it is generally other people's attitudes and reactions that create problems.

Whatever your views, bringing about changes in attitudes and reactions either in yourself or other people is a challenging matter.

Changing your own attitudes
If there is a difference between the sort of image you would like to create of your attractiveness and sexuality and what you actually do, you might like to try some changes.

Try writing down all the things you would like to do and ask yourself which of your ideas you would be happy to try out and which ones really are daydreams. Ask yourself what's stopping you from putting the realistic ideas into practice; why you're not changing your appearance, responding to friendly overtures, etc. Practise attractiveness.

When you come across an attitude or reaction in other people regarding attractiveness or sexuality that makes you feel uncomfortable or embarrassed, don't just put it to one side. Ask yourself why it makes you uncomfortable. If you don't say anything at the time think afterwards what you might have said — make it clear to yourself what your own attitude is.

Changing other people's attitudes
If you get annoyed at other people's attitudes or reactions, how often do you actually say something.

Talking to other people about your views may help to make them more sensitive to your own ways of going about things. And even if it doesn't, it helps you to let off steam.

Everybody should have the right to be personally attractive throughout life. It's a form of self expression and not one which should be denied to you by other people.

What is learning?

Learning is something which goes on all the time; it doesn't stop when people leave school. But it isn't always recognised as 'proper' learning which to so many people means just the mental drudgery of learning apparently meaningless facts by heart.

Look at this list of six activities all of which could be described as learning experiences. Tick which of them *you* would identify as such.

1. Learning new information	☐
2. Learning new skills	☐
3. Passing exams	☐
4. Gaining new experiences	☐
5. Widening personal horizons	☐
6. Following up an interest	☐

As you read the following case studies think about which of the above definitions might apply to them.

Case 1: Mary

Mary is 68. Two years ago her husband Bill died following a long and rare illness. While nursing Bill she discovered that some 750 people contracted this illness each year and that little was known about it. What is more, no-one knew of anyone who was doing any research on it. Mary knew nothing of research or medicine, but she just wanted to do something.

The first thing she did was to write an article for a women's magazine. She had never written before — she joked with friends that the longest thing she had ever written was her Christmas shopping list! She did not expect the magazine to publish her article, but writing it had made her feel better — she felt she was at least trying to do something.

To her surprise the magazine did publish her article and within a few days the local newspaper wanted to do an article about her and the local radio station wanted to do an interview.

After the dust had settled, she found that she had a steady flow of letters from other wives and husbands of sufferers. Some even phoned her to share their thoughts and feelings.

Her first thoughts were that interest would decline and that would be the end of that. But it wasn't. She continued to get two or three letters a day and several telephone calls a week.

She decided to set up a local telephone help-line through which she could provide comfort and advice to others, and where necessary could transfer them to other local agencies. She got support from the local newspaper and the local radio station, and from volunteers who were in the same situation as herself.

The telephone help-line taught her a lot about voluntary work in general, and about this kind of advisory work in particular. After two years the help-line was sufficiently well-established to run itself, but rather than letting her new skills and expertise go to waste Mary decided she would like to work with the Samaritans. She has now just started her training and although she finds it tough going she enjoys the work, and the challenge of doing something different. Mary often says now that she has never worked harder and she has learned more since her retirement and the death of her husband than she had ever learned before.

Case 2: Jack

From the age of 13 Jack had been a plumber. He had worked until he was 67 at the same firm in South Yorkshire. When he retired he was the longest serving member of the firm and a personal friend of the family which owned it. They gave him a splendid send-off — with a party and gifts of a watch, a food hamper and a wood-turning lathe.

Jack lived alone in a bungalow, one room of which was given to a workroom. His new lathe was installed there. Being a plumber for 54 years, Jack knew little about wood-turning. The first few things he tried to turn on the lathe were pretty poor. He tried to make a fruit bowl, but he didn't tool up the machine very well. The result was a large bowl with a cracked side and a hole in the bottom. His next object was a set of wooden plates — none of which looked like each other. But he kept at it.

After five months he was becoming proficient. After a year, he produced his first set of chairs with beautifully turned legs and headpieces. In fact they won a prize in a local crafts competition.

It is now five years since Jack retired and he has a full book of orders for his products. Far more, in fact, than he can ever hope, or want, to complete. He just picks and chooses what he wants to do and tends to do things straight away only for people he likes.

Case 3: Harry

Harry was a shop steward at a car factory in the Midlands when he was prematurely retired following a serious accident. At 62 he found himself out of work, out of union politics and relatively poor. What struck Harry most forcefully was the lack of information about his rights and the disorganisation of older people when it came to trying to improve their rights.

The first year of his attempts to 'improve the lot of the retired' were frustrating.

"Politicians just aren't that interested in the old. They give 'em their Christmas bonus and think that that's it."

"Trade unions are as bad. They'll negotiate for pension rights but won't organise pensioners around issues like free telephones or reduced cost TV licences or increased benefits."

"In my first year I got bitter about the attitude of my former mates in the trade unions and politics and incredibly frustrated at other retired and old people who had just given up the fight!"

Harry decided that he had to do something on his own to *"get things moving"*. He decided that the retired and elderly couldn't expect help from those at work, so they had to get their own thing going through self-help and mutual aid. He formed a Pensioner Unity Group (PUG) — taking the idea from a newspaper article he'd read.

At first he could only find seven members — most of them friends. But these seven worked hard. Within 18 months they had 98 members and regular meetings and were producing a newsletter. They had mounted campaigns about pensioner rights on local transport and television licences, had met every MP in their area and kept them up-to-date on the issues faced by the elderly.

They had also started a skills-exchange in which people offered to help others with their skills and expertise in such areas as joinery or plumbing or cake-decorating in exchange for others' goods and services.

PUG is in the middle of obtaining resources from both Urban Aid and the Manpower Services Commission for its work and is setting up a Pensioner Education Unit so that pensioners can pass on their specialised knowledge to each other.

Harry says that he and his fellow PUG workers have had to learn all the skills of setting up a self-help organisation from scratch. He says the biggest thing he has learned was just how difficult it is to keep something like a newsletter or a skill-exchange going. He's also had to deal with the tax people on more than one occasion and that meant him 'learning up the law'.

Case 4: Bernard

When Bernard retired he decided to sort out his garden. Even his best friends described his garden as 'an Amazon rain forest.'

Bernard knew nothing about gardening, but by borrowing books from his local libraries he built up a considerable knowledge of the subject. He also went along to gardening shows and listened regularly to *Gardeners' Question Time* on the radio — a programme he calls *"the Open University Gardening Course!"*

Last year, Bernard's garden took care of almost all of his own vegetable needs and produced many fine blooms. *"It's nothing special"*, says Bernard, *"but it is a lot nicer now than it used to be".*

Indeed, it isn't anything special — it just looks like any decent garden that someone has taken a bit of care over. The point is that Bernard's garden used to be a jungle — even local cats were afraid to enter it — and Bernard has had to learn about gardening from scratch. But with applicaion he managed to acquire considerable expertise.

Case 5: Angela

Angela is coming up to retirement. She has worked in a high street supermarket for nearly 20 years and is well-known both among the staff and the customers. She has no real idea of what she's going to do with her time when she finally does retire.

"I don't work for the money — I work for the company it gives you . . . I like to be with people".

Angela went to an evening class retirement course and made friends with most of the group. She discovered that although most of them did have interests they were all worried about being lonely and cut-off in their retirement. Angela suggested that they should continue to meet after the course had finished so they could follow up interests together and share their experiences.

Drawing on the interests of other members of the group Angela drew up this list of projects the group should begin.

o Help to make tape recordings for the blind.
o Join or set up a class on local industrial history.
o Learn about rockery plants.
o Learn how to do those complicated knitting patterns properly.
o Find out more about the history of Ireland (one member of the class had just been there on holiday).
o Learn more about art history.

They decided to ask visiting speakers to address their group and to approach the local education authority and ask them to provide a course in local history as there wasn't one.

Angela's main interest is in meeting other people — she wouldn't dream of reading anything about art history if she was working on her own, but doing it in a group has got her started and now she is really keen.

Case 6: Mike

Mike is 80. He describes himself as a compulsive reader. All of his life he has read books, newspapers, comics, magazines, whatever he could get his hands on. Mike has got himself a part-time job cutting newspapers for a cuttings library. He does the work at home. It doesn't pay much, but he gets six free newspapers each day. He cuts them according to instructions the library gives him, and puts the cuttings in different envelopes.

Recently they've asked him to cut out all the stories in the newspaper that mention a particular place — Ilkley Moor. In six months he has collected some 300 cuttings about this place and has become very absorbed by it. He borrowed books about the place from the library and he now claims that there is nothing he doesn't know about the moor. He gave a talk at the club about the moor and people said to him afterwards that he'd earned the nickname 'Old Moor' — that amused him.

Case 7: Doris

Doris is 60 and disabled. She's a keen member of the pensioner group at the local church. She does the flower arrangements for the church at her home with flowers collected by other church workers. At least once a week she is picked up and taken to a church service or pensioners' group meeting.

She reads a lot about religion and follows the affairs of the parish and of the church very closely. She is often visited by members of the congregation and by church office holders and her advice is much respected by both groups.

Case 8: Glyn

In his 20's, Glyn played rugby and was an active member of the rugby club. When he gave up playing at 35 he kept his membership, but only went occasionally to the club.

Now that he has retired he visits the club more regularly — mainly at lunchtimes. Recently he has been roped in on a training course for referees. He helps set up the video machines and talks about changes in the rules since he was a player. His old interest in the game has been revived and he takes a keen interest in matches played locally and covered on TV — always keeping an eye open for infringements of the rules.

The club coach says that Glyn is now an invaluable source of information about the rules of the game. Next year, he'll be a key figure in a series of classes for players on that subject.

About these cases

All these cases concern people who are coming up to retirement or who have retired. They all involve people becoming more active or remaining active.

One important link between them is learning: all of the case histories involve some new learning. For some it is a new skill or set of skills; for others, it is learning about a new subject. In some cases it is learning that hard work at something you're not sure about can pay off. And everybody learned to cope with changing circumstances.

The example of Mary shows her learning new information and new skills. She found out more about the particular illness from which her husband had died, mastered the art of writing articles and broadcasting on local radio. She coped with setting up a local telephone help-line and learned how to advise the people who rang her up.

All of this involved her in new experiences. It widened her personal horizons by introducing her to different people. She is now extending her learning further by undertaking training as a Samaritan.

In all of the examples the learning process rarely took place at a formal educational establishment. Many of those described learned simply by doing, particularly Mary, Jack, Harry and Mike. When they did require outside assistance to gain particular information or skills, they simply asked for it.

Citizens Advice Bureaux, libraries and other organisations exist to help people find out the information they need to pursue their own interests.

In some of the cases the learning was to do with acquiring physical skills — particularly in the case of Jack. In others the learning was about practical skills, or thinking skills. In many cases people were pursuing a subject just for the pleasure of learning.

Learning can thus be about thinking, feeling, coping, skills, physical activities . . . anything that enables the person to master something, even if it is just themselves.

Older and growing

Learning skills decline not so much with age as with lack of practice. People of any age can still take things in provided they set about it realistically. If learning is to take place successfully, considerations like motivation, the amount of practice the individual has had, and the individual's health are far more important than age.

Just as there are physical differences in the way different individuals change with age so there are big differences in the changing learning abilities of individuals with age.

Some people at 60 will be healthier than some people at 30. Some 80 year olds will be better learners than some 60 year olds. Some people at 60 will have better reactions and more agility than some of 18. And so on.

Although for every individual thinking and learning abilities do change with age, these changes are rarely significant when compared with the differences between individuals.

Growing and changing

Think of a task you were set at school which involved learning something off by heart. Examples might be the multiplication tables, or learning a poem.
o Did you find it an easy task then?
o Would you find it easy now?
o Do you think your ability to learn in this way has increased or decreased?

Think of a learning task you have recently undertaken. An example might involve putting up a greenhouse from kit form, complete with an inadequate instruction leaflet. Or, say, an asphalt plant was going to be installed across the road from your house and you had to learn about the official procedures for complaining.
o Did you find you were able to use any information or experience you had gained previously?
o Do you think your ability to find out

this kind of information has increased or decreased?

Learning skills don't decline with age but older people are likely to respond differently to learning tasks.

Often they will be able to complete a learning task more quickly and easily. Age brings with it an accumulation of experience and knowledge which can often be applied to new learning. For instance working out what has gone wrong with the electric toaster will be much easier if you already know how an electric fire works.

Sometimes they find things harder. Older people sometimes have to unlearn things before they can learn new ones. Think about the difference between a child of seven learning about metrication as compared with someone of 70. The child has hardly any experience of buying goods in imperial quantities (pints, gallons, gills) as opposed to somebody who has been using those measures for 60

years! Before the older person can learn about metrication they have to put to one side their imperial weights and measures.

Older learners respond better to certain types of tasks than to others. It takes them longer to learn lists, or to learn things by heart, or to learn things from which they can see no personal benefit. This could be seen as selective learning as opposed to the more uncritical learning of, say, a child of seven.

However, when older learners do see a real purpose in learning something they can show a lot more determination in their studies than is usually evident among school children.

Learning how to do new things — whether it's developing a skill at metal-working, or studying industrial archaeology — is the best possible way of keeping learning skills in practice. This applies to learners of any age.

Memory plays an important part in the learning process and is perhaps the area that causes most concern to older learners. The popular image of older people as forgetful is difficult to get away from, yet there is no evidence to suggest that memory declines with age.

The evidence points to memory declining with lack of practice, or memory being less effective when the information being memorized is not seen as relevant.

The most effective way of memorizing any information, is to make it your own — to personalise it by making it relevant to your own needs and interests. An example would be remembering a particular recipe. Using a recipe for, say, a sauce or pudding, you may simply perform the operations required with the ingredients given, so as to achieve the end product intended by the recipe writer.

Over time, you might experiment with the recipe — keeping the basic principles but adding new ingredients or flavours to suit your taste. In using the principle of the recipe and then adding other ingredients, you are remembering the essence of the recipe but are also going beyond the information given. In short, you are making the idea your own.

Recall is not, therefore, just a matter of remembering ideas or messages but is also about making use of what you have remembered.

Learning styles

Think of the last time you had to deliberately set about learning something new. Perhaps you wanted to get to grips with accounting procedures so you could talk the same language as the accountant or the tax inspector.

Perhaps you wanted to be able to speak the language of the country you plan to visit on your summer holidays. How did you approach it?

o Did you go on a course or purchase a complete home study course?

o Did you keep your eyes open and pick up at random what you saw on your subject in magazines and newspapers, in bookshops and in the libraries?

o Did you ask a friend or business associate who already had the skill you wanted to acquire, to teach it to you?

o Any others . . .

_____

_____

_____

There is no 'right' or 'wrong' way to learn. People develop different methods of learning for themselves. Individual styles of learning are as personal as eating habits.

Some researchers talk about people who learn 'serially' — that is they learn things in sequences, gradually building up a picture; others are described as 'holistic' learners — that is they learn about the whole picture, picking up the details as they go along.

Other researchers talk of 'syllabus-bound' learners, who follow learning routes dictated by others, and 'syllabus-free' learners who follow the direction that is of particular interest to them even if they are enrolled on a course which is taught by someone else.

Yet other researchers talk of 'convergent' and 'divergent' thinkers. Convergent thinkers look for one solution to a problem, think formally and conventionally.

Divergent thinkers, by contrast, think of many solutions to their problems, think unconventionally and make considerable use of their imagination when examining a problem.

For example, when asked to list possible uses of a brick, convergent thinkers tend to come up with its obvious applications in building, whilst divergent thinkers will list other, more unusual uses — paperweight, making bookshelves, pressing trousers — in addition to more formal uses.

There is no clear relationship between age and learning style. But it does seem to be the case that older people are generally more 'syllabus-bound', 'convergent' and 'serialist' in their learning. In part, this is because their own experiences of learning at school and at work, have been of this kind and, in part, because this form of learning is easier and less demanding for many than 'syllabus-free', 'divergent' and 'holistic' learning.

What is also clear is that learning styles for one topic — for instance, learning a language — may not be the same as the learning style used by the same person for another topic — for instance, learning about pension rights.

What helps a person to learn most effectively is an awareness of the style with which they feel most comfortable for a particular piece of learning and working hard within that style.

Learning about feelings

Learning is about feelings as well as about thinking. Later life brings with it just as many emotional shocks, just as many ups and downs, as any other period and responses to these new experiences need to be learned about if the problems are to be coped with.

One recently retired man observed: "*Hardly any of my friends had died before I retired, now it's a regular occurrence. None of my own kids had children when I retired, now I'm a grandfather to seven of them. None of my kids were divorced when I retired, now one of them is. I'd only been ill once before I retired but I've broken a leg and an arm in the last five years, by falling . . . . There's just so much happening, it's not surprising that I have a lot more feelings coming to the surface. More is happening to me now than ever before.*"

This man had to cope with his feelings following the death of his closest friend, with whom he had worked for 37 years. Grief was a new experience for him to deal with. But he was also able to experience again his feelings of excitement and joy at the birth of his grandchildren. For him, these grandchildren have brought as much, if not more, pleasure than the birth of his own children.

The stress which his daughter's divorce caused him was considerable. These feelings of stress were so strong that it really surprised him. He even felt physically sick at times. As for his accidents, these brought out fears which he did not know he harboured.

At first, he found it difficult sharing these feelings with his wife. Gradually, in retirement, he found ways of talking about his feelings with others that did not make him feel uncomfortable but which enabled him to come to terms more easily with these feelings and understand them better.

Feelings can significantly affect the way in which our bodies work, our thinking and our behaviour. Feelings of stress can lead to poor digestion, confused thinking and poor relations with others.

You should learn to keep your feelings in check, learn to cope with them. The death of a friend, certainly, is a time for sadness; the birth of a grandchild leads to great happiness. But it's good to keep a sense of proportion — being grief-stricken and miserable for six months does nothing to preserve fond memories; getting over-excited or too elated about something may not be very healthy either. Learn to maintain a balance.

Continuing growth

Jack Dare is 63. For most of his working life he was a publican — starting at the age of 32 and keeping a 'tidy' local pub in the Cotswolds.

Before that, he was a farm labourer, with a keen interest in athletics. In fact, he was a national champion at cross country running. When this skill declined and he could no longer run at competition speeds, he left farming and took up working in the pub, later being given his own licence.

At the pub, he developed the necessary skills for its management but also took qualifications in cellarmanship and developed a particular expertise on the subject of wine. Each year, he and his wife would travel abroad for three weeks. Many times they deliberately chose to go to a country with which they were unfamiliar and which required them to learn a new language.

They used to spend a considerable amount of their spare time learning the language — at least to a level that would get them through their holiday. Their language learning became quite a passion and between them Jack and his wife can now make themselves under-stood in 13 languages, five of which they speak fluently.

At the age of 60, Jack retired from the pub — letting his son take over. He went to live by the sea with his wife in West Wales. Their little cottage was more than adequate for their needs and needed very little doing to it. Jack found himself having some time to spare. He took up fishing for which he found he had quite an aptitude, soon working his way through local fishing competitions and becoming quite an expert on the subject.

He now works with a friend, running fishing trips from the bay. He has had to learn a few new skills and having retained his head for business, their summer industry is thriving.

Jack feels as he gets older he will not be going out on the boats quite as much. Instead, he will help set up the trips and concentrate on his own fishing. He is thinking about learning a new language — Welsh — and of helping out in the local pub.

The graph below illustrates the pattern of Jack's learning throughout his life. The peaks in the graph show the times Jack himself saw as the most significant learning periods in his life.

It shows that he was actively developing a wide range of different skills and abilities but rather than sticking with one particular line of interest, he tended to move from one to another, depending on his situation at the time, or simply on whatever caught his fancy.

Sometimes there was a direct connection between one interest and another — for instance, his job as a publican led him into developing an expertise in wines — but sometimes there was no obvious connection, as when he took up fishing.

Try drawing your own graph to indicate the most important learning periods in your own life. The vertical axis represents importance of any learning period to you on a scale between 0 to 10, the horizontal axis represents your own age.

Don't worry about your graph being absolutely precise — it should still give you the general idea.

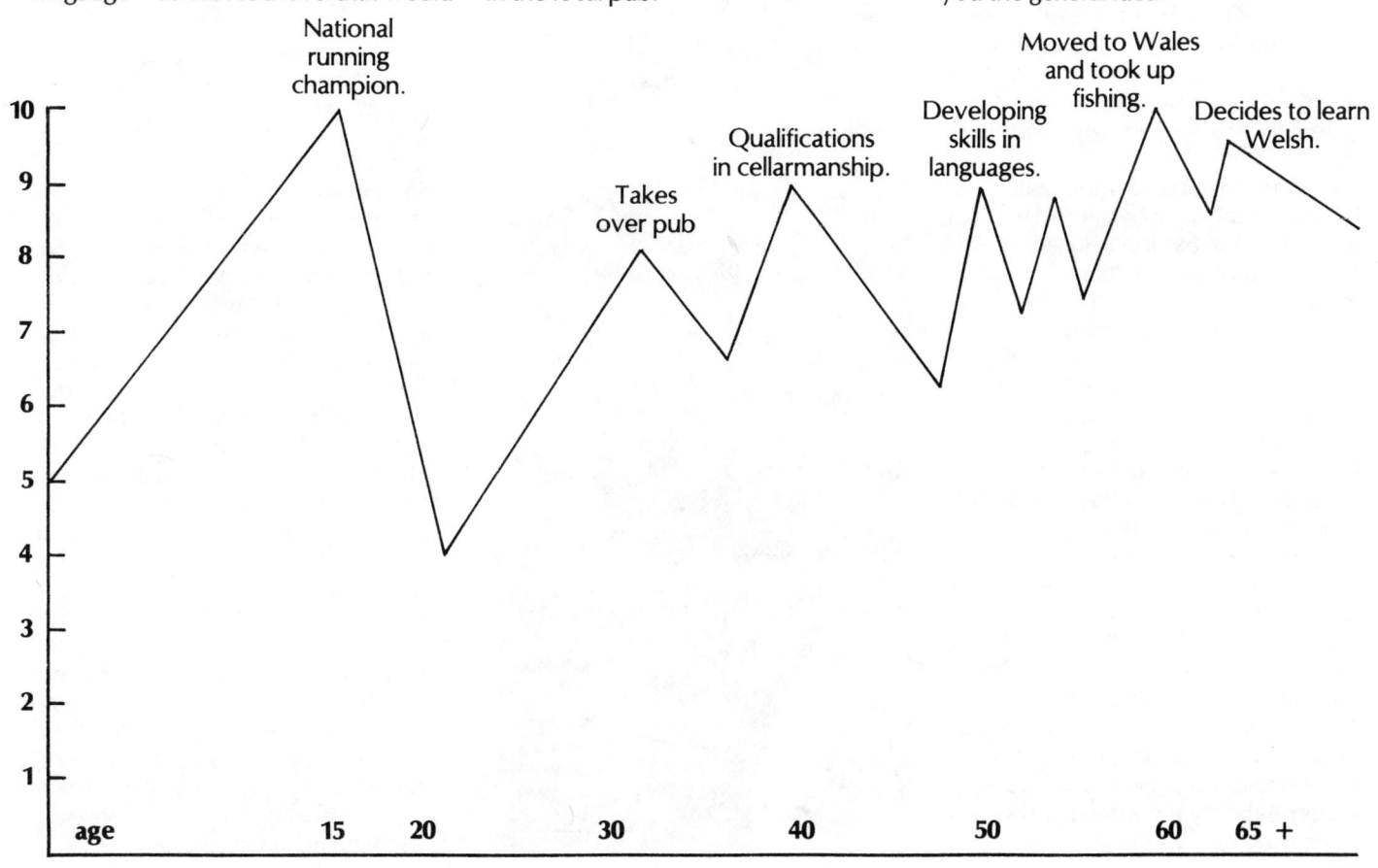

Learning opportunities

In 1980 one typical local education authority was offering 10,100 educational opportunities to adults over the age of 16. This may sound like a lot of choice and certainly many thousands of people benefit from involvement in the existing educational provision. But that provision can never anticipate everybody's needs.

Here are three examples of people who couldn't find what they wanted among 10,100 opportunities.

Mary
Couldn't find a course in Portuguese, yet was seriously thinking of retiring to Portugal, having visited it as a holiday-maker for 27 years.

Sidney
Wanted a course in BASIC computer programming for home computer users, but it had to be in the daytime.

Sandra
Couldn't find a course that specialised in home decorating that was suitable for her requirements.

So, despite the wide range of choice available, not all educational and learning needs are going to be met by formal provisions.

In some cases this is because a course on the topic a person wants to learn about is not available; in others, a course is available but not at times suited to the person who wishes to take it.

A further problem is the amount of travelling that might be needed to study a course at a particular location. And there is always a problem of cost, though on some courses there are reductions for retired persons.

Many of the courses available are vocational — they assume that if you want to learn about carpentry or about computing it is because you wish to become employed through the use of these skills. For most retired people, this is not the case and they might find the courses too demanding.

The adult education system is designed to be responsive because learning needs in the community are always changing, and because those changes are difficult to anticipate. In other words, if there is an evident need in one area for a lunchtime course on greenhouse gardening, the local education authority is obliged to do its best to provide such a course.

So a tenants' association could ask for a course on welfare rights or housing management. A pensioners' group could ask for a course on musical appreciation. A neighbourhood association could ask for a course on the production and running of a community newspaper. A group of friends could ask for a course on cricket coaching. The possibilities are endless.

All that is required is to get together a group of people — usually 12 or 13 — and apply to the local education authority. Adult education is there to serve the needs of the community, but it still needs the community to tell it what those needs are.

When looking at the educational opportunities available it may be helpful to think about it in two stages.
o How to find out what is available;
o What to do if there is no existing provision.

If you find what you are looking for in the existing provision, then you are home and dry. If this doesn't work there is another alternative — going it alone.

What is available

There are a number of different agencies providing educational opportunities. Not all of these may be active in your own area.
o The local education authority provides educational opportunities through further education colleges, community colleges, community workshops, residential adult education colleges.
o The Workers Educational Association. This is a national association formed to promote educational opportunities for working people.
o University extra mural or external studies departments. These are separate departments of a residential university providing a variety of adult education classes.
o Polytechnics and institutes of higher education often provide opportunities for adults to pursue extension studies.
o Distance learning opportunities. The Open University, the National Extension College and the registered correspondence colleges provide courses at a variety of levels for those who wish to study at home. Sometimes these courses offer the opportunity to meet with other students locally, or are linked in with a local adult education course.
o BBC Educational Programmes. These are frequently linked with a BBC book. They can provide a good introduction to a particular area of interest and deal with subjects varying from micro chips to cookery, basic education to consumer rights.
o The National Institute of Adult Education. This provides a service of information and advice to organisations and to individuals on all aspects of adult education.

A range of organisations, clubs and societies provide speakers or organise study sessions around issues of particular interest to their members.

The Women's Institute, or one of the political parties, or the church, are examples of national organisations that provide educational activities for their members. On a local level, pensioners' clubs, wine making clubs, model railway clubs or historical societies provide similar learning opportunities.

How to find out

Go direct to the college of further education, the community college, the residential college or the university extra mural department and ask for their prospectus.

If you do see a course that would suit your learning needs ask to speak with somebody who can tell you more about it — the tutor, or a previous student, or somebody at the college who is familiar with the course.

Ask the local education authority to send you details of adult education provision in the area. They will also be able to advise you on any existing or planned provision there may be for a particular interest you might wish to pursue.

Local information centres like the Citizens Advice Bureau or the library will have information on different learning opportunities in the area.

Watch out for 'open days' or 'registration days' at local colleges or adult education centres. These are often a good time to go along since they provide an opportunity to discover what's on offer, and to ask questions about it.

If there are community workshops in your area, go in and ask what facilities are available, what charges they make and what special rates they charge for pensioners.

Going it alone

There may be a variety of reasons why you decide to adopt the 'do it yourself' method. It enables you not only to learn about the subject you have chosen to study, but to organise your own time and often makes it easier for you to pursue the line of interest you think is of most value to yourself.

Some useful guidelines for self directed study are:

○ Try to set yourself realistic learning goals and stick to them.

○ Extend your own network of useful contacts whenever possible. Inquiries at the local library, a letter to the local newspaper, a call to the local radio station or a chat with the secretary of a local community organisation might reveal sources of information or the existence of other people in the area with similar interests.

○ Be prepared to learn from mistakes as well as successes. Most important, be prepared to recognise your successes and be proud of them as points of real personal achievement.

Of course, there's no reason why going it alone should not include elements of outside teaching as well. Somebody learning to type may decide to go on a crash typing course at the local college for a few days to get them started on the right lines and then do the rest by practising on their own and studying books out of the library.

The important thing is always to recognise where your own interests and learning needs lie, to think about the sort of learning pattern you would feel most comfortable with, and to use any of the educational facilities which fit in with your own requirements.

Looking ahead

Change is an individual experience. Some changes are likely to be experienced by us all at one time or another, some changes are experienced only by particular groups of people. The topics in this chapter are intended to summarise both of these sorts of experience. We ask you to read the whole chapter even though some of the topics won't apply to you directly. They should help to remind you that retired people are not just a single category but may also give you some ideas for dealing with any special concern of your own that perhaps has not been mentioned in the course.

Alone or a loner

The aim of this topic is to help you appreciate the pleasures and advantages of spending time on your own. If you are suffering from loneliness this may help you deal with it.

Do you sometimes feel that you spend too much time alone? How much privacy do you want? How much do you get? How do you spend the time you have on your own? Do you enjoy it? Even if you don't spend much time alone at the moment think about the advantages being on your own may have.

Finding yourself alone

Everybody may choose solitude at times; it is perhaps a time for privacy and relaxation, or a busy period of getting on with something you enjoy. However, quite often when you find yourself alone you may feel miserable, bored, even unloved. Time drags.

We may all feel lonely at times. There are those who are lonely because things have changed. For some this happens at retirement when work suddenly disappears. It can happen at other times, too — leaving home, moving to a new area, changing jobs, for example.

This sort of loneliness is usually temporary though it can last longer if it leads to you losing confidence in your ability to make friends. If this sounds like you, then you should find the activities suggested in this topic useful.

But sometimes loneliness is not connected with changing circumstances. Some people seem to suffer from chronic loneliness.

They may have been lonely all their lives, often finding it difficult to make and keep friends. Social situations may make them feel panicky or aggressive. They may lack conversation. They often have little self esteem. If this sounds like you the activities in this topic may not help much. You really need different assistance. Counselling can help. Training in groups in what are called 'social skills' can also be of use. If you think this applies to you, then leave the rest of this topic. Talk instead to your doctor, the Citizens Advice Bureau or 'helpline' agencies about facilities available in your area.

Solitude or loneliness

From this list of statements which describe feelings people have when they are alone, tick any that you have felt.

1	I have a chance to get on and do what I want to do without anyone interfering. ☐
2	I feel guilty because I'm not doing things for others or spending time with them. ☐
3	I seem to get a lot more done. ☐
4	I never seem to get down to doing anything. ☐
5	I know what I want to do but I never seem to get down to doing it. ☐
6	I feel strong and in control of things. ☐
7	I feel I don't have to put on an act. ☐
8	I feel really me. ☐
9	I feel relaxed. ☐
10	I feel worried and anxious. ☐
11	I feel bored. ☐
12	I feel I'm missing out on something. ☐
13	The more I'm alone, the more I want to be alone. ☐
14	The more I'm alone, the more I feel I'm left alone. ☐

Positives and negatives

If you ticked 1, 3, 6, 7, 8, 9 and 13 then you have positive feelings about being alone. You enjoy the pleasures of solitude.

If you ticked 2, 4, 5, 10, 11, 12 and 14 then you have rather negative feelings about it. Being alone probably means being lonely.

You may have ticked both positive and negative statements. For instance, you may have feelings that you can get lots done but at the same time feel guilty about not devoting your time to other people. The important thing is to find a balance that is right for you.

Balance

Peoples' feelings about time spent on their own cover a wide range. They might be very positively inclined towards solitude and enjoy immensely the opportunity to be alone occasionally. They may even feel that they don't get nearly as much time to themselves as they would like. On the other hand some people might find the idea of solitude unappealing and avoid it as much as possible, only to find on closer inspection that they gain a great deal of enjoyment from the time they spend on their own.

It can be difficult sometimes to assess exactly what your feelings are. If you are with someone they may be inclined to be dismissive, tell you that you are overreacting or are not in touch with your true feelings. Certainly your feelings may be real enough to you, but especially if you are on your own it can be useful to try and put them to the test.

A good start to achieving a balance and breaking patterns of loneliness is to look at how much time you spend alone and whether you enjoy it.

Try to keep a rough diary for a week. List:
The times when you were alone and *enjoyed it*.
The times when you were alone and *didn't enjoy it*.
What you did on these occasions.

Don't worry about times when you were alone and didn't think much about it.

Marcia Hamilton is in her early 60s and recently retired. She lives alone. Solitude was something she felt inclined to avoid though she realised that there were times when she derived great pleasure from being alone. She decided to do a detailed breakdown of the time spent on her own and her feelings about it.

Marcia enjoyed being alone for a number of reasons. It gave her a chance to recharge her batteries. She was able to devote time entirely to her own needs and wants and to do this without any interruption from other people. However, there were times when she was less happy on her own. She felt bored occasionally and missed companionship especially when she had

Below is an extract of Marcia Hamilton's diary. Try setting yours out like hers:		
	Times I was alone and enjoyed it.	**Times I was alone and didn't enjoy it.**
Wed.	Breakfast. I just enjoy the paper, toast and coffee. Lunchtime. Came in from shopping really tired and unable to string two words together. Sat down, put my feet up, had a cup of tea and had half an hour off.	
Thurs.	Breakfast, as usual. Went to the library in the morning and got a new detective novel out. Spent all afternoon reading. No distraction, no noise, bliss.	
Fri.	Breakfast, as usual. Morning. Decided to clean out the kitchen cupboards. It was a real mess but I worked out a new system and really got down to it and finished by 3 o'clock.	Evening. I'd done the kitchen cupboards and everything else. It wasn't time to go to bed, there was nothing on the television and I'd read a lot yesterday. Felt bored.
Sat.	Breakfast as usual.	Late afternoon. The kettle fuse went, didn't have another. Was upset.
Sun.	Breakfast as usual.	Evening. After my nephew and his wife had visited me, the flat felt empty. The feeling lasted several hours.

Company

If you decide to alter the balance of the time you spend with other people it may help to think about some occasions in your past life when your social circumstances changed and you had to work out a new balance of being alone or in company. Think about a time when either you felt an acute need for company or overwhelmed by people.

Moving to a new job.
The period when your children first started school.
During the war on active service doing a solitary job.
Moving to a new area where you knew few people.
A time when you felt surrounded by people, perhaps in hospital or a barracks or on a residential course.
A time when a friend or relative was ill or in difficult circumstances and made a lot of demands on you.
A time when people began to get on your nerves — say on a holiday with a group of friends.

Can you recall how you felt and what you did?

Overwhelmed?

If you are feeling overwhelmed look into the reasons for it. You may decide to do several things to provide yourself more space and time.
For instance:

o Decide how much time to devote to other people.
o Decide to cut out some of your activities if they are too demanding.
o Decide to talk to the people who may be affected by any alterations you make to your life.

Need for company?

In a situation of feeling lonely your decisions will be rather different, involving some of these actions:

o Making a conscious effort to stick to people you know already and perhaps make more of an effort to see them.
o Trying to work out closer relationships with people you don't know very well.
o Seeking out new acquaintances.

problems that she wanted to share and talk over with other people.

Marcia had considered herself to be someone who had negative feelings about being alone and seemed to have too much time to herself. Looking at her diary someone else might have thought she had quite positive feelings about being alone. No one else can really sum up your feelings on the subject. You have to work from where *you* stand.

So what Marcia set out to do was re-organise her time so as to get the maximum enjoyment out of being alone.

She listed those things that she felt good about and enjoyed by herself in an average week:

o A good selection of novels from the library.
o The Sunday paper.
o A luxurious bath.
o A phone call to her school friend May, who lived in the next town.
o A rather special meal.

She decided to try and anticipate those times that she wouldn't enjoy being alone and would most need a lift. So that when she felt down about being alone she could give herself one of these treats.

Looking back at her last week's diary, she thought it would have been a good idea to save the luxurious bath, the Sunday paper and the out of the ordinary meal until Sunday evening. That was when she felt at her lowest.

And it might have been a good idea too to save the detective novel until after the cupboards had been cleared out when she would want something to do. She also decided that in future she would phone her friend May when silly things like fuses upset her.

David Phillips' diary didn't look so different from Marcia Hamilton's. There were times when he had enjoyed being alone and times when he hadn't. Unlike Marcia though he had generally positive feelings about being alone but felt he had too much time to himself. For him the task was a question of finding a better balance between the time he spent alone and the time he spent with others.

Retirement had left him with time on his hands. Since work had disappeared he often felt at a loose end.

More contact

When trying to develop more contact with people you don't know very well:

o Make a firm invitation to do something together socially. Don't just rely on the old routine.
o Find a new activity and suggest doing it together.
o Ask for help or offer it on tasks like redecorating, car maintenance, dog walking.

For increasing your circle of acquaintances there are well trodden paths like going to new clubs and classes.

Taking up activities like adult education are obviously good ways to meet people, especially if you're a bit nervous. When you are all involved on some task together contact can be easier.

You may also find a task where there is a social scene, like helping with amateur dramatics or running church activities.

Another valuable ice-breaker is to choose an activity holiday where you have a common interest to talk to people about.

But even with these you could think of the more informal ways to show friendliness to new acquaintances.

Do you smile and act in a friendly way; speak to people or wait to be spoken to; arrive early enough to have a chat; take time to pack up so you can have a chat?

Summing it up

This topic has been about the balance between being happy on your own and enjoying company. The point is to find the balance that suits you.

Some people are natural loners. You may have noted positive feeling about being alone and enjoy spending a great deal of time on your own.

Having recently retired you may have found people concerning themselves with increasing your range of social contacts. You might have found this irritating or patronising. Remember that most people do see social contact as a good and natural thing.

Whatever your feelings, work out what is right for you.

Documents & papers

You may be a very well organised person, with everything in apple-pie order. On the other hand you may not be well prepared for sudden emergencies.

Making things easy for others

If you have ever had to take over someone's affairs you will know what a relief it is to be able to lay your hands on necessary documents. How easy would it be for someone else to deal with yours? *You* may know where all is kept, but someone not familiar with your system could find it baffling especially if they were worried or in a state of shock.

o Keep all documents relating to savings and investments together in a safe, suitable place, clearly labelled.
o As you pay quarterly bills, rates, heating, lighting, TV, and other licences, put them away together and remove the really out of date ones.
o Keep bills yet to be paid separately in an accessible place.
o Always have a current budget sheet so that anyone taking over can easily see your full range of commitments.
o Have a copy of your will (or a note about where it has been deposited).
o Make a list of people to be contacted. Attach it to your papers, together with addresses and phone numbers. The list might contain your:
  Next of kin, close friends, your doctor, priest, solicitor and bank manager.
o Tell the people you have chosen as dependable where you normally keep this information on your affairs.

Absent from home
If you are ill for a time and need hospital care, it can be comforting to know that things could continue to move smoothly.

If you plan ahead when you are well you can eliminate some of the problems that might otherwise occur. Think about the following:
o Will you be leaving a dependant able to manage to run the home alone?

o If not what arrangements can you make for emergencies?
o Would whoever is left at home have access to money for living expenses?
o If you are being helped at home by someone unfamiliar with various appliances (e.g. central heating controls, washing machine, etc) are instructions for use easily available?
o Do you have special arrangements for storing/ordering fuel?
o Are there other items you would want to add to your own written list of instructions to those who are helping you out?

Ask yourself just what would happen if you were called away tomorrow to deal with an emergency. Of course, there are almost bound to be loose ends but if it were necessary would someone else really be able to take over the running of things in your absence? Thinking along these lines can help you ensure that things are properly organised.

Easing the burden of bereavement

It is probable that as time goes on you will have to arrange a funeral for a member of the family or a close friend. Following a death there is a good deal to see to at a time when you or the deceased person's relatives are often emotionally exhausted. It may seem a dismal task but there are practical benefits to finding out at the earliest opportunity what it is necessary to do.

Charts 1 and 2 on the next page show what steps to take when a death occurs and you have to arrange a funeral.

Finding out about costs and kinds of services offered by local undertakers is also best done at a time when you are not closely involved with a death. It is probably a good idea to make inquiries about funeral directors who are members of the National Association of Funeral Directors. (The Office of Fair Trading have a leaflet which gives details of this association's code of practice.)

Chart 1

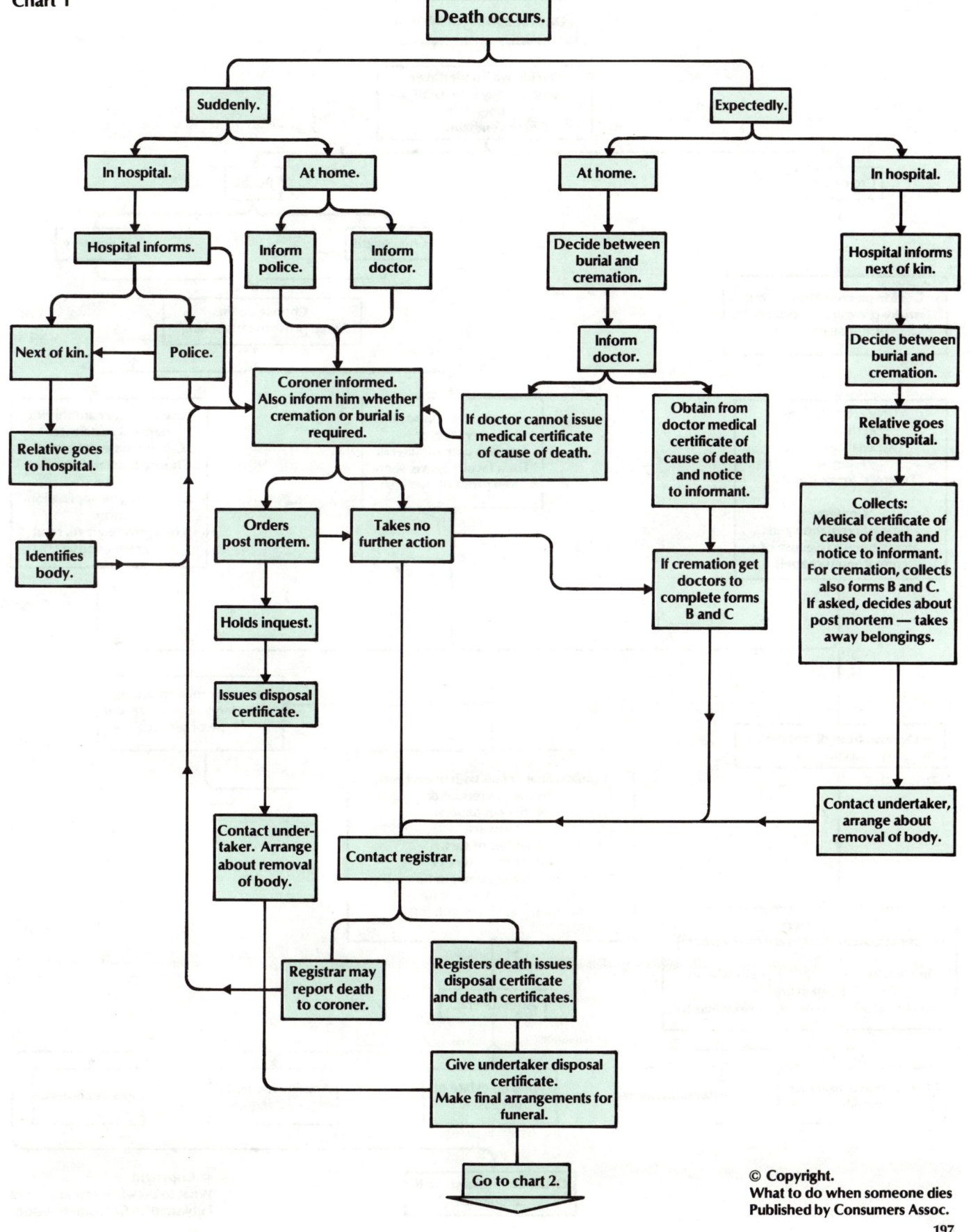

Chart 2

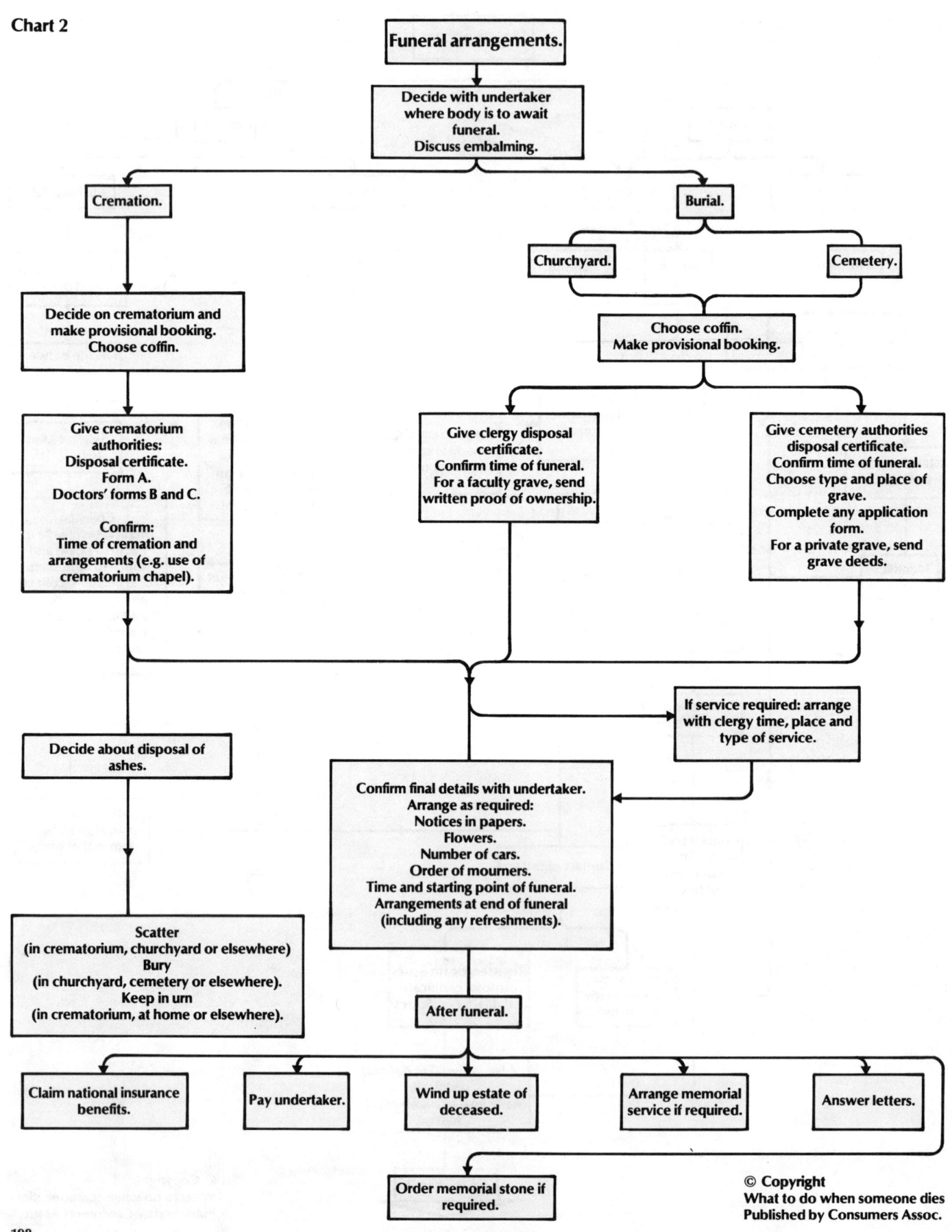

Funeral arrangements.

Decide with undertaker where body is to await funeral.
Discuss embalming.

Cremation.

Burial.

Churchyard.

Cemetery.

Decide on crematorium and make provisional booking.
Choose coffin.

Choose coffin.
Make provisional booking.

Give crematorium authorities:
Disposal certificate.
Form A.
Doctors' forms B and C.

Confirm:
Time of cremation and arrangements (e.g. use of crematorium chapel).

Give clergy disposal certificate.
Confirm time of funeral.
For a faculty grave, send written proof of ownership.

Give cemetery authorities disposal certificate.
Confirm time of funeral.
Choose type and place of grave.
Complete any application form.
For a private grave, send grave deeds.

If service required: arrange with clergy time, place and type of service.

Decide about disposal of ashes.

Confirm final details with undertaker.
Arrange as required:
Notices in papers.
Flowers.
Number of cars.
Order of mourners.
Time and starting point of funeral.
Arrangements at end of funeral (including any refreshments).

Scatter
(in crematorium, churchyard or elsewhere)
Bury
(in churchyard, cemetery or elsewhere).
Keep in urn
(in crematorium, at home or elsewhere).

After funeral.

Claim national insurance benefits.

Pay undertaker.

Wind up estate of deceased.

Arrange memorial service if required.

Answer letters.

Order memorial stone if required.

Your financial affairs

Your possessions
It may be that as time goes on you are concerned less with how and where to put your cash to work than with the problem of how to make ends meet. You may have items, inherited or bought, that have increased in value over the years. Perhaps you could sell them to increase your capital or give you some movement money — to pay an unexpected bill or take a needed holiday? But, beware of the 'con' men who knock at your door or claim they are visiting your area for one day only to purchase your 'valuables' at above market prices.

If you really need to sell any items then seek professional advice from your local resident agent or auctioneer who has a good knowledge of the item and its market value. Usually he will not charge you for this valuation service for he makes his commission on any sale which may follow. That decision is entirely yours.

Your house
If you are a house owner your home may be your most valuable asset and you could consider one of several methods of raising money on the value of your house.

It is essential to get expert advice from different sources before making a decision. Ask your Citizens Advice Bureau whether there is a money advice centre in your area. If not they will put you in touch with someone who will help. Broadly speaking the house reversion scheme is hardly ever beneficial. The House Income Plan is only really attractive to those in their seventies.

If you have no family or feel that they do not need to benefit financially from you, selling your home to buy smaller, cheaper accommodation would provide some ready cash and/or the opportunity to invest a small sum.

If you are alone and getting on in years you might find it beneficial to sell your house, invest the released capital and move into rented sheltered accommodation.

Savings and investments
You will need to review your financial affairs regularly because of changing interest rates, changing tax laws and the rate of inflation. Helpful information is always available in the press and on radio and television. Remember to take advice from more than one expert. Be prepared to move your savings and investments about to make them work in your own best interests.

Feeling generous
Sound financial planning means that you are increasing your spendable income as you get older to maintain your standard of living, and decreasing your capital. After all, what use is your capital to you after you're dead. For example you can give away up to £3000 in any tax year without attracting what is called Capital Transfer Tax (C.T.T.). A wedding in the family is an excellent opportunity for planning the avoidance of C.T.T. for you could give £5,000 to your own child, up to £2,500 to a grandchild or great grand-child and up to £1,000 to any other person.

	Method	Advantage	Disadvantage	Result for inheritors
House reversion.	Sell house to insurance company in exchange for life annuity.	Regular (fixed) income from annuity. Retain right to live in house until death.	Loss by former owner of appreciation of value of house. (N.B. amount of appreciation — if any — unknown).	Nothing to inherit.
House income plan.	Borrow — usually a loan of 80% of market value — against value of house to buy an annuity.	Regular fixed income from annuity. Retain ownership of house. Any appreciation (if any) remains the owners. If the appreciation in value is high a further loan can be taken out. If loan is paid from estate on death — loan company have no further rights on house.	Interest to be paid on loan. Disadvantage to inheritors.	Beneficiaries can either: 1 Repay the loan and keep the house. Or 2 Repay the loan by selling the house and keep the surplus if any. They are liable to repay the loan from the estate in any event.

Your will

However much or little you have to leave, it is a good idea to make a will. Leave with your papers a copy of your will or a note of where it is deposited. Check this list to see whether you need to change your will in any way.

Executor has died.
Executor is no longer willing/able to act.
Beneficiary has died.
You no longer want to leave something to a beneficiary.
You wish to change the amount of money/goods to be left to a beneficiary.
You want to leave something to a new beneficiary.
Your circumstances (e.g. family) have changed and your whole will has to be re-written.

You no longer have the money/goods you planned to leave to someone.

If you are re-writing your will consider the provisions of the Capital Transfer Act and how capital transfer tax might affect any gifts you make during your life and in your will.

Codicils

This is the official name given to changes or additions to current wills. Codicils have to be signed and witnessed in exactly the same way as a will.

Here is an example:

This is the first codicil to the will, dated 14th October 1982, of me, Pamela Sheila Berry of 26 Queens Road, Newtown, Oldshire.

1 I revoke the bequest of my niece Dorothy Elisabeth Randall.
2 I give £500 to my brother, Nicholas Robert Harrison.
3 In all other respects, I confirm my will.

Date: 4th February 1983
Signature: Pamela Sheila Berry
Signed by Pamela Sheila Berry in our presence and by us in hers:

Sarah Dell	Michael Baines
"Rose Croft"	4 High Street
Ripley Road	Newtown
Newtown	
	Restaurant
Journalist	Manager

Provision for your funeral

It may be a chilling thought but a practical one to leave a note as to your particular wishes about the type and location of funeral service, whether you prefer flowers or donations to charity. If you have paid for grave space, the 'deed of grant' should be left with your will. Remember to allow for inflation in setting aside sufficient money for funeral expenses.

Planning to keep your affairs in order will help you to feel secure even when the unexpected turns up.

Bereavement

Death is a fact of life and coping with bereavement takes time. Individual responses are different. Think about the importance of mourning and what it does or does not achieve.

For the majority the disposal of the dead becomes a ritual mark of respect, with little time for public mourning, leaving the next of kin to grieve in private — a privacy which all too often means isolation.

Most people will feel sympathy for the bereaved but even those closest will experience a sense of inadequacy arising out of the wish both to offer comfort and also to avoid triggering off further grief.

The following descriptions of two bereaved people will indicate some of the ways that grief and mourning can be experienced.

Grief restrained

Fergus Macintosh's wife died when they were both 48 years old. He refused to let it upset him or his routine. *"I ran the home by myself — our children were away at university most of the time — that and my work kept me too busy to think about my wife's death."*

He kept himself to himself and claimed he did not need other people. He appeared to be coping reasonably well. But over the years came a succession of other events that he was able to deal with less and less well. First, his mother died — his father had been dead for some time. Then his son decided to take a job some distance away from home. Finally, with his early retirement at 60 came a sense of isolation so great that Fergus had a nervous breakdown though he subsequently recovered.

Fergus's reaction to the death of his wife was a courageous attempt to keep things going as normally as possible for his family and not to affect their lives or anyone else's by his grief. But, in doing this he denied other people the means of offering help, he made for himself a burden that eventually proved too great.

Sorrow and anger

Mary Maguire nursed her husband devotedly through his terminal illness and although she knew it was inevitable she was shocked by his death when it

finally came. At first she could not believe that he was dead. The church service was a great comfort to her and friends and relatives rallied round to support her. They were so kind that it made it so much harder to admit her reaction to anyone. Because, the fact was her main reaction along with sadness and a sense of loss was to feel angry. As she told her sister finally:

"I can't help it, Maureen. I feel angry. Isn't that terrible? I loved Mick and yet I feel angry with the doctor – he could have done more I'm sure – I'm angry with the priest – he makes it sound so easy – I'm even angry with God! We've been good living people. Why should this happen to us? We've worked long and hard, brought up a family and looked for a bit of contentment together in our old age and now what?"

Mary's reaction was complex. As well as rage and anger she felt guilt. She would find herself wondering whether Mick's illness could have been prevented. Could she have done more, been kinder, more loving?

With her sister's help she began to see that her rage and anger and her guilt were unreasonable. Her sister realised that simply by listening she was helping Mary to express and contain complicated and bewildering emotions. By offering company and resisting criticism she was able to help Mary work out her grief and over time move towards a position where she could remember her husband with love and accept his death without emotional pain.

Look at these different reactions. It is fairly clear that Fergus reacted to his wife's death by suppressing his feelings and failed to go through the normal, mourning process. His breakdown probably had its roots in his having denied himself a period of mourning when his wife died. Then his growing sense of isolation was highlighted by his mother's death followed by his son's leaving home and his own retirement. His subsequent lack of experience in coping with losses of different kinds as they arose at a later stage of life.

Mary was helped by her sister's support and encouragement to experience and express her feelings and recover from the loss.

The impact of grief can be very pow-

erful. Unless it is allowed free expression the effect upon the mourner may well set up some mental disturbance.

While it is often not as extreme as in Fergus's case the bereaved may well be surprised by the unexpected feelings of hostility and anger in addition to the more usual ones of sadness and loss.

The positive side of loss

The experience of grief is difficult, slow and wearing but it can additionally be enriching. Keith Kent, an American family counsellor wrote of his emotions in mourning the death of his son. These were the benefits he felt arose.

○ An eventual release from guilt.

○ New views on life and values which were more positive than before.

○ A growth in self esteem arising from the 'bank' of love and affection that had been generated between himself and his son.

○ Acceptance of death as matter of fact.

How can you help the bereaved?

Helping the bereaved can be difficult, particularly if you feel embarrassed or afraid about death yourself. Often, those who have themselves experienced such a loss are the best support and can bring understanding, compassion and gentleness to ease the grief of others. Sometimes however people are unsure about what to do for the best.

Immediately following a death

The bereaved person needs sensitive support and practical assistance. You could help them to talk about their loss, encourage them to cry and express their feelings if they wish to and offer help with practical affairs. You might ask them to stay with you for a short period or offer to stay with them and encourage them to eat and sleep adequately.

Three to six months after the loss

This is often a time when bereaved people become socially isolated. They still need support and help. Talking about the loss and encouraging expression of feelings can be important. The best help may be that which encourages adjustments to moving back into the world again.

Social isolation

Visiting the bereaved can be very important. You can help by asking them to help with simple jobs or encouraging them to participate in activities which involve caring for others in a small way. They may respond to suggestions that they join (or take up again) a local society, club or church organisation. An offer to go along with them at least to begin with might make all the difference.

Later

Mourning can continue for a long time. People who are allowed to express grief and to mourn naturally recover more quickly. It does not help if they are turned away from being made to think of others misfortunes. Tablets from the doctor can be a helpful solution in the short run but should not be suggested automatically.

How can you help yourself?

Turning to others and accepting their help is one of the best ways of helping yourself. Try to remember the following points:

Immediately

Recognise that the immediate effects of acute grief may include a feeling of exhaustion, memory loss, nervousness, physical pain, sleeplessness, and that you need to take care of yourself physically. If you do, it will help you regain your emotional balance more quickly.

People want to help you – let them. Mourn in your own way without feeling ashamed. This is nature's way of healing.

Share your grief with those willing to accept it.

Gradually

Try to make an adjustment to normal living *before* you think you are ready or you may fall into the trap of continually putting it off.

Accept invitations even if you find it difficult. Every new attempt becomes less difficult.

After a reasonable period try to look outwards and think of others. What can you do for your children, grandchildren, neighbours, friends, the needy and disadvantaged?

Eventually

Slowly lose your image of yourself as a mourner. Become more involved in friendships among family and friends.

Actively seek new friendships by widening your contacts with people.

Become more active in any group that you have an involvement with. Consider joining at least one new organisation. Take on some voluntary work and transfer the energies formerly taken up by grief to new, positive channels of aid to others. In the long term find ways of helping the bereaved in the light of your own experience.

As the years go on the deaths of relatives and friends will be inevitable. It can particularly ease the minds of partners and close friends to discuss the possibility of bereavement.

Talk about it

Talking about death doesn't make it happen any sooner and there are advantages.

o It helps you to discuss objectively the financial and other affairs that might arise from a death. There are things to be sorted out and it is reassuring to have them clear in advance.

o On a less material level, your shared attitudes and thoughts can be - a source of strength to the survivor at the time of bereavement.

"Once the funeral was over, no one mentioned his name for six months after his death. It was as if he had never been."—a widow.

"At first, friends went out of their way to invite me round and then, gradually, it stopped."—Widower

Coping and caring

Elderly relatives, particularly parents, may need our help.

Most people value their independence and old people are no exception. Few like to be in the position of relying on others but we all need some kind of help at sometime in our lives. Often it's much harder to accept help than it is to give it.

Older people are frequently in situations where they are more dependent on others than they would wish to be, and where they are unable to give anything back. They are often aware of this — hence their fierce pride to do as much for themselves as possible.

The help that others certainly can give is to keep in touch more often by letter, telephone or visit. Or perhaps to help out in practical ways in the home, and do small jobs like shopping and cleaning.

One of the options open to some elderly people, who can no longer manage on their own, is to live with relatives. It is a decision which needs to be considered carefully by both parties and it is not the only alternative.

Problems and remedies

Harry is a widower, convalescing after a bad stroke. He has been told that he will get a lot more of his mobility back and his speech will improve, but it will take time. His son Ken and daughter-in-law Phyllis, visit him in hospital to discuss the future. At the back of their minds, is the idea that Harry might need to come and live with them.

The basic possibilities they discussed were the following.

They brought up the idea of Harry selling his house and applying to go into an old people's home or into sheltered housing where there would be help on hand and certainly they thought he would have more privacy and independence there.

However all three of them dismissed these ideas after serious discussion. They talked about various other possibilities but decided there were only two real options open to them. Either

Harry should move in with Ken and Phyllis and live with them at their home or when he was fitter he should return to his own home. This is in fact what they decided upon.

He would spend some time in the rehabilitation centre of the local hospital, getting back on his feet. In the meantime they would make arrangements for him to have a home help and a meals on wheels service. Ken was going to get a telephone installed at Harry's home and look into the possibilities of getting a toilet and shower installed on the ground floor so that Harry would not have to worry about getting up and down the stairs. Phyllis would be able to drop by three or four times a week to see how he was getting on and on the whole they were confident that things would work out alright.

However even though these arrangements did appear suitable at the moment, all three did realise that at sometime in the future Harry might still have to move in with Ken and Phyllis. So they discussed, at length, just what this would mean to them all and they needed to work out the full extent to which it might change their way of living.

Having someone to live with you can lead to major alterations in your lifestyle. Many different areas of your life are likely to be affected. There are financial considerations; how far can you afford to accommodate someone else; just how much room have you got? If you do not have a large home are you going to be treading on each other's toes all the time? Will you be able to have any privacy?

These are just the kinds of facts that were important to Ken, Phyllis and Harry in their discussions. Below are summaries of the sorts of points that were made when the three of them talked. Many may seem quite trivial or petty on the surface but underlying all of them there were these crucial issues.

What Ken, Phyllis and Harry thought

Realising that there was a possibility Harry might have to move in with Ken and Phyllis prompted all three of them to do some thinking about how they would cope.

They realised that it would bring

about a change in lifestyle. These are the changes they anticipated having to cope with.

Practical changes
For Ken and Phyllis
Room will have to be made for Harry. He will want his own things but we can't take all his furniture.

Where will we put the children and grandchildren when they come to stay?

How will he manage the stairs and getting out of the bath? Adaptations will have to be made.

Cooking and housekeeping for an extra person all the time will make extra work.

Harry's dog would have to go. Phyllis can't stand dogs.

The ideal would be to build on a self-contained flat for Harry — but there's no room, and no money to do that.

Financially — how will it affect us? Find out if we are eligible for Attendance Allowance or an Invalid Care Allowance from the Citizens Advice Bureau, or the DHSS.

Need to talk to our GP and health visitor about Harry's physiotherapy and see what else is available for him. We will be tied to the house just when we are looking forward to Ken's early retirement.

For Harry
It's a very final step to sell up and move in. What about all my furniture?

I'll always be in someone else's territory. The way they do things might not suit me, but I'd have to put up with it.

The stairs are very steep. I couldn't get to the lavatory very quickly.

It would break my heart to see my dog go.

I'll have no financial worries. Phyllis is a good cook — I'd be well looked after.

Social changes
For Ken and Phyllis
We'll lose a lot of privacy. We'll want to go out on our own, and have holidays away. Harry will be left alone sometimes — will he be too dependent? Will Ken's brother agree to have him while we go on holiday? If not, perhaps the GP would book him into hospital for a couple of weeks.

Will we get on together? We do now, but then we don't see each other every day.

Ken is still working, but when he retires, will it be easier or more difficult?

It's a lot of responsibility. Will it affect our marriage and relationship?

For Harry
I've no friends where Ken and Phyllis live. I won't be on my own, but who else will I see?

I shall be well looked after, but what shall I do with myself all day?

Will I get on all right with Phyllis? She speaks her mind and I lose my temper. It might be better when Ken's around more. I don't want to come between the two of them.

Ken and Phyllis and Harry were all well aware of the problems that could occur, but both parties also identified positive rewards.

For Ken and Phyllis
We will know we are doing the best for Harry.

We will have company as well as the responsibility.

Harry will help out in small ways.

For Harry
I shall be cared for.

I shall have company, comfort and security.

I'll do little things for them wherever I can.

What might help
Simply being aware of the possible effects living with an elderly relative can have on both parties is an important step. It helps you decide if this would in fact be the best solution, and gives the arrangement a better chance of working out successfully.

Here are listed practical suggestions that might help Ken, Phyllis and Harry to work out some of the problems they have anticipated. Tick the ones you think would be helpful and write in any other suggestions you might give them.

Harry could replace his dog with a pet that Phyllis felt happier about. ☐

Harry could keep his own TV and radio. ☐

With some of the money from the sale of Harry's house, adaptations could be made to Ken and Phyllis's house. ☐

Harry's other relations could be asked to help out — taking him for car rides for instance. ☐

They could find out if Harry might be interested in any of the local social services provisions — day centres, clubs and so on. ☐

Ken and Phyllis could make sure they had at least one evening a week out on their own. ☐

Harry could have his own friends visit him in his own room. ☐

Any others

Anything which makes the transition smoother, is likely to help both sides. As in any relationship, there needs to be give and take. Harry is giving up his independence, his dog, his furniture — all of which mean a lot to him.

Phyllis and Ken are giving up their privacy and a lot of time and energy. But there can be rewards too, for all of them.

Stresses and strains
Life does not always run so smoothly, even when things are carefully thought out. Sometimes decisions have to be made quickly because there seems no other option. The next case study looks at two people muddling along in a relationship which goes from bad to worse.

Stresses and strains

Rose is a widow in her late seventies who lives in a small terrace house in a large city. Although she has six children, and many grandchildren and great grandchildren, they rarely visit. Her divorced daughter Joan, who is in her fifties, lives upstairs and does her mother's shopping, but the two have never really got on. There are constant rows.

Rose thinks her daughter is selfish. Joan feels her mother is too demanding. The daughter has a part-time job and goes out certain evenings a week. Rose hates being left alone in the house. She is pre-occupied with the idea that her daughter will be 'mugged' when out, and that someone will break into the house. Rose has great difficulty in sleeping. Her doctor has prescribed sleeping pills and tranquillisers, but Rose often forgets to take them, and complains when she does that they make her confused.

Unable to go far herself, Rose sits nervously looking out of the window all the time Joan is out. On the rare occasions that relatives do come round, Rose's state of extreme anxiety has made her so difficult to get on with that friends and relatives are even more reluctant to visit. Joan feels that she is at the end of her tether.

Looking back
Here is a brief review of Rose's life over the past 20 years.

Age 62: Rose is well able to cope. She has a lodger and on her widow's pension, is better off than she has been for years. She's bought a new TV set. She goes to a local club every week, outings in the summer, sees friends and neighbours regularly.

Age 67: Rose's lodger moves out. Joan, her recently divorced daughter moves in. Rose had had a couple of falls — nothing serious, but the family think it's a good idea if Joan is there to help out. Rose still does her own shopping, but is more reliant on people visiting her now.

Age 74: Not nearly so mobile. Joan does all the shopping. Rose can only get as far as the end of the street. The club nearby closed down and the only other one is miles away. Friends her own age are disappearing. Still does her own cooking and cleaning.

Age 79: Rose today. She is forgetful — loses money, leaves the gas on, confuses the names of her grandchildren. She doesn't know what to do with her time. Yet she is not an invalid and her mind is active.

Looking at the problem
Imagine a long-lost friend, ten years her junior, visits Rose, is upset by the situation and talks to both Rose and Joan.

After speaking to both, Rose's friend has a clear picture of what both of them need.

Joan, it's clear, must have more time to be on her own — she certainly could use a holiday. Surely some other relatives can help out here. As for Rose, she would thrive on some new company. She needs to get out and about more — again the rest of the family could help arrange this — and she must have things to occupy her mind which is still perfectly active.

Surprising though it seems both need each other. Rose couldn't live on her own; Joan has nowhere else to live.

Ways of helping

Rose's friend lists all the things she thinks might help Rose and Joan.

Rose's home could be fitted with special locks and alarms. That way she might not be so anxious when Joan is out.

Rose could talk to the doctor about the pills he's been prescribing for her. The drugs might be making her worse. They could discuss alternative treatment.

Other relatives could be asked to visit or take Rose to their homes more frequently. This would give Joan a break and it would make a change for Rose.

Conceivably Rose might be happier in an old peoples' home. They could look into this. Certainly they can see if their local authority has a day centre Rose could go to. This would provide Rose with another opportunity to get out of the house more and could give her some new interests.

They can contact an agency such as Age Concern to see if they have any volunteers who could help. Again, this would take some of the strain off Joan and would also give Rose contact with new people.

All of these courses of action are worth considering, but complex problems like these don't have easy solutions. Putting extra locks on the doors may actually increase Rose's fears. Joan may be reluctant to allow volunteers to visit — she may feel 'guilty' or ashamed about her invalid mother. Going into an old people's home may simply increase Rose's dependence on others. The effect of Rose going into a home may increase Joan's sense of guilt and failure.

Human relationships are often very complicated. This complexity means that it's impossible to make general rules. Any decisions that are made must directly involve those particular individuals who will be affected, if they are to stand a chance of being successful.

Ken and Phyllis and Harry were all able to participate in thinking about how they would cope.

Often, as in the case of Rose and Joan, it needs someone from outside to suggest changes. This could be a friend, or it could be a social worker or a health visitor. Whoever it is, the changes that are made are unlikely to be successful if they are imposed from outside. They stand the best chance of succeeding if they take into account the personalities and the wishes of those involved.

It's awful getting old. No-one really wants you. You have to rely on other people for everything - it's not dignified.

I don't spend money on self. What's the point? I don't anywhere. Anyway, it's for the family when I'm gone.

I've had people around all my life, children, grandchildren lived nearby — even lived with me when they had nowhere else to go. Now I don't see a soul.

It's like looking after a child again. It worries me when she does things like leaving the gas on.

It's a terrible strain sometimes. People don't realise what it's like. I've got my own life to lead too.

I sometimes get resentful. Because I'm divorced, I'm the one thats taken Mum on. The others don't do their share.

Health problems

Is your health at risk? What can you do about it?

Risks to Health

Many things affect your health. They can be divided into three categories.

Some risks are *hereditary*. Some illnesses (haemophilia for example) are inherited directly. A tendency towards others such as heart disease, diabetes or asthma seems to run in certain families.

The *environment and the nature of the society* we live in are probably still the major cause of ill health. There is a relationship between health and social class. Housing conditions, jobs, where you live, air pollution, the climate and the health facilities available can all profoundly affect your health.

The last group of risks are *personal* and to do with individual habits. Smoking, drinking, being overweight, driving recklessly or taking part in risky sports all come into this category.

Each of these groups needs a different kind of action to deal with it. Inherited diseases may need medical research into their causes and treatment. They can also be helped by adopting a life style that will make them easier to cope with.

Environmental risks usually need changes in society, action by government or at the least, by local pressure groups. Personal risks are within the control of the individual. In this topic we look at the three personal areas where people most often feel the need for improvement: smoking, over-indulgence in alcohol and overeating and being overweight.

These habits can be difficult to alter but if you do manage to change them you will notice the difference in your health.

Smoking

Cigarette smoking is a major cause of ill-health. Colds, sinus trouble, bronchitis, respiratory infections of certain kinds and cancer are all connected with it. However, when people stop smoking the risk of disease is reduced. There is good evidence that older people as well as young people benefit. Whilst it is true that older people who stop smoking cannot be assured of extra years of life, at all ages people who stop smoking experience a significant improvement in their quality of life.

These are some of the possible benefits:

Save enough money for a holiday abroad.
Become fitter.
Lose your smoker's cough.

Be more attractive: no bad breath or stained fingers.
Rid yourself of the mess and smell of tobacco.
Stop children from smoking because they copy you.
Recover your senses of taste and smell.
Be proud of yourself for breaking the habit.

But you must also:

Go without a pleasure that you will miss.
Expect to find concentration hard sometimes.
Resist eating more.
Feel irritable for a while.

Gains outweigh losses for most people.

What sort of smoker are you?

People smoke for different reasons. Knowing the reasons why you smoke can help you stop by making you more aware of the situations where it will be most difficult for you to resist. Fill in the quiz to the right to find out your smoking type.

The sections in which you score the highest will provide an indication of what sort of smoker you are. Here are some suggestions for combating your particular danger areas. Try to think of some more.

Pleasure and relaxation. Make an effort and choose to do something else to fill the gap. You should be able to find something else enjoyable to do. In the car, sing along to the radio instead of smoking. Put a record on to relax at home. Carry around something to read when you might smoke.

Handling: Do something else with your hands! Keep some scrap paper handy so you can doodle. Fiddle with coins, pencils, paper clips, key rings, jewellery or special toys.

Tension: Try exercise. Arm swinging or shadow boxing is effective. Take a brisk walk. Learn relaxation exercises. Chew something — but watch out! You may substitute eating for smoking.

Stimulation: Buck yourself up with some exercises or a brisk walk, or with a cup of tea or coffee. Turn on your radio to a popular music programme and dance for three or four minutes.

Craving: Try giving up when you get a smoking related illness such as a cough or bronchitis. Work out some powerful rewards you will give yourself for each day you succeed. Make a contract to give up for someone you love.

Habit: Before you give up for good make yourself aware of when you want to light up. Watch for trigger events like using the telephone or a cup of coffee when you tend to light up automatically.

How do I actually stop?
Prepare to give up smoking in the following ways:
o Choose a date in the next few days to give up. Avoid a time when you are under a lot of stress. Write the date in here . . . .
o Between now and then, spend some time thinking about your reasons for stopping. If you really make up your mind you will succeed.
o Can you get someone to give up smoking with you? You could be a great help to each other.
o Tell people you are giving up smoking and tell them when. They could be helpful too.
o The evening before you give up, smoke your last cigarette and throw the rest away.

What if I can't give up by myself?
It is important for people who want to stop smoking to try by themselves. Many will be surprised by how easy it is but some people find it difficult. A leaflet 'Give up Smoking' or GUS by the Health Education Council will certainly help some.

Others may need further advice and help. Someone who has tried to stop smoking by themselves and has failed should contact their general practitioner and ask for an appointment with him or the health visitor. They may suggest new ways. They may suggest that nicotine chewing gum would be an appropriate aid to stopping smoking.

Some people are more strongly addicted to the nicotine in the cigarettes than others. All in all it is worth making the effort to stop smoking.

For each statement, score as follows. 1 – Never, 2 – Seldom, 3 – Occasionally, 4 – Frequently, 5 – Always.

Pleasure and relaxation
a) Smoking a cigarette is pleasant and relaxing.
b) I want a cigarette most when I am comfortable and relaxed.
c) I find cigarettes pleasurable.
Total

Handling
a) Handling a cigarette is part of the enjoyment.
b) Part of the enjoyment of smoking comes from the steps I take to light up.
c) When I smoke, part of the enjoyment is watching the smoke as I exhale it.
Total

Tension
a) I light up when I feel angry about something.
b) When I feel uncomfortable or upset I light up.
c) I smoke when I feel down or want to take my mind of worries.
Total

Stimulation
a) I smoke to keep myself from slowing down.
b) I smoke to perk myself up.
c) I smoke to give myself a lift.
Total

Craving
a) If I run out of cigarettes it is almost unbearable.
b) I am very much aware when I'm not smoking.
c) I get a real gnawing hunger for a cigarette when I haven't smoked for a while.
Total

Habit
a) I smoke automatically without really being aware of it.
b) I light up without realising I still have one burning in the ashtray.
c) I've found a cigarette in my mouth and not remembered putting it there.
Total

Alcohol — friend or foe?

Most doctors agree that alcohol taken in moderation is good for you. Unfortunately some people drink so much that their physical or mental or social well being is affected. A number of different patterns of alcohol misuse are:

o Heavy bouts leading to drinking and driving or to crime or violence in the family.
o Steady heavy drinking with effects on physical health, family life and work.
o The inability to do without drink — dependence on alcohol.

These problems can develop at any age. Although alcohol misuse is not common in retirement it is important to be aware of the problem. Loneliness, depression and feelings of uselessness are the common causes of alcohol misuse among older people.

You can help simply by being a good friend to people who feel this way. By offering friendly support you can reduce the need for alcohol. If you yourself suffer from these feelings try to increase your circle of friends rather than relying on drink to prop you up.

Early signs of mis-use

What do we mean by 'drinking in moderation', or 'drinking too much'? Everyone means different things by these statements. Think what you would define as the upper level of moderate drinking. Write it down before reading on.

Emily who never visited pubs and usually only drank at Christmas defined it as three glasses of sherry per week.

Stan who when he worked was used to taking regular pub lunches defined it as three pints of beer a day.

Arthur who mixed in 'drinking circles' defined it as more than eight pints a night.

The range of answers which people, including doctors, give to this question is always very wide. To some people, like Emily, it is immoderate to take as much as one drink daily.

For some the consumption of ten pints daily is 'moderate'. Most people would regard the daily consumption of more than five pints or five glasses of spirit or wine a day as drinking more than moderately. Rather than laying down any specific level as being the safe limit, it is better to look at changes in drinking habits or changes in the person.

Changes in the drinking habit that are indications for seeking help are:
o Getting drunk when drinking alone.
o Feeling the need for a drink before going out to a party or to see people.
o Drinking more than you drank in the year before retirement.
o Being unable to remember what happened when drunk.
o Making frequent excuses to have a drink.

Changes in the person that are indications for seeking help are:
o Deterioration in appearance.
o Financial problems.
o A change in the person's personality.
o A deterioration in physical health.

Who can help?

If the problem is not too serious people can usually help themselves. Cutting down on visits to the pub for instance. Substituting another hobby. Going to the pub just before closing time. Setting a limit on the amount of drink in the house. Seeking out new friends. And so on.

Where the problem is more serious, things can be harder. One of the main difficulties is that the person who is in need of help does not recognise that they have a problem. Others appreciate that they have a problem but are too ashamed to admit it. They may be frightened that they will be sent to a psychiatric hospital if they do.

If you can help persuade someone with a serious drink problem that seeking help is worthwhile then you will have helped them take a very large step. If you don't think you can do this yourself then try and think of someone who may be able to talk on the subject to the affected person.

The best sources of advice and help are the general practitioner, the health visitor and the local Council on Alcoholism. The council is an independent body. Its staff advise people with drinking problems and their relatives. It is a good source of advice for the person who is unwilling to admit that he has a problem or who is frightened of speaking to the doctor or health visitor. The Citizens Advice Bureau will be able to provide the address of the nearest council.

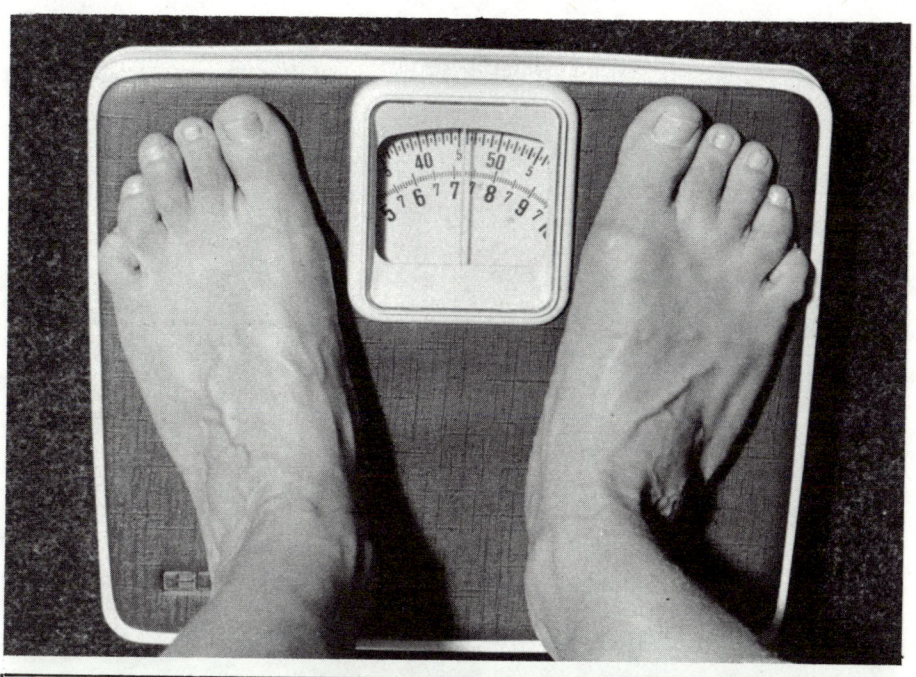

Watching your weight

Most people know if they are over-weight. A simple way of telling is to strip and to look at yourself in a mirror both from the front and from the side. Be honest. Are you overweight? If 'Yes', you need to ask: 'Do I really want to lose weight?' Many people would like to be lighter but are not prepared to change their lifestyle to do so. You must decide for yourself. If you lose weight you will:

o Reduce your risk of disease.
o Feel fitter.
o Look better.
o Feel less tired.
o Cope more easily with illnesses.

The chart on this page shows suitable weights for men and women of different heights. If you are still unsure about whether or not to lose weight or how much to lose, discuss the subject with your doctor or health visitor.

How to do it
There are three basic strategies. You should choose the one which most appeals or discuss a suitable diet with your doctor. There are many books on the market which can give you information on this subject.

1 Counting calories
The energy which food supplies to the body is measured as calories (or joules in the metric system). Special charts exist to show the calorie content of most foods and the daily calorie needs of different people. If you add up the calories in all the food you eat each day, you can keep a check on your intake and make sure that your body takes in fewer calories than it needs to keep going.

Most people will lose weight if their food contains no more than 1,000 calories each day.

This way your body has to supply the extra calories (energy) needed by burning up some of your stored fat.

2 Cutting down on energy rich foods
This is known as the *Stop, Caution, Go* system.

Stop sugar, sweets, chocolate, cakes, pastries, pies, biscuits, heavy puddings, honey, syrup, treacle, jam, marmalade,

Average weights in pounds at different ages and heights										
Height	Under 30		30-39		40-49		50-59		60+	Height
	M	F	M	F	M	F	M	F	M	F	
4' 11"	—	115	—	121	—	128	—	131	—	133	4' 11"
5ft	—	117	—	123	—	130	—	133	—	135	5ft
5' 1"	—	119	—	125	—	132	—	136	—	138	5' 1"
5' 2"	—	121	—	127	—	135	—	139	—	142	5' 2"
5' 3"	134	124	138	130	141	138	142	142	139	145	5' 3"
5' 4"	136	127	142	134	145	141	146	145	143	148	5' 4"
5' 5"	141	131	146	138	149	145	150	149	146	152	5' 5"
5' 6"	144	134	150	142	154	149	155	152	152	154	5' 6"
5' 7"	148	138	154	146	158	153	159	157	156	159	5' 7"
5' 8"	151	142	158	150	162	157	163	162	161	164	5' 8"
5' 9"	156	146	163	154	167	161	168	166	166	168	5' 9"
5' 10"	160	150	167	158	171	164	173	171	171	175	5' 10"
5' 11"	165	154	172	160	176	168	178	175	176	179	5' 11"
6ft	170	158	176	164	180	171	182	179	181	186	6ft
6' 1"	175	—	181	—	185	—	187	—	186	—	6' 1"
6' 2"	179	—	186	—	190	—	192	—	191	—	6' 2"
6' 3"	183	—	192	—	196	—	198	—	197	—	6' 3"

fruit tinned in syrup, dried fruit, cream, butter, margarine, lard, cooking oil, fat on meat, salad dressing, mayonnaise, chips, crisps, peanuts, sweet aperitifs, spirits and liqueurs, most soft drinks and mixers. *Eat as little as possible of these high calorie foods.*

Caution fatty meats, (like bacon or salami), sausages, liver paté, eggs, milk, oily fish (like herring, mackerel, sardines, tuna, salmon), cheese (except cottage cheese), thick creamy soups, nuts, bread (eat wholemeal or brown rather than white), cereals, rice, pasta (like spaghetti and macaroni), potatoes, savouries, ready made-up dishes, wines, beer and cider. *Be careful about how much of these medium calorie foods you eat.*

Go fresh fruit, salads, green and root vegetables, white fish, seafood, poultry, game, kidney, heart, brain, cottage cheese, yoghourt (natural), skimmed milk, bran, consommé and clear soups,

herbs and spices, low calorie soft drinks, coffee and tea (without milk), saccharin, water. *Eat as much as you like of these low calorie foods.*

3 Learning better eating habits
This means changing your pattern of eating. For instance, learning to:

Stop having snacks between meals.
Resist food 'just because it's there' or 'it looks so nice'.
Stop eating because you're tense, bored or depressed.
Spot hidden over-eating — for instance the 'hidden' calories of alcohol, chocolate bars or huge spoonfuls of relishes and dressings.

Counting calories will usually help you to lose weight quickly. Cutting down on energy rich foods is a more gradual method and likely to bring about a more permanent change. Learning better eating habits will usually bring about a slow but lasting change.

Whichever of the other methods you use you may also need to try this.

More information for change
In this topic we have been able to do little more than touch on the three problems of smoking, drinking and overweight. We have suggested some of the factors that may be involved in these habits and some courses of action you might take.

If you are seriously interested you will probably need more information.

It's worth going to local reliable sources, your doctor, health visitor, CAB and so on and seeking a variety of information. You may not find all the suggestions on changes appealing. Look around for ways to help yourself that suit you.

But beware of becoming the best informed person who never did anything about their problem!

Early retirement

Retirement from work, whether at the statutory ages of 60 or 65 or earlier, requires a period of emotional adjustment. But there is evidence that those who retire early adapt to changed circumstances more easily. There may be a number of reasons for this:

o The feeling that one is not old helps others to adapt to your changed situation. They are less likely to think of you as an old age pensioner.

o There may be fewer changes to cope with at one time. In most cases children will have grown and left but it may be that dependent children are still at home so delaying some of the problems attached to an 'empty nest' experience.

o Your spouse may still be working and this would ease the adjustment needed when both partners must learn afresh to live daily life in close contact.

o Your physical capacities will probably be less reduced than is likely later.

o If you volunteered for early retirement you will probably have done so on the basis that you will be able to manage financially. Sixty per cent of those who accepted early retirement have found their finances the same or better than before retirement.

o You may have been thoroughly 'fed-up' with the job (take-overs new management, unrelieved shift work, growing tiredness, lack of promotion, technological change, too much stress etc.) — and feel a new sense of morale at the thought of freedom.

o You may have felt a moral urge to retire 'if the financial terms are good enough because so many younger people are unemployed'.

So satisfaction with early retirement depends upon your own individual needs and expectations.

How do you feel about it?

A bonus: Early retirement may well allow you to move home perhaps or to become self employed for the first time or to spend more time with the family. Feeling good about early retirement will help you to seize the opportunities it offers.

A problem: If early retirement has distressed you, you may need a longer period of adjustment.

It might help to list in order of importance the problems that you find troublesome and then they may include: illness, boredom or financial difficulties.

Your own unexpected ill health can be put in perspective if you try to adjust to it. For most well people good health is not necessarily 'A1' fitness but an active ability to adapt to minor physical ailments.

Consult your doctor to see what maximum physical activity your disability will allow. Consult him too if you feel depressed over a long period.

If you have to accept an obligation to care for others, try to also provide for a life of your own. Things will be happier all round.

Wives and early retirement

Any well-adjusted couple takes early retirement in its stride, discussing joint finances, interests, travel and, often, a division of household chores.

Couples who have drifted slightly apart may need to make an extra effort to improve their relationship. However, freedom from tension, routing worry and sometimes responsibility contributes to personal tranquillity, making all of us easier to live with.

In retirement, as at any other time of change, it is a good idea to discuss money, possible alterations in lifestyle and transfers of interest from work to other pursuits before the change occurs. Wives whose main work has been in the home, may find their husbands' early retirement enriches their relationship.

Wives who have had a job as well as running a home will need to prepare for their own adjustment to retirement as carefully as their husbands and both should consider the effects upon the other. When a wife wants to go on working while her husband takes early retirement there may well be a bonus in role reversal if *both are happy with the arrangement*. If not, it is better to discuss the matter openly.

As in all aspects of retirement, planning the keynote to success lies in adopting a positive mental attitude. People who retire early are usually better able to enjoy the benefits and deal with the drawbacks.

Early retirement and money

When you retire the first essential is to tot up all the monies you have which are readily available. Then use this information with your main budget planning to consider the important decisions on broad issues like part-time work and your present and future ideas on what is an acceptable life style.

Your present age is important. Consider the length of time before you, your partner or both of you are able to receive the State Retirement Pension.

Weekly income

Pensions _____

Interest on
savings/investments _____

Spouse's regular income _____

Other _____

Total _____

Enter your estimated weekly
income here _____

Enter your estimated weekly
expenditure here _____

Balance if in Credit _____

Balance if in Debit _____

Lump sums

Special severance payment _____

Superannuation _____

Matured insurance policy _____

Ex-gratia sums _____

Other _____

Total _____

If your Weekly Balance is in debit and you do not have a lump sum or severance payment to help, then you may wish to claim all the state benefits to which you are entitled. You may also wish to consider making major decisions like moving house or earning money either through part time work or self-employment.

If you have a lump sum then you will probably want to find ways of using it to help your existing weekly budget. In the next chart follow the debit column to give you some ideas.

If your Weekly Balance is in credit follow the credit column to give you some ideas.

Remember though to seek professional advice to assist you in your decision making. Be guarded about answering newspaper advertisements. Call in at your local Citizens Advice Bureau.

Check points

o If you have only small amounts of money to put away — short term savings offering easy access are better than long term investments which tie up your money for long periods.

o Usually the higher the repayment on investment, the higher the risk.

o You need enough money readily available for known and unexpected expenses.

o Seek out inflation proof savings — and review your financial situation frequently.

o Consider investing in a personal pension plan for you or your partner.

Options

Debit weekly balance
Pay off outstanding debts.
Invest the rest to produce a high rate of income.
Save it all up until you move house or begin to earn some money again.

Credit weekly balance
Invest it all.
Invest some for a short term.
Pay off outstanding mortgage.
Buy holiday home, caravan, or boat etc.
Purchase large items for home.
Have expensive holiday.
Make gifts to family.

Your pension

The formula for calculating the maximum of benefits which can be provided in early retirement is:

$$\frac{N}{NS} \times P$$

'N' is the number of years which have been completed in service to the point of early retirement.

'NS' is the number of years which could have been completed from the date of joining to normal retirement age.

'P' is the maximum pension which could have been approved had the employee retired at his normal retiring age but based on how much he earns at the date of his early retirement.

This formula applies to both pension and cash. Any dependants' benefits are then directly related to the reduced pension. So an employee who joins a scheme at the age of 25 expecting to retire at 60, but who retires early at the age of 50 when earning £6,000 per annum may get a maximum early retirement pension of £2,857 per annum calculated as follows:

$$£6,000 \times \frac{2}{3} \times \frac{25}{35} = £2,857 \text{ per annum}$$

He could exchange part of his early retirement pension for a lump sum calculated on a similar basis as follows:

$$£6,000 \times 1.5 \times \frac{25}{35} = £6,428$$

Job release scheme

Available for men aged 64 and women aged 59 and for disabled men 60-63 years

If you want to take advantage of this voluntary early retirement your employer must — agree to the release and obtain a replacement (not necessarily for the same job) from the unemployed register.

Afterwards

You can:
Claim the small allowance available.
Claim social security benefits.
Receive industrial or war disability pension.
Receive occupational pension.

You cannot:
Have certain social security benefits.
Have statutory redundancy payments.
Take another job or set up in business.

Applications and inquiries to your Job Centre

These are the overall limits and include the value of any preserved pensions from earlier employment. The answer to the sum cannot exceed the cash/pension for a person's years of actual service with the company.

Pension entitlements

For advice about pension rights, make inquiries at your company personnel or pension fund office, your DHSS office and ask for leaflets NP.32, NI 196 and NI 208 and the Occupational Pensions Board, Apex Tower, High Street, New Malden, Surrey KTD 4DN. Tel: 01-942 8949.

Check points

o If you retire early to look after a sick relative you may be eligible for an Invalid Care Allowance.
o If you are in receipt of unemployment benefit, national insurance contributions are credited to you. If you are early retired and ineligible for unemployment benefit check that you have sufficient national insurance contributions to qualify for a full State Pension: if not you will need to pay contributions.
o If you receive an occupational pension you may also qualify for unemployment benefit but there will be reductions on a sliding scale from £35 weekly so that no unemployment benefit will be paid to a single person having an occupational pension of £57.50 or a married man with one of £71.40.
o Redundancy payments and pension lump sums will be taken into account if you claim supplementary benefit, e.g. no payments will be made if your capital exceeds £2,000. (All figures at 1982 rates)

Voluntary additional contributions

If you are considering early retirement you could ask your employer whether it is possible to increase your pension by making voluntary additional contributions.

Early retirement due to ill health

If the reason for early retirement is ill health the maximum benefits payable are those which could have been payable at normal retirement age but based, of course, on how much you are earning at the date when you decide to retire early.

Thus, a person with *potentially* more than ten years service to normal retirement age may receive a maximum early retirement pension of two-thirds of his final salary in the event of early retirement through ill health.

The same principle applies to his lump sum but should his ill health be such that his 'expectation of life is materially impaired' then he may be able to exchange the whole of his early retirement pension for an immediate cash sum, although this will not be totally free of tax. The value of the pension which, but for the seriousness of the ill health would not have been commutable, bears tax at 10 per cent.

LEISURE
Please give details of your special interests, sports and hobbies, and of membership of organisations, including any offices held

My main hobbies are gardening, making wine and beer and
studying the local natural history.
I am a member of the allotments association and between
1969 and 1972 acted as their secretary.
I am a member of a number of local and national societies
involved in natural history:
Royal Society for the Protection of Birds
Botanical Society of the British Isles
Local Natural History Society — secretary 1973 - 1977, chairman 1980—
Midlands Ornithological Society — committee member

MEDICAL

Are you willing to undergo a Medical Examination if required?	R.D.P. No.	Date Registration ends
Are you a Registered Disabled Person?		

ADDITIONAL INFORMATION
Please mention any special abilities which you feel are relevant but are not covered elsewhere

Will you serve anywhere in the British Isles?

REFEREES
Please give below the names and addresses of three people to whom we may apply for information about your work. At least one of these should relate to a previous appointment

1

2

3

Do you have any reservation about our approach to these referees?

Using your experience

Most early retirers would like to keep as active as possible. Whether your choice of activity depends upon the need to earn some money or the desire to go on using productively the skills and expertise you have built up over a lifetime in voluntary work, it is a good idea to take a personal inventory of your capacities and preferences.

Include the things you do best and enjoy and those which help your social life.

o Examine your job. You may have been trained to be an engineer or a typist but few people spend their entire working time doing the things implied by their job title. How many typists spend *all* day at a typewriter; how many electricians are unable to turn their hands to other skills; how many teachers have nothing to do outside the classroom?

o Most people are good at a wide range of tasks which may have nothing immediately to do with particular skills, or expertise.

o What additional experience have you gained from your job?

o What skills and experience have you picked up on your own initiative (e.g. building models, helping a political party, running a youth group, organising work for associations etc.)?

A personal dossier

Make your own personal dossier. This will help you to itemise your life experiences and to assess your personal qualities.

Consider the past

Write down your memories good and bad. Think back and try to recall early interests and ambitions, the places you lived in, and your experiences there, and how you 'got on' with other children and adults. Ask brothers and sisters and perhaps friends to recall what you were like.

Note your age, school, subjects and examinations passed. Don't worry if you have few formal qualifications. Think of all the activities connected with school days, whether sports, hobbies, interests. Note particularly the things you were good at. Note too the things you thought you might have been good at given the opportunity (perhaps the opportunity is *now*?) Think of the skills you have acquired after training and note down the kind of training.

Write down, in the order you did them, all the jobs you have ever done. Start with the name of your first employer. Try to recall the dates and the kind of work you did. Work through all your work experiences including war service.

Try to remember the training you did, courses you took, associations and unions you joined. Jot them down. It helps if you recall the people you worked with and spent your free time with. If you did any voluntary work or developed an absorbing interest or hobby at this time note it down.

You may recall opportunities or unexpected achievements, or periods when you felt the real 'you' had almost disappeared. You may see the present period of your life as a new opportunity to make good missed chances and realise your own potential. Now that your life is less directed by external events and the decisions of others you have a reasonable chance of controlling your own style of living.

Collect certificates, newspaper clippings, photographs and add these to your written dossier.

Consider the future

Consider your strengths and weaknesses. What action do you want to take on either of these?

Identify the ambitions and achievements of your youth and mid-life that have been neglected. Can any of these be re-established by further education or training or personal initiative?

When you are retired you can use all of these experiences for your own purposes. It does not matter whether they are noble, rewarded financially or in kind. What matters most is that they satisfy you individually.

Use your experience and personal research to transfer your abilities to new activities, do something different or even look for a new job.

Self employed

There are more than two million people in this country who are self-employed. They include building and construction workers, lawyers, doctors, actresses, artists and writers and also those who themselves employ staff in their own businesses.

If you are self-employed, the questions you must face about retirement in relation to paid work, as a full-time employee, differ slightly from those which come up when leaving an ordinary job. This topic looks at some of the business and personal decisions you will probably have to make.

Health, unemployment and pensions

Often the self-employed work extremely long hours. They rely heavily on their own abilities to maintain good health. If and when they are ill, they may get sickness benefit (if they can provide medical certificates to prove they were totally unable to work in any week) but on the other hand they know they may lose a good contract or even pick up a forfeit on a timed contract. The small village shopkeeper for example, may

have to employ temporary staff, or even close the business during the owner's period of illness.

Additionally, most self-employed people would find it difficult to collect unemployment benefit. It is virtually impossible for people, like artists or potters, to prove that they qualify for such benefits. However, people like decorators may find it slightly easier to prove they cannot find any work for a period of time.

The self-employed qualify for the minimum state retirement pension only and, therefore, need to arrange their own pensions. Fortunately, the Government is helpful in this respect.

Retirement annuities, or 'self-employed pension schemes', are contracts with a pension fund or insurance company. Through them a self-employed person may provide a personal pension which starts not earlier than his 60th birthday and not later than his 75th. The premiums attract income-tax relief. A recent incentive has been introduced by which loan-back facilities provide flexibility for those who do not wish to see their savings locked away until retirement.

But beware solving a short-term business problem by using the loan-back facility. It should not be used as the substitute for an overdraft.

Different views of retirement

Although the present statutory ages are 60 for women and 65 for men, to qualify for a state retirement pension, there are many self-employed who disregard these dates.

Easing out
Jack Davies became self-employed as a gardener when he was 34. Now, at the age of 71, he looks back to his early 60s when he, quite intentionally, refused to take on any new work. By the time he became entitled to his state retirement pension at 65, he had paced his amount of work to enable him to maintain the same level of income with his pension.

At the same time, he could have much more free time with Kitty, his wife. Retirement was a non-event, for gardening was also his hobby!

Balancing work and pension like this means taking careful notice of the earnings rule which states how much you can earn while drawing a pension before paying tax. If, like Jack, you are considering a gradual withdrawal from work, make sure you have obtained forms IR4 and IR4a from the Inland Revenue which explain this.

Handing over

Alan, the farmer, had different ideas. He enjoyed swimming, tennis and golf. When he was in his early fifties, he handed over the farm to his son Bill who had new ideas about farming and its management. Fortunately father and son were able to talk things through. Once the old farmhouse had been converted to two dwellings instead of one, father 'retired' to his sporting interests and Bill got on with his own 'new' farm.

Alan discussed the financial implications of the capital gains and transfer legislations with his accountant, who then involved Bill in the detail. For both Alan and Bill, however, it was more important to make the transfer at a time when they both felt ready for it. Money was not a problem. After talking with their accountant, they drew up plans and went ahead.

New horizons

Emily, now 58, had inherited a small woolshop from her grandparents in the village where she lived. She had no

intention of retiring from the shop until one day she received an unexpected visit from a school friend, Ethel, who she had not seen for more than thirty years. Ethel had been widowed about three years earlier and she had decided to see if she could trace one or two of her old school friends she used to think were good company. Emily was one of these and Ethel's letter to Emily had a quick response.

Not only were the old acquaintance-ships renewed but a new friendship emerged. It brought with it fresh and exciting interests, especially for Emily who had always stayed single, never really taken a holiday and seldom travelled far from the village. She determined to devote more time to developing her friendship with Ethel and to travel. At first, she thought she would sell the shop in about a year's time, when she would be 59.

Eventually however, she decided her date of retirement would be her 60th birthday and set about planning, during the next two years, for the great event.

Implications for retirement

The implications for their retirements of Jack the gardener, Alan the farmer and Emily the shopkeeper. Each in his, or her, own way, had to take a 'business inventory' and 'personal inventory' before reaching final decisions.

A business inventory

The business inventory probably included such things as:

o What is the capital taxation position when I sell or transfer the ownership of my business?

o How long do I have to keep all the paper work and records associated with my business after I sell it or retire?

o What will be the best age (from the tax point of view) or even time of the year, to sell up or retire?

o What is my financial liability with regard to my staff if I sell my business or if I close it?

All self-employed people pay income tax through an annual assessment system, not PAYE. The date on which they sell their businesses, or retire, or take a self-employed pension, all have bearings on their tax positions.

For many self-employed people, the business, the premises and its goodwill, represent their sole savings for retirement. Many hoteliers come into this category. Capital gains tax is a key factor in these cases usually with important changes to consider following any new Budget legislation.

If you have no business premises, nor goodwill to sell, the most important financial factor for you to consider is the actual date during the year you make the decision to cease paid work.

Why not draw up your own business inventory? Add to the questions on the list. Make it as detailed as you like. Then read it through again as a visual checklist against your own thoughts. Are there any gaps left? What information do you need? Which of your questions are unanswered?

You may have ideas about some. On others, you may draw a complete blank. Finding the best answers for you, always means taking some professional advice. Once you have drawn up your business inventory and thought about it, it is time to consult your accountant. Even if you have employed one particular accountant for many years, it may be worth your while and secure peace of mind, to employ two different accountants, particularly if your business is complicated, or you are in partnership. The National Federation of Self-Employed can also offer information and guidance.

A personal inventory
Here are some questions your personal inventory will probably include. Fill in those answers which occur readily to mind. Then think about and research details for the remainder.

"How will I occupy my time?"

_____

_____

_____

"Where shall I live?"

_____

_____

_____

"What about my family, will they see my point of view?"

_____

_____

_____

"What about my finances, how much income do we need to live on:"

_____

Now? _____

In five years? _____

In 10 years? _____

In 20 years? _____

"Will I continue to serve on all those committees?"

_____

"Will I start taking an interest in the political, cultural or social life which I may have missed?"

_____

Add to the questions on our list. You are an individual with a unique personal and working life. Let your personal inventory reflect this. The questions on this list may appear to be easier to answer than those on the business inventory, though you may want to discuss them with family and friends.

Taking the decision

For different people, different parts of their business and personal inventories will be most important. For some, financial decisions will be crucial. For others, personal matters will be uppermost in their minds. For one person, finding a suitable place to live may override all else. For another, it may be a question of finding a balance between the 'pull' of personal preferences and the 'push' of financial pressures. Here is how it looked to Emily, Alan and Jack.

Emily

For Emily everything revolved around where to live and the part her shop had played in her life. If she continued to live in the village, how would she feel if a new shopkeeper gave it a completely new image? Would not people in the village compare the 'old' with the 'new' and possibly suggest that it was about time that old shop had a good clean out? On the other hand, she had never lived anywhere else except in the village.

Maybe she and Ethel could find somewhere together. It was certainly an important issue they had to discuss. If she stayed in the village, would she really sever all connections with the business? It could be that the new shop owners would value her knowledge and occasional assistance. Would she like this? Or would she prefer to make a complete break?

In the end, she and Ethel did decide to live together. They bought a house in a village nearer to a town and more convenient for the larger shops which fascinated Emily. She sold her shop to a man who ran an antique business. She still visited friends in her old village but the focus of her life had changed. She was glad to be free to travel and enjoy Ethel's companionship.

Alan

Alan could have considered the setting-up of a limited company, or selling or giving the farm to his son. Whichever method he chose the financial considerations had to be weighed against his personal ones. In many ways, he had faith in his son's abilities to introduce changes where necessary, in order to keep the farm in profit. In any

case, he felt he was handing over a pretty good farm business.

He felt that he could cope with the changes better the younger he was. Financially, it might have been better to wait till he was 60 to hand over. But Alan feared that by 60 he would be set in his ways and reluctant to hand over. Bill might have become resentful of having to continue to work under his father's old methods. Personal factors meant that now was the best time to make the break.

Jack

For Jack the issue was precisely when to retire. He wanted to continue living where he always had done. His work as a gardener was an extension of his hobby. Retirement was a question of phasing out the work side of his life and phasing in the leisure side. Jack's solution is one that is often uniquely available to self-employed people. You don't have to give up work all at once.

You can take more leisure time bit by bit, according to how fit you feel and what other interests you are developing.

All this has to be planned of course and you should discuss the financial implications with your accountant. Self-employed people who have bought their way into pension schemes, can start to receive payments at any time between 60 and 75.

No company will allow the first payment to be made after 75, but they may be prepared to convert the pension into annuities. This may be worth looking at if you are still working and don't feel you need to draw on your pension savings yet.

Most self-employed people are independent and strong minded. The choice of work they have taken has made them so. They are used to looking after themselves. They know how to organise their lives.

These qualities stand them in good stead in retirement.

Changing places

This topic deals with some of the options in housing that you may find available to you if your circumstances alter. It also offers some ideas if you have to advise an elderly friend or relative about accommodation.

The best laid plans

Tess and Charlie Wall have lived in a small industrial village in the Midlands since they were married, getting on for 40 years ago. When Charlie retired two years ago they worked out their ideas about where to live. They drew up a list of what they wanted in the long term.

o A small self contained easily managed unit.
o A garden.
o No stairs (with an eye to the future).
o Convenient shopping.
o Being near friends and acquaintances.
o Convenient for their children to visit.

With the list in mind they decided not to move but to convert their house into a ground floor flat by turning two old outhouses into a shower room and dining room and then using the dining room as a bedroom. The upstairs bedrooms were only needed when there were family guests. Having done these improvements they were happy that when they did want a smaller living unit they had provided for it.

However, a year later a large waste disposal tip was opened just outside the next village two miles away. The smell was appalling especially when the wind came from that direction. Tess and Charlie said "*Last summer it was so uncomfortable sitting in the garden. You stop thinking about the summer as something you look forward to.*"

They started to look seriously into moving and thought again about some of the ideas they'd discussed and dismissed at the time of retiring, like going to North Wales. They decided there were still strong reasons against Wales, mainly the distance from family and friends. There was some talk of their son moving to Liverpool and that might have tipped the balance but eventually he decided to stay in Oxford. In fact the only thing that had changed was the waste disposal tip and its smell.

So the list was still a realistic estimate of what they needed. They applied it to their present housing needs.

o The house — a small bungalow with a garden? Somewhere where there is a chance of an allotment?
o The area — access to facilities, fairly near to where we are now — both from the point of view of family and friends?
o Out of range of the waste disposal tip.

Tess and Charlie were aware that there were a variety of different sorts of accommodation they could seek. But their original list still covered their requirements.

One bonus was that their house after the conversion, was much improved and a more attractive prospect to sell. Also in thinking about moving to a smaller house they could afford to look for one with central heating which had been one of their original intentions but they hadn't been able to afford this in the conversion.

Changed circumstances

Of course you may not have to cope with *these* sorts of changed circumstances. But in thinking about your home it's useful to look at possible changes in circumstances and think about how you'd deal with them either in your present home or with different accommodation.

Think about how any of the following circumstances might change the way you view where you live.

Public transport cuts in your area.
Selling the car.
Learning to drive.
New road opens.
Shops or facilities open or close in your area.
Compulsory purchase order on your house.
Houses put up or demolished near you.
Factory opens in your area.
You see a house or area you find very attractive.
Family moves away/nearer.
Divorced child wants to live at home again.
Grown up single child decides to leave.
Elderly relative needs looking after.
Partner or self becomes less mobile.
Living alone after lengthy period of living with others.
Need more or less space for changing hobbies and interests.
Much reduced income.
You inherit money.

Now add any issues not on the list that would lead you to think seriously about moving or perhaps altering your home.

The list above breaks down into several different concerns.

How you feel about and use the area you live in.
How your network of relatives and friends affect your views about where you live and use your home.
How personal and financial circumstances may affect your view of where you live.

Remember, what suits you now may not always suit you. You'll need to think

about the ways you could cope with any changed circumstances you face.

When considering making changes in your living arrangements you could do what Tess and Charlie did.

Think about current arrangements. What are their strengths, and what you want to carry over into your new plan?

Think about any additional benefits that your revised plan would give you (like Tess and Charlie's central heating).

Accommodation

Below are some suggestions about housing arrangements. If any interest you then check the details — having the information doesn't do you any harm.

o Many builders cater for people who want to live in small easy to run housing units. Some of these are for one person. Keep an eye open in your local paper for one and two bedroom units and have a look at them to see if they appeal.

o Special or sheltered housing schemes for older people. In these schemes there is a warden available but tenants have their own furniture and usually look after themselves. They are usually run by local authorities or housing associations. They offer a range of accommodation — from bedsitters to flats for several people.

o Housing schemes run by voluntary societies are similar to sheltered housing. Charities such as Help the Aged, or local charitable associations are a useful starting point in looking for these.

o Most local authorities have single or two person accommodation frequently available on ground floors for older people. You could investigate the possibility of a move if your present accommodation is unsuitable for you . . . and put yourself on the waiting list.

o Some counties have mobility schemes involving several local councils, which help tenants to move. Check with the Council.

> **When you are thinking of houses you can get reliable information from:**
> A Housing Aid Centre or Housing Advice Centre. These are provided by the borough council and can help you find the information you need. (Check if there's one in your area.)
> Your local Citizens Advice Bureau.
> Your local authority housing department.

o If you own your own house you may be able to sell it to the council and become a council tenant. Find out if such a scheme exists in your area.

o You might be able to exchange houses of flats with someone in another area or in the same area. Some local authorities even have exchange bureaux.

o You might consider living with other members of your family perhaps in a self contained unit or lodging with a family or in a boarding house.

o New towns will consider applications from the retired particularly if they have relatives in the town . . . apply to the appropriate New Towns Development Corporation. Check with your council about being nominated. Check with the Development Corporation on houses for sale.

o Residential homes often limit space and you may not be able to take many of your belongings with you.

o Privately run homes usually cater for small numbers, often fewer than 20. They vary greatly and it's a good idea to shop around.

o If you live in a house that seems far too big you could donate it to a charity, for instance Help the Aged. Part of the house would then be converted into a modernised and usually self-contained flat for you. The portion you don't need is converted for the use of retired people. Do seek independent professional advice, preferably from your solicitor before undertaking this step.

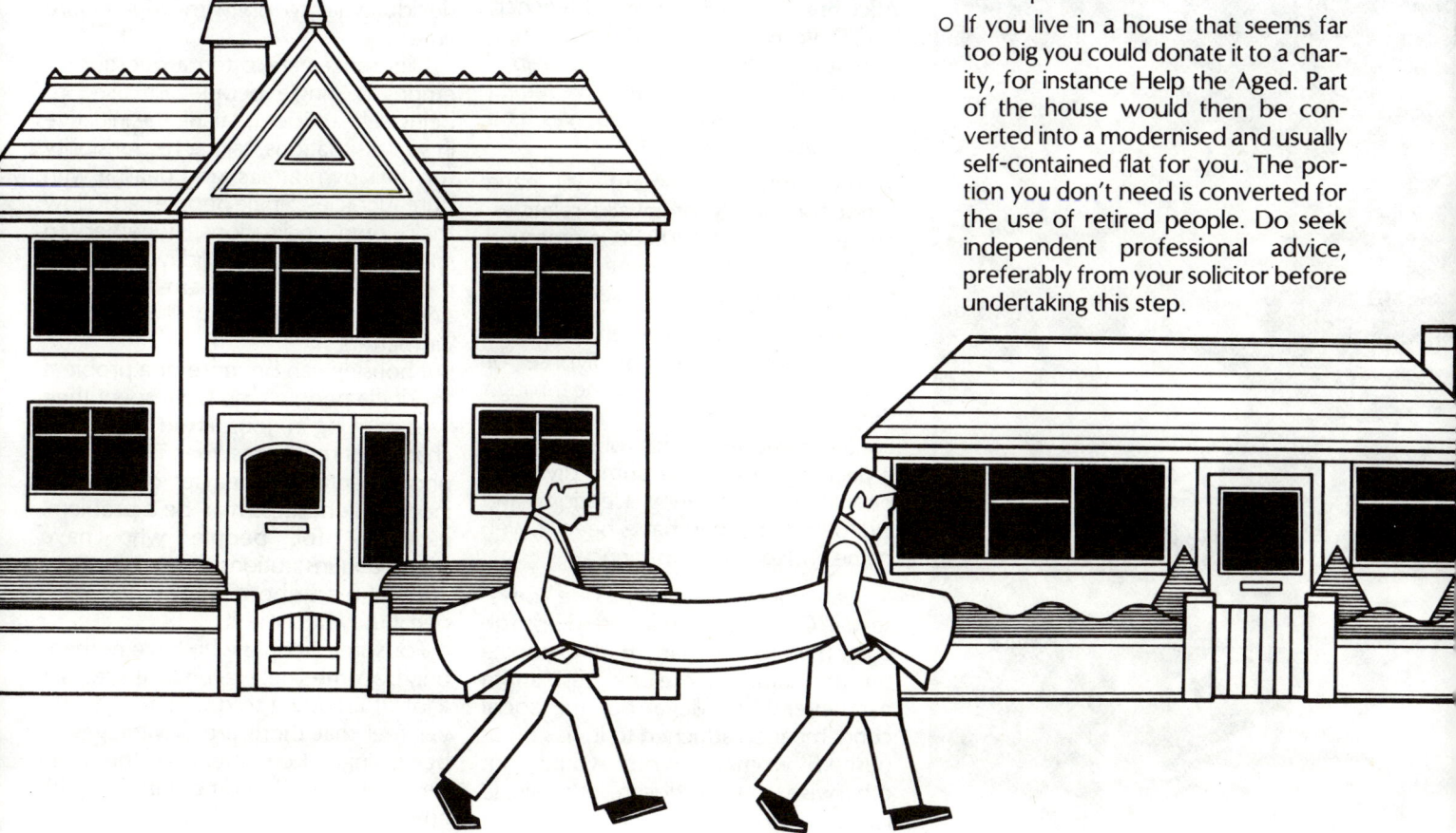

Single people

Retirement is often thought of as a time for re-discovering the pleasures of a wife or husband's company. But many people are single. Many of the issues they face are exactly the same as for married people. But there are differences too. Being single can be a source of both strengths and weaknesses in retirement.

How many single people are there?

The 1971 census showed that:

18% of 60–69 year olds lived alone (almost 1 in 5)

30% of 70–79 year olds lived alone (almost 1 in 3)

35% of over 80s lived alone (over 1 in 3).

Many of the people in the first age group will have been single throughout life, or since an earlier divorce or widowhood. In the older two age groups, many will have become single through bereavement.

This topic looks at the first group — people already single around the age of retirement.

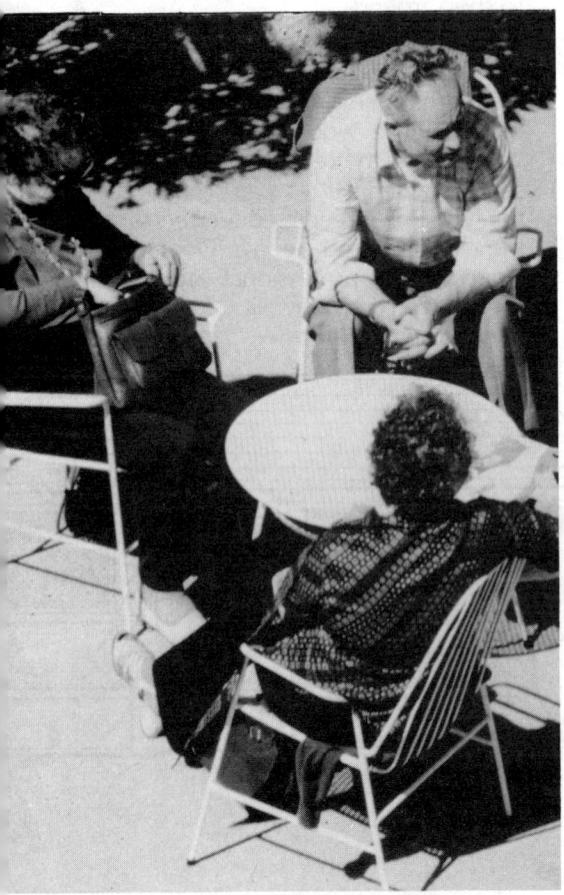

Who are the single people?

There is an image of the single, as lonely, isolated, maybe eccentric. They may be treated as odd individuals who know nothing of love, children, relationships, sex or family life. There can be few single people who can't recall, without irritation, some social occasion where their being single was seen by others as being a problem.

Single people are not a simple category. Some have been married, some have not, some do have children, some work, some don't. They are as likely to have as varied an experience of life, love, relationships, work and family, as any other part of the population.

Many people are single through choice. They have simply not wanted to get married or settle down with one other person. Some may be women who have chosen a career. The pleasure, variety and stimulation of working life is, for many, as attractive as the prospect of bringing up children.

Alice Brackley, a 57 year old teacher, said, *"I've worked in a lot of different jobs. I've been a companion help. I taught children in Kenya and I've taught in this country. My last job was as a matron in a prep. school"*.

Some (mostly women) will have cared for elderly or invalid relatives. There are currently 300,000 unmarried women acting as housekeeper/nurses to their parents or other relatives.

Some are men or women who have become single through divorce or widowhood. All will have gone through the process of adjusting to life alone. For those widowed, this will have been a painful process. For some divorced people, re-discovering freedom and independence may have been a welcome and exciting experience.

Some may be people who are homosexual. Growing up in a period less tolerant than today, many had no choice but to adapt to life alone. Lesbianism has never been illegal but the social condemnation attached to it, has often pushed women, who would not otherwise have so chosen, into a single life.

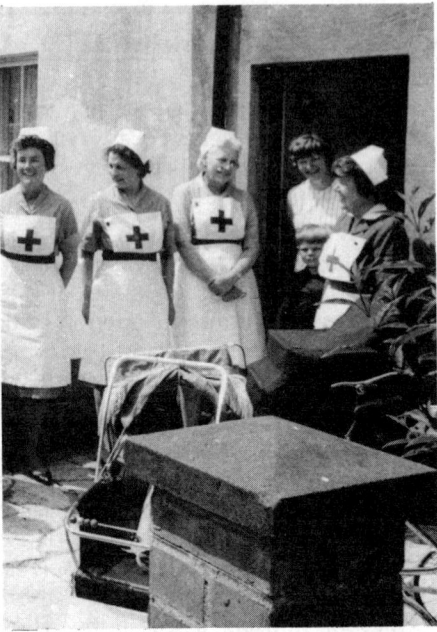

What's so different?

Many aspects of retirement will be exactly the same for single people as for couples. You have to decide where to live; adjust to the loss of work companions; adjust to a change in income; decide what to do with your leisure time.

Differences are often a question of emphasis. Single people are used to being self-sufficient, taking the initiative in social situations, taking responsibility for their own affairs, and dealing with bureaucracies. Single people can follow their own inclinations, whether to spend money on a holiday or a lawn mower. They can suit themselves emotionally and socially, as well as in practical matters.

But housing can be more of a problem for single people who have spent their lives in 'living-in' jobs. Fixed household charges of rent, rates, fuel, TV and telephone rental, fall heavier on a single income. Loneliness may be a problem, especially for people who have worked in institutions. For some there are real fears about what would happen if they became ill.

For some people who have perhaps only become single recently, there is still a lot of adjusting to do. They may not yet feel that there are advantages to being single. Retirement for them can be a time to become familiar with advantages.

How important are the differences?

Here are some of the advantages and disadvantages of being single in retirement.

For each one that is very important, score 2, important, score 1, or irrelevant/unimportant, score 0. As an example, the chart is filled in for Alice Brackley, who has spent a varied life in a number of different jobs, some abroad and mostly of the 'living-in' type. Add up your total for advantages and for disadvantages.

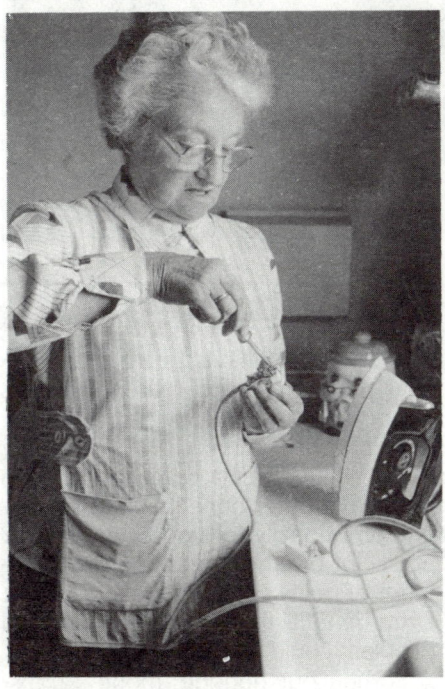

More advantages?

If you scored more on advantages, then you are probably an independent and self-sufficient person, with few practical worries.

Equal scores?

If you scored the same for advantages and disadvantages, then you're probably approaching retirement with a fair degree of confidence in your ability to handle situations, but you also have some significant worries that you need to deal with.

More disadvantages?

If you scored more for disadvantages, then you need to look carefully at how each of these disadvantages will affect you and plan to minimise their effects.

Advantages

As a single person.	This is very important.		This is important.		This is irrelevant/ unimportant.	
	You	Alice	You	Alice	You	Alice
Being used to handling my own affairs.				1		
Being used to going out and making friends.				1		
Having only myself to think of.						0
Being used to being resourceful.		2				
Already having a wide network of friends.				1		

	You	Alice
Total		5

Disadvantages

As a single person.	This is very important.		This is important.		This is irrelevant/ unimportant.	
	You	Alice	You	Alice	You	Alice
Having to live on a single retirement income.				1		
Work has been the main focus of my life and I will lose all that.				1		
Being worried about living alone in case I become ill or have an accident.		2				
Afraid of being lonely.						0
Housing may be a problem for me.		2				

	You	Alice
Total		6

Sorting out disadvantages

Here are some suggestions for first steps you might take to deal with issues that you think are serious disadvantages to being retired. They may not be appropriate for you — but you might find it useful to write down your own series of first steps:

o Check carefully all rights and benefits you could receive to help your financial situation. Work out a budget after retirement.

o Work out how you will keep contact with work, clubs and societies you could continue to attend, occasions when you might meet work friends.

o If you worry about falling ill, or having an accident, work out a lifeline scheme with friends and neighbours. (Could be phone calls, keeping an eye on each other's houses and so on.)

o Check out times when you *do* feel lonely. Decide to go out or find something specific to do at those times.

o It's worth doing plenty of shopping around if housing is a problem. It can have a very important effect on your social life and contact with others — not to say your budget!

Alice Brackley's experience

Alice scored slightly more for disadvantages (6) than advantages (5). The social aspects didn't worry her. She was confident in her ability to make friends and had few fears of being lonely. Her biggest worries were housing and living alone. Her working life had taken her all over the place and she had no firm base and insufficient money to purchase a home of her own. She was worried about high rents and also about living alone.

She suffered from osteo-arthritis and there was a history of heart disease in the family. Another worry was financial — working abroad and frequent job changes, meant she had a poor contributions record. But overall, she was optimistic, *"I'm not mean, but I am careful!"*.

Dealing with worries

For Alice it was important to deal with these worries before retirement. She realised that, if she could sort out her housing problem, her other worries would become more manageable. She

could establish a circle of friends and neighbours. Frequent contact with other people would ease her worries about living alone. She would also be able to budget properly.

Alice managed to set things in motion a few years before she retired. She decided to go back to the town where she'd been born and still had relatives, and where she felt at home. She started by visiting the town one holiday and visiting local estate agents, looking for private rented accommodation. The results were disappointing — expensive or unsuitable. However, she also put her name on the council house list and wrote to the National Federation of Housing Associations to see if there were any housing associations in the area that provided for people in her circumstances.

A few months before she retired, Alice was offered a flat by a housing association. With this major problem out of the way, the advantages of being single quickly came to the fore. She made contact with her neighbours and located the Geological Society (a particular hobby of hers) and a bridge course. She also made enquiries about doing work with handicapped children. For Alice, once the practical problem of housing had been settled, finding friends and ways of occupying herself presented no difficulties.

What about you?

If like Alice you have a particular practical problem about retirement, it is important to start taking steps to cope with it before you retire.

The solution of a practical problem may have other benefits, both socially and emotionally for you. So look back at the list of advantages and disadvantages of being single. Think about what extra benefits the solving of a practical problem could bring for you.

Sorting out housing, money, transport, perhaps having a telephone for instance, can make you feel better about being alone, if you feel that to be a problem.

Emotional and social problems can be harder to grapple with than practical ones but solving the practical ones to begin with can remind you of the strengths that you have — independence, resourcefulness and so on.

Whatever the disadvantages are of being single in retirement, it is important to remember and build on the advantages. Some of them are real strengths, not to be underestimated, which will give you the edge on many a married couple.

As one man put it, *"It sounds a bit arrogant but I felt that if I couldn't manage for myself — oh dear me, I might as well stop"*.

Partners

Most people think of 'partners' as married couples. But any two people who live together have some kind of partnership, two sisters, a mother and son or two friends. There will be different degrees of involvement in the other's life. But among the elements shared will be the companionship, the practical and emotional support you give each other and the give and take of everyday life.

When your circumstances change, on retirement, it's worth thinking about the way that everyday concerns are going to have an impact on your relationship with your partner.

If your expectations haven't been talked about then it's easy for misunderstandings to arise.

Living together

People who have lived together for some time have usually developed a fairly agreeable set of working arrangements about how much time they spend together and apart, what their routines are, and who does what around the house. After retirement, these working arrangements may need adjusting.

There follows a chart containing expectations people may have about life together with their partner after retirement. All the statements involve ideas about how time is organised and the expectation each partner has about their own and the other's time.

Put a tick to show whether you agree or disagree with each point. When you've done this, cover your own answers with a piece of paper and ask your partner to do the exercise too.

Even if only one of you has so far retired, try and complete the exercise in terms of what your expectations are likely to be. Also, complete the three points at the foot of the list, in that case.

Compare your answers. See how much agreement there is between you and your partner. Where you and your partner do agree, is this because you've already talked about it? Or do you just know instinctively what the other thinks and expects?

Expectations in retirement	Partner		You	
	Agree	Dis-agree	Agree	Dis-agree
Both partners at home.				
Now we're both retired I expect my partner will generally spend more time with me.	☐	☐	☐	☐
Now we're both retired I expect my partner will spend less time with his/her friends and more time with me.	☐	☐	☐	☐
Now we're both retired I expect we shall do more things together.	☐	☐	☐	☐
Now that we're both retired I expect we'll be less tied by routine and 'jobs' and will just be able to get up and go out without having to plan in advance.	☐	☐	☐	☐
Even though we're both retired I wouldn't like to be at my partner's beck and call all the time.	☐	☐	☐	☐
Even though we're both retired I wouldn't like to see my partner much more during what used to be working hours.	☐	☐	☐	☐
Now we've both retired I expect my partner and I will work together at various 'jobs' in the house.	☐	☐	☐	☐
Though we've both retired I expect that we will both do the same 'jobs' we've always done.	☐	☐	☐	☐
Now we're both retired I expect we'll have less privacy than we've been used to.	☐	☐	☐	☐
When only one partner has retired.				
I would expect the other partner to give up his/her job now.	☐	☐	☐	☐
I would expect household chores to be done in the same way as they've always been.	☐	☐	☐	☐
I would expect the retired partner to take on all the household jobs	☐	☐	☐	☐

It's a good idea to talk about these things now you have both done this exercise, because you will be clearer in your own mind, about how you see things happening and what you both expect. Where you disagree on some issues — a problem could arise. If you have different expectations of each other in retirement, or if you know how your partner will react and resent their attitude — then again you could take this opportunity to talk it over.

Obviously there are other things that aren't included in the list that you may also like to talk about — financial matters, missing work, how to manage depression or boredom if it arises, and especially discovering if you do share the same expectations.

Sometimes differing expectations can lead to problems. The following three case studies concern themselves with differing expectations in the areas of companionship, how routines are going to be altered, and how jobs are going to be done.

Companionship

Kath Evans retired a few months ago from a part-time job about a year after her husband. Harry expects her to be around the house. He needs company and sees Kath as the obvious person to supply it. She feels guilty about going out even though she'd previously had a strong established social life with women friends of her own.

Kath misses seeing her friends as much as she used to. Harry doesn't like most of them. When Kath's friends call, he is often rude and anti-social. Harry doesn't understand why she needs to see so much of her friends now he's at home and feels she should concentrate her attention on him. And Harry still complains about having nothing to do even though Kath devotes a lot of her time to keeping him company. Kath says "Harry doesn't seem to understand. He never felt guilty about being out at work all those years after the children left home. Before I got my job I was in all the time. Anyway, I like seeing my friends."

It is Kath who has had to make all the efforts to accommodate Harry's demand for companionship. And this has left her feeling rather resentful.

Routines

Dave Forrest retired a few years ago at 63. His wife Margaret is 10 years younger. She still had several years to work before her retirement. The Forrests came to an arrangement that they both found satisfactory. Dave would take over the management of the house.

Margaret has just retired herself. The first few weeks have been wonderful, but she now feels she'd like to do more in the house herself. However, Dave is resisting the pressure. He feels that anything Margaret does is a criticism of the way he's managed the house. Also, over the years he has developed a firm routine for running the house. He remembers the very empty feeling he had at retirement until he had got himself sorted out. If Margaret now starts taking work on round the house it will, he feels, leave him with too much time on his hands.

Another area of friction was that Margaret was expecting to see much more of the grandchildren when they had both retired but to her surprise she found Dave wasn't keen to have them over. It was as though, fond of them as he was, he didn't want his quiet routine disrupted.

Jobs

Len and Jean are brother and sister and share a house left to them by their parents. Jean has always been the housekeeper, and Len the handyman. They've lived independent lives, but have got on reasonably well together over the years.

Jean imagined that once Len retired he would take over a share of the household chores. This didn't happen. Len saw retirement as an opportunity to rest up a bit, do the things he liked doing. He'd never had much to do with the running of the house; Jean seemed to have it all under control, so where was the point in trying to change things?

Jean was appalled by his attitude and thought he was going into a decline — staying in bed till mid-morning and watching TV or reading the newspaper until the pub opened in the evening. Jean herself had always been active and expected Len to *do* something in retirement.

Adapting

These problems have arisen out of one or both parties feeling unhappy about the changes that retirement has brought. Any two people living together may have difficulties at some stage in their lives adapting to each other and to changed circumstances.

Adapting to change is a gradual process of slipping into a different routine, accepting a different set of circumstances, altering the way you relate to the people around you. Sometimes you need to think back to particular changes that have happened, to be able to remember what you did at that time.

Dave and Margaret Forrest thought about some of the major changes in their lives and how they'd coped at the time.

Getting married.

"At last! After that long engagement! Honeymoon period was bliss, but getting used to each other wasn't quite what we'd expected."

Nowhere to live — two years living with Margaret's parents.

"All the problems of living with in-laws. Used to argue with Margaret's parents. Margaret tried to stay out of it and not take sides."

Having children and moving house.

"Lovely! But there was so much work to do — we had very separate jobs. Children brought us closer together."

Dave unemployed for one year.

"Bad time. Dave depressed, put great strain on family. We had a lot of rows at this time. Found him things to do, boosting his morale. Tried to be understanding."

Children leaving home.

"This threw me completely. I leant on Dave for support. Eventually got a job and felt much more independent."

Daughter moving in after her divorce.

"Bad patch for us. Dave did not have much sympathy. I took our daughter's side and became involved in sorting out her problems. Dave felt excluded — as if there was a rift between him and I."

Margaret in hospital.

"Made us very close. Margaret's convalescence was difficult for me rushing home to cook meals. But I found I quite enjoyed organising the running of the house. Margaret let me spoil her and take over for a while."

You can see that Dave and Margaret coped in different ways at different times in their lives; Margaret avoided confrontation with Dave over her parents, and much later on, over his running of the house. She gave Dave support when he was unemployed, but desperately needed *his* when the children left home.

Dave let off steam about things when living with Margaret's parents and they had quite a few rows over the years but when their daughter moved in for a

while, Dave chose to keep out of the way. No doubt Dave and Margaret will find similar solutions to the problems they've come up against in retirement.

Think about changes you and your partner have adapted to in the past and write down the ways you did this.

Getting it straight
When you and your partner talk about the changes in your circumstances that retirement brings, consider these points:

o What you have done for your partner in the past as well as being practical may also have been a way of showing affection. So the other partner contributing or taking over certain domestic tasks may deprive you of the means of doing this.

o On the other hand, you may want your partner to take over some of the responsibility for domestic tasks as a way of showing your respect and affection.

o Your routine and way of doing things has been worked out over a number of years. A disruption to it may make you feel that your way of going about things isn't valued any more.

o Perhaps if your partner tries to keep the relationship ticking over the way it always has, you may feel that he or she doesn't see retirement as an opportunity to bring you together.

o Plans for spending time together need to be worked out in consultation: otherwise the adjustments being made may largely be one-sided, one partner doing all the alterations to life style.

o Spending time away from each other with separate interests and separate friends doesn't mean you are no longer interested in each other. It can be a very worthwhile way of recharging batteries so that the time you spend together is all the more highly valued.

Disagreements
It may be that you discuss the way retirement will affect your life with your partner and find that you cannot agree about how you are to adapt. It might be the case that you know instinctively how your partner will react to retirement and don't feel happy about that either. Retirement sometimes exaggerates things that have always been present in your relationship.

When one or both of you is at work all day, you don't spend as much time in each other's company — and you may prefer it that way! Many marriages are quite satisfactory to the partners in a state of 'companionable isolation'.

Harry and Kath
In this couple's case, the marriage had jogged along well enough, mainly because they had led separate lives. Kath was a sociable person, Harry was not. But this routine had broken down in retirement.

Is Harry being selfish or is Kath? Which one should give way to the other — or can they reach a compromise?

Harry and Kath could talk about their needs as individuals, as well as what they expect from each other.

Harry needs Kath's company, perhaps more at first, but less as he gets used to being retired.

Kath can give Harry more time at first, but still keep up her own friends.

Harry would be in a better position if he didn't lean on Kath to meet all his needs. If anything happened to her, he would really be at a loss.

Len and Jean
It might have helped if Jean and Len had talked about Len's retirement in advance. Even so, talking is not doing. Len might have expressed willingness to help out a bit more — and then done nothing. Or if Len had learnt of Jean's intentions for *his* retirement, he might have become very angry and things might have been even worse.

Was it unrealistic of Jean to expect Len to change the habit of a lifetime — leaving all the domestic matters to her? Was it unfair of Jean to want Len to lead an active retirement? Or was Len being thoughtless — and sinking into the kind of rut that it would be difficult to get out of?

Len and Jean could look back to times when they've made adjustments to their lifestyles — when they first moved in together; when they both cared for their invalid father. How did they cope then — was there more give and take at those times?

Each has to respect the personality of the other. Jean's a doer — Len watches the world go by. If the way the other lives irritates — it's possible to learn to switch off.

Jean could put her foot down and not do Len's washing, iron his shirts. But would she be prepared to do her share of mending the gutters, painting the house?

If things did not get better — they could lead more separate lives which would be one way of working out a peaceful co-existence.

Working out ways of adjusting to these kinds of problems with your partner needs time, understanding and tolerance. A change in your life — like retirement — can make you stop and think. You may not be happy with everything you see. A change in circumstances provides you with one opportunity to make the kind of changes in your relationship with your partner that you both want.

Picking up the pieces

For anyone who has lived with another person, picking up the pieces when that partnership is over can be a lengthy and difficult process.

This topic looks at that process. It concentrates mainly on picking up the pieces after the end of a marriage. But parts of it could be applied after the end of any close partnership.

What does marriage mean to you?

Here are five general statements about marriage. Tick the one that you feel is closest to your own point of view.

a **Marriage is a sacrament binding you for life to the partner.** ☐
b **Marriage is an intense, emotional commitment that you expect only once in a life time.** ☐
c **Marriage is a way of stating publicly that a relationship is special and important.** ☐
d **Marriage means different things to different people and there are many kinds of marriages.** ☐
e **Marriage is a financial and social arrangement that has little to do with people's feelings for each other.** ☐

If you ticked a or b:

It seems likely that your way of adjusting would be to accept that future relationships would be of a different order. But there is no reason why such relationships could not satisfy you socially and emotionally. But the prospect of remarriage for instance is likely to be much against your values.

If you ticked c or d:

It seems that you could seek to replace the relationship with another of a similar type. The emotional, social and practical needs that you have could be satisfied by a new, close relationship, possibly remarriage.

Benefits This activity looks in detail at some of the possible benefits of marriage. Read through the list and tick whether each item is important or not to you.	Important	Not Important
1 Marriage makes me feel I have a place in society.		
2 My husband/wife and I share common hobbies and interests.		
3 Being married means we can go out and enjoy ourselves with other couples.		
4 Marriage gives me an enjoyable sexual relationship.		
5 Marriage gives me closeness, warmth and intimacy.		
6 Marriage gives me friendship.		
7 Marriage means there is someone to look after me if I am ill.		
8 Marriage means there is someone to share household chores.		
9 Marriage protects me from loneliness.		
10 Marriage gives me someone to share troubles with.		

If you ticked e:

Your views about the intimacy of relationships are not closely connected with the institution of marriage itself. Therefore remarriage would be a practical consideration.

Benefits

Items 1 and 3 refer to the social status that marriage can bring. For many people this is more important than they care to admit. Marriage can make you feel you 'fit'.

Item 4 is often easier too, within the bounds of marriage. Sexual relationships are often easier to maintain within marriage. The tolerance given to the younger generation is often not extended to their parents. Gossip can be hurtful if not harmful and many people prefer the social acceptance that marriage brings.

Robert and Betty

Take the example of Robert and Betty. Robert's wife died when he was 58. A year later Betty's husband died suddenly. The two couples had been close friends. Their social life had centred round a country dance club made up almost entirely of couples. When his wife died Robert found the club with its emphasis on married couples a difficult place to be. Many people were unsure how to treat him and he stopped attending many of the functions. When Betty's husband died a year later, Robert became her main support and companion, returning the help that he had received when his wife died. Two years later they married. They were not 'in love' as they both had been when they married their original spouses. But they were very fond of each other and marriage brought them companionship and protection from loneliness. They took up new social interests, joined other clubs and enjoyed the welcome that they received as a couple.

It is easy to condemn a society that isolates the unmarried, much harder to live within it. For Robert and Betty, accepting a different kind of marriage made all the difference to them.

Hilda

Items **5, 7, 8** and **10** are all benefits that people expect from marriage. For many people marriage is the main relationship that can satisfy these needs, but they are benefits which can be provided by other relationships too.

Take the example of Hilda. She was 63 when her husband Edward died. Hilda believed strongly that marriage was a relationship that happens to you only once. She accepted that other people found married couples easier socially but did not want to marry again for this reason. Neither did she want to remarry for what she called her own convenience — the fact that marriage provided friendship, support and sharing. After living alone for 18 months after Edward's death, she and her widowed sister Sarah agreed to live together in Hilda's house. They have always been close and felt their relationship was both warm and intimate. The relationship did not 'compete' with their previous marital relationships and it did provide support for each of the sisters. Practically too they found household tasks easier and were both less worried about illness. They shared common interests and built up a social life together.

George

Items **2, 6** and **9** are benefits which aren't generally accepted as being limited to marriage in any way. They represent needs which can easily be satisfied outside marriage.

Take the example of George. His wife died when he was only 60. They had shared everything as a couple and to George it was inconceivable that anything other than marriage could provide any satisfaction. A year later he contacted a number of marriage bureaux and friendship groups. He met all kinds of people and experimented with a social life that his quiet daughter, Joan, found rather alarming. She felt that the whole venture was undignified and could hardly keep track of the women friends George introduced to her. George however was enjoying himself enormously, discovering in himself a new person, humorous outgoing, popular. After a year or so he came to realise that he was enjoying his varied and stimulating social life for itself and that it wasn't really remarriage he desired. He took up more new interests always thinking about the social side of things. By this time he had a wide social circle and felt happy with life.

Reactions—changes and adjustments

From these very different people only Robert and Betty decided to remarry. But any of them may have been faced with reactions from others about their ways of picking up the pieces. George's daughter Joan was shocked. Hilda and Sarah's decision may have been seen by others as a clear statement that both rejected the idea of remarriage.

For people who consider remarriage, the issue may be complicated by strong reactions from others — relatives, friends, acquaintances and neighbours. While some may express great pleasure and say so, others may be prejudiced against the idea. They might think that it devalues the memory of the previous spouse. Practical issues may have to be brought up like the inheritance of property.

If a family do not welcome remarriage it may place a strain on relationships with them and perhaps in the marriage too.

Robert and Betty may have asked themselves:

o How favourable would family and friends be to the idea of this marriage?

o Do we mind what other people say?

o How could we overcome any opposition?

In fact for them the main problem involved their social life. Their children were delighted that they could find such pleasure in a second marriage.

As single people they had found themselves feeling awkward at the country dance club. When they decided to marry they realised they would again be a couple but wondered whether some of the reactions might be malicious, and so they made a resolve to move out of a circle which had known them as parts of other couples.

They talked between themselves about adjustments, changes and compromises they felt they might have to make in their new relationship. They realised that because they were two different people:

o The adjustments might not be the same as they had been in their previous marriages.

o The working arrangements did not have to be the same as they had had in their previous marriages.

o Each might have personality characteristics the other had not encountered in their previous close relationships.

o A new close relationship did not have to be the same as a previous one to be good.

o Most close relationships have some aspects that are not satisfactory to both partners. These may differ from unsatisfactory aspects of previous relationships.

Away from it all

Cut off

This topic looks at some of the problems of rural isolation and ways of tackling them.

If you live in the country and have done all your life, you will know the benefits and the problems that rural living brings. You may be quite happy with your lifestyle and not want to change it. Or you might wonder if retirement will alter things and make you feel rather isolated.

You may be considering moving to the country now that you are about to retire. The peace and tranquillity of rural surroundings may attract you. But think about the problems that distance can cause before you take this step. Remember too, that some rural areas possess a lively sense of community whilst others seem 'dead'.

"One is one, and all alone . . ."

Being physically distant from other people does not mean you will necessarily feel isolated or lonely. It's yourself, your surroundings, and other people in the locality that can turn isolation into loneliness.

o Being alone is not the same thing as being lonely. You can be on your own for long periods and enjoy your own company. When you feel lonely, you want and need the company of other people. Anyone who has experienced such feelings knows just how painful they can be.

o Someone living in a large city can still feel isolated. You need contact and involvement outside the narrow walls of your home. Sometimes the feeling of being cut off makes you feel unwanted. You may begin to lose confidence in yourself, think that nothing you do is worthwhile, become generally depressed. Everyone has these feelings at some time but if you have them regularly, your health and sense of well being can be affected if you do not seek help.

If you moved now, in a few years time do you think you would identify with the following statements:

"We bought this house in the heart of the country and had the happy years, then my husband became disabled. We've no family. I feel buried alive."

"This village used to be a thriving community but now the youngsters have left for the towns and the holiday homes are empty most of the year."

So — what can you do?

Even deciding that for you isolation is a problem, means that you have taken the first step.

Secondly, you need to make an effort to do something about it, and not become apathetic.

Listed below are some of the things you can do if you feel lonely or isolated. Tick the boxes of those you would be most likely to do and put your reasons in the space provided. Two examples are given to start you off.

Ways of coping

Some of the suggestions below will help almost immediately. They may do the trick by just lifting your mood.

Some might make your feelings disappear temporarily, but offer no real solution.

Some may actually offer an opportunity to extend your social circle. So if it's contact you desire don't give up on these. Such small steps can over a period of time give you more social contact. Perhaps though you may want to take bolder steps now.

You may have thought of most of these options already, tried them, and still feel lonely and isolated.

Activity		Comments
Go and visit a relative.	☐	I can't do this often enough because my only relations live 70 miles away.
Go and visit a friend.	☑	I could do this, yes, but my best friend lives with her married daughter and I don't like to intrude too often.
	Tick	
Visit a relative.	☐	
Visit a friend or neighbour.	☐	
Telephone a relative.	☐	
Telephone a friend.	☐	
Write a letter.	☐	
Go shopping.	☐	
Do the house-work/ DIY/ gardening.	☐	
Read a book.	☐	
Make something.	☐	

Activity		Comments
Go for a walk.	☐	
Watch television.	☐	
Listen to the radio.	☐	
Go out for a drink.	☐	
Have a drink at home.	☐	
Take pills (tranquillisers, anti-depressants etc.)	☐	
Do nothing in particular.	☐	

Do you have any other ideas for activities that take you out of yourself?

Review your contacts

The activities which you have just completed are concerned solely with your first step, with providing immediate aid for solving the problems of feeling lonely or isolated. It could be useful for you now to make a systematic investigation into your contacts.

Who you meet and what you do with other people will affect how isolated you feel. Use the checklists below to build up a picture of the amount of contact you have over a typical week.

Tick the appropriate boxes

	You visited them.	They visited you.	Every day.	3 or 4 times a week	1 or 2 times a week	Not at all.	Comments.
Neighbours.	☐	☐	☐	☐	☐	☐	
Other friends.	☐	☐	☐	☐	☐	☐	
Postman.	☐	☐	☐	☐	☐	☐	
Milkman.	☐	☐	☐	☐	☐	☐	
Mobile shop.	☐	☐	☐	☐	☐	☐	
Mobile library.	☐	☐	☐	☐	☐	☐	
Salesman.	☐	☐	☐	☐	☐	☐	
Health visitor.	☐	☐	☐	☐	☐	☐	
Social worker.	☐	☐	☐	☐	☐	☐	
Priest.	☐	☐	☐	☐	☐	☐	
Doctor.	☐	☐	☐	☐	☐	☐	

Others (write in).

	You visited them.	They visited you.	Every day.	3 or 4 times a week	1 or 2 times a week	Not at all.	Comments.
	☐	☐	☐	☐	☐	☐	
	☐	☐	☐	☐	☐	☐	
	☐	☐	☐	☐	☐	☐	
	☐	☐	☐	☐	☐	☐	

Of course, some people are so isolated that even contacts of these sorts are minimal. A whole range of different problems arise for them to deal with.

John and Alice Kemp live in a remote hill farm, their nearest neighbours some twenty miles away. John, an amateur radio enthusiast, boasts that he has 24 hour access to the world. Although they have not yet met he has built up a close friendship with Jock a member of the Radio Amateur Invalid and Bedfast Club. Alice is a volunteer weather recorder and finds this absorbing. She doesn't mind that it is time consuming and restricts her to home — "I wasn't going anywhere anyway" she says. Alice is also a member of a Correspondence Club and along with writing and receiving news she has learned glass

London Borough of Barnet Library Services
Mobile Library

engraving, at the suggestion of her pen friend. *"What I like about it is that you don't need a lot of equipment — just a stylus, a bit of black felt, a piece of greaseproof paper, poster paint and brush and you're off!"*

You can take on a home based voluntary job — many hard up voluntary charities need people who will type up reports, address and stick envelopes. Others would be delighted to receive hand made gifts of, say, toys, embroidered clothes, models etc. for fund raising efforts.

In some parts of the country there are voluntary groups running jigsaw puzzle libraries for the housebound. If you are a keen 'puzzler' you could help in checking puzzles as they are returned. Check at your library or your volunteer organisation to see if such a group works in your district.

Do you find the contacts you usually have satisfy your need for company and conversation and a sense of being in touch. If not, think about what steps you could take to improve matters.
o Chatting to more mobile people when you see them keeps you in touch with what is going on in the neighbourhood. Being in on 'the grapevine' makes sure you get and transmit all news and receive help when you need it.
o Are there any changes you could make? Could you visit more, write more letters (and get more answers). Perhaps you could make more effort to make it known that you would like to be visited. Perhaps you could press the Parish Council to consider services (e.g. mobile library, library by post) which are not available to you.

What else can you do?
o If you have a car, be prepared to share journeys with isolated neighbours.

o If you don't have a car, offer another mutually agreed service in exchange for sharing journeys.
o Make a formal request to your local council for a solution to your problem.

On the road: a campaign that succeeded

In many rural areas, organising transport is the only real solution to the problem of being cut off.

A group of people in a sparsely populated area in the Pennines were successful in getting themselves provided with transport. This is what they did:
o After informal talks with the local vicar a small group approached a voluntary action committee and outlined the transport problem in their district.
o As a result of presenting their case the voluntary action committee were given a community minibus by a commercial bus company and the local authority jointly. The local authority met the immediate deficit.
o Now seven remote villages can connect with commercial bus services and the inhabitants have access to social and other services.
o Because the minibus has volunteer drivers, the project hopes to pay off the reducing deficit and buy another minibus.
o The project has brought people together.
o New ideas for money raising have arisen and provide a common interest in a widely scattered area. For instance the minibus and a volunteer driver will take tourists on a conducted tour of an isolated 'working farm' in the summer.

Is there anyone in your area you could approach who might be able to help? Do you know others like yourself who'd be prepared to try and do something? You could advertise in the local paper — perhaps get them to do an article on transport in your area. Getting together with other people may not solve all your problems straightaway, but it may help just talking about it.

Still feel lonely?

Most peoples circumstances aren't nearly so extreme as John and Alice Kemps', of course.

Even so, you may need to take a bolder step, by finding out more about what's going on where you live and then deciding to get involved.

Get down to work and find out precisely what provisions for activities and meeting people are available in your area.

Project search

Take a look at what's on offer in your locality. Is there a regular meeting place for community activities near you — a village institute, church hall or community centre? Do you know what goes on there? You may not think of yourself as the sort of person who joins groups — but anything is worth a try.

If you are thinking of moving into an isolated area check beforehand what amenities there are.

Make a list of all the premises in your area — your nearest village or small town if you are quite isolated — where meetings are held and activities take place. If you do not know where to start, ask all or some of the following people: nearest librarian, doctor, vicar, priest, social worker, shopkeeper, teacher, postman, parish councillor.

This is what **Charlie Allen** found out when he did his own small survey in the village three miles from his home. He enjoyed doing it and got talking to a lot of people he only knew by sight.

Do the same as Charlie did. Ask people. If you are not interested in what is on offer, you may have some good ideas that others want to hear. Could you start up some group or activity yourself?

Building	What goes on there	Distance from home	Would I be interested in going?
Church hall.	Women's Institute (Mon).	3 miles.	No.
	Cubs & Brownies (Tues & Thurs).	—	No.
	Choir practice (Wed Eve).	—	Perhaps. I used to enjoy singing.
	Senior Citizens club (Wed pm).	—	I don't want to join but I might be able to help out.
	Youth club (Sat).		No.
	Old time dancing (Fri).	—	What me!
Blue Boar Inn.	Darts night (Tues).	2 miles.	Yes.
	Folk club (Fri).	—	Would they all be youngsters?
Conservative Club.	Members only — meetings & social events.	—	Not really.
School room.	Evening classes: pottery, car maintenance, animal husbandry, foreign languages. (Tues & Thurs).	2½ miles.	Might think about doing car maintenance next year.
Room above old police station.	"After 8 Club". organises fortnightly (Sat). Whist drives, bridge, canasta. Also talks by local people. Slide shows	4 miles	I'll think about this one. I enjoy card games but not many men seem to go.

Absorbing interest

Most people have interests or hobbies of some kind. But some people use retirement to turn a spare-time interest into something that totally absorbs them.

This topic looks at two cases where people have retired and become absorbed in a particular activity or interest. The examples are given so that you can assess the effect retirement has had on these people, and think about how the lessons learned from their experience might be useful to you.

An interest expanded

Frank Hobbs worked all his life for an electricity board but his real interest always lay with his beekeeping. As he says:

"The day I walked out of the office it was, to me, as though a book was closed and finished with."

He had looked forward to retirement

and when it came his life really opened out.

"I'm beginning to wonder now how I ever found time to go to work."

He can now spend considerably more time with his bees when he wants to, and he is able to adopt a different attitude.

"How can I put it. . . when I was working and I went to examine the bees it was a matter of 'I must do it tonight or I shan't be able to get it done', and you tended to skip through them."

"Now I can take a more leisurely approach. Before I start working with the bees I can sit down and see what's going on and take a much greater interest."

But there's another side to it as well. Frank has become increasingly involved in the administrative work of the local Beekeepers Association. As he puts it:

". . . It kind of snowballed from the ordinary beekeeping to being Chairman of the local association, which again involves being the representative on the county committee. And now we've started running classes for beginners at the local community centre. . ."

Frank is now keen on organising an advanced one day course at the community centre, bringing in two outside experts to talk about the techniques of queen bee rearing — an area he himself is increasingly interested in.

These commitments have their own effect on his social life. The more inexperienced beekeepers come to him for advice or for emergency assistance, for instance if they get a swarm and don't have a spare hive.

"There's a kind of freemasonry among beekeepers. Everybody's prepared to help one another.

"The beginners, they often see me if they've got any problems, and they'll say 'If you've got five minutes drop round'. . . and of course five minutes tends to turn into an hour."

Frank is also finding that retirement has given him more time to spend with his family — especially with his grandchildren.

"In my case when my two daughters were younger, I was that busy working to get some money to pay the mortgage off that I'm afraid that a lot of my time was taken away from the family.

Now I find I can spend more time with them. One of my granddaughters, she won't be four 'til May but I'm even getting her a bit interested in bees."

Frank's overall comment on the first four years of his retirement. . .

". . . I thought I'd have a lot more spare time that I've got. . . I'm busy all the time but I'm doing things I choose."

Retirement has provided Frank with an opportunity to develop those areas of activity he feels most comfortable in. Work never had a lot of attraction for him. He enjoyed the company of his work mates and still goes back to see them every now and again, but he never felt that the description 'employee of the Electricity Board' summed him up very well. So, when he finished work it was *"as though a book was closed."*

His beekeeping had always been an important part of his life, but now it has become central. Retirement has enabled him to be the sort of person he wants to be. He is now: 'The Chairman of the local Beekeepers Association', or 'Mr Hobbs who runs the classes down at the Community Centre', or 'The chap who is organising a discussion on Queen rearing', or 'Frank who will be able to lend me one of his hives'.

Job descriptions

It is our own actions which help to tell other people who we are. Work provides the most common setting in which this can take place. The first description that comes to mind for a person who is working is usually their trade or profession. So we say — 'she's a solicitor in the town', or 'he's a factory worker'. This is usually the first piece of information you get about people. After that you might learn what *sort* of worker the person is — 'she's a steady reliable worker', 'he tends to cut corners', and maybe a bit about what they do in their spare time — 'she runs an evening class on citizen's rights', or 'he gives good tips on the horses'.

Few people are fortunate enough to choose their own work role, yet it is used as a label throughout life. Retirement means that, probably for the first time, you can choose your own labels.

Frank's example

Frank was set the task of choosing the six labels that he thought would best describe himself before retirement to a total stranger.

He arranged in order of priority his list of the descriptions that summed up best how he saw himself.
Beekeeper
Family man
Gardener
Labour voter
Employee of Electricity Board
Ex-seaman

The fact was that whilst his neighbours would have fully gone along with those descriptions, they would have put them in a very different order. They saw him first and foremost in terms of his job, an employee of the Electricity Board, whereas in Frank's own eyes that was only marginally more *him* than the fact of his having served for a time in the Navy many years before.

Only six months after retirement however, Frank's neighbours had come to see Frank in the way he saw himself — as first and foremost a beekeeper and family man.

Retirement has given Frank the opportunity to develop those activities that he prefers and to be accepted by others as "Frank the beekeeper."

New development

Winifred Butler came to live in Brixham at the suggestion of her son David, who is married with a young family. He works part of the year as a fisherman and spends the other half taking tourists on trips during the holiday season. The idea was that her husband Tom would be able to help with the fishing and the pleasure trips when he wanted to.

". . . it's useful for David — he can find things for his father to do and his father likes to be busy. It's nice to feel needed and useful."

This worked well for Tom, but Winifred found herself in a new town, her husband out of the house most days, and without the friends and neighbours she was accustomed to in London. It had been entirely for Tom's benefit that Winifred had agreed to the move at all:

"My mother lived to be 92, and my father had a long illness. We'd had some very difficult years. My husband was a great support. Without him I couldn't have looked after my parents, and I felt — if he wants to move, we'll move. But if I said I didn't miss my friends — because we'd always lived in the same place — it wouldn't be true."

For many years Winifred had been an active member of the Mothers Union, and of the local church, but most of these activities had been dropped during her parents' illness. Now she saw the opportunity of returning to those activities, and she joined the most active of the churches in the area.

"*They were most welcoming and I was very grateful.*" After two meetings they asked her to become the diocesan representative. "*Well I nearly dropped out because it was not my intention to come and take on that kind of job – I'd left all that behind me you see.*"

She then found that the diocesan representative automatically goes onto a Deanery Committee, and because she was on the Deanery Committee she also had a place on the local Mothers' Union Committee.

"*So in agreeing to do one job I found myself doing three jobs. But I must say I'm enjoying it very much indeed.*"

Winifred's previous experience in voluntary work means that she is now much in demand to help with the organisation of local groups. On several occasions she had had to turn down invitations to join local groups, in order to preserve some time to spend with her own family.

"*I'm a great believer in doing one or perhaps two jobs well. There are people who get very much over-involved, and don't do any thing properly.*"

She is also conscious that she doesn't want to live life at the same pace as she once did. She prefers to take things a little more gently now. "*You do slow up, but if you've got any sense you don't allow yourself to stop.*"

New roles

For Winifred this involvement has re-awakened old interests. But there have been new developments too.

The local Mothers' Union were short of a speaker one day and asked her to address their meeting.

"*Well of course one thing leads to another and to my utter and complete amazement I'm being called upon to act as a speaker in the district, not just to Mothers' Union. It's an entirely new venture as far as I'm concerned.*"

And it's an interesting new area for Winifred – she notices a big difference between working for the church in a large city compared to a small town.

"*The sort of problems you have in London are not the same as you have in a semi-rural area, so I've learned a lot.*"

Winifred's example

Winifred was also set the task of listing descriptions that she thought would best sum herself up for a total stranger.

Before retirement when she was in London nursing her elderly parents, Winifred would have described herself along these lines:

Wife and mother
Church member
Friend and neighbour
Ex-secretary
Member of voluntary organisations
Gardener

As you can see, she had always regarded her connection with the church as very important but, within a short while of moving she found herself becoming far more *active* in this role. Also, she would have put rather higher on her list her position as an *active* member of voluntary organisations. She could continue to develop her role as friend and neighbour but in new circumstances and with new people.

Winifred had worked as a secretary in London during some of the time that her children were growing up, but she always thought of her church and voluntary group work as more rewarding and important. Caring for invalid parents had interrupted this work for several years. When she found herself suddenly in a new town, without commitments and with time on her hands, she was able to use her existing skills to establish herself in a new community. Retirement gave Winifred the opportunity to rediscover an old interest that had lain 'dormant' over the years. Becoming immersed in that interest enabled her to establish herself in a new neighbourhood as the sort of person she likes to be known as.

Following the examples of Frank Hobbs, and Winifred Butler, write down the six descriptions you think would best portray you to a total stranger. Now arrange them in an order of priority that suits you best. Is the pattern of your day-to-day activities accurately described by this list? Are there ways you would like to see it change? With more time to yourself after retirement, you can choose how to spend it and decide what you want to get involved in.

For Frank and Winifred, their respective interests provided them with a rewarding occupation in itself. But it also gave them a way of telling other people who they were through their actions, without having to use labels like 'I used to be a secretary' or even simply 'I'm retired.' In retirement they found an identity they enjoy.

Conclusion

Thinking things over

Moving from one way of life to another often stimulates you to think again about your overall aims. You may begin to ask yourself questions about where you fit in to the general scheme of things, to think over just what your beliefs and values are.

Goals and values

Retirement offers unique opportunities, either to reinforce the beliefs and values you have accumulated over a lifetime or to accept the challenge of further self exploration. Retirement offers both the freedom and the time to think again about those questions which a work-filled life often denies.

This course has indicated some practical ways in which the search for information can be satisfied and has shown the need to seek out the companionship of others so that you can communicate your ideas.

But what about the more elusive questions like *"Who am I and what have I made of my life?"* Most people look back at a picture of small achievements and small failures − even the most successful have to live with the fact that what they have become may often fall short of what they would have wished to become. Coming to terms with this can be a positive step towards self knowledge.

The activity on the right could help you to think about the sort of goals that are important to you in life. It also asks you to rate them in order of importance.

You might also consider whether the order of importance of these goals for you has changed over the course of your life.

The kinds of goals you mark as important say a good deal about you as a person. How many of these will you continue to pursue in retirement? The course 'Planning Retirement' has frequently pointed out the need for continuous adjustment to change. A clear idea of how you want to be as a person gives you the confidence to do this.

Your values have been forming themselves over the years. During that time, your attitudes will no doubt have altered and your beliefs been modified

Look at the list of personal goals below and mark them in order of importance to you. (No. 1 is of major importance and so on.)	
Security — To feel secure in your home life and in your social relationships outside the home. To feel you "know where you are" financially.	☐
Service — To help others in any way you can; to be more concerned with others' happiness than your own.	☐
Leadership — To organise, control, lead others to achieve goals of various kinds.	☐
Pleasure — To enjoy life to the full; to take every opportunity to experience the good things of life.	☐
Affection — To give and attract affection in relationships with family and friends.	☐
Duty — To be dedicated to your chosen ideals, values and principles.	☐
Wealth — To build up a financial estate.	☐
Expertness — To become an expert in at least one special subject, skill or accomplishment or to go on working to this end.	☐
Self development — To work towards developing your latent powers and capacities. To seek opportunities for growth and realisation of your own potential.	☐
Prestige — To become well-known and "looked up to".	☐
Independence — To be "your own boss", have freedom to think and do what you want.	☐

by some of the experiences you have had and some of the people you have met.

Some events which affect people significantly are common experiences. Starting work for the first time, getting married, becoming a parent, being called for service in a war, losing the people you care for are commonplace enough but all involve a considerable change.

All call out for a new view of yourself, involve new relationships, new obligations, new rewards. Life changes of these kinds can be disturbing, even when enjoyable. They pose new questions, present new problems for solution; challenge whatever comfortable certainties may have gone before; force you into meeting the challenge of the unknown and make demands upon your inner resources.

The individual dramas, the unique personal experiences are often the ones that affect you most and move you to think deeply about the realities and what stance you want to take.

Retirement is a commonplace event but for everyone certainly going through it, it is a unique personal experience. Only you can answer the question of what you want to do with it.

Traditions and change

What was the tradition you grew up in? How have you developed it since? Your values and beliefs may well be based on one of the great faiths — Jewish, Christian, Hindu, Moslem — or upon Humanism. Add to this the cultural traditions of your race. You may be content to simply maintain these traditions within your own personal life. On the other hand you may feel that they are valuable enough to pass on within the family or the wider community.

It is considered old fashioned to refer to the 'wisdom' of the older generation and their obligation to pass it on but the young are often reassured to find some continuity, intrigued by family history and want to know how changes have affected the lives and thoughts of those who have experienced a different way of life. The bond between grandparents and grandchildren is a strong one and the relationship often a good deal easier than that between parents and children. Often we find immigrant or rural communities that recognise the value of maintaining traditions by bringing the generations together as families in cultural activities. Older members maintain links and strengthen or reassess lifelong beliefs and values. Younger ones are able to compare cultural attitudes and begin to formulate their own approach to life.

There is a growing awareness that there is a vast store of experience and information lying dormant among the retired. You may decide to accept the role of an 'elder' in your community and make that information and experience available.

Maintaining traditions — of all sorts — needs no justification: its value is obvious.

If maintaining traditions is important it is equally necessary to recognise the new.

Coming to terms with a changing society can be a dynamic experience. Being open to the new patterns of behaviour, lifestyles, opinions, methods of organisation and all the new shifts of emphasis that indicate a new generation, can offer interesting new

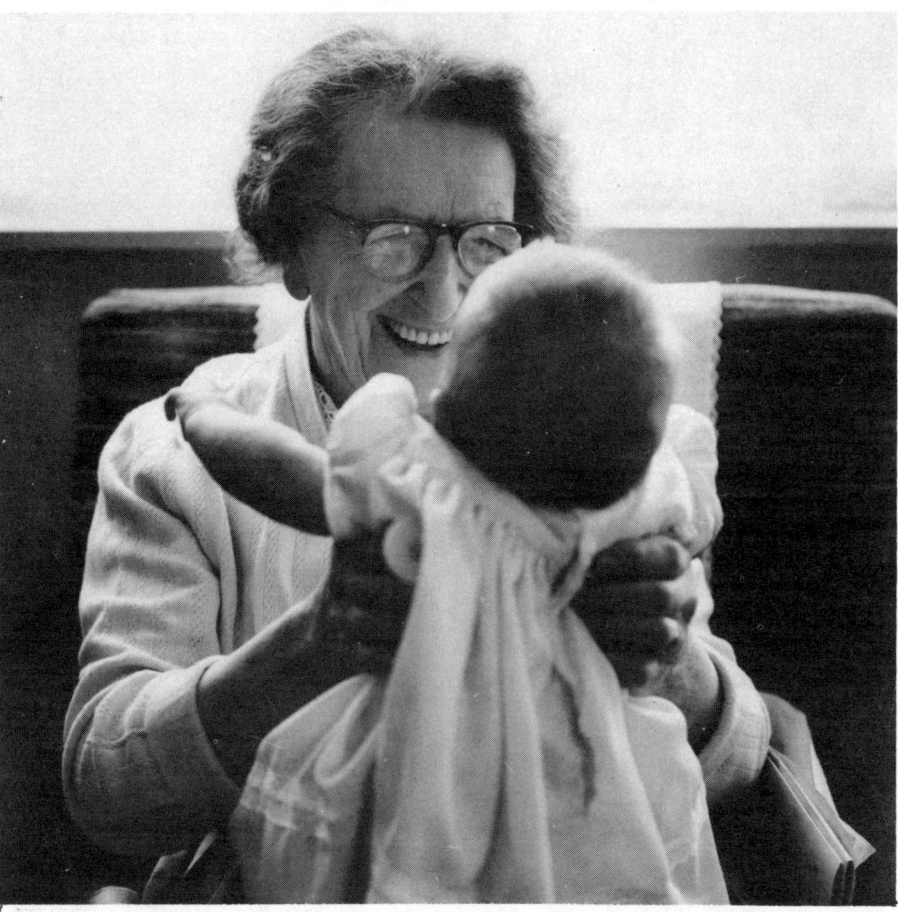

perspectives on what had become familiar in your own life. There will be opportunities to learn. It may be sometimes necessary to 'unlearn'.

We live at a time when, because of new technology, the younger generation may have much to teach the older generation. Certainly both will have much to gain from shared experiences. If the new morality seems to by-pass the virtues you value, tolerance is more likely to keep you in touch with the younger generation than a closed mind.

It may not be enough simply to allow for the changes that will affect you immediately. In our society today it is not the fact of change that is remarkable but the accelerated rate of change.

Being aware of changes in, for example, technology, science and the arts, noting alterations in moral attitudes and behaviour, taking an interest in current affairs, the changing fashions and trends enriches life at any time.

Opting out leads to social isolation. More than that, it is a signal that you no longer feel any responsibility to society — that you have retired, not simply from work but from life!

Accepting the fact of change — along with the right to approve or disapprove — and being involved enough to want to find out more, keeps you in touch with life, keeps you mentally alert and can provide the stimulus to continue to seek to attain your life-goals

through the whole of your retirement. In the early active years you may choose an active involvement through part-time work, voluntary work, hobbies, interests or in continuing your education. This will involve you with a range of other people, whether through a service offered, or responsibilities and commitments accepted. In the late years of retirement when advanced age of necessity reduces your physical activities it's still possible to be alert and interested in what is going on. The experience of how your own set of values has worked for you may well be of interest to others of all ages.

The goals you set up in your private life will affect your actions and relationships in your more public life. Being actively involved with life will offer a continuing challenge to test out your attitudes and beliefs.

Retirement is for the rest of your life. You have a wide range of choices for action ahead of you. In planning your future you have had to look back upon a whole lifetime's experience and ask many questions in order to throw light on the decisions that lie ahead. This book has asked you to think about what you see as your purpose in life. As the years go on you will get nearer to being able to define your purpose if you retain enough curiosity to go on posing questions.

What next?

This is a guide to sources of information and help that's available from people, places and books.

Organisations

Pre-Retirement Association of Great Britain and Northern Ireland
19 Undine Street
Tooting
London SW17 8PP

Health Education Council
78 New Oxford Street
London WC1 1AH

Scottish Health Education Group
Woodburn House
Canaan Lane
Edinburgh EH10 4SG

Department of Health and Social Security
England — Alexander Fleming House
Elephant and Castle
London SE1 6BY

Scotland — 3 Lady Lawson Street
Edinburgh EH3 9SH

Wales — Government Buildings
Gabalfu
Cardiff CF4 4YJ

Northern Ireland — Dundonald House
Upper
Newtownards
Road
Belfast BT4 3SF

Community Health Council Headquarters
126 Albert Street
London NW1

Sports Council England
70 Brompton Road
London SW3 1EX

Sports Council Scotland
1 St Colne Street
Edinburgh EH3 6AA

Sports Council Wales
Dophia Gardens
Cardiff CF1 9SW

Sports Council Northern Ireland
49 Malone Road
Belfast BT9 6RZ

CRUSE
The Charter House
6 Leon Gate Gardens
Richmond
Surrey TW9 2DF

National Council for the Single Woman and her Dependants
29 Chilworth Mews
London W2 3RG

Royal Society for the Prevention of Accidents (ROSPA)
Cannon House
The Priory
Queensway
Birmingham B4 6BS

Action on Smoking and Health (ASH)
27 Mortimer Street
London W1N 7RH

Inland Revenue
Somerset House
Strand
London WC2

Consumers Association
14 Buckingham Street
London WC2N 6DS

REACH (Retired Executives Action Clearing House)
Victoria House
Southampton Row
London WC1B 4DH

Employment Fellowship
Drayton House
Gordon Street
London WC1

The Money Advice Centre
The Birmingham Settlement
3/8 Summer Lane
Birmingham 19

Department of Education and Science
Elizabeth House
York Road
London SE1 7PH

Scottish Education Department
43 Jeffrey Street
Edinburgh EH1 18H

The Open University
Walton Hall
Milton Keynes MK7 6AA

Workers Education Association (WEA)
Temple House
9 Upper Berkeley Street
London W1H 8BY

Small Firms Centres
Birmingham, Bristol, Cambridge, Cardiff, Glasgow, Leeds, Liverpool, London, Manchester, Newcastle, Nottingham.

Information and counselling services operated by the Small Firms Division of the Department of Industry. Dial 100 and ask for FREEPHONE 2444 for all locations. In Scotland the Small Firms Services is provided by the Scottish Development Agency.

In Wales, the Welsh Office provides this information. The Welsh Development Agency provides counselling. In Northern Ireland an information service is provided by The Department of Commerce.

National Federation of Housing Associations
30–32 Southampton Street
Strand
London WC2E 7HE

Confederation of British Industry
Centre Point
103 New Oxford Street
London WC1A 1DU
(Wide range of services for small firm members)

Council for Small Industries in Rural Areas (COSIRA)
141 Castle Street
Salisbury
Wiltshire SP1 3TP

Note also in your local area
Your local library
Your Citizens Advice Bureau (CAB)
Your Housing Department (Housing Aid Centre)

Your Department of Health and Social Security (DHSS)
The Samaritans
The Volunteer Centre
The Leisure Centre

Look in the phone book for all of these.

Books

The Good Health Guide – The Open University – (Harper and Row 1980)

Exercise, The Facts – E J Bassey and P H Fentem – (Oxford University Press 1981)

Fitness on Forty Minutes a Week – Malcolm Carruthers and Alastair Murray – (Futura 1980)

In the Pink – Dr Beric Wright – (Choice Magazine, Pre-Retirement Association 1979)

Stress and Relaxation – Jane Madders – (Martin Dunitz 1981)

Everything you Need to Know to Ensure Health Wholesome Eating – Paul Simons – (Thorsons 1978)

Nutrition – John Yudkin – (Hodder and Stoughton 1977)

The Health Rights Handbook — Gerry and Carol Stimson — (Penguin 1980)

Caring for Elderly Dependants — Heather Mackenzie and Dr Muir Gray — (Allen and Unwin and Beaconsfield 1980)

Filling in Your VAT Return — Leaflet form (free) HM Customs and Excise — addresses in local telephone directories under 'Customs and Excise'.

Changing Your Job — Godfrey Golzen (Kogan Page for Daily Telegraph).

Dismissal, redundancy and job hunting — Consumers Association (publishers of WHICH?) 14 Buckingham Street, London WC2N 6DS (Registering for employment, finding a job, retraining etc)

The Good Job Guide — The New Opportunity Press Limited in association with The Sunday Times (for qualified, experienced people. Includes self analysis, where to look, training opportunities for mature students, the job market).

Guide to Early Retirement — Incomes Data Services Limited, 140 Great Portland Street, London W1.

Money and Your Retirement — Edward J Eves — (Choice Publications Limited 1982)

Consumer Decisions — Open University Education Short Course (Open University, Walton Hall, Milton Keynes MK7 6AA)

Your Pension is For You — National Federation of Old Age Pensioners Association 1981

Money in the 1980's: How to Make it, How to Keep it — William Davis — (George Weidenfeld and Nicholson Limited 1981)

Supplementary Benefits Handbook (HMSO)

A Housing Rights Handbook — Marion Cutting — (Penguin 1979)

Where to Live after Retirement — (Consumer Publications 1979)

Your Pension — Pensioner's Voice (National Federation of Old Age Pensions Association)

Booklets available from the Department of Industry for the self-employed
— Setting up a new business.

— Marketing.
— Elements of bookkeeping.
— Management accounting.
— Microprocessors and the small business.
— Selling to large firms.
— How to start exporting.
— Employing people.

All the above booklets are free.

Looking Ahead, A Guide to Retirement — Fred Kemp and Bernard Buttle — (Macdonald and Evans 1980)

Working at Home for Profit — Joanna Johnson — (Basil Blackwell 1980)

Voluntary Social Services, A Directory of National Organisations — (National Council for Social Service)

Retirement Briefing File — (Retirement Choice Magazine) regularly updated

Disability Rights Handbook — (Disability Alliance, Cambridge Terrace, London NW1 4JL)

Your Rights (For Pensioners) — Anne Eblett — (Age Concern)

The Joy of Sex — Alex Comfort — (Quartet Books 1975)

Community Education Courses at the Open University

This book forms part of an Open University short, home-study course. The course package also includes an audio cassette and accompanying notes, a booklet giving details of helpful organisations and books, a set of computer marked assignments and a number of information sheets and leaflets.

"Planning Retirement" is only one of a range of Community Education courses dealing with the practical concerns of everyday life. All the courses come in attractive, easy-to-follow packs which help you get to the root of matters that concern you, and decide what's best for your own situation. Courses are currently available on parenthood, from pre-pregnancy through pregnancy and childbirth, to the first years of life, the pre-school years, childhood 5–10 and the teenage years. There are also courses on consumer and health issues, and one for school governors.

If you are not already a registered student on Planning Retirement and would like to find out more about this or any other course in the Community Education programme, write to:

ASCO, PO Box 76, The Open University, Milton Keynes MK7 6AA.

Each course is designed primarily for a specific target group: parents, consumers, or people who are retiring themselves. However, many professionals use them in their own field of community or education work. The Community Education Office can offer advice and assistance in using the course materials in this way. To purchase parts of the course materials or to find out more about using the materials as a resource: write to:

The Community Education Office, The Open University, PO Box 188, Milton Keynes MK7 6AA.